“The sum of wisdom, says Calvin, consists in the knowledge of God and the knowledge of ourselves, though today it is hard to say which is more contested. What is humanity, that God is mindful of us and gracious toward us? This volume offers a much-needed Reformed-catholic retrieval of a much-disputed doctrine. Like the doctrine of God, theological anthropology touches every part of Christian theology and is indispensable to any coherent theological system. In the absence of creedal formulations, Sutanto's concluding twelve theses are especially welcome.”

KEVIN J. VANHOOZER
Litfin Divinity School, Wheaton College

“Drawing from the riches of the catholicity of the Reformed tradition, Sutanto offers a wealth of wisdom for both the enduring questions of theological anthropology and the pressing questions of our own time. With theological clarity and pastoral wisdom, this wonderful book provides a biblically rich, deeply traditioned, holistic account of our humanity. In any age—but especially our own—this is a gift.”

JESSICA JOUSTRA
Calvin Theological Seminary

“Far deeper than a mere introduction, *For Us and for Our Salvation* beautifully unpacks the riches of Reformed-catholic theological anthropology. Sutanto's engagement with Scripture is exemplary, his exposition of the tradition is illuminating, and his application to contemporary concerns is wise and measured. There is so much here for both students and scholars to feast on. I highly recommend it!”

UCHE ANIZOR
Talbot School of Theology, Biola University

“The publication of Sutanto's book on the doctrine of humanity is reason enough for gratitude since we have lacked an up-to-date Reformed introduction to the doctrine for decades. But beyond gratitude for the publication of a timely and useful resource, this book merits praise. It not only addresses topics of both perennial significance and contemporary controversy with insight and good judgment. This book also exemplifies the virtues of theological reasoning at its finest, grounding its conclusions in biblical exegesis, attending to the wisdom of the church catholic and Reformed, and drawing forth prudential applications for life, ministry, and worship, all the while helping its readers cultivate the same virtues through its example. Three cheers for Sutanto's *For Us and for Our Salvation*."

SCOTT R. SWAIN
Reformed Theological Seminary, Orlando, Florida

"A fresh and engaging survey of the doctrines of sin and salvation from the perspective of the Reformed tradition (including neo-Calvinism). Sutanto is a sure-footed guide as he breaks down the big doctrines of the faith. Throughout, he mines Scripture for all its worth, bringing out new treasures as well as old. Students will find much to learn, and even experts will appreciate Sutanto's analytic clarity and expositional insight. This is a helpful book indeed!"

HANS MADUEME
Covenant College

N. GRAY SUTANTO
(PhD, University of Edinburgh) is associate professor of systematic theology at Reformed Theological Seminary in Washington, DC. He has translated, edited, or written numerous books, including *The Essential Herman Bavinck* (with Gayle E. Doornbos) and *Neo-Calvinism: A Theological Introduction* (with Cory C. Brock).

FOR US AND FOR OUR SALVATION

THE BIBLICAL DOCTRINE OF HUMANITY AND SIN

WE BELIEVE

STUDIES IN REFORMED BIBLICAL DOCTRINE

John McClean and Murray J. Smith, series editors

We Believe is a series of eight major studies of the Christian faith's primary doctrines as confessed in the Nicene Creed and guided by the Reformed tradition. In each volume, trusted authors engage a major creedal doctrine in light of its biblical-theological foundations and historical development, drawing out its spiritual, ethical, and missional implications for the church today.

1
One God Almighty
The Biblical Doctrine of the Triune God

2
Maker of Heaven and Earth
The Biblical Doctrine of Creation and Providence

3
The Lord Jesus Christ
The Biblical Doctrine of the Person and Work of Christ

4
For Us and for Our Salvation
The Biblical Doctrine of Humanity and Sin

5
He Will Come Again in Glory
The Biblical Doctrine of the End

6
The Giver of Life
The Biblical Doctrine of the Holy Spirit and Salvation

7
He Spoke Through the Prophets
The Biblical Doctrine of God's Self-Revelation

8
One, Holy, Catholic, and Apostolic Church
The Biblical Doctrine of the Church

FOR US AND FOR OUR SALVATION

THE BIBLICAL DOCTRINE OF HUMANITY AND SIN

N. GRAY SUTANTO

Baker Academic
a division of Baker Publishing Group
Grand Rapids, Michigan

Published by Baker Academic
a division of Baker Publishing Group
Grand Rapids, Michigan
BakerAcademic.com

Printed in the United States of America

Library of Congress Cataloging-in-Publication Data
Names: Sutanto, Nathaniel Gray, 1991– author
Title: For us and for our salvation : the biblical doctrine of humanity and sin / N. Gray Sutanto.
Description: Grand Rapids, Michigan : Baker Academic, a division of Baker Publishing Group, [2026] | Series: We believe : studies in Reformed biblical doctrine | Includes bibliographical references.
Identifiers: LCCN 2026000301 | ISBN 9781540971432 cloth | ISBN 9781493457076 ebook | ISBN 9781493457083 pdf
Subjects: LCSH: Theological anthropology—Biblical teaching | Theological anthropology—Reformed Church | Reformed Church—Doctrines
Classification: LCC BS661 .S88 2026
LC record available at https://lccn.loc.gov/2026000301

26 27 28 29 30 31 32 7 6 5 4 3 2 1

For Covenant City Church, Jakarta, Indonesia

CONTENTS

BIBLICAL EXPOSITIONS

SERIES INTRODUCTION

Your word is a lamp to my feet
and a light to my path.
—Psalm 119:105

The unfolding of your words gives light;
it imparts understanding to the simple.
—Psalm 119:130

AN INVITATION TO CONFESSIONAL THEOLOGY

We Believe is a series of eight studies of the primary doctrines of the Christian faith as confessed in the Nicene Creed and received in the Reformed tradition. The series marks the 1,700th anniversary of the Council of Nicaea (AD 325) by reaffirming and advancing the Church's confession.[1] The title of our series is drawn from the first words of the Creed—the single Greek verb Πιστεύομεν—which introduces what has become the classic confession of the Christian faith. Since the Church's confession neither began at Nicaea, nor ended with its creed, *We Believe* examines the biblical foundations of the Church's faith, traces its development (especially in the Reformed tradition), and applies its truths to the worship, life, and mission of the Church today. Since true theology begins in prayer and worship of the God who has revealed himself, each volume opens with a theme prayer, shaped by Scripture and the Church's confession. Further, since even the deepest truths of the faith need

1. For the history of the Nicene Creed, which received its final form at the Council of Constantinople (AD 381), see D. Fairbairn and R. M. Reeves, *The Story of Creeds and Confessions: Tracing the Development of the Christian Faith* (Baker Academic, 2019), 48–79.

to be simply expounded so they can be clearly grasped and faithfully lived, each volume closes with a series of theses, which summarize the doctrine covered in the book. *We Believe* provides a comprehensive and integrated biblical, theological, and missional treatment of the major doctrines of the Christian faith.

BIBLICAL REVELATION

The Church's confession is rooted in and ruled by God's revelation in Scripture. The Scriptures are "the Word of God written" and "the rule of faith and life" (Westminster Confession of Faith 1:2). The first part of each study, therefore, is devoted to a fresh examination of biblical revelation.

Fundamentally, our studies are tethered to the text of Scripture, and each volume in the series includes expositions of the primary biblical texts which form the doctrine under consideration.[2] Moreover, since Scripture is the only "infallible rule" for its own interpretation (Westminster Confession of Faith 1:9), our studies seek to interpret Scripture by Scripture, initially by embracing the discipline of Biblical Theology.[3] We begin—where God's people have always begun—with the recognition that Scripture is God's inspired and authoritative word. We proceed by tracing God's progressive revelation of himself and his purposes in the organically unfolding canon of Scripture, taking full account of its varied forms, while especially recognizing its fundamental, Christ-centered unity. This procedure is one we learn from Scripture itself. The Bible regularly claims that its revelation forms a single coherent narrative climaxing in the gospel of Christ, even as it also indicates that this narrative has many dimensions and is revealed in a diversity of literary forms.[4] Faithful Christian readings of Scripture—from Irenaeus

2. For convenience of reference, these biblical expositions are highlighted in text boxes. Several key biblical texts are important for more than one doctrine, but to avoid repetition, these are treated only once in the series.

3. We understand this discipline along the lines sketched by Geerhardus Vos in his 1894 Inaugural Lecture at Princeton Theological Seminary. G. Vos, "The Idea of Biblical Theology as a Science and as a Theological Discipline," in *Redemptive History and Biblical Interpretation: The Shorter Writings of Geerhardus Vos*, ed. R. B. Gaffin (P&R, 1980), 3–24; *Biblical Theology: Old and New Testaments* (Eerdmans, 1948), 3–18.

4. See, for example, Deut. 26:5–11; Josh. 24; 1 Sam. 12:6–18; Pss. 78; 105–6; 136; Neh. 9:7–37; Acts. 7; 13:13–43; Heb. 11.

and Augustine to Calvin and Kuyper—have, therefore, always recognized a fundamental unity within the rich diversity of Scripture—a unity which is conceptual (in that the Scriptures speak of the same God relating in consistent ways to the same created world), and narratival (in that the Scriptures narrate a single redemptive-history).[5]

In the first part of each study, then, we look for the organic unfolding of God's revelation from its seed form in the garden of Eden (Gen. 1–2) to its full flowering in the garden-city of the New Jerusalem (Rev. 21–22). As Augustine said, "In the Old Testament the New is concealed, in the New the Old is revealed."[6] So we read Genesis in the light of the Gospels, Exodus in the light of the Epistles, and Ruth in the light of Revelation. We follow the rich network of citations and allusions—the "inner biblical exegesis"—by which Scripture interprets Scripture.[7] We outline the primary biblical themes relevant to each doctrine—God's kingdom and covenant, God's creation and blessing, God's Son and people, God's Spirit and temple—together with their many related subthemes, as they inform and shape the Church's confession. We use Scripture's own words and categories to trace the drama of redemption from creation to new creation centered on Christ.

Following this approach, we recognize that the Bible fundamentally structures its own unfolding narrative, and organizes all its major themes, around God's two primary covenants with Adam and Christ (Rom. 5:12–21; 1 Cor. 15:22). Reformed theology came to characterize these as the "covenant of works" and the "covenant of grace," confessing that, from start to finish, God has related to his people and his world by way of covenant (Westminster Confession of Faith 7:1–6).[8] Scripture thus presents each of the major

---

5. See C. H. H. Scobie, "History of Biblical Theology," in *New Dictionary of Biblical Theology*, ed. T. D. Alexander and B. S. Rosner (InterVarsity, 2000), 11–20.

6. Augustine, Quaest. in Hept. 2: 73: *Novum Testamentum in Vetere latet, Vetus Testamentum in Novo patet.*

7. The phrase "inner biblical exegesis" was coined by M. A. Fishbane, *Biblical Interpretation in Ancient Israel* (Oxford University Press, 1985). See further: G. K. Beale and D. A. Carson, eds., *Commentary on the New Testament Use of the Old Testament* (Baker Academic, 2007); G. K. Beale, *Handbook on the New Testament Use of the Old Testament: Exegesis and Interpretation* (Baker Academic, 2012); G. E. Schnittjer, *Old Testament Use of Old Testament: A Book-by-Book Guide* (Zondervan, 2021).

8. See esp. G. P. Waters, J. N. Reid, and J. R. Muether, eds., *Covenant Theology: Biblical, Theological, and Historical Perspectives* (Crossway, 2020); H. Perkins, *Reformed Covenant Theology: A Systematic Introduction* (Lexham, 2024).

post-fall biblical covenants—God's covenants with Abraham, Israel, David, and the new covenant—as successive administrations of the single covenant of grace: the covenant which was first promised in the garden (Gen. 3:15), climactically sealed by the blood of Christ (Matt. 26:28 and Mark 14:24 with Exod. 24:8), and which ultimately will be fulfilled in the new creation when the Triune God comes to dwell with his people at last (Rev. 21:3).[9]

Above all—and consistent with the covenant theology we have just sketched—we take Jesus's own word as our guide, and look for him, the Lord Jesus Christ, "in all the Scriptures" (Luke 24:27). Following Jesus and his apostles, we recognize that God "promised . . . the gospel . . . beforehand through his prophets in the Holy Scriptures" (Rom. 1:3–4; cf. Luke 24:44–49; Gal. 3:8; 1 Cor. 15:3–5; 1 Pet. 1:12). Christ himself—his person, his work, and his kingdom—is the climax and goal of the Triune God's gracious plan to redeem his people and his world. Indeed, Christ is the very "substance" of biblical revelation (Col. 2:17; cf. John 5:39; Rom. 10:4; 1 Cor. 10:4; 2 Cor. 1:20; 2 Tim. 3:15; 1 Pet. 1:10–12). The grace of God in Christ was not merely foreshadowed and prophesied in the Old Testament; it was mediated in advance to the saints of old, by the Spirit, through the "promises, prophecies, sacrifices . . . and other types" given to God's people in that period (Westminster Confession of Faith 7:5–6). We therefore affirm that the Old Testament is *both* Christo-telic (in that it points forward to Christ as its goal), *and* Christo-centric (in that its types and promises really mediated God's grace in Christ, through the Spirit).[10] Thus, with John Calvin, we are right to "seek in the whole of Scripture . . . truly to know Jesus Christ, and the infinite riches that are comprised in him and are offered to us by him from God the Father."[11]

9. For the central covenant promise—"I will be your God and you will be my people" (or variations), see Gen. 17:7–8; 28:15; 31:3, 5, 42; 39:2–6, 21–23; Exod. 6:7; 29:45–46; Lev. 11:45; 25:38; 26:11–12; Deut. 23:15; 26:17–18; 29:12–13; 2 Sam. 7:23–24; 1 Chron. 17:22; Ps. 95:7; Jer. 11:4; 24:7; 30:22; 31:1, 33; 32:38; Ezek. 14:11; 34:24, 30–31; 36:28; 37:23, 27; Zech. 2:11; 8:8; 13:9; Hos. 1:8–2:23; Matt. 1:23; 18:20; 28:20; 2 Cor. 6:16; Rev. 21:3.

10. See P. A. Lillback, ed. *Seeing Christ in All of Scripture: Hermeneutics at Westminster Theological Seminary* (Westminster Seminary Press, 2016); L. G. Tipton, "Christocentrism *and* Christotelism: The Spirit, Redemptive History, and the Gospel," in *Redeeming the Life of the Mind: Essays in Honor of Vern Poythress*, ed. J. M. Frame, W. A. Grudem, and J. J. Hughes (Crossway, 2018), 129–45.

11. From Calvin's preface to Pierre Olivétan's French translation of the New Testament (1534) in *Calvin: Commentaries*, ed. and trans. J. Haroutunian and L. P. Smith (Westminster 1958), 70.

In thus seeking Christ in all the Scriptures, we find that later revelation in Scripture interprets earlier revelation in ways that are consistent with its original meaning; the later revelation shows the "true and full sense" (*sensus plenior*) in light of the fulfillment in Christ (Westminster Confession of Faith 1:9). The New Testament offers no radical reinterpretation, much less correction, of the Old, but unfolds the full meaning of God's inspired word. As B. B. Warfield put it, the Old Testament is like a room "richly furnished but dimly lighted," such that "the introduction of light [from the New Testament] brings into it nothing which was not in it before," but "brings out into clearer view much of what is in it but was only dimly or even not at all perceived before."[12] As we read the Scriptures as the unfolding narrative of God's redemptive purpose, we learn to see, again and again, that Christ is the center and substance of the Scriptures, and so the center and substance of the Church's faith.

DOGMATIC DEVELOPMENT

The Church confesses not only what is "expressly set down in Scripture" but what "by good and necessary consequence may be deduced from Scripture" (Westminster Confession of Faith 1:6). The second part of each study in the *We Believe* series, therefore, is devoted to an account of the dogmatic development of the doctrine under consideration. Far from being opposed to each other, Biblical Theology and Systematic and Confessional Dogmatics actually need each other; there is a necessarily reciprocal relationship between the two.[13] While both disciplines deal with God's special revelation in Scripture, they analyze it according to different principles. The primary

12. B. B. Warfield, "The Biblical Doctrine of the Trinity," in *Biblical Doctrines: The Works of Benjamin B. Warfield*, vol. 2 (Oxford University Press, 1932), 141–42.

13. For reflection on the relationship between the two disciples in the Reformed tradition, see esp. Vos, "Idea," 3–24; J. Murray, "Systematic Theology," in *Collected Writings of John Murray*, vol. 4, *Studies in Theology: Reviews*, ed. I. Murray (Banner of Truth, 1983), 1–21; R. B. Gaffin, "Systematic Theology and Biblical Theology," *Westminster Theological Journal* 38 (1975–76): 281–99. For review of these contributions and a constructive proposal, see M. Allen, "Systematic Theology and Biblical Theology—Part One," *Journal of Reformed Theology* 14 (2020): 52–72; Allen, "Systematic Theology and Biblical Theology—Part Two," *Journal of Reformed Theology* 14 (2020): 344–57. Note also J. McClean, "Of Covenant and Creation: A Conversation between Systematic Theology and Biblical Theology," in *An Everlasting Covenant: Biblical and Theological Essays in Honour of William J. Dumbrell*, ed. J. A. Davies and A. M. Harman, RTR Supplement Series 4 (Reformed Theological Review, 2010), 187–227.

organizing principle for Biblical Theology is history—the organic unfolding of God's work of redemption and his interpretation of the same in his inspired word. The primary organizing principle of Dogmatics is logic—the rational organization of God's revealed truth. As Geerhardus Vos observes, while Biblical Theology constructs a historical "line," Christian Dogmatics constructs a logical "circle."[14] Thus, while Christian Dogmatics, including the Church's creeds and confessions, generally follow the redemptive-historical shape of biblical revelation, it self-consciously sets that redemptive history within the reality of the Triune God and his relations to his world as these are revealed in all of Scripture.[15] In the same way, while Christian Dogmatics fundamentally expresses itself using biblical language, it also employs extrabiblical language to summarize and synthesize biblical teaching, especially where Scripture uses a variety of expressions for the same reality, or where this is necessary to refute error.[16] Since "the word of God is living and active" (Heb. 4:12), the God-given language of Scripture remains primary. Faithful Dogmatics rightly recognizes what John Webster calls the "rhetorical sufficiency" of Scripture.[17] Indeed, since "the Old Testament in Hebrew . . . and the New Testament in Greek" were "immediately inspired by God," the final court of appeal for all Christian Dogmatics is the words of Scripture in the original languages (Westminster Confession of Faith 1:8). Yet still, the same theological judgment can be expressed in a range of different conceptual and linguistic forms, and the faithful presentation and propagation of biblical truth sometimes requires extrabiblical expression.[18]

There is, moreover, a real history of doctrinal development to be traced through the ages of church history. As the very word of the living God, the Scriptures possess an inexhaustible depth. As the Church reads and rereads God's word in an ever-changing world, we find that there is always more to confess regarding God and his ways in the world, and always more to celebrate

14. See Vos, "Idea," 23; cf. Murray, "Systematic Theology," 9.

15. Cf. Allen, "Systematic Theology—Part Two," 355–56.

16. Cf. Allen, "Systematic Theology—Part Two," 355.

17. J. Webster, "Biblical Reasoning," in *The Domain of the Word: Scripture and Theological Reason* (T&T Clark, 2012), 131.

18. See D. S. Yeago, "The New Testament and Nicene Dogma: A Contribution to the Recovery of Theological Exegesis," *Pro-Ecclesia* 3 (1994): 87–100. Compare B. B. Warfield's comments to this effect on the doctrine of the Trinity (Warfield, "Trinity," 133).

in the depths of his "being, wisdom, power, holiness, justice, goodness, and truth" (Westminster Shorter Catechism 4). Herman Bavinck states it well:

> Scripture is not designed so that we should parrot it but that as free children of God we should think his thoughts after him. . . . So much study and reflection on the subject is bound up with it that no person can do it alone. That takes centuries. To that end the church has been appointed and given the promise of the Spirit's guidance into all truth.[19]

As each generation has read the Scriptures, confessed the faith, proclaimed the gospel, instructed children, discipled converts, and refuted errors, the Church—under the oversight of its living Lord, and by the enabling of his Holy Spirit—has deepened in its grasp of biblical truth.[20] The Church has learned again and again that "the Lord hath yet more light and truth to break forth from His Word."[21] The foundational doctrines of God and Christ were fundamentally established in the Church's early centuries, and codified in the ecumenical creeds, such that they received only incremental refinements thereafter. Other doctrines, however, no less crucial to the life of the Church—for example, the doctrines of Scripture and authority—received considerable development in the medieval, Reformation, and modern periods.

Doctrinal development, however—at least where it can be considered faithful—never moves beyond Scripture; it only ever penetrates more deeply into its truth. Faithful Dogmatics is thus not the imposition of a foreign grid onto Scripture, but a complementary means of interpreting Scripture by Scripture. In doing so, we make use of sanctified human reason. For while the fall has corrupted the human mind (Rom. 1:21–23; Eph. 4:17–18), that same mind is renewed in Christ and by the Spirit (Rom. 12:2; 1 Cor. 2:10–13; Eph. 4:23), and as such can play the role of servant in the task of theology. Thus Francis Turretin helpfully distinguishes between revelation as the "foundation of faith" and reason as the "instrument of faith," which can serve to "illustrate"

19. H. Bavinck, *Reformed Dogmatics*, vol. 1, *Prolegomena* (Baker Academic, 2003), 83.

20. The role of the Spirit in doctrinal development is helpfully emphasized by Murray, "Systematic Theology," 1–21, esp. 6.

21. G. Rawson, "We Limit Not the Truth of God" in *Leeds Hymn Book*, 1853, no. 409.

and "collate" biblical passages or arguments, to draw out "inferences," and to help assess whether various positions agree or disagree with what has been revealed.[22]

The Church has been at this task for nearly two thousand years, and there is a great deal to be learned from the wisdom of the ages. For this reason, each volume in the *We Believe* series provides a survey of the historical development of the doctrine under consideration. In charting this development, we give the Church's creeds and confessions pride of place. For while Augustine, Aquinas, Luther, Calvin, Turretin, and Bavinck—among a host of others—have provided significant insight into biblical truth, the Church's creeds and confessions reflect the official teaching of the Church *as* Church or—perhaps better—the common teaching of the Church's elders, that is, the teaching of those appointed by the Spirit, and charged with guarding and promoting the apostolic gospel and, indeed, "the whole counsel of God" (Acts 15:1–35; 16:4; 20:27–28; 1 Tim. 3:2; 5:17–18; 2 Tim. 2:2; Titus 1:9).[23]

The Church's teaching is always subordinate to Scripture. Scripture is the magisterial authority, the "rule that rules" (*norma normans*); the Church's teaching is a ministerial authority, "the rule that is ruled" (*norma normata*). In the order of authority, "the Supreme Judge, by which all controversies of religion are to be determined, and all decrees of councils, opinions of ancient writers, doctrines of men, and private spirits, are to be examined, and in whose sentence we are to rest, can be no other but the Holy Spirit speaking in the Scripture" (Westminster Confession of Faith 1:10). At the same time, in the order of knowing, there is wisdom in beginning with the Church's confession. We rightly take the Church's teaching as our guide in reading, interpreting, and applying Scripture. We learn the truth from our elders as they teach us the truth from God's word. This yields an iterative process: The Scriptures form our confession; our scripturally formed confession provides the lens through which we read the Scriptures; and our further reading of the Scriptures further refines our confession.[24]

22. F. Turretin, *Institutes of Elenctic Theology*, trans. G. M. Giger, 3 vols. (P&R, 1992–97), §§ 1.8.3, 6–7; 1.12.15.

23. See M. S. Horton, *The Christian Faith: A Systematic Theology for Pilgrims on the Way* (Zondervan, 2011), 211–18.

24. S. Swain, "A Ruled Reading Reformed: The Role of the Church's Confession in Biblical Interpretation," *International Journal of Systematic Theology* 14 (2012): 177–93.

We Believe stands unashamedly in the Reformed confessional tradition, and seeks to defend and advance it. There are, of course, significant differences between the various Christian confessions. While the whole Church receives the doctrine of the ecumenical creeds (the Apostles', Nicene, and Athanasian creeds, together with the Definition of Chalcedon), the later confessions present divergent views on a host of significant matters. It is our conviction that the Reformed confessions, especially the Three Forms of Unity and the Westminster Standards, present the best—that is, the most fully biblical—account of Christian truth. That very tradition, however, has always aimed to contend for "the faith that was once for all delivered to the saints" (Jude 3) and has thus championed a kind of Reformed catholicity.[25] Our approach in the *We Believe* series is therefore irenic, and ecumenical. We write *from* the perspective of the Reformed tradition, but *for* the Church catholic.

Moreover, while the Reformed confessions of the sixteenth century are a high point in the development of the Church's doctrine, they are not the end point. The body of Christ will not "attain to the unity of the faith and of the knowledge of the Son of God, to mature manhood, to the measure of stature of the fullness of Christ" (Eph. 4:13) until Christ fully unites us to himself by his Spirit, when he raises his people from the dead and perfects us by his glorious presence (1 Cor. 15:42–49; Phil. 3:20–21). The bride of Christ will not be fully purified, "without spot or wrinkle," until the Lord returns and presents us to himself "in splendour" (Eph. 5:27; Rev. 21:2, 9). The city of God will not be complete until God himself comes to dwell among us in all his fullness and illumine us with his light (Rev. 21:3, 22–23). A Reformed commitment to the creeds and confessions is, therefore, not an end point, but a stimulus to further biblical exposition and dogmatic clarification.[26] As a work in Christian Dogmatics, *We Believe* does not merely aim to retrieve or to repristinate the Reformed tradition, but to constructively develop it, always under the authority of God's word. If this series makes a modest contribution to the Church's pilgrimage to maturity in Christ, it will have achieved its goal.

---

25. Horton, *Christian Faith*, 30–32. Cf. M. Allen and S. R. Swain, *Reformed Catholicity: The Promise of Retrieval for Theology and Biblical Interpretation* (Baker Academic, 2015); *Christian Dogmatics: Reformed Theology for the Church Catholic* (Baker Academic, 2016).

26. See Bavinck, *Reformed Dogmatics*, 1:31.

TRUTH FOR WORSHIP, LIFE, AND MISSION

The Church's maturity in Christ involves far more than doctrinal faithfulness and clarity. The drama of redemption, which forms the Church's doctrine, aims ultimately at discipleship and doxology.[27] The third part of each study in the *We Believe* series, therefore, briefly considers the ways in which the doctrine under consideration shapes the Church's worship, life, and mission. While the discussion here is necessarily indicative rather than exhaustive, we aim to demonstrate how biblical doctrine creates a moral vision for all of life. This includes, at the broadest level, observing the way in which the particular doctrine provides the basis for biblical principles for Christian worship, life, and mission, whether these are given explicitly in the biblical text (e.g. Matt. 7:12, the "golden rule"), or summarized from biblical revelation as a whole (e.g. "the sanctity of life").[28] It includes, more sharply, consideration of the way in which Christian doctrine grounds the moral law, summarized in the Ten Commandments, and further summarized in the two great commandments of love for God and neighbor (Westminster Confession of Faith 19.2, 5; see esp. Exod. 20:1–17; Deut. 5:6–21; Matt. 22:37–40; Rom. 13:8; Gal. 5:14; James 2:8). It also includes, further, consideration of the wealth of biblical examples which illustrate—both positively and negatively—the wisdom of life according to God's law. Crucially, since Reformed theology has always emphasized the necessity of the work of the Spirit in enabling faith and renewing those who were lost in sin by uniting them to Christ, this section also considers the way in which each doctrine highlights the gracious work of God in enabling his people "to live and work for his praise and glory" (*A Prayer Book for Australia*).

Each of the authors for the series subscribes to one or more of the major Reformed confessions, and shares the general approach to Scripture and theology we have just outlined. At the same time, each author has approached the task in their own way, and—within the rich agreement just sketched—there are differences between us at the level of detail. We have deliberately

27. For this alliterative summary—"drama, doctrine, doxology, and discipleship"—see Horton, *Christian Faith*, 13–27.

28. See J. Murray, *Principles of Conduct: Aspects of Biblical Ethics* (Tyndale, 1957), 78–140.

assembled a company of authors who are experts in either Biblical Theology or Dogmatics on the conviction that in the Reformed tradition scholars must have a facility in both, even while maintaining their own expertise. The books aim to show the necessary integrity of Biblical Theology and Systematic Theology, to introduce students to biblical-confessional theology, and to help enrich and expand Reformed theology, while serving as a resource and reference for pastors, elders, and thoughtful Christians. We're thankful to Lexham Press, and especially our expert editor Dr. Todd Hains, for their partnership in this venture. Our hope and prayer is that these eight *Studies in Reformed Biblical Doctrine* might serve to ground the Church more firmly in the truth of God's word, that together we might "glorify God and enjoy him forever" (Westminster Shorter Catechism 1).

Almighty God, you are enthroned on the praises of Israel,
and all nations will worship and glorify your name.
Grant us counsel, instruct us, and reveal yourself to us,
that we would enjoy and glorify you in heart, soul,
and mind in this life and forever.
Through Jesus Christ our Lord,
who lives and reigns with you
and the Holy Spirit, one God,
now and forever.
Amen.

John McClean
Vice Principal and Lecturer in Systematic Theology and Ethics
Christ College, Sydney

Murray J. Smith
Lecturer in Biblical Theology and Exegesis
Christ College, Sydney

PREFACE

Belief in God and an appropriate estimation of who we are go together. We are, after all, worshiping creatures. Take God away and we are predisposed to worship something else in God's place, and usually, because we are created as God's image-bearers, we end up worshiping ourselves. Left to our own devices, however, we are a riddle to ourselves—we feel, in a singular moment, that we are dependent and yet in control, physical and yet transcending matter, inconsequential and yet the center of our own story. It is no wonder that in contexts where the biblical confession of faith is in decline, confusion with respect to human nature tends to arise.

What, then, do Christians confess about who we are? And how does that Christian confession make sense of our daily experience?

This book introduces and advances a broadly Reformed-catholic account of humanity as created and fallen. I hope to show that this Protestant tradition possesses a wealth of wisdom for understanding who we are and that, by drawing from this tradition, certain questions that one may have about, say, human existence, dignity, diversity, or sexuality—questions that continue to plague the modern social imaginary—are not shunned but are probed and effectively explored. To do this well, it is necessary to mine Christian teachings on anthropology's biblical roots and historical expressions. As I continue to say in the introduction, books that introduce and argue for the Reformed tradition's approach to theological anthropology are few and far between. I wrote this, therefore, for theological students with the hope of drawing them to the riches of the primary texts of the Reformed-catholic tradition.

I am thankful to the editors of the We Believe series, John McLean and Murray Smith, for approaching and entrusting me with writing on the important topic of theological anthropology. I started thinking about this book in the spring of 2019 following a conversation with John over coffee at Plaza Indonesia in Jakarta. While this topic has been in the forefront of my mind ever since I explored the epistemology of Herman Bavinck for my first book, I felt the acute pressure and weight appropriate to writing an introduction like this one. I knew, therefore, that I needed further reflection and to write a more technical work before undertaking the writing of this particular volume. That led me to dive deeper into Bavinck's primary texts and some contemporary issues on theological anthropology, including race, affect theory, the cognitive science of religion, covenant, and the beatific vision. That research turned into the book *God and Humanity* (T&T Clark Explorations in Reformed Theology [Bloomsbury T&T Clark, 2024]). I direct readers who would like to read a more technical study after this one to consult that particular work, which I take to be the terrain for which this book is an entryway. The editorial comments from John and Murray made this book far better. Thanks as well to Todd Hains and the team at Lexham Press and Baker Academic (especially Eric Salo) for shepherding this book to completion. An earlier version of chapter 7 has also been published in *Themelios*.[1] Thanks to the editors for the permission to include a revised form in this volume.

My thanks go to John Fesko and Jennifer Patterson for reading the entirety of this manuscript and for offering helpful suggestions and comments. I am also grateful to Michael Allen, Scott Swain, Josh Malone, Harrison Perkins, Steven J. Duby, Thomas Keene, Peter Lee, James Eglinton, Cory Brock, Marinus de Jong, Rachel Gilson, Rebecca McLaughlin, and D. Blair Smith for either reading sections or chapters, engaging in constructive conversations, or providing feedback. As ever, Reformed Theological Seminary, Washington DC, has been a wonderful place to undertake this research, and I'm grateful to my colleagues Scott Redd, Paul Jeon, Peter Lee, Thomas Keene, Jennifer Patterson, Stephanie DiMaria, Jenny McGahey, Elizabeth Wagner, and Mike Park for being such encouraging presences. Kimberley Stephenson, our trusted librarian, was always prompt in providing research material and ordering

1. See N. Gray Sutanto, "Cultural Mandate and the Image of God: Human Vocation Under Creation, Fall, and Redemption," *Themelios* 48 (2023): 592–604.

the books that I needed for the completion of this project. Isaac Whitney did wonders in helping to produce the glossary of terms. Steven Preston also helped edit the manuscript. I am grateful, too, to my wife, Indita Probosutedjo, for her unending patience with me as I carried on writing, and for Atari Probosutedjo, Scott and Jennifer Redd, and Retno Sulistiowati for their hospitality, help, and encouragement as we transitioned to DC.

This book is dedicated to our church family back home in Jakarta, Indonesia—Covenant City Church. My years there taught me humility and allowed me to receive radical hospitality, friendship, and grace, and thus gave me a profound insight of what it means to be human.

ABBREVIATIONS

BTCB	Brazos Theological Commentary on the Bible
NICNT	New International Commentary on the New Testament
NICOT	New International Commentary on the Old Testament
NIGTC	New International Greek Testament Commentary
RD	Herman Bavinck. *Reformed Dogmatics*. Edited by John Bolt. Translated by John Vriend. 4 vols. Baker Academic, 2003–8.
TPT	Petrus van Mastricht. *Theoretical-Practical Theology*. 5 vols. Reformation Heritage Books, 2018.
WBC	Word Biblical Commentary
WCF	Westminster Confession of Faith

A PRAYER FOR THE STUDY OF HUMANITY AND SIN

O LORD, our Lord,
how majestic is your name in all the earth!
You have set your glory above the heavens.
Out of the mouth of babies and infants,
you have established strength because of your foes,
to still the enemy and the avenger.
When I look at your heavens, the work of your fingers,
the moon and the stars, which you have set in place,
what is man that you are mindful of him,
and the son of man that you care for him?
Yet you have made him a little lower than the heavenly beings
and crowned him with glory and honor.
You have given him dominion over the works of your hands;
you have put all things under his feet,
all sheep and oxen,
and also the beasts of the field,
the birds of the heavens, and the fish of the sea,
whatever passes along the paths of the seas.
O LORD, our Lord,
how majestic is your name in all the earth! (Psalm 8)

Gracious God, illumine us to understand ourselves in light of your word. Grant us grace to see the majesty and humility of our constitution, the depths of our sin in our fallen condition, and the great mercy with which you have saved us in Christ Jesus, that we may embrace who we are as image-bearers who receive the grace of the gospel and follow Christ's lead and example to your glory. Through Jesus Christ our Lord, who lives and reigns with you and the Holy Spirit, one God, forever and ever. Amen.

INTRODUCTION

WHAT IS HUMANITY? (PSALM 8:4)

ADVANCING A CHRISTIAN AND REFORMED ANTHROPOLOGY

What does it mean to be a human being? Who am I as made in the divine image?

Few questions are more central than these, and perhaps defining the meaning of our human existence has never been more acutely needed than it is today. According to the Christian tradition, to be made in God's image is to be imbued with both humility and dignity, to straddle between spiritual and material realities, and to find our end in the God we are meant to image. To be made in the divine image, then, is both indicative of our being and an imperative to pursue a particular purpose. We are most human when we have a reference point beyond ourselves, and we are less human to the extent that we curve inward in the attempt to deny that we are signs that point to our Maker.

Secular modernity's departure from the biblical moorings of anthropology as made in the image of God has introduced reductionist accounts of our human nature that are often neither coherent nor existentially satisfying. On the one hand, we are reduced to our material origins and are deemed nothing more than the aggregate sum of our physical parts. Meaning, consciousness, and normativity are thus illusory. On the other hand, because there is nothing transcendent about us, we are told to define ourselves, to rely on our own willpower to bring forth some purpose for our existence. If existence precedes essence, however, and there is no essence except one that is willed by our own freedoms, what is that essence but a mere cry into the void and a pointless rebellion against the futility of our existence? Humans are considered nothing, and yet we are called to create our own meaning, as if we were ourselves divine.

The denial of our psychosomatic unity—that we are embodied souls—has produced a volatile dialectic that oscillates between naturalistic materialism and divine-like responsibility, between meaninglessness and the pressure to create meaning for ourselves. This is both incoherent and unlivable, and there is a need to recover the biblical teaching that humans are made in the image of God. This book hopes to fill that need. Here, I offer an introduction to a Christian and Reformed account of theological anthropology. As such, it seeks to recover that sense of being made in the divine image, its biblical moorings, its reception within the broad Reformed and catholic tradition, and its contemporary application. The three sections of this book correspond to those three aims.

THE ANTHROPOLOGICAL QUESTION TODAY: IN THREE PARTS

In comportment with the goal of the We Believe series, this book is thus an exposition of the clause in the Nicene Creed that Christ came down "for us and for our salvation." What constitutes humanity, and how should we understand human nature in terms of its creation and then its fall into sin—which makes salvation for us necessary?

BIBLICAL REVELATION

Section 1 provides a panoramic overview of the scriptural texts that form the foundation for a Reformed theological anthropology. The first chapter thus offers a biblical-theological reading of important passages on created humanity, the second chapter focuses on the first sin and the consequent corruption of human beings, and the third on postlapsarian humanity as preserved and redeemed. This section presupposes the unity of the whole canon and the divine authorship of Scripture that provides the basis and, indeed, a mandate for a theological interpretation. The scriptural texts considered in this section are what Alexander Pruss has called "seminal texts"—texts that are particularly generative and fecund within the Christian tradition.[1] A minimalist reading that limits the sense of the text to its historical author's intent (often speculatively reconstructed from historical backgrounds), while ignoring the witness of the catholic tradition's reception of these texts, is not merely unduly narrow in scope but also unfaithful given the ontology of Scripture. The same Spirit who inspires the Scriptures, after all, also illumines the church's reception of the same. Thus, I draw conclusions from the biblical witnesses not just with respect to the sense of the immediate context but also from their theological implications on, say, human dignity, personhood, or the nature of sin.

DOGMATIC DEVELOPMENT

Section 2 presents a dogmatic sketch of a Reformed anthropology. This section covers human nature as created, original sin, corruption, and its transformation by grace. Chapters 4–6 present a Reformed-catholic account of human nature and the image of God. Chapter 7 considers the cultural mandate, human vocation, and the corporate image of God. Chapter 8 outlines and defends the doctrine of original sin. Chapter 9 is on human corruption and common grace, actual sin, and the redeemed human nature. Because other volumes in this series treat the doctrines of creation, Christology, and salvation, some areas that could well have been explored are not treated (e.g., the font of human nature in the divine ideas, or our union with Christ), and readers are encouraged to pick up the other volumes for such topics. And although the book discusses sin's corruption of our human nature, a further

1. Alexander Pruss, *One Body: An Essay in Christian Sexual Ethics* (University of Notre Dame Press, 2013), 3–5. See also Ryan S. Peterson, *The Imago Dei as Human Identity: A Theological Interpretation* (Eisenbrauns, 2016). On reading the Bible as Christian Scripture, see Kevin J. Vanhoozer, *Mere Christian Hermeneutics: Transfiguring What It Means to Read the Bible Theologically* (Zondervan, 2024).

analysis of sin in itself, actual sin, and all of its consequences (whether social or environmental) must await another project.

I am persuaded that a renewal of theological anthropology for contemporary concerns necessitates the work of retrieval. If the recent years of evangelical theology have exposed a certain forgetfulness with regard to theology proper, the same could be said about the doctrine of humanity.[2] This can be seen, for instance, in the common deployment of the taxonomy offered on the different models for the image of God along the lines of the structural, vocational (functional), and the relational. Structural accounts of the image of God locate the image in the structure, nature, or part of the human being (usually in the soul); vocational or functional accounts locate the image in some calling or representational responsibility; relational accounts have to do with how the image refers to the relations one has with others, God, and Christ. This taxonomy is virtually ubiquitous in contemporary textbooks or introductions to theological anthropology, and readers are then encouraged to locate thinkers or traditions into a particular category, usually with a reminder that the structural perspective is no longer an option due to a lack of exegetical support.

While it may be helpful to think of the structural, vocational, and relational as aspects of the image, identifying the image along the lines of this taxonomy would have been quite alien to the Christian tradition. Indeed, as I will show, even Augustine, who is usually identified as a primary representative of the structuralist position because of the way in which he identifies the image with the intellectual soul, immediately goes on to emphasize that the soul's well-being is contingent on its relation to God, which in turn makes it possible for the soul to conform to God well and to turn toward its neighbor in rightly ordered love. Later theologians in the Reformed tradition would emphasize not one but multipronged aspects of the image of God, involving the metaphysics and faculties of the soul, the proper virtues accruing to those faculties that order one's self toward God (original righteousness), the relation of the soul to the body, the proper exercise of stewardship and

2. "There is very little in print on human nature in Reformed thought." Paul Helm, *Human Nature from Calvin to Edwards* (Reformation Heritage Books, 2018), xi. For an exemplary work of retrieval in relation to theology proper and Christology, see Steven J. Duby, *Jesus and the God of Classical Theism* (Baker Academic, 2023).

dominion over creation, and the blessed end of humanity with God in resurrected eternal life. The perceived separation between structural, functional, and relational accounts has also often led to the eclipse of one aspect, as if vocational and relational tasks do not presuppose an account of human nature, or as if the metaphysics of who we are do not bear inherent ethical or corporate responsibilities. The tendency of contemporary systematic theology to bypass earlier accounts of the metaphysics of human nature for a functional or relational anthropology, then, seems to live on the "borrowed capital" of the traditioned presentation.[3]

Indeed, the Reformed tradition is much more holistic in its presentation. We do well, then, to recover the scope of a properly Reformed account of theological anthropology by attending to the primary sources, especially in the Reformed tradition's confessional and high orthodox expressions. Recent scholarship has shown that one could not limit or reduce the Reformed tradition to the magisterial Reformers but should attend to its formalization and development as that tradition stabilized both ecclesiastically and academically. Further, the work of translation in recent decades has nurtured a recovery of these post-Reformation orthodox divines, which prompts theologians to mine these formative influences that have often been unwittingly left behind. Hence, this second section devotes much space to flesh out the doctrine of the image of God and human nature by attending to the accounts of those doctrines from the Reformed confessions, the Leiden Synopsis, Francis Turretin, Petrus van Mastricht, and Herman Bavinck. This second section is also introduced by attending to the Augustinian and Thomist (dualist and hylomorphist) precedents for these Reformed reflections on human nature. As we shall see, though the Reformed tradition does form a doctrine of humanity that accents original righteousness and depravity in ways that distinguish it from its Roman Catholic counterpart, it is important to show that a Reformed theological anthropology still stands in broad continuity with the earlier catholic (and Augustinian) tradition. Indeed, if a result of this volume is that readers would be led to read these primary sources, then I would consider the book to have accomplished its task.

---

3. Kelly Kapic, "Anthropology," in *Christian Dogmatics: Reformed Theology for the Church Catholic*, ed. Michael Allen and Scott R. Swain (Baker Academic, 2016), 170.

As I articulate at the beginning of chapter 4, because theological anthropology is a distributed doctrine that effects virtually every loci of theology and is not the main subject of creedal developments (which would be the Trinity and Christology), one would have to go to particular theologians to find the dogmatic elaborations on the doctrine. It would be counterproductive and not pedagogically useful, however, to survey every major Christian thinker on this topic. Thus, my selection of thinkers here, from Augustine and Thomas to the high Reformed orthodox theologians and the late-modern Herman Bavinck, is an attempt to present a synthesized and accessible account of a broad Reformed-catholic anthropology and human nature, and these thinkers present representative mature statements. There are other works that have focused on, say, the anthropology of Gregory of Nyssa, Calvin, Schleiermacher, or Barth, but there is little that presents, in a concise and introductory way, a theological anthropology of the Reformed-catholic tradition. This volume, including the chapters on dogmatic development, is written toward that end.

The task of retrieval is for the sake of renewal and development.[4] Herman Bavinck's theological anthropology made advancements on this topic in his emphasis on the corporate and organic character of the image of God. This development has led to generative neo-Calvinistic teachings on correspondingly corporate dimensions of human vocation, responsibility, and sin. This second section is thus attentive to these contributions, outlining a dogmatic exposition of the relation between the image of God and the cultural mandate before the fall, common grace, and the Great Commission as well.

TRUTH FOR WORSHIP, LIFE, AND MISSION

The third and final section engages two important contemporary issues: that of gender and sexuality on the one hand, and race on the other. In the former chapter, I provide a biblical and theological account of sex that seeks to do justice to the interplay of nature and culture for a well-formed understanding of the male and female in relation. I also provide a preliminary response to

4. I am presupposing Herman Bavinck's account of the development of doctrine here. On this, see Cameron Clausing, *Theology and History in the Methodology of Herman Bavinck: Revelation, Confession, and Christian Consciousness* (Oxford University Press, 2023).

revisionary and trans-inclusive definitions of gender. In the latter chapter, I examine and critique the construct of a "gradation of existence" between the races, show that race is ultimately a "true myth" in the sense that it is a social fiction that has malformed our imaginations, and then present Herman Bavinck's view on human diversity as a way toward a Reformed account of the same.

The three sections are intertwined. While the first section focuses on scriptural and biblical-theological observations, it anticipates the dogmatic and applied material. The dogmatic section discusses and presupposes the foundation of Scripture and is also never unconcerned with contemporary application. I hope to write a textbook that thus indicates the organic relation between biblical theology and systematic theology, along with the ethical pressure they exert on readers. Humans are made in the image of God, after all, and in Scripture we hear the divine voice that discloses not only who God is but also who we are called to be.

While there is indeed little in print on the image of God and human ontology from the Reformed tradition, Paul Helm's *Human Nature from Calvin to Edwards* is a wonderful initial contribution. However, while Helm focuses on many authors, the selectivity of his topics (and seemingly ad hoc organization to parts of the book) makes it difficult reading for the uninitiated, and I hope this present volume, which covers both biblical material and a more constrained set of topics and historical figures expounded in a more developed and systematic fashion, will be more immediately useful for readers. Further, because the topic of theological anthropology in general represents quite a large field, the book does not (and cannot) engage with all the live contemporary debates or arguments.[5] The book does, however, hope to prepare the reader to begin engaging with the field and such debates from a Reformed outlook. While the book does aim to make some contributions to theological anthropology from a Reformed perspective, the primary audience for this book remains the theological student.

Finally, as I write this book, I am in constant awareness of Gregory of Nyssa's observation that humanity is a mystery. Because we are image-bearers

5. For recent introductions that offer a broad entryway into the live issues, see Joshua Ryan Farris, *An Introduction to Theological Anthropology: Humans, Both Creaturely and Divine* (Baker Academic, 2020); Marc Cortez, *Theological Anthropology: A Guide for the Perplexed* (Bloomsbury T&T Clark, 2010); and Lucy Peppiatt, *Imago Dei: Humanity Made in the Image of God* (Cascade Books, 2022).

of an incomprehensible God, it would be surprising if we, who are formed as an "imitation of the archetype," should be comprehensible.[6] There is much more that can be said about humanity as created and fallen, and this book, indeed, could serve only as a mere starting point. I pray, however, that it might invite readers to the wonders of who we are, precisely because we are signs that point to our Maker.

6. Gregory of Nyssa, "On the Making of Man" 11.3, in *A Select Library of Nicene and Post-Nicene Fathers of the Christian Church*, 2nd series, ed. Philip Schaff and Henry Wace, 14 vols. (Christian Literature, 1890–1900; repr., Hendrickson, 1994), 5:396.

1

HUMANITY: CREATED IN THE IMAGE OF GOD

THIS FIRST CHAPTER comments on important passages on created humanity, covering the creation of humanity in the image of God; the scriptural emphasis on human nature as a body-soul unity; human vocation in light of the biblical themes of temple, covenant, dominion, and representation; dignity and personhood; and the ways in which Jesus Christ is the true image of God. The next two chapters shall focus on fallen and redeemed humanity, respectively. Because the orders of sin and grace presuppose the order of creation, these chapters set the backdrop for the proceeding material.

Christian theology describes humanity as made in the image of God. This directs us toward divine revelation, for image-bearers have a reference point outside of themselves—we are essentially *religious* creatures. We do not form meaning for ourselves creatively. Rather, we are called to recognize the kind of beings that we are. God, after all, is the Creator, and he has made all things "according to their kinds" (Gen. 1:11–12, 21, 24–25). The divine word carves up reality according to its joints, as it were, as that word discloses and describes the natural kinds that God has created. Human naming, then, is an act of recognition. Words refer to things, and human predication is truthful insofar as it thinks God's thoughts after him in an ectypal, analogous fashion. We do not know as God knows, but we know according to our finite capacities, with the revelation that God has accommodated to us.[1] True description of reality is possible because all things refer back to the divine eminence and volition as the first cause of all created existence. This first part thus appropriately presents the scriptural and textual grounds for the dogmatic exposition that follows in the second section.

GENESIS 1 AND 2—ON THE CREATION OF HUMANITY AND THE IMAGE OF GOD

Genesis 1:26–28

Humanity was made to image God, to relate with him, and to represent him. The creation of humanity breaks the rhythm of a series of creative acts. In the first five days, God creates with "Let there be . . ." iterations that bring forth light, the chasm between the skies and seas, land and vegetation, the celestial lights, and animals of all kinds. When God turns to the human being in Genesis 1:26, however, "the voice switches from the imperative to the subjunctive . . . having set the stage . . . God deliberates and announces his own particular project, the particular work of God."[2] As the text says:

> Then God said, "Let us make man in our image, after our likeness. And let them have dominion over the fish of the sea and over the birds of the heavens and over the livestock and over all the earth and over every creeping thing that creeps on the earth."
>
> So God created man in his own image,
> in the image of God he created him;
> male and female he created them. (Gen. 1:26–27)

The break in rhythm indicates that God is doing something different with the creation of the human being. "This particular attention devoted to the origin of man," Bavinck observes, "serves already as evidence of the fact

1. For the distinction between archetypal and ectypal theology, see Franciscus Junius, *A Treatise on True Theology*, trans. David C. Noe (Reformation Heritage Books, 2014); and Herman Bavinck, *Wonderful Works of God*, trans. Henry Zylstra (Westminster Seminary Press, 2020), 153.

2. John Behr, "Humanity," in *New Cambridge Companion to Christian Doctrine*, ed. Michael Allen (Cambridge University Press, 2022), 39.

that man is the purpose and end, the head and crown of the whole work of creation."[3] The divine annunciation of the creation of human beings bears several features that require exposition: (a) on the first person plural reference ("Let us make"), (b) on the sense and relation of "likeness" and "image," (c) on the embodied character of image-bearers as male and female, and (d) on the dominion given to humanity. I shall comment on the first two in this section and the latter two in the next sections.

A few options have been offered in more recent scholarship on the sense of the first person plural: Perhaps the reference there is a "royal we" or about a council of angels that God is addressing before making the human beings.[4] The majority report of premodern and Reformed exegesis, however, would emphasize that the first person plural here is a Trinitarian reference—a point we will return to in the dogmatic section of this book. The Triune God is making humanity in his image. Although the Trinity is merely adumbrated in the Old Testament and finally disclosed in the New Testament, there is a single divine author behind the whole of Scripture, and Christians are warranted in taking into account the fullness of the scriptural data when reading this opening chapter of Genesis.

While Van Mastricht rightly notes that some premodern exegetes have argued that image and likeness are distinguished, with image referring to our conformity to God by nature and likeness "in the things of grace," he also notes the alternative reading of considering the use of these two terms for "rhetorical amplification, so that they mean an especially similar image."[5] This latter reading is to be preferred, for the language of "image" is used elsewhere to refer to the idols or statues of other gods (e.g., 2 Kings 11:18), and "likeness," too, is used similarly to refer to idols as copies of gods (Isa. 40:18) or of the "likeness" between human fathers and sons (Adam and Seth,

---

3. Bavinck, *Wonderful Works*, 166.

4. Cf. Gordon Wenham, *Genesis 1–15*, WBC (Zondervan, 1987), 27–28; Gerhard von Rad, *Old Testament Theology*, vols. 1 and 2, trans. D. M. G. Stalker (Prince, 2005), 145–46. Van Mastricht already notes the other options, including (1) the address to the angels, (2) an address to nature (3), the royal use of the first plural "in the custom of great men," and (4) to emphasize merely the "excellence of man"; nonetheless, Van Mastricht continues to side with Augustine and "most modern theologians" who "most solidly deduce the mystery of the Trinity from this passage." Petrus van Mastricht, *Theoretical-Practical Theology*, vol. 3, *The Works of God and the Fall of Man*, ed. Joel Beeke, trans. Todd M. Rester (Reformation Heritage Books, 2018), 247–48 (hereafter *TPT*).

5. Van Mastricht, *TPT*, 3:250. Cf. R. R. Reno, *Genesis*, BTCB (Brazos, 2017), 51–52.

per Gen. 5:3).[6] Hence, as Bavinck notes, despite some nuances, "there is no essential material distinction to be made between ["image" and "likeness"] either. They are used interchangeably, and alternate for no specific reason."[7] Likewise, the Westminster Assembly's annotation on this passage makes the same point: "Image and likeness are not two diverse things, but the same more fully and clearly expressed in two words than in one."[8] "Likeness" and "image" are thus adjacent or synonymous terms, and recent commentators confirm this reading.[9] The sense is that humans have a reference point outside of themselves—we are in relation to God, called to commune with God, and we represent God. Made in the image of God, we are dignified as the pinnacle of creation, representing God's lordship over it, and are somehow analogous or similar to him; but as image, we are humbled as servants, requiring God for our own flourishing and obedience to God for proper cultivation over creation. We are meant, therefore, to be imitators of God on a creaturely level (Exod. 20:11; Eph. 5:1–14). Further, though humans are indeed made with certain capacities and responsibilities (which will be further fleshed out below and in later chapters), the emphasis here is on the way in which the whole of the human being, as created, is made in the image of God and refers back to him.[10]

It follows, therefore, that humanity is essentially religious. As image-bearers, we are created to worship God and enjoy him, as the Westminster

---

6. Stephen G. Dempster, *Dominion and Dynasty: A Theology of the Hebrew Bible* (IVP Academic, 2003), 58–59.

7. Herman Bavinck, *Reformed Dogmatics*, vol. 2, *God and Creation*, ed. John Bolt, trans. John Vriend (Baker Academic, 2004), 532 (hereafter *RD*). So G. C. Berkouwer: "Because of the variable usage of the two terms in Genesis, it is difficult to escape the conclusion that it is impossible to hold that '*tselem*' and '*demuth*' refer to two different things." *Man: The Image of God*, trans. Dirk Jellema (Eerdmans, 1962), 69.

8. Westminster Assembly, *Annotations Upon All the Books of the Old and New Testaments: This Third, Above the First and Second, Edition So Enlarged, as They Make Commentary on the Sacred Scripture, Never Before Published in English* (Evan Tyler, 1657), annotation on Gen. 1:26.

9. Kleinig concurs: Image and likeness are "virtual synonyms"; John Kleinig, *Wonderfully Made: A Protestant Theology of the Body* (Lexham, 2021), 27. And Marc Cortez: "Contemporary exegetes . . . agree that these two terms are largely synonymous and that we should not read any strong distinction into their use in this text." Cortez, *Theological Anthropology: A Guide for the Perplexed* (Bloomsbury T&T Clark, 2010), 16.

10. Ryan S. Peterson, *The Imago Dei as Human Identity: A Theological Interpretation* (Eisenbrauns, 2016), 84. Although the Reformed theologians surveyed later do not use this language, Peterson's construal of the image of God in humanity as constitutive of human identity is thus helpful in framing the way in which our capacities, functions, and relations are not to be isolated.

Shorter Catechism states. What we shall see in the chapters that follow is that when humanity fails to worship God, it will inevitably worship something else within creation, idolizing creatures with divine properties (Rom. 1:21–23).

Genesis 2:7

The divine annunciation mentions humanity's creation as male and female, referring to their embodiment. Two further points expand on the goodness of humanity as a created, embodied psychosomatic unity from Genesis 2:7: The first point is based upon the "breath" of God that makes humanity into a "living being," and the second on the emphasis and care with which God creates humankind in its embodiment.

First, Genesis 1 discloses a cosmic perspective that points to humanity as the terminus of God's creative work, whereas chapter 2 offers a more intimate, zoomed-in perspective, as it were.[11] Genesis 1:26–27 shows that God announces his creation of humanity poetically, and Genesis 2:7 highlights the intimate process by which he bestows life on the first human. The name of Adam, after all, connotes not merely a proper name but who he is as representative of humanity, the human representation of the earth, and human nature as a whole.[12] "Then the Lord God formed the man of dust from the ground and breathed into his nostrils the breath of life, and the man became a living creature" (Gen. 2:7). The "breath" (נשמה) of life here has a wide semantic range and could be used to refer to the literal breath of a living person (e.g., Gen. 7:22; Deut. 20:16; 1 Kings 17:17; Isa. 2:22) or to refer to the power of God that can give life or destroy (e.g., Ps. 18:15; Job 4:9; Isa. 30:33). Other animals are also called living beings (e.g., Gen. 1:20; 2:19); importantly, the animals also have the breath of life (Gen. 1:30; 6:17; 7:15, 22). That we are made with the same breath and with the same earthly materials explains why it is that we share so much, biologically speaking, with other material creatures. However, it is important to note that with respect to human beings, the breath of life is associated in Scripture with

11. Cf. Abigale Favale, *Genesis of Gender: A Christian Theory* (Ignatius, 2022), 36–37; Bavinck, *Wonderful Works*, 166.

12. Cf. Kleinig, *Wonderfully Made*, 26.

the gift of understanding and the capacity for wisdom, making us unique among the animals as well.[13]

Consider, for instance, Job 32:6–9, where the prophet Elihu rebukes Job's three friends with wisdom—a wisdom that he identifies with the gift of God's breath of life:

> And Elihu the son of Barachel the Buzite answered and said: "I am young in years, and you are aged; therefore I was timid and afraid to declare my opinion to you. I said, 'Let days speak, and many years teach wisdom.' But it is the spirit in man, the breath of the Almighty, that makes him understand. It is not the old who are wise, nor the aged who understand what is right."

Elihu associates the "spirit" (רוח) in someone with the breath (נשמה) of God, which gifts them understanding. John Hartley notes, therefore, that the very breath of God "which gives human beings life (cf. Gen. 2:7), also inspires the human spirit with insight."[14] The mention of the spirit in a person also calls to mind Proverbs 20:27 and Paul's discussion in 1 Corinthians 2:10–16: It is the locus of "a person's reflective thought."[15] This breath, when associated with humanity, thus corresponds with the capacity for understanding, and God is the one who moves to gift the exercise and actualization of wisdom. The breath of God is associated not just with the bestowal of life, distinguishing a living person from the dead, but also with the capacities of the embodied soul. Wisdom is not mere calculated reasoning for the sake of producing the most efficient forms of action; rather, it stands in an organic connection to righteousness and holiness (Eph. 4:24; Col. 3:10). Indeed, wisdom issues from the godly fear of the Lord (Prov. 9:10).

When Elihu then turns to Job in the next chapter, he counsels Job to listen to him because he speaks words from the "uprightness" of his "heart" (Job 33:3), with sincere lips, and again invokes the "Spirit of God" who has made him and the "breath of the almighty" that gives him life (Job 33:4) to fortify his claims.[16] John Kleinig points to these same passages and observes rightly:

13. *Pace* Wenham, *Genesis 1–15*, 60–61.
14. John Hartley, *The Book of Job*, NICOT (Eerdmans, 1988), 434.
15. Hartley, *The Book of Job*, 434.
16. Cf. Hartley, *The Book of Job*, 438.

"The breath of life that he breathes into them, makes them what they are, with all their physical and mental powers."[17] The older tradition that includes the human "joint capacity of will and reason" in the image of God is thus not without grounds, given the exposition of Genesis 2:7 in Job 33:3–4 and the way in which such capacities are presupposed in the vocational call of humans to represent God and to obey his will, conforming themselves to him.[18] The Westminster divines, commenting on Genesis 1:26, argued that the image includes several important features and cannot be reduced to one capacity or the mere presence of life: "A spiritual and immortal substance, and endued with three faculties understanding, will, and memory, as the Deity has three Persons, Father, Son, and Holy Ghost, and in the now supernatural endowments of divine knowledge, righteousness and true holiness (Eccles. 7:29; Eph. 4:24), and lastly in authority and government of creatures."[19] Clearly, the breath of God in Genesis 2:7 signifies life in its fullest sense and is expanded on in Scripture as distinct from the breath God has given to other animals, imbuing humanity with vital life (like the animals) but with the *kind* of being humans have as vice-regents and responsible, religious agents.

The human as a living "being" here is a translation of the word נפש (*nephesh*). נפש likewise has a wide range of meaning, and exegesis has disclosed that it could refer to the vitality of life (as opposed to inert, dead objects), to thirst and hunger, to desire and need, and also to the sense of a conscious soul that animates and directs the whole body.[20] While this recent material is concerned with ensuring that contemporary readers not eisegete the sense of נפש with Greek or even contemporary intuitions on a separate, immaterial substance alongside the body, נפש has a broad semantic range and can and often does connote the inner sense of self-consciousness and mental activity, without isolating such activity as an independent substrate: "It might more sensibly be read as 'person' or 'self' or by such personal pronouns as 'I' and 'myself.' . . . In those cases it is correct to suppose that the term stands for the whole person rather than for some immaterial part or

17. Kleinig, *Wonderfully Made*, 31.
18. Bonaventure, *Breviloquium*, trans. Dominic V. Monti (Franciscan Institute, 2005), 85.
19. Westminster Assembly, *Annotations*, Gen. 1:26.
20. See Hans Walter Wolff, *Anthropology of the Old Testament*, trans. Margaret Kohl (SCM, 1947), 10–25.

aspect."[21] It is in this sense, therefore, that one's נפש observes the testimonies of God (Ps. 119:129) and loves them (Ps. 119:167).

Second, note the emphasis and care with which the text depicts God's fashioning of the human body in Genesis 2. Gerhard von Rad describes it eloquently:

> It is particular in the picture of the creation of man and woman that this account [in Genesis 2] is fully detailed and bold in its vividness, for it depicts God the creator as completely applied to his work without the slightest reserve, and occupied in shaping it . . . like a potter. The material utilized is the ground—but man became a "living being" only by God's breathing into him his own divine breath from his own mouth. Verse 7 which recounts this thus contains a precise definition—a rare thing with the Jahwist. Compared with Gen. 1:26f., here the creation of man is pictured on the one hand as much more personal and indeed much more intimate act of God.[22]

God creates the body with a loving attention and care. The body is *good*, and God delights in it. Psalm 139 also highlights this care, declaring with praise that humanity was "fearfully and wonderfully made":

> For you formed my inward parts;
>   you knitted me together in my mother's womb.
> I praise you, for I am fearfully and wonderfully made.
> Wonderful are your works;
>   my soul knows it very well.
> My frame was not hidden from you,
> when I was being made in secret,
>   intricately woven in the depths of the earth.
> Your eyes saw my unformed substance;
> in your book were written, every one of them,
>   the days that were formed for me,
>   when as yet there was none of them. (Ps. 139:13–16)

---

21. John Cooper, *Body, Soul, and Life Everlasting: Biblical Anthropology and the Monism-Dualism Debate* (Eerdmans, 2000), 39.

22. Von Rad, *Old Testament Theology*, 1:149.

1 Corinthians 11:7

First Corinthians 11:7 mentions the image of God and, at first glance, seems problematically to exclude women from the image. The text reads: "For a man ought not to cover his head, since he is the image and glory of God, but woman is the glory of man." The mystery of this passage is compounded by the similarly perplexing material in the surrounding context: the appeal to the angels in verse 10, the prohibition of exposed heads for women prophesying in verses 5–6, and the apparent disgracefulness of men having long hair in verse 14.

The history of Christian interpretation has offered numerous options on the sense of 1 Corinthians 11:7, and it is difficult to assert with certainty what this text has in mind. Let me briefly mention some interpretive options before setting forth some parameters.

In Augustine's reading, women are created in the image of God and are equal to men. Hence, he warns that taking 1 Corinthians 11:7 to mean that women were not created in the image of God is "in contradiction both to Christian good sense and to the text of Gen. 1:27."[a] What, then, does the text mean? Augustine believes that men and women share the same intellectual nature and are thus called to contemplate eternal realities, but the woman signifies the function of the intellect that regards "the management of temporal affairs," which can lure one away from contemplation.[b] The head covering thus points allegorically to the virtuous curbing of the intellect so that it considers bodily ends as subordinated to the eternal. Both men and women, to be clear, are called to the same contemplation of God, but the distinction of the sexes *signifies* different functions of the intellect: contemplation of eternal things, on the one hand, and temporal matters, on the other.[c] This is not to say that women are called to temporal matters while men are called to eternal matters: Both are called to attend to eternal matters first—but their bodies serve as distinct pedagogical reminders of the priority of the eternal over the temporal.

Calvin argues that this text is not so much on the createdness of women—for then they would be identical with men—but on their domestic role.[d] Men and women are created ontologically equal yet have different roles assigned to them.

Bavinck's interpretation, in my view, is the most promising. Indeed, Bavinck offers a balanced reading: "The woman, accordingly, is very much a partaker of human nature and of the image of God . . . and in solidarity with man. . . . [The man] is nevertheless incomplete without the woman, for she is the mother of all living (1 Cor. 11:7–12; Eph. 5:22ff.)."[e] While acknowledging Calvin's perspective, he suggests that here the text is referring to Adam's federal headship—and Adam is the representative of all of humanity (per Rom. 5:12, 18–19).[f] The language of the head is referring to Adam, not males in general.

Lucy Peppiatt, finally, suggests that Paul is not indicating his own theological position here but is rather citing an opponent for the sake of argument.[g] While this does remove the difficulty, it's a more novel interpretation and, like the others, cannot be confirmed with certainty.

Whatever we might say about the text, some clear parameters are established once we consider the whole scope of scriptural teaching and the immediate context. One should stress the clear text of Genesis 1:27 over 1 Corinthians 11:7 in our interpretive efforts—the clear illumines the obscure (WCF 1:9).[h] Excluding women from the image of God is not an option, given the clear passages in the creation accounts. Further, despite the mysterious character of the verse and the surrounding context, notice that 1 Corinthians 11:7 is couched between strong claims on the mutual and complementary nature of the male-female relation. First Corinthians 11:4–5 affirms the mutual prophesying of males and females, which harkens us back to the common mandate (and thus common relation) they have from and with God (Gen. 1:28).[i] Then, 1 Corinthians 11:8 and 11–12 affirm the mutual dependence between male and female. Though woman was made out of man (appealing to Gen. 2:18–25), Paul argues that man is now not "independent of . . . woman; for as woman was made from man, so man is now born of woman" (1 Cor. 11:11–12). The clause that the woman is the "glory of man" (1 Cor. 11:7), therefore, seems to imply that, just as humanity was made to disperse in order to represent God on earth, the woman was created so that God's image-bearers can be generative to that end; created humanity is the glory of God, the manifestation of his presence, and it is through the woman that the manifestation and dispersal of humanity is possible. Far from rendering the woman subordinate to the man, her creation as "second," as it were, is the *fulfillment* and *glory* of humanity. Here, as elsewhere, the Reformational principle of letting the clear passages of Scripture interpret the more obscure is helpful.

a. Augustine, *The Trinity* 12.3, trans. Edmund Hill (New City Press, 1991), 329.
b. Augustine, *The Trinity* 12.3.10 (Hill, 330).
c. Augustine, *The Trinity* 12.3.19 (Hill, 336).
d. John Calvin, *Commentaries on the First Book of Moses, Called Genesis*, trans. John King (Printed for the Calvin Translation Society, 1850), 90–100; Turretin and Van Mastricht argue that this text teaches that men have (benevolent) dominion over women in their marital relation (Turretin, *IET*, 1:465; Van Mastricht, *TPT*, 3:288).

e. Bavinck, *RD*, 2:578.
f. Bavinck, *RD*, 2:578.
g. Peppiatt, *Imago Dei*, 103–6. See also her *Women and Worship at Corinth: Paul's Rhetorical Arguments in 1 Corinthians* (Cascade Books, 2015).
h. Peppiatt, *Imago Dei*, 105.
i. Amy Peeler, "Imaging Glory: 1 Corinthians 11, Gender, and Bodies at Worship," in *Beauty, Order, and Mystery: A Christian Vision of Human Sexuality*, ed. Gerald Hiestand and Todd Wilson (IVP Academic, 2017), 151–64.

Such texts indicate that, beyond humanity's function or calling, God delights in us as his creation—in what we are and who we were created to be. There is no sense of oppositional dualism between the soul-ish (or spiritual) aspect of who we are and our material embodiment, as if the soul is good and the material body is less than good. All of what we are is called "good." Even while some in the Christian tradition have emphasized the importance of the intellectual soul, they have also, as we shall see, sought to account for how that soul is fitted and holistically connected to the body. This affirmation of the goodness of human materiality has led some past interpreters to reflect on the stature or uprightness of our bodies,[23] and Gregory of Nyssa would note that even in its weakness, the body discloses its eminence over the rest of creation, for what "seems to be a deficiency of our nature, is a means for our obtaining dominion over the subject creatures . . . the needful services of our life are divided among the individual animals that are under our sway."[24] The structure of the body discloses the uniqueness of human nature. Unlike the angels, our bodies allow us to be morally responsible for one another and to wisely order ourselves in relation to both spiritual and material realities.[25]

Later chapters will discuss the theological and ethical significances of our embodiment and sexed creation in more detail. For now, it is worth noting that the inclusion of "male and female" in Genesis 1:26–27, in conjunction with the command to be fruitful and multiply, illumines the created goodness of our embodied selves. The creation accounts of Genesis 1 and 2 emphasize the goodness of our sexed bodies and the unity-in-difference

23. E.g., Bonaventure, *Breviloquium*, 89; Van Mastricht, *TPT*, 3:255.
24. Gregory of Nyssa, "On the Making of Man" 11.3, in *A Select Library of Nicene and Post-Nicene Fathers of the Christian Church*, 2nd series, ed. Philip Schaff and Henry Wace, 14 vols. (Christian Literature, 1890–1900; repr., Hendrickson, 1994), 5:392.
25. For an elaboration of this point concerning human uniqueness vis-à-vis the angels, see Bavinck, *RD*, 2:461–63.

of males and females. Victor P. Hamilton comments that this is Genesis's way of putting a distinguishing marker on human beings: "Unlike God, *man* is characterized by sexual differentiation. Unlike animals, *man* is not broken down into species (i.e., 'according to their kinds' or 'all kinds of'), but rather is designated by sexuality: *male and female he created them.*"[26] Alexander Pruss concurs: "Maleness and femaleness are the very first individual features of human beings mentioned in Genesis. The fact that humans are distinguished in this way seems to have some textual connection with human beings' being created in the image of God—interestingly, Genesis 1 does not emphasize sexual distinction in any other species."[27] Despite the existence of diversity within the Christian tradition on whether the body should be included in the image of God, this text suggests that there is good reason for its inclusion—not because God is essentially a body but because of the formal eminence of the body, its fecundity, and its representative function on earth.[28] To say it another way, the designation of humankind as created as "male and female" in Genesis 1:27 indicates that embodiment is important and not accidental for what it means to be made in the image.[29]

HOLISTIC DUALISM OR TRICHOTOMY?

The Old Testament characterizes the body-soul relation holistically. Von Rad accents that the image of God "refer[s] to the whole of man and do[es] not relate solely to the spiritual and intellectual being."[30] The whole person is denoted by terms like נפש, despite the rendering of נפש into "soul" or "spirit" in English translations. The "heart" (לב), too, is often invoked not just to refer to the organ in our chest area (e.g., Jer. 4:19) but also as the "hidden

26. Victor P. Hamilton, *The Book of Genesis: 1–17*, NICOT (Eerdmans, 1990), 138. On the same page, he qualifies, "Sexuality is applied to animal creatures, but not in the Creation story, only later in the Flood narrative (6:19)." This observation indicates the grain of truth in Barth's account of the image of God in Barth, *Church Dogmatics*, vol. III/1, *The Doctrine of Creation*, ed. Geoffrey W. Bromiley and T. F. Torrance (T&T Clark, 2004), 183–92.

27. Alexander Pruss, *One Body: An Essay in Christian Sexual Ethics* (University of Notre Dame Press, 2013), 88.

28. "As the command 'be fruitful and multiply' emphasizes, we are physically equipped to live in the image of God, because we possess the potential for new life." Reno, *Genesis*, 56.

29. Kleinig, *Wonderfully Made*, 29.

30. Von Rad, *Old Testament Theology*, 1:145.

control-center of the whole human being."[31] Hence, the psalmist asks the Lord to search his heart (Ps. 139:23), the locus of his thoughts, and asks God for a clean heart (Ps. 51:10).

This does not mean that there is no distinction, however, between body and soul. John Cooper is right to term Scripture's presentation of the body-soul relation as "holistic dualism."[32] Scripture emphasizes the vital and organic relation between body and soul while affirming the possibility of its unnatural separation, especially witnessed in death. The thief on the cross is present with Jesus immediately upon death (Luke 23:43), after all. Geerhardus Vos's opening lines on anthropology in his *Reformed Dogmatics* point to Genesis 3:19, Ecclesiastes 12:7, and 2 Corinthians 5:1, along with texts that indicate the continuation of the soul apart from the body after death, to show that the soul is connected to and yet distinct from the body.[33] Though much of the relation between body and soul is a "mystery," what is clear is that despite their distinctness, there is a vital unity between them: "The union between [body and soul] is a life-unity." The biblical picture of the soul is thus opposed to Plato's dualism (where the soul and body are related oppositionally), materialism (where the soul is reduced to the body), and idealism (where the body has no real existence apart from minds). Vos goes on to term the scriptural view "realistic dualism."[34]

Scripture is thus opposed to what has come to be known as "trichotomy." While dualism affirms the existence of both body and soul, trichotomy observes that there are really three parts to the self: body, soul, and spirit. Such confusion stems from noting the use of both "soul" and "spirit" in reference to the human being: רוח and נפש or πνεῦμα and ψυχή. First Thessalonians 5:23 is usually taken to be proof of trichotomy: "Now may the God of peace himself sanctify you completely, and may your whole spirit and soul and body be kept blameless at the coming of our Lord Jesus Christ" (cf. Heb. 4:12). The soul is meant to indicate the animate life that distinguishes bodies from corpses (and in that case, animals, too, have souls), whereas the spirit refers

31. Cooper, *Body, Soul, and Life Everlasting*, 42.

32. Cooper, *Body, Soul, and Life Everlasting*, 66.

33. Geerhardus Vos, *Reformed Dogmatics*, vol. 2, *Anthropology*, trans. Richard B. Gaffin (Lexham, 2014), 1.

34. Vos, *Reformed Dogmatics*, 2:1–2.

to human consciousness, with an intellect and will.[35] As such, the spirit is seen to hover, as it were, above the material aspects of the human body as a "third, independent principle."[36]

In response, it is worth noting that taken on their own, 1 Thessalonians 5:23 and Hebrews 4:12 say nothing about how the mentioned terms of "soul," "spirit," and "body" are to be related. The texts say little to nothing to indicate whether the terms amplify or refer to one another (as in a hendiadys or a synecdoche), or whether each has a distinct point of reference. One needs to bring other theological and philosophical judgments and scriptural texts into the conversation to read the passages in one way or another. Hence, as Cooper notes, 1 Thessalonians 5:23 is not only consistent with trichotomy but could well be compatible with monism, according to which the soul and body are really identical: "Strictly speaking, no clear and distinct philosophical implications flow from this text."[37] Bavinck makes a similar point: "Hebrews 4:12 and 1 Thessalonians 5:23 no more contain a list of all the essential constituents of man than, say, Luke 10:27, and therefore do not prove anything."[38] Bavinck and Vos both note the Platonic influences behind trichotomy, which motivates emphasizing the independence of spirit from matter.[39] If oppositional dualism fuels trichotomy, Scripture's organic holism motivates Vos's realistic dualism.

Indeed, Scripture often uses "soul" and "spirit" (ψυχή and πνεῦμα) interchangeably. Bavinck catalogs some examples:

> One moment "body and soul" constitute the nature of man, the next it is "body and spirit" (Matt. 10:28; 1 Cor. 7:34; James 2:26). Psychic activities are in turn attributed to the spirit and to the soul (Ps. 139:13ff; Prov. 19:2 and 17:27; Ps. 77:6; 1 Cor. 2:11; Num. 21:4 and Job. 21:4; 1 Sam. 1:10 and Isa. 54:6; Luke 1:46–47; etc.). Dying is called both the surrender of the soul (Gen. 35:17; 1 Kings 17:21; Matt. 20:28; Acts 15:26; 20:10) and the surrender of the spirit (Ps. 31:5; Matt. 27:50; Luke 8:55; 23:46; Acts 7:59). Sometimes the spirit and sometimes the soul is called immortal (Eccles. 12:7; Matt. 10:28); the dead are called "souls" (Rev. 6:9; 20:4) as well as "spirits" (Heb. 12:23; 1 Pet. 3:19).[40]

35. Vos, *Reformed Dogmatics*, 2:2.
36. Vos, *Reformed Dogmatics*, 2:2.
37. Cooper, *Body, Soul, and Life Everlasting*, 104.
38. Bavinck, *RD*, 2:556.
39. Bavinck, *RD*, 2:555; Vos, *Reformed Dogmatics*, 2:2.
40. Bavinck, *RD*, 2:556.

While Bavinck does concede that at times "spirit" is used to emphasize the result of the נשמה (breath) of God that quickens the human being uniquely and "soul" emphasizes the connectedness of that spirit with the body, the two terms do not refer to anything that is "essentially different."[41] The soul, then, is fitted to the body, and the body is not a prison of the soul. Further, the whole soul animates the whole of the body, and their separation at death is an unnatural rupture due to the fall.

That the soul is at home with the body entails the goodness of the body. This goodness is further emphasized by two more strands, which will be further elaborated upon in chapter 3 along with the dogmatic section on incarnation and resurrection. God himself was made "flesh" (John 1:14). A sign that humans are made in the image of God is that the human body is fitted to be inhabited by the divine—as we shall see, the human body is a temple. As von Rad aptly observes, the Old Testament considers "man as theomorphic."[42] In other words, it was fitting for God to be incarnate in a human nature because the body itself is that through which humans image God. Moreover, because the body belongs properly to us, God is committed to the resurrection of the body, and that resurrected body is a "spiritual" body already anticipated by the physical body in creation (1 Cor. 15:44), guaranteed and foreseen by Christ's own resurrected body.

Cooper thus concludes that the Old Testament vision of holistic dualism implies a modification of "something between Plato and Aristotle or perhaps some combination of the two." In a way that anticipates this book's dogmatic section, Cooper then points to Augustine and Aquinas, and the broader Reformed tradition (including neo-Calvinism) after them, as offering precisely the kind of ontology of the soul that mirrors the holistic dualism of the body-soul relation of Scripture.[43] Despite the differences in philosophical language deployed within the history of Christian theology, there is thus a majority report that recognizes the holistic dualism of the scriptural witness on the relation between body and soul.

---

41. Bavinck, *RD*, 2:556.
42. Von Rad, *Old Testament Theology*, 1:145.
43. Cooper, *Body, Soul, and Life Everlasting*, 72. Cf. Bonaventure, *Breviloquium*, 91.

TEMPLE AND COVENANT, DOMINION AND REPRESENTATION

With the creation and nature of humanity established, this section highlights the vocation and responsibilities of the first humans in Genesis 1 and 2. Two observations are in order here: that Adam is created as a king-priest-prophet in a temple, and that his context in the state of innocence implies a covenantal arrangement. Both of these highlight that humans were created to be in relation with God and to be visible representatives of the invisible God.

First, then, human beings were made as prophets-priests-kings in a temple-garden. The sense of "image" in Genesis 1:26–28, connected with the command to lay dominion over the earth, connects with the ancient Near Eastern context, in which there was a "common practice for ancient rulers to place statues in conquered lands representing their rule."[44] Kings used these icons or statues to point to their sovereignty and, in turn, the kings would refer to themselves as representatives of the gods.[45] Genesis 1:26–28, then, when read in this background, is a kind of subversion of an ancient Near Eastern polytheistic milieu—for it asserts all human beings as representatives of the one true God, whose sovereignty knows no bounds (further explicating the second commandment, not to make carved images of God). The creation of humanity, therefore, is connected with its dominion in Psalm 8. This sense of representation is further clarified when Adam's sonship is in view. Adam is made in the likeness of God and is called the son of God (cf. Gen. 5:1–3; Luke 3:38)—not in the sense of being physically from God the way human progeny stem from their parents, but in the sense of being created to represent and honor God.[46]

Moreover, Scripture describes the garden as a primordial temple (e.g., Ps. 36:7–9; Ezek. 28:13–18).[47] The combination of the two verbs that character-

44. Richard Lints, *Identity and Idolatry: The Image of God and Its Inversion* (IVP Academic, 2015), 69.

45. Cf. John F. Kilner, *Dignity and Destiny: Humanity in the Image of God* (Eerdmans, 2015), 55–58.

46. Lints, *Identity and Idolatry*, 72.

47. For a concise presentation of the scriptural data on Eden as a temple-garden, see G. K. Beale and Mitchell Kim, *God Dwells Among Us: A Biblical Theology of Temple* (IVP Academic, 2021), 5–12. For an expanded account, see G. K. Beale, *The Temple and the Church's Mission: A Biblical Theology of the Dwelling Place of God* (IVP Academic, 2004).

ize Adam's task to "work and keep" (עבד and שמר) the garden (Gen. 2:15) is used elsewhere to describe the tasks of the Israelite priests (e.g., Num. 1:53, 18:5–6).[48] Humanity's role as priest over the garden is further confirmed when the divine prohibition against the eating of fruit from the tree of knowledge is given in conjunction with the mandate to cultivate the earth in Genesis 2:16–17. As G. K. Beale and Mitchell Kim comment: "Just as the priests were to keep guard over the temple (Num. 18:5) by obeying God's commands, so Adam as a priest guards the Garden-temple of Eden by keeping God's commands. Adam works out God's priestly purposes through obedience to his word."[49] As the priest-king, Adam also has the prophetic responsibility to communicate God's word (and the potential consequences of violating that word) to Eve and their progeny. Hence, the work of representing God on earth, obeying God's word, and conveying that word indicates that God created humanity to be a king, priest, and prophet in creation.[50]

It is worth emphasizing, therefore, that Adam was created not neutrally but in a positive relation to God—he was, after all, created "very good" (Gen. 1:31).[51] He was made a representative, and God walked with him in Eden as a temple-garden. Adam was made to enjoy Sabbath in the divine presence and dwelling.[52] Since humankind fell into sin, the salvation given to us reshapes us into the image of God typified by Adam before the fall and now modeled in the second Adam, Jesus Christ, in knowledge, righteousness, and holiness (Eph. 4:24; Col. 3:10). Adam, as the Reformed tradition would argue, had original righteousness, and he would have passed that righteousness down to his posterity had he remained upright as the prophet-priest-king in the garden.

Adam's life, however, was not yet consummate existence. This brings us to the second point. The Westminster Confession of Faith 7:2 describes Adam as within a "covenant of works," who would merit a higher, spiritual existence conditioned on his perfect obedience. The tree of life prefigures this reward

---

48. See also Michael Morales, *Who Shall Ascend the Mountain of the Lord? A Biblical Theology of the Book of Leviticus* (IVP Academic, 2015), 53.

49. Beale and Kim, *God Dwells Among Us*, 13. Cf. Dempster, *Dominion and Dynasty*, 62–63.

50. Cf. Brandon Crowe, *The Lord Jesus Christ: The Biblical Doctrine of the Person and Work of Christ* (Lexham, 2023), 13–14.

51. John Murray, *Collected Writings of John Murray*, vol. 2, *Systematic Theology* (Banner of Truth, 1977), 40.

52. Morales, *Who Shall Ascend*, 45–47.

(Gen. 2:9). Paul's argument in 1 Corinthians 15 indicates that humanity's pre-fallen condition was good, but not yet consummate. Consider the passage:

> If there is a natural body, there is also a spiritual body. Thus it is written, "The first man Adam became a living being"; the last Adam became a life-giving spirit. But it is not the spiritual that is first but the natural, and then the spiritual. The first man was from the earth, a man of dust; the second man is from heaven. (1 Cor. 15:44–47)

The existence of a protological natural body, Paul argues, implies the existence of a higher, consummate, spiritual body. Though glory exceeds protology, protology anticipates glory. The conditions of Genesis 2 and 3 are non-ideal compared to glory. Adam did not yet partake of the tree of life (Gen. 3:22; Westminster Larger Catechism Q&A 20), and death was threatened upon the eating of the tree of knowledge; Adam had a mutable existence and was corruptible; Adam was in a garden, not yet a city; Adam had to subdue a crafty serpent, who was free to tempt.[53]

The contrast in 1 Corinthians 15:47 between the earthly man and the man "from heaven," then, should be taken as a *qualitative* contrast rather than a contrast of *origin*.[54] In other words, the body of the first man Adam was earthly in quality, whereas the second (and last) Adam has a qualitatively heavenly body. While fallen humanity is in view in 1 Corinthians 15:20–23, Paul pivots into a discussion of the creational body in 15:35–49. First Corinthians 15:20–23, like Romans 5, focuses on the contrast between Adam as the head of fallen humanity and the resurrected Christ as the firstfruits of the redeemed, the first among many to be resurrected from the dead. In 1 Corinthians 15:35–39, however, Paul deals with a contrast between humanity as created and the heavenly body as the qualitatively superior, eschatological body. The particular kinds of bodies in 1 Corinthians 15:36–41 show that God has designed each body to have its own distinct forms of glory, without the fall. Moreover, Paul appeals explicitly to Genesis 2:7 in 1 Corinthians 15:45, a passage that locates Adam in the prelapsarian order, in order to ground

---

53. This paragraph and the following couple of paragraphs draw from my essay "Consummation Anyway: A Reformed Proposal," *Journal of Analytic Theology* 9 (2021): 223–37.

54. Marc Cortez, *Resourcing Theological Anthropology: A Constructive Account of Humanity in Light of Christ* (Zondervan Academic, 2017), 72.

his argument that the natural comes first, before the spiritual in 1 Corinthians 15:44 and 46. The contrasts Paul observed in 1 Corinthians 15:42–43 thus denote the distinction between created and consummate bodies: The former is "perishable, dishonourable, and weak, unlike the spiritual which is imperishable, glorious, and powerful."[55]

The upshot, especially in view of the "if-then" logic of 1 Corinthians 15:44, is that "Jesus comes not just as the one who addresses what went wrong in the fall (15:20–23), but also as the one who advances creation toward its intended telos (15:35–49)."[56] Vos concurs and notes the following on this passage: "It will be noticed, however, that in verses 45, 46 the Apostle generalizes the antithesis so that it no longer concerns the body exclusively, but the whole contrast, that relating to the pre-eschatological period, so as to make it cover no longer the reign of sin, but the order of things established in creation."[57] Indeed, commenting on this same passage, Marc Cortez observes that "Paul is outlining the only true telos of the human person: eschatological consummation."[58] The contrast between the created body and the heavenly body is a contrast between the state of innocence (or protology) and the state of glory (eschatology). Moreover, there is a clear logical link between the two, as established in 1 Corinthians 15:44: *If* there is a natural, *then* there is a spiritual—namely, *if* there is a creational order, *then* there is an eschatological consummation that moves natural, created bodies into heavenly, glorious bodies. WCF 7:2 was denoting this eschatological consummation by its reference to the "life promised to Adam."

The commands in Genesis 1:26 ("Let them have dominion") and 1:28 ("Be fruitful and multiply") highlight that humanity's image-bearing, positive relation, and obedience to God have an intrinsically teleological function.

55. Cortez, *Resourcing Theological Anthropology*, 81. To say it another way, I suggest that the pivot from predication on the fallen body to the created body occurs in verse 45—though one could argue that the antithesis of the "natural" versus "spiritual" in verse 44 already has the created body in view. The description of the body as not merely imperishable but "dishonourable" is due to Paul's generalized use of the term "natural" to include both the created and fallen states. The upshot, in other words, is that the spiritual body is superlative, not merely compared to the fallen body (which should be obvious) but also compared to the *created* body.

56. Cortez, *Resourcing Theological Anthropology*, 83.

57. Geerhardus Vos, "The Eschatological Aspect of the Pauline Conception of the Spirit," in *Redemptive History and Biblical Interpretation: The Shorter Writings of Geerhardus Vos*, ed. Richard B. Gaffin (Presbyterian and Reformed, 1980), 106.

58. Cortez, *Resourcing Theological Anthropology*, 83.

The command to be fruitful and multiply implies that the earth is not yet filled, and the command to subdue implies that it is not yet cultivated. This is the work that Adam and his progeny were to carry out. As humanity thus represents God in their dispersal throughout the world, the glory of God will also fill the world (Ps. 8).

Genesis 1:26–28 thus looks forward to the filling of the earth with representations of God, anticipating a time when the will of God is carried out on

Psalm 8

Psalm 8 is a meditation on the formation and location of humanity, as it were, within the order of creation. The passage teaches that humanity is imbued with both *dignity* and *humility*. On the one hand, humans have a humble place within creation. We are small and insignificant, especially when compared with the moon and the stars (Ps. 8:3), such that the psalmist is amazed that God is mindful of us (v. 4). Yet humans were created as the pinnacle of the material world, with glory: "You have made him a little lower than the heavenly beings and crowned him with glory and honor" (v. 5). Although our lives are short and we are dust, connected to the material world the way angels are not, we were created to steward a dominion over "the works of [God's] hands" (v. 6). The psalm, then, connects our image-bearing with the so-called cultural mandate, and as we work and fill the globe, we represent God, such that his name would be made manifest "in all the earth" (vv. 1, 8). As image-bearers, humans are directly connected with God, and in that sense they are like the angels and are crowned with glory. But precisely because they are made *in* the image, humans are dependent, accountable to God, and earthly. Passages like this are why, classically, humans have been described as straddling the heavenly and the earthly—representing both as a kind of "microcosm" of all creation.

Jesus Christ, ultimately, is the one who represents God on earth perfectly, as the second Adam.[a] Hebrews 2:5–8 cites this psalm and points to Jesus, who "for a little while was made lower than the angels, . . . crowned with glory and honor because of the suffering of death, so that by the grace of God he might taste death for everyone" (Heb. 2:9).

a. I discuss Jesus as the son of Adam in chapter 3. See also Joel Marcus, "Son of Man as Son of Adam," *Revue biblique* 110 (2003): 36–61 (especially the comments on Ps. 8 and Heb. 1–2 on 54–56) and "Son of Man as Son of Adam, Part 2: Exegesis," *Revue biblique* 110 (2003): 370–86.

earth fully just as it is in heaven. Looking ahead, the promise of the restoration of the world by the redemption of the sons of God is thus a restoration and consummation of this Adamic trajectory. The new heavens and new earth are, in the words of Beale and Kim, "Eden completely expanded."[59] The life promised to Adam is given in conjunction with humanity's spread and obedience globally: "Adam was created in the image of the triune God to indicate his presence and rule over the earth."[60] The image corresponds to a task, a mandate from God in relation to the earth—and God remains committed that humans represent him even after the fall (Gen. 9:1–7). As representatives of God, humanity is to "work and keep" the ground (Gen. 2:15). Implicit in these mandates is that eschatological vision of image-bearers representing God across the globe, and in diverse ways. This mandate also grounds the goodness of the diversity of cultures and the natural formations of the peoples in languages (especially seen in the redemption of the Tower of Babel in Pentecost; Gen. 11; Acts 2). Cultures are restored and consummated in tribes, tongues, and nations represented in the eschaton (Rev. 7; 21).

The call to dominion, of course, in light of sin can easily be misunderstood and abused, turned into hubris by pride. Two markers from the text disallow taking that dominion into that misdirection. First, humans are images of God and so are dependent on God. Humans do not create out of their mere imagination or power but must recognize reality as God intended it to be. God is the author of nature, and humans must work along its grain. Second, the call to work and keep the ground is a priestly work. This is further signified by the conjunction of this command to work the garden alongside the prohibition from God in Genesis 2:16–17—God is the one who imbues meaning on the trees. The first humans were not to eat of the tree of the knowledge of good and evil and were thus bound to the word of God for their destinies and for the authoritative interpretation of created nature.

True dominion, therefore, presupposes obedience to God, and hubris is the result of disobedience. Failure to heed the word of God leads humans to reinterpret and instrumentalize nature for unnatural and selfish ends. Hence, the call to *dominion* should perhaps be termed as a call to *cultivation* (Gen. 2:5). We must listen to God's intentions and work in accordance with the

59. Beale and Kim, *God Dwells Among Us*, 125–34.
60. Beale and Kim, *God Dwells Among Us*, 18.

norms and bounds he has set for us. Adam's naming of the animals in Genesis 2:20 itself presupposes preexisting "kinds" that God has set before him, and Adam does not name or bless himself.[61] This obedience to God by naming the animals is itself another indicative of Adam's conformity to God—what later theologians, again, would refer to as his original righteousness.

The upshot of this section is this: God has created human beings to be the visible representations of himself on earth.[62] We are called to image God, to represent the divine will, and to exercise an analogous responsibility to cultivate creation. As human beings disperse throughout the globe, so the image and representation of God is manifested throughout the globe.[63]

The vocational and the ontological coalesce. This representational vocation presupposes both a particular human nature with the capacities necessary to represent God—as the text of Job 32:8 observed above indicated.[64] Human beings are persons, with the capacities of the intellect and will—and they are meant to exercise those capacities to cultivate creation, represent God, and commune with God. Ephesians 4:24 and Colossians 3:10 suggest that the virtues of right knowledge (wisdom) and righteousness, for instance, correspond to the proper exercising of the intellect and will. Humans are agents, with self-consciousness and moral responsibility, and are the appropriate subjects of communion, guilt, and redemption. If what it means to be human is that we are made in the image of God, then human beings are inherently related to God—whether in conformity or in rebellion—and have their meaning and significance as a gift to them. They exist in the image of God, and they flourish when they commune and

61. Cf. Reno, *Genesis*, 73.

62. Recent biblical scholarship observes that "image" language implies a vocation: "The general consensus among contemporary biblical scholars is that the image of God in Genesis 1 should be understood in a primarily functional sense." Cortez, *Theological Anthropology*, 30. Cf. Wenham, *Genesis 1–15*, 31–32; Hamilton, *Book of Genesis*, 138; Reno, *Genesis*, 53; J. Richard Middleton, *The Liberating Image: The Imago Dei in Genesis 1* (Brazos, 2005).

63. Reno, *Genesis*, 53.

64. Matthew Levering, *Engaging the Doctrine of Creation: Cosmos, Creatures, and the Wise and Good Creator* (Baker Academic, 2017), 190. Gijsbert van den Brink argues that the functional or vocational sense is clearly in view in this passage but nonetheless concedes that our relation with God "cannot be conceived of without specific capacities. Thus, to be able to live in accordance to our calling, we have been endowed with many special substantive and structural characteristics that, though not unique in kind, are still unique in degree." *Reformed Theology and Evolutionary Theory* (Eerdmans, 2020), 157.

walk with God.[65] Images and icons, after all, have meaning precisely from what they image. The image of God, therefore, carries both ontological and ethical implications—a point that was captured well by the patristic, medieval, and Reformed divines.[66] There is thus no need to pit the vocational aspects of image-bearing with its ontological structure, for human nature is designed in order to fulfill those vocational responsibilities to which God has called humanity.

DIGNITY AND PERSONHOOD

The dignity and personhood of humanity indicates the ontological significance of humans made in the image of God. Human dignity, therefore, consists not in autonomy but in the ontology and identity received, as humans are set apart for fellowship with God himself.[67] Every human being shares the same human nature and blood in Adam (Acts 17:26). Because humans are meant to have an everlasting communion with God, human death is tragic and unnatural. God prohibits humans to murder one another, for "God made man in his own image" (Gen. 9:6). James 3:9 thus warns that we control the tongue, lest we curse those who are made in the image of God. Such scriptural teachings have been key cornerstones for Christian moral teaching on the sanctity of life and human rights.[68] Human dignity, then, as an entailment of our creation in the image of God, is a "feature of creation, not an achievement."[69] It is not one's instrumental value that determines one's dignity—one's *existence* as such is dignified.

Indeed, the goodness and dignity of human life is presupposed in the second table of the Ten Commandments. God prohibits human murder (Exod. 20:13), and, classically interpreted, the commandments also entail positive

65. Christa McKirland, *God's Provision, Humanity's Need: The Gift of Our Dependence* (Baker Academic, 2022), 47.

66. Bavinck, *RD*, 2:533. Horton's framing of ontological versus relational (and covenantal) accounts of the image of God is thus, in my view, unnecessary. See Michael Horton, *The Christian Faith: A Systematic Theology for Pilgrims on the Way* (Zondervan, 2011), 381, 389, 393, 395.

67. See John Webster, "The Dignity of Creatures," in *God Without Measure: Working Papers in Christian Theology*, vol. 2, *Virtue and Intellect* (Bloomsbury T&T Clark, 2016), 29–48.

68. Cf. Nicholas Wolterstorff, *Justice: Rights and Wrongs* (Princeton University Press, 2008).

69. Christopher Watkin, *Biblical Critical Theory: How the Bible's Unfolding Story Makes Sense of Modern Life and Culture* (Zondervan, 2022), 88.

obligations toward the flourishing of human life. The Westminster Larger Catechism Q&A 153 indicates that the sixth commandment entails duties for the "sober use of meat, drink, physic, sleep, labor, and recreations," along with "charitable thoughts, love, compassion, meekness, gentleness, kindness." It thus warns against sins of speech against one's neighbor. Indeed, the sanctity of human life is also behind the commandments against adultery, for one should not objectify one's neighbor; against stealing, for one should care for the needs and property of one's neighbor; against bearing false witness, for one should care for the good name of one's neighbor; and against coveting, for one should rejoice at the well-being of one's neighbor. The fifth commandment, on honoring parents, reminds us that we are all connected to one another and have all sorts of duties in accordance with our social places.[70]

It has become commonplace for critics of those who include the structure or ontology of the human being into the image of God to argue that such a move introduces a gradationed or exclusionary account of the image of God. In other words, if the image of God essentially includes the soul's faculties of intellect and will, so this misunderstanding goes, then does not this exclude those with cognitive or physical disabilities? Does this also imply that those who exercise their intelligence to a higher degree possess more of the image than others? The older metaphysical accounts of the image, therefore, seem to smuggle in ableist biases, so the charge goes.

Two brief responses are in order here. First, including the capacities of the human being within the image of God is a distinct claim from whether one would actualize those capacities. The older scholastic categories of act and potency are useful here. An active potency is "strictly speaking, a kind of act or actuality . . . more precisely, it is a kind of act relative to the substance possessing it, though a kind of potency relative to the action it grounds."[71] To identify the potency of a thing is to determine what that thing is ontologically, as distinguished from other particular things.[72] Humans, for instance, are the kinds of beings that are endowed with the potency for wisdom, but the

70. Carmen Imes argues well that our creation as image-bearers means we have to take relationships more seriously in her *Being God's Image: Why Creation Still Matters* (IVP Academic, 2023).

71. Edward Feser, *Scholastic Metaphysics: A Contemporary Introduction* (Editiones Scholasticae, 2014), 43.

72. Favale helpfully refers to this as an "Essential Potential," which in turn refers to an "inherent potential or possibility a thing has." *Genesis of Gender*, 116, 119, respectively.

actualization of those potencies is a distinct matter. Edward Feser clarifies: "In arguing for the existence of active potencies or causal powers, Scholastic writers emphasize the point that a cause is not always bringing about its characteristic effect. . . . My power to write must therefore be distinguished from this or that actual, particular *action* of writing, as a standing precondition of the latter."[73] Infants or those in a comatose state due to some serious injury, for that matter, continue to be image-bearers, even while the power to reason or will morally are not actualized.

Those who are cognitively impaired, likewise, still have the power for wisdom and volition, even as the actualization of that potency differs from others and even if perhaps the exercise of those powers is only actualized in the resurrection—one still engages with them as *humans* and *persons*. If humans are the particular creatures that are called to be in communion with and representatives of God, then such potencies are precisely those which are presupposed as the "standing precondition," which in turn makes them fitting for the task. In that sense, the very description of "neurodivergence" confirms this point. Cats, which lack higher-order cognition, are not described that way because they lack the potency, or "innate potential," to do so.[74] Likewise, we may fail to respond appropriately to God when we sin, but we are still ontologically image-bearers—the proper functioning of our essential capacities refers to active potency in a secondary sense, presupposing the capacity itself.

To illumine the point, then, a hypothetically resurrected ant will still not actualize any higher-order thinking because it was never in its substance to think. Ants might have the active potency to create a complex underground nest or to lift objects much heavier than their bodies, but ants do not have the power of intellectual reasoning. This focus on what human beings *are*, with our attendant formal capacities (or essential potencies), then, does not introduce a gradation for the image of God but rather complements and grounds the emphasis on human dignity. Every human is made in the image of God, whether or not they actualize wisdom or righteousness.

Second, I am not persuaded that focusing the image on the relational aspects of who we are avoids the worry of introducing a gradation. As Harriett

73. Feser, *Scholastic Metaphysics*, 46.
74. Favale, *Genesis of Gender*, 121.

Harris has shown, defining the image in terms of the relations that we have with one another risks reducing us to our existing relations—we would thus be defined by the relations that we enter into, along with relations that we do not choose. Ironically, the relational view of the image, therefore, risks defining a woman, for instance, in terms of who she is in relation to men.[75] More recently, Joanna Leidenhag has argued that relational accounts also risk excluding persons with autism, who may lack the actualization of forming second-person relations.[76] Whatever gradation-related worries thrown at structuralist accounts, therefore, can be parried back to other models. Rather, I suggest that to imbue the sense of the image of God with the metaphysics of what we are, therefore, is not only necessary to account for the functional, vocational, and relational dimensions of what we are but also better grounds dignity and inclusion. No human, *qua human*, is excluded from the *imago Dei*.

CHRIST AND THE IMAGE

Before bringing this chapter to a close, it is important to take a look at 2 Corinthians 4:4 and Colossians 1:15, as these texts refer to Christ as the image of God. Second Corinthians 4:4 refers to Christ as the image and states that the god of this world is blinding unbelievers from recognizing him in the gospel. Colossians 1:15 claims that he "is the image of the invisible God, the firstborn of all creation." Passages such as these have led some recent theologians in the line of Barth to suggest that perhaps humankind was made after the image of Christ or that Christology is in some way prototypical for humanity's creation.[77] As G. C. Berkouwer's work on the image of God would observe: "The Incarnation is described as consanguinity *with us*. Barth, however, formulates the matter in the opposite way, so that Jesus does not participate in our nature, but *we in His*."[78] The question is, Is Christ made into

75. Harriett A. Harris, "Should We Say That Personhood Is Relational?," *Scottish Journal of Theology* 51 (1998): 214–38.

76. Joanna Leidenhag, "The Challenge of Autism for Relational Approaches to Theological Anthropology," *International Journal of Systematic Theology* 23 (2021): 109–34.

77. E.g., Cortez, *Resourcing Anthropology*, and, in a more thoroughgoing fashion, Bruce McCormack, *The Humility of the Eternal Son: Reformed Kenoticism and the Repair of Chalcedon* (Cambridge University Press, 2021).

78. Berkouwer, *Man*, 95 (emphasis original).

the likeness of humanity, or is humanity, even human nature, patterned after the likeness of Christ's humanity?

I shall handle the issue of whether humanity is made in the image of the Trinity or of the Son more extensively in the dogmatic section of this book (specifically chaps. 4 and 5). For now, a few exegetical comments will suffice.

We should be careful to distinguish passages in which Christ is referred to as the divine Son of God in his preexistent state, on the one hand, and according to his incarnation and the economy of the gospel, on the other. In other words, when one claims that Christ is the image of God, we should ask the question: In which respect, and according to which nature, the divine or human? Second Corinthians 4:4 is about the latter, as the context indicates, and as such he came *after* the pattern and failed representation for the first Adam. The Son, in this sense, was made in the "likeness of men" (Phil. 2:7–8) and in the Word was made "flesh" (John 1:14). He was made like us in every way (Heb. 2:14–17) so that he might be the great high priest who sympathizes with us. As the one who succeeded where Adam failed, then, he shows us *perfect human obedience* and is, as such, the norm for all human beings.[79] He is the last Adam (1 Cor. 15:45–49), and we will be made like him (Rom. 8:29) in death and resurrection (Rom. 8:17; 1 John 3:2). The incarnation was for the redemption of humans from sin (1 Tim. 1:15).[80] As Berkouwer notes, "In [Bavinck's and Calvin's] thinking they always approach the Incarnation from a consideration of man's fall and guilt."[81] In this sense, therefore, though Christ is the norm and standard for perfect human obedience, his human nature can be understood only by looking at that nature first, for he was made *like us*.[82]

Colossians 1:15, however, considers Christ as the eternal, preexistent Son of God. Herman Ridderbos's comment is apt: "When Paul speaks of Christ as Image of God, he describes him thereby not, as is the case when he calls

79. Cf. Guy Prentiss Waters, "Ephesians," in *A Biblical-Theological Introduction to the New Testament: The Gospel Realized*, ed. Michael J. Kruger (Crossway, 2016), 280–81.

80. First Timothy 1:15 is an important passage that grounds the infralapsarian Christology of both Bonaventure and Aquinas. See Justus H. Hunter, *If Adam Had Not Sinned: The Reasons for the Incarnation from Anselm to Scotus* (Catholic University of America Press, 2020).

81. Berkouwer, *Man*, 97.

82. *Pace* Kilner, *Dignity and Destiny*, 52–53.

him the last Adam (1 Cor. 15:45ff.), as the second or last man, but, at least in Colossians 1:15 (and Phil. 2:6) as the Pre-existent One in his glory."[83] Colossians 1:15–20 is divided into two units: Verses 15–17 identify the divine nature of the Son, whereas verses 18–20 identify the human nature and the Son's Adamic representation as the head of the church. In Colossians 1:16, then, the divinity of the eternal Son is in view, for Paul conjoins the acts of creation and providence (Col. 1:16–17) to the Son, who is the image of God—and the Son does this not by way of his human nature but by his preexistent divine nature.

The Christian tradition has thus always recognized that the eternal Son is the unique image in a way that humans are not: "The Son of God is the essential image of most perfect equality, having the same numerical essence with the Father. Adam is the accidental and analogical image of inadequate and imperfect similitude (as to nature, gifts and state)."[84] Technically, the Son is *the* image of God, whereas humans are made *in* the image of God (ectypally). Bavinck says it this way: "The former is the eternal only begotten Son; the latter is the created Son of God. The former is the image of God *within* the divine being, the latter, *outside* of it."[85] Just as the Son flows from and perfectly reflects the Father in eternal generation, so humans, in an analogical fashion, are created by and are called to image God and are adopted through the gospel as sons (Gal. 4:4–7). It is fitting that the eternal Son should become the incarnate Son to make us the sons of God. This eternal Sonship, however, is unique to the Son. The preexistent Son is in the very form of God (Phil. 2:6–7), the imprint of his being (Heb. 1:1–3), and one substance with the Father (John 10:30).

CONCLUSION

This chapter has considered the creation of humanity in the image of God, the biblical descriptions of its nature as a holistic unity of body and soul, humanity's vocation and relation to God by way of covenant, the dignity and personhood of every individual, and the uniqueness of the Son of God as the

---

83. Herman Ridderbos, *Paul: An Outline of His Theology* (Eerdmans, 1975), 71.

84. Francis Turretin, *Institutes of Elenctic Theology*, vol. 1, *First Through Tenth Topics*, ed. James T. Dennison, trans. George Musgrave Giger (P&R, 1992), 465.

85. Bavinck, *RD*, 2:533.

eternal image. Along the way, we have seen that humanity is created with a unique nature, such that it has the capacities for wisdom and righteousness, ordered toward the fulfillment of its vocation to represent God on earth. God creates each of us with a soul that is fitted for a body, with a unique dignity and responsibility to cultivate the world in a way that is pleasing to him. Much of the dogmatic teachings of the Christian faith on human nature, vocation, and destiny are thus already present in the opening chapters of the book of Genesis. This is not, however, the end of the story. The next two chapters consider humanity as fallen and then redeemed in Christ.

FURTHER READING

Beale, G. K., and Mitchell Kim. *God Dwells Among Us: Expanding Eden to the Ends of the Earth*. IVP Academic, 2014. A standard, accessible work that expands on the imperatives to be fruitful and multiply as God's representations on earth.

Reno, R. R. *Genesis*. BTCB. Brazos, 2017. An insightful commentary that brings out the theological and ethical implications of the seminal texts in the opening chapters of Genesis.

Kilner, John F. *Dignity and Destiny: Humanity in the Image of God*. Eerdmans, 2015. A survey textbook that details the biblical teachings on the image of God.

Vos, Geerhardus. *Biblical Theology: Old and New Testaments*. Banner of Truth, 2014. The best introduction to the theological plotline of Scripture, but beyond that, chapters 1–4 still represent the best concise expositions of "pre-redemptive" special revelation—including discussions on the creation of humanity, the covenantal significance of the garden of Eden, and pre-redemptive eschatology.

Peterson, Ryan S. *The Imago Dei as Human Identity: A Theological Interpretation*. Eisenbrauns, 2016. Perhaps the best recent monograph that combines exegesis and theological concerns on the subject of interpreting Genesis 1:26–28.

2

HUMANITY: FALLEN IN SIN

HUMANS FAILED TO RETAIN their original innocence. This chapter considers the first human sin in Scripture and the consequences of that sin on humanity. The first section thus deals with the seminal texts of Genesis 3 and Romans 5:12–21, and the second section traces the corruption of human nature and the spread of sin by surveying some important passages across the biblical corpus.

THE FIRST HUMAN SIN: GENESIS 3 AND ROMANS 5:12–21

God has made all things good (Gen. 1:31). Scripture is adamant about the contingency and alien character of sin to an otherwise good creation. God takes no delight in evil, for he is pure (Hab. 1:13). God is light, "and in him there is no darkness at all" (1 John 1:5; cf. Rev. 21:23). God, therefore, "tempts no one," because "God cannot be tempted with evil" (James 1:13).

Van Mastricht observes that denying God is the author of sin is a basic feature of Christian orthodoxy: "Scripture (e.g., Ps. 5) as well as by the nature of God, insofar as he is the highest good, God cannot be the author of sin, which is acknowledged by all."[1] Indeed, Berkouwer describes this denial of

1. Van Mastricht, *TPT*, 3:334.

God as the author of sin as the great biblical "a priori" when one broaches the topic of sin's origins.[2] As we will further explore in the dogmatic section of this book, while the Reformed tradition teaches that Scripture affirms the sovereignty of God over all that comes to pass (e.g., Prov. 21:1; Isa. 45:7; Lam. 3:37–38; Eph. 1:11), it remains adamant on the basic asymmetry between God's sovereignty of the good, on the one hand, and evil, on the other. That God is not the author of sin, as we shall see, will also prove significant for a proper account of the metaphysics of sin: If God is the Creator of all things (John 1:1–4; Col. 1:15–16) and God is not the author of sin, then it follows that sin is not a thing—that is, not a substance.

The first human sin thus involves an upright humanity who fell away from that condition by freely choosing to disobey God. Two texts in particular are of foundational importance on the first human sin and the ensuing "fall": Genesis 3 and Romans 5:12–21.[3] A "crafty" serpent tempted Adam and Eve by questioning God's word and its proper interpretation, as it were, of the tree of the knowledge of good and evil (Gen. 3:1–2). The serpent twisted the word of God by adding prohibitions to God's word. Whereas God said they may eat of any tree except one (Gen. 2:16), the serpent suggested that God prohibited eating from any tree (Gen. 3:1). The serpent succeeded in influencing Eve, for, even as she asserted that God allowed eating from every tree (Gen. 3:2), she added that God prohibited touching the tree at the middle of the garden, not just eating from it (Gen. 3:3). "Eve is beginning to play along, with the result that the wedge of mistrust is driven further between God and his creatures."[4] The temptation of the serpent was already making its way into the consciousness of the first humans.

The serpent then directly contradicted the word of God by asserting that humans would be "like" God, and not "surely die," if they looked at the tree for themselves and ate of it (Gen. 3:4–5). The craftiness of the serpent is seen in this assertion because it masks the temptation with a sense of piety—were not Adam and Eve created to be in the "image and likeness" of God, per Genesis 1:26–27? Surely, then, eating the fruit would cause them to become what

2. G. C. Berkouwer, *Sin*, trans. Philip C. Holtrop (Eerdmans, 1971), 27.

3. Cf. Henri Blocher, *Original Sin: Illumining a Riddle* (IVP Academic, 1997), 32.

4. Christopher Watkin, *Biblical Critical Theory: How the Bible's Unfolding Story Makes Sense of Modern Life and Culture* (Zondervan, 2022), 112.

they were meant to be—that is, to be "like God." But the serpent was masking an equivocation here: To *image* God is not meant to indicate that human beings *are* themselves God, as if humans and God could belong in the same category of being. Humanity was made to be images of God and not like God himself—they were meant to be dependent and subordinate to God, as creatures in his likeness and as stewards and representatives of him, not divine. The serpent, in effect, was promising humanity that they would transcend their creatureliness and become like the Creator. Eve then proceeded to interpret the tree for herself (Gen. 3:6), as if her reasoning and direct experience of the tree would produce a counterhypothesis to God's own word about it. In effect, she was now putting herself as the proper interpreter of nature, giving it her own meaning as if she were God, instead of recognizing what nature really was in accordance with divine revelation.[5]

Adam, instead of exercising his stewardship and declaring the word of God (which gives nature its proper meaning, for nature itself flowed from the word and ideas of God), sat idly by and silently acquiesced to the serpent and Eve. They were not content to image God by obeying his word—they wanted to be the giver of the divine word themselves. Genesis 3 indicates, therefore, that sin is not just about disobedience to God but also a resistance to nature as God created it. There is an inversion of the created order, where humankind listens to creatures instead of the Creator.[6]

As humanity resists God and nature, sin corrupts its being. This temptation appealed to the whole human person as a body-soul unity: "the body with its appetite for enjoyable food, the mind with its quest for more knowledge, and the soul with its trust in God and his word."[7] The consequences of this first human sin confirm this: The union between Adam and Eve was ruptured, and they blamed one another. Indeed, the serpent had already begun to subvert their relation by addressing the woman and not Adam, who represented her and was entrusted with communicating the word of God to her. They became

---

5. For more on the epistemological consequences of Gen. 3, see Watkin, *Biblical Critical Theory*, chap. 5. Watkin is drawing out the implications of Van Til's reading of Genesis 3: Cornelius Van Til, "Nature and Scripture," in *The Infallible Word: A Symposium by Members of Westminster Theological Seminary* (P&R, 2003), 263–301.

6. Gordon Wenham, *Genesis 1–15* (Zondervan, 1987), 75. See also the parallel comments in Derek Nelson, *Sin: A Guide for the Perplexed* (Bloomsbury T&T Clark, 2011), 23.

7. John Kleinig, *Wonderfully Made: A Protestant Theology of the Body* (Lexham, 2021), 40.

self-conscious about their bodies and desired to cover their shame with fig leaves (Gen. 3:7, 10–11): "The trust of innocence is replaced by the fear of guilt. The trees that God created for man to look at (2:9) are now his hiding place to prevent God seeing him."[8] The harmony found in original creation is now lost.

The body bears the consequences of sin. As Paul would indicate, corruption inflicts our bodies. It is a body of death (Rom. 7:24), a body of sin (Rom. 6:6), and the Genesis narrative indicates this by the pronouncement that humanity will return to the dust (Gen. 3:19). The woman will carry the pain of child-bearing and birthing (Gen. 3:16), and the earth will no longer be receptive to the work of humanity (Gen. 3:17–19). Human lives are like vapor—indeed, they are short—and death punctures human existence like an unwelcome thief (Isa. 40:6–7; James 1:10–11). The narrative on the murder of Abel follows immediately after the first sin (Gen. 4). A cycle of death ensues in Genesis 5.

Sin also breaks the relationship between God and humanity. We now have a mind that is hostile to God (Col. 2:13; Eph. 4:18). Adam and Eve hid from him instead of walking in communion with him as they did before (Gen. 3:8). God barred them from eating of the tree of life (Gen. 3:22), and they were cast out of the garden, bound to live east of Eden (Gen. 3:24). Stephen Dempster is correct in noting that, while the term "the fall" does not show up in the text, it is surely an apt description of the events; describing it as a fall could even be considered a "euphemism," especially when one considers the ensuing corruption after Genesis 3.[9]

That the name of Adam also means "humankind" indicates that Adam acted not as a private person but as a representative for the human race.[10] Romans 5:12–21 is a pivotal text on the origin of human sin and its consequences while highlighting Christ's role as a second Adam, especially as it parallels the one man, Adam, with the one man, Jesus Christ: "Therefore, as one trespass led to condemnation for all men, so one act of righteousness leads to justification and life for all men. For as by the one man's disobedience the many were made sinners, so by the one man's obedience the many will be made righteous" (Rom. 5:18–19). While commenting on every detail

8. Wenham, *Genesis 1–15*, 76.

9. Stephen G. Dempster, *Dominion and Dynasty: A Theology of the Hebrew Bible* (IVP Academic, 2003), 66.

10. Cf. Blocher, *Original Sin*, 51–52.

of this passage will go beyond the purposes of this section, a few observations are in order. Adam was "a type of the one who was to come" (5:14). The Reformed tradition has taken this to mean that Adam was a representative of the human race, being the first, just as Christ will be the representative for his people, being the last Adam (1 Cor. 15:44–58). This does not mean that Eve was uninvolved in the "one trespass" (Rom. 5:18), but the reference to Adam as the one who is the type of Christ identifies Adam's position as a unique federal head.[11]

The emphasis in Romans 5 is Adam's guilt, both his own and that of his posterity, and the gift of justification that Christ brings. Notice the parallels—Christ provided salvific solutions that corresponded to the problems brought about by Adam's fall. Adam committed "one trespass," whereas Christ offered "one act of righteousness" (5:18); Adam disobeyed, whereas Christ obeyed (5:19); Adam's trespass brought about condemnation and death, whereas Christ brought "justification and life" (5:17–18); through Adam's disobedience, the "many were made sinners," while through Christ's obedience, "the many will be made righteous" (5:19). The sense of being "made sinners" and "made righteous" here (καθίστημι) has forensic significance, as the sense of the verb is to *constitute* or *appoint* humans as sinners or righteous.[12] As I suggest in the dogmatic chapter on original sin later, it is unpersuasive to argue that Adam merely transmitted a corrupted nature to his progeny, for, as Thomas Schreiner also notes, "It is hard to see why people would receive a corrupt nature if they were not guilty of Adam's sin."[13] This verb informs the Reformed tradition's emphasis that the passage refers to the *imputation* of Adam's sin or Christ's righteousness, and not merely to the transmission of corruption: "The work of each representative has been imputed or reckoned to those whom each represents."[14] Adam's trespass led to the many being rendered guilty and condemned—a forensic declaration—and Christ, correspondingly, brings about a forensic

11. For a thorough exegesis of this passage, see John Murray, *The Imputation of Adam's Sin* (Presbyterian and Reformed, 1959).

12. Cf. Thomas Schreiner, *Romans*, 2nd ed. (Baker Academic, 2018), 294–95; Douglas Moo, *The Letter to the Romans*, 2nd ed., NICNT (Eerdmans, 2018), 371–72, on the interpretive debates and a defense of the forensic reading of Rom. 5:19.

13. Schreiner, *Romans*, 295.

14. Guy Prentiss Waters, "Romans," in *A Biblical-Theological Introduction to the New Testament: The Gospel Realized*, ed. Michael J. Kruger (Crossway, 2016), 187.

declaration of righteousness to those who are found in him (cf. Rom. 4:24–25).[15]

The biblical teachings on the fall into sin have an equalizing effect, just as much as its doctrine of the *imago Dei* does. If the latter doctrine teaches that all humans are equal in dignity and are in relation to God, the doctrine of sin in Scripture teaches that all humans are guilty and, indeed, corrupted before God: "There is no one who does not sin" (1 Kings 8:46; cf. Job 14:4; Ps. 103:3; Eccles. 7:20). Everyone is accountable to God.

THE CORRUPTION AND SPREAD OF SIN

Old Testament Witnesses

The Bible's understanding of sin is holistic as much as it is pervasive: It deals not just with individual acts of sin and all of their diverse instantiations and motivations but also with sin as it pollutes the self and community. The human is now a "sinner," "defiled," and guilty, and has incurred a heavy debt—indeed, a debt so heavy that only God can remove it.[16] After a brief discussion of some key terms that denote sin, we turn to a selective survey of important passages in the Pentateuch, the Prophets, the historical writings, and then the poetic and wisdom literature, focusing specifically on the corrupted human nature and the sin that springs forth from that corruption.

In the Old Testament, "sin" is often the translation of חטא, which refers to missing the mark, deviating from some goal or good. While the word is at times used to refer to physical objects missing the mark by going off their proper trajectory (e.g., Judg. 20:16), when used in reference to sin, the mark or good from which one deviates is God himself (e.g., Gen. 20:9; Lev. 4:13–14), or other persons (e.g., Gen. 31:36), or both (e.g., Ps. 51:1, 3). While חטא emphasizes the objective character of sin as deviating from a mark, פשע emphasizes the sense of sin as willful "rebellion" (also often translated as "transgression"—as in 1 Kings 12:19; Isa. 1:2; Hos. 7:13). עון (e.g., Gen. 4:13)

15. "Accordingly, salvation is the reversal of condemnation. It is cast in *legal* categories. . . . Salvation is, for Paul, much broader than merely legal in nature. But it is not less than that." Thomas H. McCall, *Against God and Nature: The Doctrine of Sin* (Crossway, 2019), 90.

16. Cf. Keith L. Johnson and David Lauber, eds., *T&T Clark Companion to the Doctrine of Sin* (Bloomsbury T&T Clark, 2016); Nelson, *Sin*, 17–35; McCall, *Against God and Nature*, 33–39.

is applied "not simply to the sin but also the penalty that results from it."[17] Here, the sense is that sin incurs a burden and a heavy weight, polluting the sinner and condemning his conscience, such that only God can take away the sinner's iniquities (e.g., Exod. 34:7; Num. 14:18).

Jay Sklar reminds readers that these terms should not be isolated from the biblical narratives, and read in that light, a diverse array of metaphors emerge describing sins as rupturing one's relation to God:

> If he is our king, then sin is an act of rebellion against him (Num 14.9; Deut 1.26); if he is our faithful spouse, then sin is an act of spiritual prostitution (Exod 34.17; Lev 17.7; 20.5; Deut 31.16). Idolatry especially is considered to be a highly relational sin and is therefore described with highly relational language: it is a "serving" of other gods (Exod 23.24, 33; Deut 7.4; 13.6), instead of faithfully serving the Lord as a son does the father he loves (Exod 4.23); it is a "forsaking" of the Lord for other gods (Deut 31.16), instead of "cleaving" to the Lord in faithful love as one might do with a spouse (Deut 10.20; 13.4 [13.5]; 30.20 cf. Gen 2.24). While sin is sometimes thought of today as the breaking of a rule, these metaphors emphasize that it is the breaking of a relationship, an act of treachery against the Lord, the faithful covenant king and father and husband.[18]

The events of Genesis 3, which initiated this breaking of humanity's relationship with God, have serious consequences east of Eden and create what von Rad has described as an "avalanche" of the spread of sin that affects all of human history.[19] Humanity is separated from the covenant presence of God and is cast out of the temple-garden. These consequences are immediately and viscerally recounted: "As the story unfolds in Genesis, we see illustrated both the universal spread and the vicious character of sin. No sooner do we get outside of Eden (in the canonical narrative) before the oldest son of Adam and Eve murders his younger brother (Ge. 4:1–10)."[20] Sin is perpetuated from one generation to another. Just as Adam avoided responsibility and shifted

17. Jay Sklar, "Pentateuch," in *T&T Clark Companion to the Doctrine of Sin*, ed. Keith L. Johnson and David Tauber (Bloomsbury T&T Clark, 2016), 5.

18. Sklar, "Pentateuch," 6.

19. Gerhard von Rad, *Old Testament Theology*, vols. 1 and 2, trans. D. M. G. Stalker (Prince, 2005), 154. Cf. Nelson, *Sin*, 21–23.

20. McCall, *Against God and Nature*, 41.

the blame to God (Gen. 3:12), so does Cain, the son of Adam, shift the blame after the murder of his brother: "Am I my brother's keeper?" (Gen. 4:9). As Cain murdered his younger brother Abel, so does his descendant Lamech murder a young man (Gen. 4:23).

C. John Collins describes the destructive consequences of Adam's sin: "The hiding from God in Genesis 3:8; the fear and blame game of 3:10–13; the solemn sentences of 3:14–19; the evil deeds of chapter 4: all of these are in jarring discord with the idyllic scene of blessing and benevolent dominion (1:28–29) and innocent enjoyment (2:8–9, 18–25)."[21] Sin is now likened to a power, seeking to devour humanity in Genesis 4:7. By Genesis 6, "The LORD saw that the wickedness of man was great in the earth, and that every intention of the thoughts of his heart was only evil continually" (Gen. 6:5). This evil, now parasitically animating human nature, continues on even after the flood, despite the warnings and judgments of God: "The intention of man's heart is evil from his youth" (Gen. 8:21). This evil manifests itself in rebellion against God. Though we were made in his image and were meant to multiply and disperse across the globe while flourishing in the divine presence, humanity gathered together to form a name for itself by building the Tower of Babel (Gen. 11:4). The presence of sin brings about death, as seen in the genealogy of Genesis 5 with the repetition of the phrase "and he died," signifying that humanity now lives under a different epoch, a post-fall "world under curse with no relief in sight."[22]

The covering of Adam and Eve with skin after their first sin in Genesis 3:20 shows that God deals patiently with them by providing a substitute that covers them from immediate judgment. The rest of the Pentateuch expands on this: "For the Israelites, properly addressing the sin required both confession (which presumes repentance) (Lev. 5:5) and sacrifice. By these means, the sin was atoned and the sinner forgiven (4:20, 26; 5:10; Num. 15:25)."[23] This remains the case for both unintentional sins (e.g., Lev. 4:2) and intentional sins (Lev. 5:1; 6:1–7). The access to God by way of offering blood sacrifices for sin is itself made possible by God's gracious initiative (Lev. 17:11); God

21. C. John Collins, "Adam and Eve in the Old Testament," in *Adam, The Fall, and Original Sin: Theological, Biblical, and Scientific Perspectives*, ed. Michael Reeves and Hans Madueme (Baker Academic, 2014), 21.

22. Dempster, *Dominion and Dynasty*, 71.

23. Sklar, "Pentateuch," 15.

resides in the holy of holies within the tabernacle (which corresponds to heaven), and sacrifices and priestly work mediate access to God in the outer court (which corresponds to earth as the dwelling of God's pilgrim people).[24] Atonement is necessary for communion with God, as indicated by Leviticus 16, the literary center of the Pentateuch.[25] These old-covenant provisions are ultimately meant to point the Israelites to a truer and greater sacrifice and priest in the incarnate Christ. Unlike the priests of Israel, who "daily" make sacrifices for their own sins "and then for those of the people," Christ was sinless (Heb. 7:27). Unlike the sacrifices of "goats and calves," Jesus offers "his own blood" (Heb. 9:13). There are, however, high-handed sins that can lead to sins of apostasy (Num. 15:30–31), which, as Bavinck notes, was exemplified by Pharaoh's resistance against God, a sin of hardening one's heart (e.g., Exod. 4:21; 7:13), and is connected to "the unpardonable sin . . . as blasphemy against the Holy Spirit (Matt. 12:31–32; cf. Heb. 6:4–8; 10:25–29; 12:15–17; 1 John 5:16)."[26] It is a grave sin to reject in obstinance the salvation that God reveals.

The prophetic writings further indicate that the corruption of sin that leads to the violation of Israel's covenant relation with God is not reducible to actions but is rooted in something deeper: "Israel's prophets attributed wickedness to an evil heart."[27] Indeed, Jeremiah 17:9 exclaims that the "heart is deceitful above all things, and desperately sick; who can understand it?" such that God promises the writing of the law in human hearts in the new covenant so that we might be able to obey God (Jer. 31:31–34). Ezekiel records that God likens the restoration of his people to the enlivening of bones, a movement from death to new life: "And I will put my Spirit within you, and you shall live, and I will place you in your own land. Then you shall know that I am the Lord; I have spoken, and I will do it, declares the Lord" (Ezek.

24. G. K. Beale and Mitchell Kim, *God Dwells Among Us: A Biblical Theology of Temple* (IVP Academic, 2021), 43–44.

25. L. Michael Morales, *Who Shall Ascend the Mountain of the Lord? A Biblical Theology of the Book of Leviticus* (IVP Academic, 2015), 23–38.

26. Herman Bavinck, *Guidebook for Instruction in the Christian Religion*, ed. and trans. Gregory Parker Jr. and Cameron Clausing (Hendrickson, 2022), 93.

27. Tatha Wiley, *Original Sin: Origins, Developments, Contemporary Meanings* (Paulist Press, 2002), 29. Thus, as William M. Wood notes, the prophets also depict Israel's sin in terms of adulterous infidelity, especially in Hosea 1–3 and Jer. 2: "Breaching the Covenant: Sin in the Prophets," in *Ruined Sinners to Reclaim: Human Corruption in Historical, Biblical, Theological, and Pastoral Perspective*, ed. David Gibson and Jonathan Gibson (Crossway, 2024), 336–43.

37:14). Sin so corrodes our nature that nothing short of divine intervention can restore it. These latter prophetic texts point back to the Deuteronomic witness that the human heart requires circumcision, a covenant sign that points to one's death and resurrection, "so that you will love the Lord your God with all your heart and with all your soul, that you may live" (Deut. 30:6).

Alongside this tracing of sinful acts to a sinful heart, the prophets also emphasize a connection between false worship and social injustice or, as Mark Boda describes it, the "intertwining of the vertical and horizontal axes" of ethical behavior (e.g., Isa. 1:10–31; 65:11; 66:24; Jer. 7:6, 9; Ezek. 18:5–9; Amos 5:21–24; Mic. 2:1–2, 8–9).[28] Israel was meant to be God's covenant people, having God alone as their God and thus directing their worship to him exclusively.[29] Love of God, therefore, should lead to love of those made in his image: "The prophets will consistently attack Israel for dividing worship and ethics, the vertical and horizontal axes, and seek for reintegration."[30] Sins are against God and are thus often connected to sins against his image-bearers, or as the Westminster divines put it: "The cause of all wickedness is infidelity."[31] Thus, the prophetic literature is sensitive to not only the theological direction but also the societal and generational impact of sin (Isa. 13:16; 14:21; 65:6–7; Jer. 2:9; 11:22–23; Ezek. 20:21–24; Amos 7:17).

The historical writings witness to the social and generational impacts of sin, especially by way of representation, imputation, and imitation. Exodus 34:7 has already indicated that sins of one generation can influence and impact the next: "[God] will by no means clear the guilty, visiting the iniquity of the fathers on the children and the children's children, to the third and the fourth generation." This passage does not indicate that God is flippantly punishing the children for the sins of their parents (for that would contradict the beginning of the text that God is slow to anger). Rather, as Sklar notes, the passage is embedded within a narrative of the way in which children tend to imitate the sins of their parents, and hence would become vulnerable to the same punishments: "*The family unit is cohesive and the effects of sin impact*

28. Mark Boda, "Prophets," in *T&T Clark Companion to the Doctrine of Sin*, ed. Keith L. Johnson and David Tauber (Bloomsbury T&T Clark, 2016), 36.

29. Richard Lints, *Identity and Idolatry: The Image of God and Its Inversion* (IVP Academic, 2015), 79–101.

30. Boda, "Prophets," 35.

31. Westminster Assembly, *Annotations*, Ps. 14:1.

more than the sinner himself or herself."[32] We already noted the way in which corruption spreads through the human race after the fall, such that, by the time of the record of the book of Judges, "Everyone did what was right in his own eyes" (Judg. 17:6; 21:25). Sin, as Cornelius Plantinga Jr. argues, is fruitful because human beings are made to be fruitful and multiply: "Like a virus, it attaches the life force of its host. Sowing and reaping, human longing, children's natural trust of their parents—such things belong among the springs and roots of a good creation. Sin does not remove these things; it attaches them and converts them to new uses."[33] Sin is parasitic on the fruitfulness of created natures.

The books of 1 and 2 Kings specifically emphasize the generational and imitative impact of the sins of unfaithful kings. This includes the consequences of the sins of David and Solomon (2 Sam. 12:10–14; 1 Kings 11:11–13), which led to the divided kingdom, and within that period, sin's corrosiveness continued unabated. The sin of Manasseh is one such example, as he raised altars to other gods and offered his own "son as an offering and used fortune-telling and omens and dealt with mediums and with necromancers" (2 Kings 21:6). This not only provoked God's anger toward him and the whole southern kingdom of Judah (2 Kings 21:10–16), but it is also the reason for the ultimate exile of that kingdom (2 Kings 24:3–4). In fact, even his good son Josiah, though he restored significant Deuteronomic (monotheistic) worship back to Judah (2 Kings 22–23), was unable to mend the spiritual damage caused by his father. Ultimately, the good of Josiah could not cleanse the people from the idolatrous ways of Manasseh (2 Kings 23:12, 26–27). Boda aptly observes that in these writings, sin "and its accompanying guilt and punishment is understood in terms of corporate solidarity."[34]

Two key texts are relevant on the imputation of sin, both of which mirror the imputation of Adam's sin: the sin of Achan and the sin of David's census. Achan "coveted" and kept, in disobedience against God, the spoils of "a beautiful cloak from Shinar, and 200 shekels of silver, and a bar of gold weighing 50 shekels" (Josh. 7:21). God counted his sin as Israel's sin, and due to his sin,

32. Sklar, "Pentateuch," 20 (emphasis original).

33. Cornelius Plantinga Jr., *Not the Way It's Supposed to Be: A Breviary of Sin* (Eerdmans, 1995), 90–91.

34. Boda, "Prophets," 32.

the Israelites lost thirty-six men. As a result, the Israelites put Achan and his whole family to death by stoning (Josh. 7:1, 5, 22–26). In 2 Samuel 24:10–15, God responded to David's sin by sending a pestilence that killed seventy-thousand men. These texts show that God is in covenant with his people, and the sin of the one may implicate or be imputed to the whole. The biblical text cuts against the grain of the Western prioritization of individuality and autonomy.[35] Further, the observation of sin as both individual and corporate will inform our retrieval of Bavinck's account of human nature and culture in later chapters of this book: "There is growth, expansion, progression in the life of sin, albeit toward further corruption; there are individual sins, but also family, class, social, and national sins (*volkszonden*)."[36]

Finally, I turn to the poetic and wisdom literature, focusing on the Psalter and the book of Proverbs. The psalms in particular "[assume] that all humans suffer from innate sinfulness. Nonetheless, their 'moral equipment' may be sensitized, even rehabilitated through relationship with YHWH and knowledge of his will."[37] Psalm 14 portrays this innate sinfulness and "universality of corruption"[38] vividly: "They are corrupt, they do abominable deeds; there is none who does good. The Lord looks down from heaven on the children of man, to see if there are any who understand, who seek after God. They have all turned aside; together they have become corrupt; there is none who does good, not even one" (Ps. 14:1–3; cf. Ps. 53). The only hope in the face of human wickedness is a salvation that comes from the outside—from God himself: "Oh, that salvation for Israel would come out of Zion!" (Ps. 14:7). Sin is debilitating, such that sinners hate what is good (Ps. 25:19; 34:21; 50:17–18); evil deeds come from a love of evil (Ps. 11:5; 52:3–4). The wicked exult with "arrogant words; all the evildoers boast." They spread social injustice: "They kill the widow and the sojourner, and murder the fatherless," all the while denying God's existence (Ps. 94:4–7). Psalm 51:5 shows that sinners are such at conception. As the Westminster annotations on this passage observe: "[The psalmist] here brings all his actual transgressions to the fountain of them,

35. See especially Alistair McFadyen, *Bound to Sin: Abuse, Holocaust, and the Christian Doctrine of Sin* (Cambridge University Press, 2000), 14–42.

36. Bavinck, *Guidebook for Instruction in the Christian Religion*, 92.

37. Christopher B. Ansberry, "Writings," in *T&T Clark Companion to the Doctrine of Sin*, ed. Keith L. Johnson and David Tauber (Bloomsbury T&T Clark, 2016), 47.

38. John Goldingay, *Psalms*, vol. 1, *Psalms 1–41* (Baker Academic, 2006), 214.

original corruption."[39] Sin is a recalcitrant stain, and thus God himself is needed to bring renewal and restoration (Ps. 51:6–10). Christopher Ansberry sums up the teachings of the Psalter on sin poignantly "*as an all-encompassing, embodied phenomenon*. Sin affects one's character, cognitive faculties, attitudes, desires, tastes, speech, actions, and moral vision."[40]

These holistic consequences of sin go beyond the individual. Ansberry goes on to note that the Psalter also has in view generational sins when it refers to sin as "rebellion" and "amnesia."[41] Psalm 78 thus warns future generations, "The children yet unborn . . . so that they should set their hope in God and not forget the works of God, but keep his commandments; and they should not be like their fathers, a stubborn and rebellious generation, a generation whose heart was not steadfast, whose spirit was not faithful to God" (Ps. 78:6–8). Psalm 95 also reminds its hearers of the sins of their "fathers" so that they do not imitate the past generation (Ps. 95:9). Psalm 106, likewise, identifies the present generation with the sins of their fathers, so that they might remember the faithfulness of God toward them, especially in their deliverance from the Egyptians at the Red Sea. In all of these granular reminders, sin is depicted as being against God, against the community, and thus a pollution that latches onto multiple generations. Sin is a power that leaves an impact; it has "the capacity to infiltrate the structures of the community and overpower its constituents."[42]

The book of Proverbs provides the emphasis that the wicked are foolish. Sin is folly, cultivating false speech and violence—that is, "self-destroying practices, leading to living death."[43] "Fools," in the wisdom literature, refers to "human creatures who scorn their vocation to be wise in their practices for the well-being of the quotidian."[44] The vertical axis of proper worship of God leads to the horizontal axis of wise human living within the natural limits of that human existence. "The fear of the Lord is the beginning of knowledge; fools despise wisdom and instruction" (Prov. 1:7; cf. 1:29–30). Folly

39. Westminster Assembly, *Annotations*, Ps. 51:5.
40. Ansberry, "Writings," 48 (emphasis original).
41. Ansberry, "Writings," 50.
42. Ansberry, "Writings," 51.
43. David Kelsey, *Eccentric Existence: A Theological Anthropology*, vol. 1 (Westminster John Knox, 2009), 408.
44. Kelsey, *Eccentric Existence*, 408.

loves company, and the wise should resist their enticement (Prov. 1:10–12, 22; 2:12–15). Folly has its own path, while wisdom seeks another way, the path of justice and righteousness (Prov. 1:15; 2:8, 20). The whole person is involved in folly: The mouth babbles foolishly (Prov. 10:10) and stirs up violence (Prov. 10:11); sin mangles one's perception (Prov. 26:12, 26), raises "haughty eyes, a lying tongue, and hands that shed innocent blood" (Prov. 6:17), and comes from an evil heart (Prov. 6:14, 18). Folly, in turn, ruptures relations (Prov. 11:8; 14:21), resists order in the community (Prov. 11:11), and "perverts the ways of justice" (Prov. 17:23).[45]

In sum, the Old Testament witnesses to sin as an all-corrosive power that marks human nature after the fall. Though the Old Testament recognizes different kinds of actual sins (e.g., unintentional versus high-handed), acts of sin come from an evil heart that hates and resists God. Because human beings are image-bearers of God, sin is folly against our nature and best interests and leads to humanity's destruction as we turn to idols. Because sins are against God, they are also against one's neighbor, who is made in his image. Sin leads to God-forgetfulness, an amnesia of who we are and what God has made us to be, and as such sin also leads to social injustices, causing ripple effects that stain generations. Because of our sins and sinfulness, we incur a guilt that we cannot blot out and are separated from the divine presence. Divine grace alone can be the ground of hope for forgiveness, renewal, and moral renovation.

New Testament Witnesses

Several New Testament terms refer to sin or the sinfulness of humanity. ἁμαρτία (or cognates), which means to miss the mark, to fail, and to be culpable, is frequently the word in use (e.g., Matt. 1:21, 3:6; Mark 3:28; Luke 17:3). Other times, sin is described as a debt by the word ὀφείλημα, as in the Lord's Prayer (Matt. 6:12). Sin is described as depravity or wickedness, as expressed in the word πονηρία (e.g., Matt. 22:18; Mark 7:22; Luke 11:39), and as unrighteousness, as denoted by the word ἀδικία (e.g., Luke 13:27; Acts 1:18;

45. Stephen M. Coleman, "The Folly, Mystery, and Absurdity of Sin in the Wisdom Literature," in *Ruined Sinners to Reclaim: Human Corruption in Historical, Biblical, Theological, and Pastoral Perspective*, ed. David Gibson and Jonathan Gibson (Crossway, 2024), 320–21.

Rom. 1:18; 3:5) and other cognate forms. The Synoptic Gospels emphasize that sin "is a universal human condition, besetting Jesus' disciples, adversaries, and the populace at large."[46] They warn against love and trust of wealth as an alternative to true monotheistic worship (Matt. 6:24; 19:16–30; Mark 10:17–31; Luke 16:30; 18:18–30), identify one's response to Jesus as the marker of whether one is persevering in fidelity to God (e.g., Matt. 10:39; 11:27–29), highlight the internal origin and nature of sin (especially in the Sermon on the Mount, e.g., Matt. 5:38–39, 43–44), and warn against self-righteousness, which leads to failure to see one's own need for divine forgiveness (e.g., Matt. 3:7–10; 8:10–12; 18:21–35; Mark 2:23–3:6; 12:38–40; Luke 16:15). The sin against the Spirit, which is deemed unforgivable (Matt. 12:31–32; Mark 3:28–29; Luke 12:8–10), is precisely that "defiant, relentless, repudiation of the salvation offered by God's spirit" and is connected with high-handed sins denounced in Numbers 15:30–31, discussed above.[47]

The Johannine literature uses the dark (σκοτία) as a way of describing sin and sinfulness, emphasizing that sin is against God's revelation and light, which exposes the dark (e.g., John 1:5; 6:17; 12:46; 1 John 1:5; 2:8, 9, 11; 3:19).[48] First John also defines sin tersely as lawlessness: ἡ ἁμαρτία ἐστὶν ἡ ἀνομία (1 John 3:4). John, too, emphasizes the universality of sin, such that the denial of one's sinfulness is really a form of self-deception (1 John 1:8). God sending his Son to save the world presupposes the darkness of that world (John 3:16; 1 John 4:10). Those now in the light have an advocate in Christ, through whom they have forgiveness (1 John 2:1, 12). Those in the light also hope to be purified, so that they shall be more and more conformed to Christ (1 John 3:2). The descriptions of sin as lawlessness, darkness, disobedience, and lovelessness in John inform the traditioned account of sin as privation,

46. C. Clifton Black, "Synoptic Gospels," in *T&T Clark Companion to the Doctrine of Sin*, ed. Keith L. Johnson and David Tauber (Bloomsbury T&T Clark, 2016), 63–64.

47. Black, "Synoptic Gospels," 76.

48. "The Johannine view of sin has been recast by the Gospel's dualism; the human problem is born from the harsh division between light and darkness, truth and falsehood, to which humanity is captive." Gary M. Burge, "The Gospel and Epistles of John," in *T&T Clark Companion to the Doctrine of Sin*, ed. Keith L. Johnson and David Tauber (Bloomsbury T&T Clark, 2016), 94–95. On this theme of light and the world, see especially the insightful comments on John 1:1–18 in Edward W. Klink III, *John* (Zondervan Academic, 2017), 83–122. See also Murray J. Smith, "'Everyone Who Practices Sin Is a Slave to Sin': Sin in the Johannine Literature," in *Ruined Sinners to Reclaim: Human Corruption in Historical, Biblical, Theological, and Pastoral Perspective*, ed. David Gibson and Jonathan Gibson (Crossway, 2024), 381–431.

as an antithesis, as deviation, and thus as something inscrutable apart from God, his goodness, and his law.[49]

Σάρξ (*sarx*) is another way in which the New Testament refers to sin, especially in Paul's writings. While *sarx* can be used to refer to our body (as in 2 Cor. 4:11, where it is used *interchangeably* with "body," or John 1:14: "the word became *flesh*"), the "flesh" is more often used by Paul to refer to the present post-fall redemptive-historical order, which differs from the creational and will be superseded by the new creation. It refers to a "historically or temporally qualified sphere of existence" and reflects "an atmospheric quality."[50] In 1 Corinthians 1:18–23, for example, the people "according to the flesh" are seen as wise "in this present aeon, this present world-age . . . 'Flesh' brings into view man . . . in this world, human nature 'in this age.'"[51] This is not to say that human nature has always been sinful but that "the original creation order has become subject to corruption; the order of fallen Adam and his posterity has become the order of sin and death."[52] There is the act of sin, the human nature qualified by sinfulness, and the whole order of creation in the postlapsarian state, and *sarx* often refers to this latter sense.

In the Pauline texts, sin is so ingrained in our nature that it is recalcitrant to the truth and is often inscrutable. Though Ephesians 2:1–3 and Romans 7:14–25 are covered in the exegetical notes that follow, for the sake of space I will limit myself to two important passages from the book of Romans here: Romans 1:18–32 and 3:9–20.

Romans 1:18–23 indicates that one of the manifestations of sin is in the way in which we suppress our natural knowledge of God. What can be known about God "is plain" because "God has shown it to [humanity]," such that we are "without excuse" (1:19–20). The reason why no one, left to one's self, turns to God is not because God has left himself without a witness—everyone, in fact, knows God because "God has shown it to them." The suppression of verse 18 presupposes the possession and holding on of that which is suppressed, which is the knowledge of God: his divine nature (1:20), the way in which we fail to image God and thus incur his wrath (1:18, 32). "Because the law

49. Berkouwer, *Sin*, 256.

50. Richard B. Gaffin Jr., *In the Fullness of Time: An Introduction to the Biblical Theology of Acts and Paul* (Crossway, 2022), 350–51.

51. Gaffin, *In the Fullness of Time*, 351.

52. Gaffin, *In the Fullness of Time*, 352.

Romans 7:14–25

Following a defense of the intrinsic goodness and spiritual character of the law, Romans 7:14–25 is a vivid description of the "bondage of sin," as Paul describes his own struggle between what he delights in in his mind and the sin that resides in his members.[a] There has been, however, an interpretive debate on whether Paul is here reflecting on his pre-conversion, unregenerate life or his post-conversion, regenerate life.

Two promising lines of interpretation are consistent with the Reformed tradition. Petrus van Mastricht's comments on this passage reflect a traditioned Reformed interpretation, appealing to Romans 7:24–25 to introduce the topic of the state of sinfulness that all humans are in, including the regenerate Christian: "He is not speaking about himself as still unregenerate, for it does not belong to such to acknowledge, sense, and complain of their misery."[b] Given the reality of the polluting powers of sin, it is impossible for those without spiritual regeneration to concede of their sinfulness, declaring that the body is now a body of death (Rom. 7:24–25; cf. Rom. 6:6). As Guy Waters remarks, "Paul declares a consent to (Rom. 7:16), delight in (7:22), and service of (7:25a) the law of God that he later affirms is categorically impossible for the unbeliever (8:7)."[c] That the mind can now "delight" in the law thus indicates that this is Paul describing a post-conversion experience. Though this inner self wants to do good (7:18) and delights in the law of God (7:22), there is still sin that "dwells within [him]" (7:17); it dwells in his "members" (7:23), for he has a "body of death" (7:24). In other words, and as we shall explore in the next chapter, regeneration is true only for the inner self—that is, for the heart or ego that drives the functioning body, though the body is still a body of sin (6:6), marked by concupiscence, decay, and bound for death. That sinfulness still abides residually within one's members is not incongruent with the resurrection life detailed in Romans 6, for there Paul consistently indicates that the regenerated human must still put to death the body's "passions" (6:12), which must be resisted (6:19). The believer, in other words, is no longer a slave to sin but still resides in a body "sold under sin" (7:14). That's why it is "no longer I who do it, but sin that dwells within me" (7:17).[d]

Tom Schreiner and Will Timmins offer comments on this text to show that the inability of the Christian to obey the law, despite delighting in it in his inner self, is due to the present anthropological condition of Christians living in a postlapsarian era and body.[e] As Schreiner summarizes: "The text depicts the anthropological condition of human beings, and a fleshliness that as an Adamic inheritance persists in Christian believers this side of the resurrection of the body. As long as human beings are in the body, their struggle with sin persists."[f] Timmins appeals to the already / not yet of the Christian's regenerate experience. Though renewed inwardly, regeneration is a down payment for a future, glorified bodily existence, such that believers participate in but do not "possess" new life.[g] That full glorified existence is granted in the resurrection (Rom. 8:23), which is anticipated in Paul's cry for deliverance from this present sin-indwelled body (7:24–25). To sum up, and to anticipate the discussion of the regenerate person's existence in the next chapter, regeneration is granted *in* the body but not yet *for* the body. The problem here is not the body as such, but the body that has been implicated and qualified by the inherited corruption that all humans share after the fall of Adam.

Dennis Johnson offers an alternative reading that considers the "I" in Romans 7 to refer to the unregenerate person. He argues that the main rhetorical function of this text is to vindicate the law's goodness as a *standard*, but lack of power as a *command* and means of salvation.[h] Johnson argues that the language of slavery to sin and the sinner's fleshliness (Rom. 7:14, 23–25) stand in stark contrast to the liberation of slavery that Paul already emphasized for believers in Romans 6:11–12 and 17–18. The language of the body of death in Romans 7:25 specifically refers not to bodily death, for Johnson, but to "the death that consists in the inability to do what the law demands, and the condemnation resulting from that failure (cf. 5:12–21)."[i] This state of condemnation anticipates the relief of life in Christ in Romans 8:1–3. How, then, can the unbeliever be said to delight in God's law, when Romans 8:7 says that the mind cannot submit to the same? Johnson argues that Paul, in "pastoral wisdom," is observing the Jewish observance and admiration of the law, already discussed in Romans 2:17–29, which "only compound the culpability of those who teach others while failing to conform their own behaviour to the God-given norms they propound."[j] Similarly, Romans 10:2–3 witnesses to the Jews who have a zeal for God, but not according to knowledge. The sinful mind might consent to the law's goodness with their conscience but, instead of confessing one's inability to follow that law, uses the law to fuel their self-righteousness. Johnson's comments here, coupled with the observation that Romans 7 lacks any reference to the Spirit, seem to suggest that this pericope refers to the unregenerate life, rather than that of Christian experience.

Both of these readings are consistent with the Reformed emphases on the radical powers of sin and the necessity of regeneration for faith in Christ.

a. Blocher, *Original Sin*, 99.

b. Van Mastricht, *TPT*, 3:519. Dennis Johnson, however, rightly observes that recent interpretations of this passage do not track neatly with preexisting commitments to an overall doctrine of salvation, whether Arminian or Reformed. See his "The Function of Romans 7:13–25 in Paul's Argument for the Law's Impotence and the Spirit's Power, and Its Bearing on the Identity of the Schizophrenic 'I,'" in *Resurrection and Eschatology: Theology in Service of the Church; Essays in Honor of Richard B. Gaffin Jr.*, ed. Lane G. Tipton and Jeffrey C. Waddington (P&R, 2004), 7.

c. Waters, "Romans," 188.

d. *Pace* McCall, *Against God and Nature*, 366. See also Moo, *Romans*, 445–48. Indeed, McCall seems to miss that the indictments of Romans 7 are not applied to the "I" (which is indeed freed from sin, as Rom. 6 attests), but to the I's *members*.

e. Schreiner, *Romans*, 369–92; William N. Timmins, *Romans 7 and Christian Identity: A Study of the "I" in Its Literary Context* (Cambridge University Press, 2017), 148–207.

f. Schreiner, *Romans*, 387.

g. Timmins, *Romans 7*, 97.

h. Johnson, "The Function of Romans 7:13–25," 42.

i. Johnson, "The Function of Romans 7:13–25," 48.

j. Johnson, "The Function of Romans 7:13–25," 51.

of nature has been given to us by an imprinting of the eternal light, and by means of that light we receive the teaching of divine law."[53]

We are culpable not because we are ignorant and fail to find God by our own efforts or intellectual diligence but rather because, as those who have received this implanted knowledge of God, we fail to acknowledge God or properly give thanks to God (Rom. 1:21). The present active participle κατεχόντων (1:18), which is often translated "suppress" in modern English translations (NIV, ESV, CSB), has the sense of "holding on" or "restrain" (thus KJV: "who hold the truth in unrighteousness"), such that the sinner retains this knowledge while holding it unethically by ignoring it or misusing it in unrighteousness.[54]

53. Bonaventure, *Collations on the Ten Commandments*, trans. Paul J. Spaeth (The Franciscan Institute, 1995), II.2.

54. David C. Noe, "Suppress or Retain? Theodore Beza, Natural Theology, and the Translation of Romans 1:18," in *Theodore Beza at 500: New Perspectives on an Old Reformer*, ed. Kirk Summers and Scott M. Manetsch (Vandenhoeck & Ruprecht, 2021), 139–57. I agree with Noe with a caveat: Noe overemphasizes the distinction between the noetic and the ethical, for the two cannot be so neatly separated. Indeed, because sin impacts the whole self, noetic and psychological consequences (as seen in suppression) presuppose and are the result of the unethical ignoring and misuse of the implanted knowledge of God. Hence, while Noe is correct that one retains the knowledge of God, this retaining is not in contradiction with suppression, and that suppression never succeeds in eliminating the internal knowledge (e.g., in cases of self-deception). The sinner suppresses the knowledge of God *while* also retaining it. Suppression is thus futile, yet always engaged, and is thus folly. Further, the ethical misuse of the knowledge retained can also

Ephesians 2:1–3

Ephesians 2:1–3 is an important witness on the holistic character of sin. Indeed, this is the first passage to which Westminster Divine Anthony Burgess appeals to prove that there is, in fact, an original corruption that plagues humanity.[a] The descriptions of Ephesians 2:2–3 refer to the state of being spiritually "dead in the trespasses and sins," which is true of the Christian before conversion, "like the rest of mankind" (Eph. 2:3). Post-fall humanity is walking in trespasses and sins (cf. Ps. 1), assenting to the social direction of the world, a kind of "malformation" that is "systemic" in character, referring to the ways in which "cultural structures incentivize or nudge us toward particular behaviors."[b] The cultures of the world are in turn following supernatural forces at work in nurturing disobedience. This description shows that demonic activity manifests itself precisely in the inclination to sin, and not necessarily in paranormal appearances that puncture ordinary experience. Supernatural forces opposing God is common indeed, as pervasive as air.

Sinful humans, however, are culpable—they are, after all, transgressing and actively walk in a way that follows the "passions of our flesh," which in turn results in the works of the flesh (cf. Gal. 5:19–21). The flesh, here, does not refer to the mere appetites that may have gone awry but includes the command and consent of the mind to elevate creaturely realities over the divine. The world, the flesh, and the devil all overlap in producing the nexus of the sinful conditions of human existence. Such teachings anticipate the doctrine of total depravity in the Reformed tradition—that sin is radical and has corrupted everything. Such activity, then, rightly merits the wrath of God (Eph. 2:3).

The transition to verse 4 indicates the only solution to the problem of sin: the grace of God, which makes us "alive" (Eph. 2:4–10). Given the fallen condition of humanity, we are incapable of changing ourselves and require regeneration from God himself. Indeed, regeneration, therefore, precedes faith: "Though this faith be in us, yet it is not of us, that is, not from the power of nature, but that it is merely the gift of God; and this is to be meant not only of the habit of faith, but the very act."[c]

a. Anthony Burgess, *A Treatise on Original Sin: Proving That It Is, by Pregnant Texts of Scripture, and Vindicated from False Glosses* (Anchora Spei, 1658), 2.

b. Michael Allen, *Ephesians*, BTCB (Brazos, 2022), 32.

c. Westminster Assembly, *Annotations*, Eph. 2:8.

Bonaventure, then, argues that the teachings of Romans 1 show that God is the first thing known to the human mind, and this knowledge is never extinguished but presupposed while sinners desire "to worship an idol."[55] The will's ethical turn away from this implanted knowledge leads to suppression.[56] Only God's regenerating work re-enables sinners "to re-enter the mirror of our mind in which divine realities shine forth."[57]

In the unregenerate state, while knowing the true God, we deceive ourselves into acting as if God does not exist or is not the source of all that is good.[58] John Murray's comment is perceptive: "The inexcusableness resides in the fact that being in possession of this knowledge they did not render to God the glory and the thanks which the knowledge they possessed ought to have constrained."[59] Sin is thus not limited to isolated acts but resides much deeper: It infects our thinking and darkens our hearts, and we repress in futility the inextinguishable knowledge of the very God that we were created to image.

J. H. Bavinck argues that the sinner's unrighteousness is so radical and subtle that it cannot be considered primarily noetic or epistemic, but he connects this suppression of the knowledge of God to psychological repression:

> Suppression occurs so directly, so spontaneously, so simultaneously with the "understanding and seeing clearly" that at the precise moment that people see, they no longer see; at the exact moment that they know, they already no longer know. Psychologically considered, this is in and of itself entirely possible. . . . In this connection one could even say that human beings, in being addressed by the world around them, always suppress

lead to wrong propositional inferences, which is the basis for the distinction between *theologia falsa* and *theologia vera*, and regenerate natural theology and unregenerate natural theology.

55. Bonaventure, *Disputed Questions on the Mystery of the Trinity*, ed. George Marcil, trans. Zachary Hayes (The Franciscan Institute, 1979), q. 1. a. 1, ad. 3. See also Bonaventure, *Itinerarium Mentis in Deum*, ed. Philotheus Boehner and Zachary Hayes, trans. Zachary Hayes (The Franciscan Institute, 2002), V. 3. Cf. Christopher Cullen, *Bonaventure* (Oxford University Press, 2006), 63–65.

56. Nathaniel Gray Sutanto, "Questioning Bonaventure's Augustinianism? On the Noetic Effects of Sin," *New Blackfriars* 102 (2021): 401–7.

57. Bonaventure, *Itinerarium*, II, 13.

58. For an analysis of sin as self-deception, see William Wood, "Sin as Self-Deception," in *T&T Clark Handbook of Analytic Theology*, ed. James M. Arcadi and James T. Turner Jr. (Bloomsbury T&T Clark, 2021), 335–45; and Greg L. Bahnsen, "The Crucial Concept of Self-Deception in Presuppositional Apologetics," *Westminster Theological Journal* 57 (1995): 1–31.

59. John Murray, *The Epistle to the Romans* (Eerdmans, 1997), 41.

> an instance of their becoming aware as an instance in which God, who is present everywhere and in everything, presents himself and manifests himself to them in a very evident way.[60]

Bavinck concludes that, according to this passage, "there is something distorted in the human condition. People have been resisting, suppressing. They have done so unconsciously." A traumatized individual learns to cope with a troubled memory by repressing it. In the long run, that repression could become unconscious, even second nature, until and unless a particular event or person triggers the memory. In the same manner, the sinner represses the awareness of their ruptured relation with their Maker—and we were born as skilled suppressors (cf. Eph. 2:1–3; 4:18). According to Paul here, the indication that the suppressed knowledge of God would always be present and reemerge is in the ineradicable drive to worship something as a substitute of God.[61] If image-bearers do not worship God, then they will worship something else—"images resembling mortal man" and other creatures:

> Humanity has abandoned its intended function of pointing beyond itself to the one true God and instead has taken on the role of pointing to, or representing something *within creation*. No longer does humanity "image" God, conducting itself as the glory of God in all of its activity, but now "images" something within the created order—whether human or animal. This, as Paul goes on to show, is a tragic move with devastating bodily consequences. This exchange entails viewing the human body not as the representation of God designed to relate to others and care for creation in line with God's character. Rather, the human body is pointing beyond itself to something within creation, or perhaps even *pointing to itself* as the ultimate end of creation, which is a surrender of the true glory of humanity in exchange for shame.[62]

Paul may be alluding to the events of Genesis 3—instead of imitating God and listening to his word, Adam and Eve listened to the serpent. As Greg

60. Johan Herman Bavinck, "Religious Consciousness and Christian Faith," in *The J. H. Bavinck Reader*, ed. John Bolt, James D. Bratt, and Paul J. Visser (Eerdmans, 2013), 284.

61. Cf. Lints, *Identity and Idolatry*, 110–11. See also N. Gray Sutanto, *A Sense of the Divine: An Affective Model of General Revelation from the Reformed Tradition* (Cambridge University Press, 2025).

62. Timothy G. Gombis, "Paul," in *T&T Clark Companion to the Doctrine of Sin*, ed. Keith L. Johnson and David Tauber (Bloomsbury T&T Clark, 2016), 99 (emphasis original).

Beale pithily summarizes it: We become what we worship.[63] The iterations of God's wrath "giving up" (Rom. 1:24, 26, 28) humanity to its worst impulses leads them to unnatural acts of sin, expressed in forms of sexual immorality, which are direct consequences of suppressing the natural knowledge of God. Departure from God, ultimately, leads to a departure from nature, for God is the author of nature.[64] When we reject God, we end up worshiping the thing closest to us: ourselves, his image-bearers—which is why Paul refers to sexual sin in particular as the natural conclusion of idolatry. As Bavinck recognized already in 1904, the decline of the Christian faith leads inevitably to the erosion of nature, and especially of a coherent sense of *human* nature "when all rule, all order, all measure, all logos is gone from nature and therefore nature itself is gotten rid of."[65] This self-deception and denial of nature ultimately lead to not merely enjoying the acts of sin but also approving those who "practice them" (Rom. 1:32).

Romans 3:9–20 then declares the universality and totality of sin in the clearest terms: No one does good—in fact, all have turned aside. Paul is citing and alluding to passages like Psalm 14:1–3 (cf. Ps. 53:1–3); Psalm 5:9; Psalm 10:7; Ecclesiastes 7:20; Isaiah 59:7–8; and Psalm 36:2.[66] Sin is universal, such that no one is righteous, and sin is total, such that every part of ourselves has been affected: Our throats, tongues, feet, and eyes are mired in sin. "This is unqualified godlessness."[67] Observing Romans 3, Peter Martyr Vermigli comments that all "these things sufficiently point to the utter corruption of human nature."[68] Indeed, the totality with which sin has infected our faculties indicated here forms the basis for the Reformed teachings on original sin and total depravity that will be explored in later chapters. Unregenerate sinners, thoroughly stricken by the power of sin, lack the freedom to choose between spiritual good and evil but are inclined only to sin. Hence, no one will be seen as righteous when judged on the basis of the law (Rom. 3:20). As

63. Greg Beale, *We Become What We Worship: A Biblical-Theology of Idolatry* (IVP Academic, 2008). Cf. Matthew Roberts, *Pride: Identity and the Worship of Self* (Christian Focus, 2023), 15–33.

64. On this point, see Carl R. Trueman, *The Desecration of Man: How the Rejection of God Degrades Our Humanity* (Sentinel, 2026).

65. Herman Bavinck, *Christianity and Science*, trans. and ed. N. Gray Sutanto, James Eglinton, Cory C. Brock (Crossway, 2023), 200.

66. See Moo, *Romans*, 211–13.

67. Murray, *Romans*, 105.

68. Peter Martyr Vermigli, *On Original Sin*, trans. Kirk Summers (Davenant, 2019), 8.

Douglas Moo comments, "Nothing a person does, whatever the object of obedience or the motivation of that obedience, can bring him or her into favour with God."[69] The guilt of sin points humanity to a salvation that must come from something other than the performance of the law: "The law provides no resources to recover [human beings] from their lost condition. It serves only to underscore their plight."[70] The penalty of sin is death (Rom. 6:23).

Romans 7:24 thus underscores that the fallen human nature is now a "body of death," and sin continues to dwell in our members, even as Christians. Our own desires lead us to perpetuate sin: "But each person is tempted when he is lured and enticed by his own desire. Then desire when it has conceived gives birth to sin, and sin when it is fully grown brings forth death" (James 1:14–15). Such passages will signal to the Reformed that the tendency to sin itself—that is, concupiscence—is illicit and culpable, already a feature of our fallenness rather than natural to our created natures.[71]

GOD'S COMMITMENT TO FALLEN IMAGE-BEARERS

Things seem dark indeed, and the realities and consequences of sin are stark. It must be emphasized, however, that God is committed to his good creation and to his fallen image-bearers. Derek Nelson reminds us that sin actually implies good news, precisely because it "brings God back to the picture of moral fault, and thus [the doctrine of sin actually] reintroduces the language of hope, forgiveness, and reconciliation into the experience of suffering and human misery."[72] Without the doctrine of sin, our sense that there is something wrong with the world and with ourselves, and that things are not the way they are supposed to be, would itself be illusory, pointing to no solutions. In that case, we are left in despair. But if our sense of shame, wrong, and misery is not illusory, and is rather an indication that we do indeed know that God exists and that we have violated his moral law (Rom. 1:19–20, 32; 2:15), then there *are* solutions and a good to which our deviations point.

---

69. Moo, *Romans*, 220.

70. Guy Prentiss Waters, "Romans," in *A Biblical-Theological Introduction to the New Testament: The Gospel Realized*, ed. Michael J. Kruger (Crossway, 2016), 185.

71. Cf. Blocher, *Original Sin*, 24.

72. Nelson, *Sin*, 16.

Furthermore, sin's evil actually highlights the dignity of human beings—the fall is tragic *because* we are made in God's image. And despite that fall, we remain image-bearers (Gen. 9:6; James 3:9) with dignity and moral accountability.

CONCLUSION

This chapter has surveyed the key biblical texts on the origin of sin and the spread and corruption of sin on human nature through the Old and New Testaments. Along the way, we have seen that sin is not reducible to particular acts of sins—actual sins arise from an evil and sin-stricken human nature. Sin is thus often described as a power and a stain, which leads to humanity's separation from God, guilt, and the corresponding need for atonement and for an intercessor who mediates between sinful humanity and God. The next chapter highlights God's commitment to the spread and restoration of his image-bearers after the fall.

FURTHER READING

Gibson, David, and Jonathan Gibson, eds. *Ruined Sinners to Reclaim: Human Corruption in Historical, Biblical, Theological, and Pastoral Perspective*. Crossway, 2024. Especially pages 251–510. The second part of this tome on the doctrine of sin offers a helpful survey of the seminal biblical texts on sin in context, while providing readings that also draw from the Reformed tradition.

Wiley, Tatha. *Original Sin: Origins, Developments, Contemporary Meanings*. Paulist Press, 2002. A standard survey text that includes not only the biblical material on sin but also the later debates on the doctrine from ancient to modern theology.

Murray, John. *The Imputation of Adam's Sin*. Presbyterian and Reformed, 1959. A classic work defending the Reformed doctrine of the imputation of Adam's sin by providing an incisive exegesis of Romans 5:12–21.

Plantinga, Cornelius, Jr. *Not the Way It's Supposed to Be: A Breviary of Sin*. Eerdmans, 1995. Perhaps the most accessible introduction to the biblical depictions of sin—an ideal starting point for the new reader.

3

HUMANITY: PRESERVED AND RENEWED IN CHRIST

THE FIRST CHAPTER sketched the biblical teachings on the image of God, the creation of the human being, and the purpose of humanity to fellowship with God and carry out the cultural mandate in order to spread the glory of God across the whole world as his representatives. The second chapter observed that humanity has rejected this call from God, seeking instead to go their own way, imitating other gods and pointing to themselves rather than God. After the fall, sin has corrupted humanity universally and totally, and now humans live under the curse of sin, deserving the just penalty of death. God, however, is not done with humanity and remains committed to his image-bearers. This chapter thus turns to God's preservation of humanity, witnessed in the storyline of Scripture, before zooming in on the teachings of the New Testament on God's renewal of human nature through the work of the Spirit of Jesus Christ.

GOD'S PRESERVATION OF IMAGE-BEARERS

The story of humanity continued despite the tragedy of the fall. "Immediately after the fall, we see that God comes to man, seeks him, and guides him back into his fellowship (Gen. 3:7–15)."[1] God did not leave humanity to its own devices, nor does God abandon his plan to have humanity represent him across the whole world. In other words, God is committed to dwell with his people in a holy land, through a representative seed. Two themes emerge: God's commitment for humanity to bear a seed that will finally represent God and humanity perfectly, and God's commitment to have his glory proclaimed through all the earth by the representation of image-bearers in the world (Ps. 8). Though a full biblical theology of the renewal of God's image-bearers is impossible here, we shall focus on two loci for the sake of space: the primordial history of Genesis after the fall and until the call of Israel, and Jesus Christ as the second Adam of a new humanity, especially witnessed in the implications of his death, resurrection, and ascension.

Seed and Land—From Adam to Israel

Writing on the consequences of the fall and God's dealings with humanity, Herman Bavinck shows that the biblical narrative depicts the interweaving of both sin and good, grace and wrath throughout human history as the curse of the fall is suspended in part by common grace: "God committed himself thereby to creation, in spite of its apostasy, to preserve it and make its path straight. Even the punishment—which was pronounced upon the serpent, the woman, and the man, after the transgression—was mixed with blessing and grace."[2] Indeed, Adam and Eve did not suffer the wrath of God unilaterally after their sin. Adam and Eve did lose their communion with the life-sustaining Spirit, and their physical death was now certain. Yet, God promises them a seed that would crush the serpent in what is considered the first proclamation of the gospel: "I will put enmity between you and the woman, and between your offspring and her offspring; he shall bruise your head, and you shall bruise his heel" (Gen. 3:15). The narrative of the Old Testament focuses on this question: Who shall be the promised seed of the woman, who crushes the serpent? The naming of Eve by Adam as the "mother" of the living (Gen. 3:20) is, as Dempster observes, a "genuine act

1. Herman Bavinck, *Guidebook for Instruction in the Christian Religion*, ed. and trans. Gregory Parker Jr. and Cameron Clausing (Hendrickson, 2022), 97.

2. Bavinck, *Guidebook*, 95–96.

of faith" on the promise of God for this seed who would reverse the fall and provide renewal.[3] The description of Eve as the mother of the living is thus a "soteriological statement."[4] The promise of seed also indicates God's gracious and unwavering commitment to the call of humanity to be fruitful and multiply—that fruitfulness and multiplication after the fall, however, will now be complicated by sin and destruction.

The genealogy of Genesis 4:17–24, after Cain's murder of Abel, indicates the simultaneous spread of sin and the natural human enactment of the cultural mandate. On the one hand, the genealogy begins with the consequences of Cain's sin of murdering his brother, which was Cain building a city in exile (Gen. 4:17). The genealogy then ends with the prideful Lamech, a descendant of Cain, who himself killed a "young man" (Gen. 4:23). Sin spreads like a moral infection. On the other hand, this exile was also a result of God's patience with Cain and fallen humanity. The sinful city of Cain is also the locus for the developments of culture: infrastructure and agriculture from Jabal, "the father of those who dwell in tents and livestock"; music from Jubal, "the father of all those who play the lyre and the pipe"; and craftsmanship and technology from Tubal-cain, "the forger of all instruments of bronze and iron" (Gen. 4:20–22). The genealogy juxtaposes the mixed character of blessing and curse—the blessing of the development of culture coincides with the deadly corruption of sin.[5] Sinful cultures still comprise image-bearers. The presence of sin does not impede the development of culture, and even the most sinful of cultures continue to witness, however parasitically, to the good gifts of the Creator.

The existence of civilization in Cain's line along with the preservation of his life (Gen. 4:15) inform what would later be called the doctrine of "common grace"—God gifts fallen humanity such that remnants of human nature and its function are still intact, witnessed in the ability of sinners to continue to enjoy relative peace, work, multiply, and acknowledge at least some aspects of the natural law, despite failing to give thanks to God for these things (cf. Rom. 1:18–23; Acts 17:24–28). John Murray rightly points to Romans 2:14–15 to show

3. Stephen G. Dempster, *Dominion and Dynasty: A Theology of the Hebrew Bible* (IVP Academic, 2003), 68.

4. Michael Lefebvre, "Adam Reigns in Eden: Genesis and the Origins of Kingship," *Bulletin of Ecclesial Theology* 5 (2018): 52.

5. Dempster, *Dominion and Dynasty*, 70.

that the moral law has been written on human beings by nature, such that the "divinely established norms of conduct have relevance to, and even effect upon, those who are outside the pale not only of redemptive grace but also of that special revelation that is the medium of its application in the hearts and lives of men."[6] Romans 1:24, 26, and 28 show us that the wrath of God gives us over to our sinful impulses, which means that we are dependent on God's kindness in restraining our sins. God, after all, "makes his sun rise on the evil and on the good, and sends rain on the just and on the unjust" (Matt. 5:45). Bavinck is thus well justified in his argument that common grace and special, redemptive grace are poured out from God immediately after the fall; the genealogies of the exiled city of Cain alongside the presentation of the line of Seth in Genesis 4–5 are indicating the intertwining of common grace and special grace.

This passage on the city of Cain is immediately followed by the arrival of another seed from Eve, named Seth (Gen. 4:25–26). Genesis 5 presents an alternative genealogy, which recalls the promised seed of Genesis 3:15. It ends with the birth of Noah and the introduction of his sons (Gen. 5:32), which prompts the question of whether Noah will be the redemptive seed. What follows in Genesis 6–9 even positions Noah as a redeemer figure in the midst of a spiritually decaying humanity. God saves Noah and his family, along with the animals, from God's judgment in the form of a flood, and upon the reestablishment of a new world order after the flood (2 Pet. 3:5–6), God issues "new commands" that "echo old creation imperatives, namely to be fruitful and multiply" in Genesis 8:16–17:[7] "Go out from the ark, you and your wife, and your sons and your sons' wives with you. Bring out with you every living thing that is with you of all flesh—birds and animals and every creeping thing that creeps on the earth—that they may swarm on the earth, and be fruitful and multiply on the earth." Genesis 9:1–6, 8–17 reiterates this command of preservation in the establishment of the Noachian covenant. The covenant with Noah establishes him as an Adam-like figure.[8] God "blessed" him as he did Adam, and God reissued the same command to

6. John Murray, *Collected Writings of John Murray*, vol. 2, *Systematic Theology* (Banner of Truth, 1977), 109.

7. Dempster, *Dominion and Dynasty*, 73.

8. G. K. Beale and Mitchell Kim, *God Dwells Among Us: A Biblical Theology of Temple* (IVP Academic, 2021), 28.

Noah as he did to Adam: "Be fruitful and multiply and fill the earth." But this new creational imperative features elements that presuppose a post-fall reality, with sanctions on the shedding of blood (Gen. 9:6). In contrast to the commands given to Adam, humanity is now exposed to the animal world in a life-threatening way, and the declaration of the dignity of the image of God here is given in the context of a "sanction against murder rather than as a celebration of wonder."[9] The persistence of sin in this postdiluvian reality is seen again as Noah sins just as Adam did, though now not in a garden but in a vineyard (Gen. 9:20–21), showing that a truer and better redemptive representative seed is still to come.

The corruption of sin continues until the narrative of the Tower of Babel in Genesis 11, and God judges the people in this account by dispersing them (Gen. 11:9). But even here, God's introducing multiple languages to "confuse" them and his dispersing them discloses not merely judgment but also mercy, as it compels the people to multiply across the earth fruitfully instead of settling in one place, in accordance with God's command in Genesis 1:26–28.[10] The focus on the call of Abraham and the covenant that God establishes with him for the next ten chapters of Genesis answers the question: How will the mandate be carried out to all the earth? It also furthers the emphasis on "geography and genealogy" as this focus on one man is instrumental for the filling of the earth.[11] Through him and his seed, the whole world will be blessed. God promises land to him and his children (Gen. 12:7; 15:18). The language of Genesis 17:2 and 6 echoes the call of Adam to be fruitful and multiply: "That I may make my covenant between me and you, and may multiply you greatly. . . . I will make you exceedingly fruitful, and I will make you into nations, and kings shall come from you."[12] Then, despite Abraham's impatience and Sarah's faithlessness, God delivers on his promises by giving them a son, Isaac, only in their old age (Gen. 21:1), as if to communicate, as Augustine comments, that the child is a "gift of God, and was not due to men and was the gratuitous largess of grace . . . it was requisite that a son be given in a way which no effort of nature could compass."[13] The call of the next chapter to sacrifice this

9. Dempster, *Dominion and Dynasty*, 73.
10. Beale and Kim, *God Dwells Among Us*, 28.
11. Dempster, *Dominion and Dynasty*, 76.
12. See Beale and Kim, *God Dwells Among Us*, 29.
13. Augustine, *The City of God*, trans. Marcus Dods (Random House, 1993), 14.3.

promised son "juxtaposes the height of blessing (the birth of the seed) with the depth of the curse (the attack upon the seed)," foreshadowing that the seed of Eve, who brings about the restoration of the people and world, will have to die to bear the curses of that people and world.[14]

Because of Abraham's faith, God spares Isaac's life and reiterates the promises of fruitfulness for the sake of the nations to Jacob, Isaac's son (Gen. 26:3–4). Jacob is renamed Israel, and he will be made into a nation (Gen. 28:13–14; 32:28). When Moses is called to rescue the Israelites from Egypt, God says that "Israel is my firstborn son" (Exod. 4:22). "Israel is a first-born son, a new humanity among the nations, one in whom the image of God is transmitted."[15] The rescue of Israel from Egyptian slavery echoes the narrative of the flood and the call of Abraham—just as Noah and Abraham were called to be a distinct people and given a mandate to obey as a blessing to the world, so is Israel redeemed in order that they might be a distinct people (Exod. 19–24). "Because Israel is son of God, they should obey God from the heart (see esp. Deut. 8:5–6, 14:1–2). If Israel disobeyed, they would be turning their back on the covenant, and it would be as if they were no longer God's children (Deut. 32:4–6, 18–20)."[16] This obedience was ordered toward Israel's role as the mediator of blessing toward the whole world (Exod. 19:5–6). They are a "kingdom of priests," a "holy nation," to whom belong the patriarchs and oracles of God (Rom. 9:4), such that they were meant to be a prophetic light to all the nations. As a chosen people, therefore, Israel, like Adam, was called to be a prophet, priest, and king.[17]

Israel, however, ultimately fails to obey God and is cast into exile for violating God's covenant—Israel failed to be a holy people, and by the end of 1 and 2 Kings, Israel had become like the other nations.[18] The latter prophets depict the promised land as a new Eden from which Israel is cast out, failing to keep

14. Dempster, *Dominion and Dynasty*, 84.

15. Dempster, *Dominion and Dynasty*, 98.

16. Brandon Crowe, *The Lord Jesus Christ: The Biblical Doctrine of the Person and Work of Christ* (Lexham, 2023), 9–142.

17. "Every Christian theology must have a significant place for such realities as the God of Israel, the exodus, the Torah, the Temple, the Davidic Kingship, and the promised land. A covenant-based Christian theology will track God's covenants with Noah, Abraham, Moses, and David, as fulfilled by Christ and the Church." Matthew Levering, "Israel," in *The New Cambridge Companion to Christian Doctrine*, ed. Michael Allen (Cambridge University Press, 2023), 54.

18. Dempster, *Dominion and Dynasty*, 150–56.

themselves holy by breaching the covenant (e.g., Isa. 1:2–9; cf. Deut. 30:19).[19] The corporate failure of Israel coincides with the sins of its representatives. David committed grave sins and failed to be the king who obeyed God fully (2 Sam. 11; Ps. 51), and Solomon, too, failed by clinging to the idols of the many foreign women he married (1 Kings 11). Again, the question reemerges: Who then will be the faithful son of God who will obey where Adam and Israel failed? And how would the everlasting kingdom promised to David come to pass (2 Sam. 7)? Who would be the truer and greater David?

Christ as Second Adam

The previous section has underscored the importance of God's mandate, as given to Adam, as God is committed to further the execution of that mandate through the seed of the woman who would reverse the failures of Adam. Through this seed, a new humanity will emerge that will be a blessing to all the nations. Due to space, we cannot outline the way in which the rest of the Old Testament traces the lineage of Eve in search of the promised seed who would crush the serpent and restore image-bearers and their place in God's world and in fellowship with God. When Jesus enters into the picture, however, he is decisively positioned and described in the New Testament as the new Adam, that promised seed of the woman. Christ's Sonship is thus multilayered. To put it in christological terms: Jesus is not merely the eternally begotten Son in his preexistent divine nature; he is also the true and obedient Son of God who obeyed where Adam had failed in his human nature. Jesus is the image of God par excellence, as exemplified in his perfect life and obedience.

Like Adam, the Bible depicts Jesus as a new and climactic representative of God's people: "With the appearance of Jesus as the fully obedient Son of God, we encounter a new day in the history of redemption—a day of eschatological salvation secured by the Messiah."[20] More specifically, Jesus is Messiah

19. On the prophetic literature's depiction of Israel's sin as the breaking of a covenant, see William M. Wood, "Breaching the Covenant: Sin in the Prophets," in *Ruined Sinners to Reclaim: Sin in Historical, Biblical, Theological, and Pastoral Perspective*, ed. David Gibson and Jonathan Gibson (Crossway, 2024), 323–52.

20. Brandon Crowe, *The Last Adam: A Theology of the Obedient Life of Jesus in the Gospels* (Baker Academic, 2017), 81. See also Brandon D. Crowe, *The Obedient Son: Deuteronomy and Christology in the Gospel of Matthew* (De Gruyter, 2012); *The Lord Jesus Christ*, 9–142.

because, as the obedient Son, he is the "embodiment of true humanity, and the truly obedient man."[21] Luke traces Jesus's genealogy back to Adam (Luke 3:38). As with Israel, God calls Christ out of Egypt (Matt. 2:15) and the Spirit leads him to the wilderness temptations in order to recapitulate the trials of Adam in the garden (Luke 4). Christ crushes the serpent, and this is what his death on the cross has accomplished: His death succeeded because by it he "disarmed" the rulers and authorities by "canceling the record of debt that stood against us" (Col. 2:13–15). The "Son of God" came to "destroy the works of the devil" (1 John 3:8; cf. Ps. 91). Indeed, he subdued the serpent (Rev. 12:9–11). This is the promised seed that would crush the serpent and bruise his head, per Genesis 3:15. If Eden was a garden-temple where God's presence dwelled with his covenant people, Jesus is the perfect presence of God, through whom God will dwell with his people consummately as the true temple (John 2:21).

The Gospel of John also has suggestive descriptions of Jesus's work that connect him to Adam. Edward Klink III detects certain clues in John 19–20 that merit our attention.[22] First, in John 19:5, Pilate proclaims to the Jews and Romans about Jesus: ἰδοὺ ὁ ἄνθρωπος ("Behold, the man!" John 19:5). As Klink comments, the "particle of exclamation, 'behold,'" here is used in John when "there is a challenge to perceive with the mind a truth not outwardly evident to human eyes," as in John 1:29: "Behold, the Lamb of God."[23] "Speaking beyond himself in a manner similar to Caiaphas (see 11:49–52), Pilate not only introduces this title with emphasis, but directs his listeners to see in it a deeper truth and reality about the person to whom it is applied."[24] Second, Klink detects in this text an echo of God's judgment of Adam in Genesis 3:22, where "Behold, the man" serves to introduce a declaration of "Adam's alienation from God and existence in a state of death."[25] The echo serves as a reversal of that Adamic declaration. Third, after the resurrection, Jesus appears on the first day of the week, thereby establishing a new day of worship, and "blows"

21. Crowe, *The Lord Jesus Christ*, 58.

22. Edward W. Klink III, "Genesis Revealed: Second Adam Christology in the Fourth Gospel," *Bulletin of Ecclesial Theology* 5 (2018): 27–42.

23. Klink, "Genesis Revealed," 33. See also the comments in Edward W. Klink III, *John* (Zondervan Academic, 2016), 777–79.

24. Klink, "Genesis Revealed," 33.

25. Klink, "Genesis Revealed," 34.

(ἐμφυσάω) the Spirit on his disciples (John 20:22), connecting his finished work with the life-giving Spirit of Genesis 2:7, "where the exact verb is used [in the LXX]. . . . The Gospel is guiding the reader to see an act of (re)creation."[26]

If Jesus is the true Adam, then the Gospel is signifying that he, too, will be the head of a new humanity. God's image-bearers will once again image God not merely by their ontology but also by their Spirit-infused ethical conformity to God. "That is, Jesus is established by the Spirit his Body—the Body of Christ—as a ministering agent in the world, and by the same Spirit Jesus is empowering this new humanity to do what Adam and his descendants had failed to do: to be God's representatives and ministers in the world."[27]

Fourth, such observations are strengthened when one sees the way John depicts Jesus as a gardener in John 20:15. This reference "directs the reader not only to the biblical garden, but also to the (original) biblical gardener, Adam. . . . For Jesus had fulfilled in his person the demands of God, and therefore had become the second Adam, the Gardener assigned by God (see Gen. 2:15). . . . In the second Garden, the Gardener himself [as the incarnate one] came to tend his (new) creation (Gen. 2:15; Rev. 21–22)."[28] Adam was cast out of the garden and into exile, but Jesus enters this garden as the resurrected, vindicated, and obedient Son. A new creation is commencing because of Jesus's resurrection.

Jesus is therefore the prophesied "Son of Man" of Daniel 7:13–14, who would be "given dominion and glory and a kingdom, that all peoples, nations, and languages should serve him; his dominion is an everlasting dominion, which shall not pass away, and his kingdom one that shall not be destroyed." The Son of Man fulfills the Adamic task of representing God's authority as God commissions him to do in Genesis 1–2, which Psalm 8 echoes by way of royal imagery in the context of ruling the fauna (see also Ps. 80:17).[29]

The Gospels record that Jesus refers to himself as the Son of Man (Matt. 26:64–65; Mark 14:62; Luke 22:69–71). As the "Son of Man, Jesus fulfils the intended destiny of the royal dominion of humanity."[30] Hence, Jesus introduces the Great Commission by proclaiming that all authority in heaven and

26. Klink, "Genesis Revealed," 34.
27. Klink, "Genesis Revealed," 35.
28. Klink, "Genesis Revealed," 39–40.
29. Crowe, *The Last Adam*, 39.
30. Crowe, *The Last Adam*, 43.

earth has been granted to him (Matt. 28:18). This commission is to call the nations, to make disciples and to baptize them in the Triune name of Father, Son, and Spirit—we proclaim the gospel so that God's image-bearers will once again bear his name and reflect his character, in conformity with what they were made to be.

Jesus was thus like us "in every respect . . . yet without sin" (Heb. 2:17; 4:15). As the head of the new humanity, the Spirit conforms his people to Christ's example (1 Cor. 15:45; Rom. 8:29). Through him the new creation has come, a new eon, as it were, and a new epoch of God's redemptive history (2 Cor. 5:21). He came in the fullness of time (Gal. 4:4) and is the turning point of the ages, from the former times to "these last days" (Heb. 1:1–2). God calls the church, as those in union with Christ in this new age and new covenant, to behold "the glory of the Lord," such that they might be "transformed into the same image from one degree of glory to another. For this comes from the Lord who is the Spirit" (2 Cor. 3:18).[31] John Kilner's summation of Christ as the image of God in the sense of being the "standard for what God's image should look like" is apt.[32] "Christ illustrates God's purposes and goals for humanity. As the fulfilment of humanity's vocation—of God's call upon people, Christ demonstrates who people can be. Christ both is and illustrates human destiny."[33] Gaffin expresses Paul's declaration tersely: "Christ is literally the eschatological man."[34] As the eschatological human, his example is the standard for renewed humanity.

It is through the preaching of this gospel, the word of God, that the Spirit regenerates and transforms sinners to Christ's image. Beale and Kim have shown that the book of Acts in particular echoes the mandate of Genesis 1:26–28 and applies that language to the fruitfulness and multiplication of people by the word of God: "Unlike Genesis 1:28, the word of God, not people, bears fruit and multiplies in Acts."[35] Indeed, the Septuagint uses the verbs αὐξάνω ("to cause to be fruitful") and πληθύνω ("to multiply") in Genesis 1:28,

31. On the redemptive-historical significance of this passage, see Richard B. Gaffin, *In the Fullness of Time: An Introduction to the Biblical Theology of Acts and Paul* (Crossway, 2022), 341–43, and the exegetical note below.

32. John F. Kilner, *Dignity and Destiny: Humanity in the Image of God* (Eerdmans, 2015), 72.

33. Kilner, *Dignity and Destiny*, 73.

34. Gaffin, *In the Fullness of Time*, 340.

35. Beale and Kim, *God Dwells Among Us*, 24.

and again in Exodus 1:7, to describe the growth of the Israelites in Egypt. The same terms are used in Acts 6:7: "And the word of God continued to increase [ηὔξανεν] and the number of the disciples multiplied [ἐπληθύνετο] greatly in Jerusalem, and a great many of the priests became obedient to the faith" (cf. Acts 12:24). As one commentator puts it, the word of God here "is viewed as a vital force, reaching into people's lives and transforming situations according to God's will . . . the church which is the creature of the word grew."[36] The Spirit is at work to apply that word to its hearers, causing it to take root in hearts and minds.

Before the fall, image-bearing was natural and multiplied by means of procreation. After the fall, image-bearing in the ethical sense requires the reception and preaching of the gospel in Spirit-wrought effectual calling. In the postlapsarian order, we bear God's image ontologically but not ethically. Before the fall, the word of God gave Adam life; after the fall, the word of God restores spiritual life by regeneration. Grace restores nature, and the gospel restores our image-bearing direction.

THE RENEWAL OF HUMAN NATURE

The first part of this chapter treated God's commitment to the spread of his image-bearers even after the fall. God promises a seed that would crush the serpent and restore God's people by being a better and truer representative than Adam, and that person is Jesus Christ. By accepting Christ in the gospel, Christians are being conformed to his image and thus are becoming truly human, imaging God both naturally and ethically. How, exactly, does God confer renewal on human nature? The New Testament, and especially the Pauline Epistles, zoom in on this issue in detail. We will first treat the topic of regeneration and then consider Paul's language of the "inner man" and the new "I" of the Christian.

Regeneration

God, as Petrus van Mastricht identifies, is the "principal cause of our faith," for God is the Father of lights, from whom comes every saving good

36. David Peterson, *The Acts of the Apostles* (Eerdmans, 2009), 236.

(James 1:17), and the Spirit of faith (2 Cor. 4:13), who restored us when we were blind and dead in sin (Ezek. 11:19; Eph. 2:1–2; 4:18).[37] This effectual call of God leads to regeneration and faith in Christ, conversion and repentance, and the ongoing moral renovation of sanctification.

Sin, as we saw in the previous chapter, blinds us to the truths of God, and we are thus "dead," incapable of following God because we are inclined away from him (Rom. 8:7). Our act of faith is thus the result of God making us "alive" (Eph. 2:4–7), such that we can now obey his will. No one can come to God unless the Father draws him (John 6:44, 64). God *regenerates* sinners as part of his larger work of renewing all things: God "saved us, not because of works done by us in righteousness, but according to his own mercy, by the washing of regeneration and renewal of the Holy Spirit" (Titus 3:5; cf. James 1:18).[38] The regeneration of creatures thus points to the final restoration and consummation of creation and is by the power of the Spirit that blows wherever it wishes (John 3:3–8). Commenting on the language of John 3:3, John Murray argues that regeneration is a radical work of God: "It is not a continuation or development of the natural life of the person concerned. It informs us that no amount of education, manipulation or nurture of the powers resident in man's natural life can produce it."[39] Becoming Christian is a matter not of incremental natural advancement but of foundational spiritual change.

The Spirit who resurrected Christ from the dead and consummated his human nature is the same Spirit who is now at work in the believer, working from within to conform them to Christ's image (2 Cor. 3:17–18). The believer can now bear the fruit of the Spirit (Gal. 5:16–26). That is, the life of the age to come and the renewal of the world, where the sinner will be consummately sanctified, is already inaugurated in the believer's life now, such that we are able to follow the Spirit of Christ, walking with him and in him.

When God regenerates sinners, then, they are considered new creatures (2 Cor. 5:17) with a new life, and even a "new self" (Eph. 4:24; Col. 3:10), patterned after the image of God, such that we can now perform good works (Eph. 2:10) in righteousness, holiness, and knowledge. These qualities, as

37. Petrus van Mastricht, *Theoretical-Practical Theology*, vol. 2, *Faith in the Triune God*, trans. Todd M. Rester, ed. Joel R. Beeke (Reformation Heritage Books, 2019), 14.

38. See Murray, *Collected Writings*, 2:167–201.

39. Murray, *Collected Writings*, 2:179.

2 Corinthians 3:17–18 and 1 Corinthians 15:45

> Now the Lord is the Spirit, and where the Spirit of the Lord is, there is freedom. And we all, with unveiled face, beholding the glory of the Lord, are being transformed into the same image from one degree of glory to another. For this comes from the Lord who is the Spirit. (2 Cor. 3:17–18)

Second Corinthians 3:17–18 is significant because it denotes the relation between Christ, who is the Adamic and obedient image of God in his human nature, and those who are being transformed into "the same image." But what does it mean that Christ here "is the Spirit"? And what are the implications of this identification? Richard B. Gaffin Jr. is helpful here. First, he reminds readers that the identification of Christ with the Spirit is already present in 1 Corinthians 15:45, where Paul teaches that "the last Adam became a life-giving spirit." From the context of 1 Corinthians 15, Paul is showing that Christ is the "first instance of the Spiritual body that believers will receive in their future resurrection."[a] His body is from heaven, as it were, whereas Adam's was earthly and natural. Paul is teaching that believers in union with Christ their head, too, will receive a spiritual body like his.

Second, Gaffin shows that the sense of "life-giving Spirit" here does not primarily denote the function of Christ's preexistent divine nature, nor his incarnate human existence per se, but specifically the exalted state of his resurrected life. It is as the "firstfruits" (1 Cor. 15:20) that Christ is so: "His resurrection is clearly the timepoint when Christ became the life-giving Spirit."[b] The passage is clearly *not*, then, about the life of God in himself (for the Father, Son, and Spirit are eternally one substance) but about the economy of Christ's Adamic, human existence, and more specifically about the new resurrected state.

The identification of Christ and the Spirit, therefore, is brought about by virtue of his resurrection: "For Christ, the resurrection resulted in (1) an unprecedented possession for the Spirit and (2) and unprecedented transformation *by* the Spirit."[c] Gaffin continues:

> This possession and transformation was so climactic, so complete and permanent, that Christ and the Spirit are now one. Paul deems that oneness expressed adequately and appropriately by saying that Christ, as the last Adam, became the life-giving Spirit. This oneness, however, exists in a specific respect; it consists in the activity of giving life. If we look for labels for

this oneness or equation, in terms of the classical theological distinction between the *ontological* and *economic* Trinity, this equation reflects the latter (economic), always keeping in mind that it concerns the transformation experienced by Christ in his humanity.[d]

This does not mean, as Gaffin clarifies, that the Spirit was not life-giving before the exaltation of Christ, but it does mean that the Spirit gives life on the "stable basis of the finished, once-for-all work of Christ in his earthly ministry and . . . as the Spirit is the transformer of Christ in his humanity."[e]

The sense of 2 Corinthians 3:17–18 becomes straightforward with this exposition of 1 Corinthians 15:45 in hand. The object of the believer's hope is to behold the glory of the resurrected and exalted Christ, which we apprehend now by faith. As believers focus on Christ, they become conformed to his image (per Rom. 8:29; 1 Cor. 15:49). It is this ascended Christ, transformed and in possession of the Spirit, who gives freedom (cf. Rom. 8:2). "In 1 Corinthians 15:45, that conjoint activity [of Christ and the Spirit] consists in giving resurrection life. In 2 Corinthians 3:17, in view is the eschatological 'freedom' inherent in that life."[f]

a. Gaffin, *In the Fullness of Time*, 335.
b. Gaffin, *In the Fullness of Time*, 335.
c. Gaffin, *In the Fullness of Time*, 336 (emphasis original).
d. Gaffin, *In the Fullness of Time*, 336–37 (emphasis original).
e. Gaffin, *In the Fullness of Time*, 339–40.
f. Gaffin, *In the Fullness of Time*, 341.

mentioned in Ephesians 4:24 and Colossians 3:10, refer to the proper functioning of the image once again—as we are made new (indicative), we are called to live in accordance with this reality (imperative): Put off the old man, and put on the new. This restoration of the proper functioning of the image of God in the new man will be the backdrop of the Reformed teachings on the "narrow" sense of the image of God. Though we never lost the broad image of God (ontology), we lost the narrow sense (conformity to God) in the fall, and this narrow sense is restored decisively in regeneration, progressively in sanctification, and consummately in resurrection. We are thus called to consider ourselves dead to sin but alive before God (Rom. 6:11)—or, as Vermigli describes it, "In the process of regeneration, we receive the gift of the Holy Spirit, who breaks the power of concupiscence so that, though it clings to us, it does not rule. This is what Paul is talking about when he exhorts the faithful not to let sin reign in their mortal body."[40] Sin has lost its power on the renewed person. She is free to obey God.

The New Man and the Inner Self

Talk of a "new man" or a "new creation" should not be misread as if our human nature itself is replaced with another. Christians are still human beings. Christians are still the same persons as their former, non-Christian selves, but now are reformed and redirected. Regeneration does not transmute us from humans to angels, or something wholly other, but rather conforms us to who we were made to be. The "newness," in other words, refers to the *spiritual qualities* that now mark out the human nature of the believer as the Spirit is given; these qualities are the firstfruits and down payment, as it were, of the consummated human nature of the age to come (Rom. 8:23).[41] Likewise, we should take care when talking about our sinfulness. We should not think of our fallen state as bestowing upon us a "sin nature" alongside our human nature. Yes, we are by nature children of wrath, and we have a body of sin (Rom. 7:24), but sin, as we shall show in a later chapter on corruption, is parasitic upon the good and does not have a nature or substance of its own, for then God would be the author of sin (for God creates all that is not God). Augustine, then, argues that the "creature, which cleaves to God, differs from those who do not, not by nature, but by fault."[42] As Thomas McCall has helpfully argued, we have to remember that any talk of sinful nature presupposes that "our natures, originally created as *good* and called such by God, have become corrupted by sin."[43]

The new self of Ephesians 4:24 and Colossians 3:10, then, should be compared with the "inner self" of 2 Corinthians 4:16: "So we do not lose heart. Though our outer self is wasting away, our inner self is being renewed day by day." Gaffin connects this passage to Paul's references to the inner self in Romans 7:22 and Ephesians 3:16. First, he argues that this distinction between inner and outer self is not partitive but aspectival. There is no dual-personality

40. Peter Martyr Vermigli, *On Original Sin*, trans. Kirk Summers (Davenant, 2019), 28–29.

41. See especially Herman Bavinck, *Reformed Dogmatics*, vol. 4, *Holy Spirit, Church, and New Creation* (Baker Academic, 2008), 92–95.

42. Augustine, *City of God*, 12.1.

43. McCall, *Against God and Nature: The Doctrine of Sin* (Crossway, 2019), 217 (emphasis original).

here between the inner and outer selves. Rather, inner and outer refer to two "aspects" of the whole self.[44] If the outer self is the functioning "I," the inner self refers to the "heart" of a person, the dispositional aspect of one's self that directs the functional and "finds expression through that functioning."[45]

The renewal of the inner self, therefore, decisively redirects the believer toward the things of the Spirit: "What the believer is in Christ and by faith is true—and is only true—*in* the body, but it is not (yet) true *for* the body. In terms of the anthropological distinction basic for Paul, the renewal true of the 'inner self' is truly only *in* the 'outer self,' but that renewal is not (yet) true *for* the 'outer self' (2 Cor. 4:16)."[46] The renewal of the inner disposition of the self anticipates the resurrection of the outer self. The body, the outer self, is still subjected to the ongoing presence of sin, marked by death and decay, and is as such characterized by the present "evil age" (Gal. 1:4).

Second, Gaffin warns against identifying this inner self with Paul's language of the "old man." That old man has not been regenerated and is indicative of the post-fall, non-regenerated state of human nature and is as such always following the passions of the flesh, the sinfulness of this present age of redemptive history. For the person united to Christ, this old self has been crucified with Christ (Rom. 6:6), undergoing a decisive transition from the old self to the new, and it is this new human that has an "inner" self that anticipates the resurrection of the body.[47] This resurrected body, in turn, is that glorious body which Adam would have obtained without death had he remained obedient. Christ restores us to our consummate bodily destiny. Stephen Davis, commenting on Paul's logic in 1 Corinthians 15, says it this way: "The new 'glorified' or 'spiritual body'. . . is a transformation of the old body rather than a *de novo* creation, much as a stalk of grain is a transformation of a seed of grain; that is, it exists because of changes that have occurred in the seed and can be considered a new state of the seed."[48] Regeneration consists in the renewal of human nature, not a replacement.

44. Gaffin, *In the Fullness of Time*, 315.
45. Gaffin, *In the Fullness of Time*, 316.
46. Gaffin, *In the Fullness of Time*, 388.
47. Gaffin, *In the Fullness of Time*, 316.
48. Stephen T. Davis, "Redemption, The Resurrected Body, and Human Nature," in *The Ashgate Companion to Theological Anthropology*, ed. Joshua R. Farris and Charles Taliaferro (Routledge, 2016), 300.

Revelation 21:22–27

> And I saw no temple in the city, for its temple is the Lord God the Almighty and the Lamb. And the city has no need of sun or moon to shine on it, for the glory of God gives it light, and its lamp is the Lamb. By its light will the nations walk, and the kings of the earth will bring their glory into it, and its gates will never be shut by day—and there will be no night there. They will bring into it the glory and the honor of the nations. But nothing unclean will ever enter it, nor anyone who does what is detestable or false, but only those who are written in the Lamb's book of life. (Rev. 21:22–27)

Revelation 21:22–27 focuses on the multicultural character of the new Jerusalem, fulfilling what was inaugurated through Pentecost and Peter's teaching in Acts 10:34–35. Indeed, the redeemed will fill the new creation from every tribe, nation, and tongue (Rev. 5:9–10; 7:9). God will finally dwell with his people, and his people will walk by his light, imaging him in perfect conformity as his representatives.

God alone consummates creation, and this renewed world is not progressively brought about by human or Christian labor. However, Revelation 21:24 also communicates that the "glory" of the kings of the earth (and, by representation, the nations) will be brought into it. Richard Bauckham's comments on this passage are instructive, as he walks the balancing act of recognizing that this new Jerusalem is both the consummation of what began in Genesis and a city brought about by God alone:

> In the beginning God had planted a garden for humanity to live in (Gen. 2:8). In the end he will give them a city. In the New Jerusalem the blessings of paradise will be restored, but the New Jerusalem is more than paradise regained. As a city it fulfils humanity's desire to build out of nature a human place of human culture and community. True, it is given by God and so comes down from heaven. But this does not mean humanity makes no contribution to it. It consummates human history and culture insofar as these have been dedicated to God (cf. 21:12, 14, 24, 26) while excluding the distortions of history and culture into opposition to God that Babylon represents (cf. 21:8, 27; 22:15). It comes from God in the sense that all good comes from God, and all that is humanly good is best acknowledged to come from God. But the city that both includes paradise unspoiled and is adorned with the beauty of paradise

points to that harmony of nature and human culture to which ancient cities once aspired but which modern cities have been increasingly betrayed.[a]

As Bauckham observes, the city "comes down from heaven," and yet there is something that is brought into it that shows its continuity with humanity now. We should be wary here and not overly speculate. As we say elsewhere, "The first word of eschatology is modesty."[b] Kuyper warns that it is not as if the paintings we make or the chairs we build will be transferred over into heaven, though the "germ," or seed, of our labors, or the direction of them, will be consummated (see 2 Pet. 3:11).[c] Further, the glorified self will be in continuity with the regenerated self, and the good works that characterize the regenerate will be consummated there (e.g., Phil. 2:13–14; Eph. 2:10). The sanctified will experience eschatological purification. And that eschatological vision of the new humanity includes the cultural and linguistic diversity of the people of God.

a. Richard Bauckham, *The Theology of the Book of Revelation* (Cambridge University Press, 1993), 135.

b. Cory C. Brock and N. Gray Sutanto, *Neo-Calvinism: A Theological Introduction* (Lexham, 2023), 167.

c. Abraham Kuyper, *Common Grace*, vol. 1, *God's Gifts for a Fallen World*, trans. Nelson D. Kloosterman and Ed M. van der Maas, ed. Jordan Ballor (Lexham, 2015), 545, 550.

It is fitting, then, that though Christians will be at home with the Lord when they die and their souls are unnaturally separated from their bodies (2 Cor. 5:8), in this intermediate state (which we will discuss in chapter 9), they long for their resurrection bodies (Phil. 3:10–11). The resurrection of the body and the renewal of the whole world is the decisive reversal of sin and the consummation of creation—the fitting consequence of the obedience of the true Adamic king, Jesus Christ. There, we will not only receive the glorified existence that Adam should have acquired for his progeny but also a life free from the consequences of Adam's sin: "Death is swallowed up in victory. O Death, where is your victory? O death, where is your sting? The sting of death is sin, and the power of sin is the law. But thanks be to God, who gives us the victory through our Lord Jesus Christ" (1 Cor. 15:54–57).

CONCLUSION

This chapter has explored the biblical teachings on God's commitment to the spread of his image-bearers, on Christ as the true Adamic representative, and on the believer's renewal in Christ by the Spirit. We have seen that, though humanity has become corrupt and guilty due to Adam's sin, God remains committed to the calling of humanity to be fruitful and multiply as representatives of God, and he preserves a remnant humanity toward that end. Noah, Abraham, and Israel are all Adamic sons, called to represent God to the whole world, and all failed in that calling, pointing us to the truer and greater Adam in Christ Jesus. In and through Christ, the Spirit renews the elect so that they can be ethically conformed into the image of God once again.

As such, I conclude this first section on the biblical material on humanity and sin. We have explored the creation, calling, nature, and destiny of humanity in chapter 1, the entrance and corruption of sin in the previous chapter, and the restoration and renewal of human beings in Christ in this present chapter.

FURTHER READING

Beale, G. K. *The Temple and the Church's Mission: A Biblical Theology of the Dwelling Place of God*. IVP Academic, 2004. A wonderful narration of God's commitment to the mandate of Genesis 1:26–28, even after the fall into sin.

Bavinck, Herman. *The Wonderful Works of God*. Translated by Henry Zylstra. Westminster Seminary Press, 2019. Especially chapters 13–14, "Sin and Death" and "The Covenant of Grace." Though this work is a concise dogmatics, Bavinck prioritizes the exegesis of particular scriptural texts and the narrative of Scripture to show God's gracious dealings with fallen humanity in these chapters.

Dempster, Stephen. *Dominion and Dynasty: A Theology of the Hebrew Bible*. IVP Academic, 2003. Perhaps the most accessible introduction to the theology of the Old Testament and its themes on the expansion of Adam's progeny and land.

Klink, Edward W., III. *John*. Zondervan Exegetical Commentary on the New Testament. Zondervan Academic, 2017. This commentary is exemplary in showing the theological implications of John's Gospel and the way in which John is depicting Jesus as the true and greater Adam.

4

HUMANS, BODY AND SOUL: PRECEDENTS IN AUGUSTINE AND AQUINAS

INTRODUCTION

The Scriptures present much material for theological reflection on humanity and sin. To begin this section on a Reformed dogmatic outline of humanity as created and fallen, it is wise to highlight the contributions of Augustine (354–430) and Thomas Aquinas (1225–1274) on human nature, for much of what they say is formative for the Reformed tradition. Augustine was an African bishop of Hippo and Aquinas was a medieval theologian of the Dominican order. Indeed, much of the Reformed tradition refines, formalizes, and follows what Augustine and Thomas say, and they reflect fruitfully and vitally on the whole scope of biblical teaching on these topics. Though the Reformed tradition would accent certain teachings on original righteousness, original sin, and redemption that would form a distinct anthropology from their Roman Catholic counterparts, it is important to show that basic features of their doctrine of human nature are still in continuity with the broader (pre-Reformational) catholic tradition.

The next three chapters focus on a presentation of a Reformed account of human ontology and the image of God, as informed by this Augustinian trajectory. To elaborate on what I had mentioned in the introduction to this volume, this presentation of a Christian and theological account of human nature is necessarily selective. While there are descriptions of human nature in the creeds or confessions of the church, a fuller exposition of, say, what it means to be image-bearers or the body-soul relation can mainly be found in the writings of particular theologians. The creeds, after all, focus primarily on the development of theology proper and Christology. It would thus be overwhelming and not pedagogically helpful to survey every Christian thinker on the subject. Instead, I have chosen to select just some of the most influential or representational thinkers to form a Reformed-catholic theological anthropology. For this reason, I have chosen Augustine first not only as a mature representation of the church fathers on this topic but also as the most formative figure for the medieval and Reformational periods, and Aquinas as one authoritative medieval Augustinian on the subject. When we turn to the Reformed tradition in the next two chapters, I shall present some of the confessional teachings on human nature as created and fallen and elaborate on the same by highlighting the contributions of Francis Turretin (1623–1687), Petrus van Mastricht (1630–1706), the early seventeenth-century codification of Reformed orthodoxy in the Leiden Synopsis, and finally turn to the writings of the modern Reformed theologian Herman Bavinck (1854–1921).

This is not to suggest that, say, Calvin or Luther had nothing to say with respect to human nature—the seventeenth-century Reformed scholastics, in fact, presuppose their insights and developments. However, the high Reformed orthodoxy of the seventeenth century does present a mature, developed, and codified account of human nature that represents the Reformed tradition at its most crystalized. Furthermore, Herman Bavinck, in the nineteenth century, represents the continuation of that tradition in the modern context as the main dogmatician of the Dutch neo-Calvinist movement that sought to revitalize Reformed orthodoxy in light of modernity. There are also many works that focus on, say, the contributions of Irenaeus, Gregory of Nyssa, Gregory of Nazianzus, Luther, Calvin, Schleiermacher, or Barth on theological anthropology,[1] but, as noted in the introduction, there

1. For treatments of Gregory of Nyssa, Luther, Schleiermacher, and Barth, for instance, see Marc Cortez, *Theological Anthropology: A Guide for the Perplexed* (Bloomsbury T&T Clark, 2010); Cortez, *Christological Anthropology in Historical Perspective: Ancient and Contemporary Approaches*

is very little that presents a Reformed orthodox or neo-Calvinist account of human nature in a concise, introductory, and synthesized way. The chapters on human nature in this book seek to fill precisely that gap.

To turn to the substantive matters, there are at least two reasons for devoting three whole chapters to human ontology—that is, human *nature*. First, all accounts of sin and redemption, of anti-nature and the restoration of nature, presuppose ontology. The logical ordering here follows the biblical exposition in the first section of this book: Humankind was created good, with an intelligible nature given from God and oriented toward him, and it is precisely that nature which is marred by sin and restored in salvation.

The second reason is best articulated by John Webster's account of the implications of postmodernity for the human person: "The dissolution of anthropology marks one of the primary fissures between modernity and postmodernity."[2] If modernity sought to replace an anthropology conditioned by the order of the divine and the revealed by way of a universal, rational humanity that is free to conduct itself beyond authority, "radical postmodernity," in contrast, seeks to deconstruct notions of humanity or being as such. Modernity has projected a universal human nature, which really veils the product of a particular European imagination, and in reaction, postmodernity has unmasked the veil and rejected notions of humanness altogether: "There is no human nature, no substrate to human history, just as there is no trajectory along which humankind moves."[3] The rejection of Christian theism has led to the demise of human nature as such, and without a recognition of human unity, new and often conflicting categories are willed into existence, whether of gender or race, that have produced more confusion

to *Theological Anthropology* (Zondervan, 2016); and Daniel Pedersen, *Schleiermacher's Theology of Sin and Nature: Agency, Value, and Modern Theology* (Routledge, 2020). For Irenaeus and the later patristics, see, for instance, M. C. Steenberg, *Of God and Man: Theology as Anthropology from Irenaeus to Athanasius* (Bloomsbury T&T Clark, 2009); on Gregory of Nazianzus, see especially Gabrielle Thomas, *The Image of God in the Theology Gregory of Nazianzus* (Cambridge University Press, 2019); for Calvin, see, for example, Steven Tyra's *"Neither the Spirit Without the Flesh": John Calvin's Doctrine of the Beatific Vision* (Bloomsbury T&T Clark, 2024). For the contributions of Herman Bavinck in greater detail, see my *God and Humanity: Herman Bavinck and Theological Anthropology* (Bloomsbury T&T Clark, 2024). As mentioned in the introduction, for a brief and broad sampling of the Reformed tradition on human nature, see Paul Helm, *Human Nature from Calvin to Edwards* (Reformation Heritage Books, 2018).

2. John Webster, "The Human Person," in *The Cambridge Companion to Postmodern Theology*, ed. Kevin J. Vanhoozer (Cambridge University Press, 2006), 221.

3. Webster, "The Human Person," 222.

and violence rather than unity or hospitality. To address such issues, then, it is important to retrieve a theological (and not a projected) account of the human person and of that human nature that renders all persons equal and accountable before God.

The literature on Augustine and theological anthropology is legion, and there are many texts from which one can draw from Augustine's corpus, from earlier to more mature writings.[4] The literature on Thomas, too, is similarly manifold. This chapter thus has modest aims and seeks to provide an introductory sketch of an Augustinian account of humanity, drawing primarily from his middle to later writings, and in ways that anticipate the rest of the book. Here, then, I first exposit Augustine on the image of God and the body-soul relation, and then I move to the will and its tethering to humanity's fourfold existence. Along the way, I note Augustine's critical engagements with (neo-)Platonism, Manicheanism, and Pelagianism, which were formative for his own description of theological anthropology. In a final section, I show the ways in which Aquinas generally stands on this Augustinian tradition, while adopting Aristotelian hylomorphism (that forms exist in matter, as that which give a particular matter its shape and identity) to articulate the body-soul relation, according to which the soul is the form of the body. The focus on Thomas in this section is not meant to suggest that he is the only one who utilized hylomorphism (many other medieval divines did), nor is it to suggest that Thomas is the most important medieval figure (for he stands alongside others, such as Bonaventure, Henry of Ghent, and John Duns Scotus, who critiqued, differed, or improved him in important ways), but Aquinas's hylomorphism is instructive because of its clarity and overlap

4. I draw from some recent helpful offerings: Matthew Drever, *Image, Identity, and the Forming of the Augustinian Soul* (Oxford University Press, 2013); Gerald Boersma, *Augustine's Early Theology of Image* (Oxford University Press, 2016); Jesse Couenhoven, *Stricken by Sin, Cured by Christ: Agency, Necessity, and Culpability in Augustinian Theology* (Oxford University Press, 2013); Han-Luen Kantzer Komline, *Augustine on the Will: A Theological Account* (Oxford University Press, 2020); Rowan Williams, *On Augustine* (Bloomsbury, 2016); John Cavadini, *Visioning Augustine* (Wiley-Blackwell, 2019). See also Robert Dodaro and George Lawless, eds., *Augustine and His Critics* (Routledge, 2000). Charles Mathewes, *Evil and the Augustinian Tradition* (Cambridge University Press, 2001). One important hinge in Augustine's earlier and later writings is the maturation of his theology of sin, grace, and election. See William Babcock, "Augustine's Interpretation of Romans (A.D. 394–396)," *Augustinian Studies* 10 (1979): 55–74; and Carol Harrison, *Rethinking Augustine's Early Theology: An Argument for Continuity* (Oxford University Press, 2008).

on this specific topic with later Reformed theology.[5] This Augustinian and hylomorphist trajectory, broadly considered, will form the precedence for the Reformed tradition's reflection on theological anthropology in the following two chapters.

AUGUSTINE: THE IMAGE OF GOD

Augustine's doctrine of the image of God emphasizes the priority of the soul and its relational proximity to the God it images.[6] We shall focus on this aspect first, before observing the importance of the body in Augustine's anthropology.

Augustine's gloss of Genesis 1:26–28 in his *Literal Meaning of Genesis* is a fitting place to start to consider his exposition of the image of God. He interprets the first person plural to refer to the creation of humanity after the image of the *Triune* God—and in this he anticipates the same exegetical tendency as many in the Reformed tradition: "Scripture would indicate by this the plurality of Persons, the Father, Son and Holy Spirit. . . . [The writer of Genesis] does not say that the Father made man to the image of the Son, or the Son made him to the image of the Father; otherwise the expression *to Our image* would not be correct if man were made to the image of the Father alone or the Son alone."[7] Augustine then turns to the Pauline passages of Colossians 3:10 and Ephesians 4:24 to argue that the proper locus of this image is in the "reason, or mind, or intelligence," according to which "man has been created to the image of God, since it is not by any features of the body but by a perfection of the intelligible order, that is, of the mind when illuminated."[8] The language of

5. See, e.g., Carl A. Vater, *God's Knowledge of the World: Medieval Theories of Divine Ideas from Bonaventure to Ockham* (Catholic University of America Press, 2022); Nathaniel Gray Sutanto, "*Gevoel* and Illumination: Bavinck, Augustine, and Bonaventure on Awareness of God," *Pro Ecclesia* 30 (2021): 265–78.

6. As Boersma notes, for Augustine, "an account of 'human nature' must transcend the human person; it finds intelligibility in its exemplar, the Holy Trinity." *Augustine's Early Theology of Image*, 255.

7. Augustine, *The Literal Meaning of Genesis*, vol. 1, trans. John Hammond Taylor (Paulist Press, 1982), 3.19.29. See also Augustine, *The Trinity*, 12.2.7.

8. Augustine, *Literal Meaning of Genesis*, 3.20.30. See also Augustine, *The City of God*, 12.23, and *The Trinity*, 12.2.12. So, Drever: "Though Augustine's version of Genesis 1:26 uses the generic *homo* as the locus of the *imago dei* and thus does not specify which dimension is the divine image, Augustine reads the verse through Paul (Ephesians 4:23–24, Colossians 3:10), arguing

the illuminated soul points to the way in which the language of image picks out ontological, relational, and ethical implications. The image is located in the intellectual soul (which exercises intellectual vision, above corporeal or imaginary); the soul reflects God in its being and requires loving contemplation of God for its well-being.

Augustine is sensitive to note elsewhere, however, that the language of "image" is used to refer to the Son in a superlative and unique way, and that we are the image in a distinct sense, as seen in the way in which he calls the Son *the* image whereas we are made *in* the image. The Son is the image of God because he is *of* the divine substance in a begotten way, but we are images of God in the sense of being his unique creatures:

> Let us copy the example of this divine image, the Son, and not draw away from God. For we too are the image of God, though not the equal one like him; we are made by the Father through the Son, not born of the Father like that image; we are image because we are illuminated with light; that one is so because it is the light that illumines, and therefore it provides a model for us without having a model itself.[9]

As Drever rightly notes, Augustine is sensitive that though we are created from (*ex*) God, we are not created out of (*de*) or from the divine substance but from (*de*) nothing. As such, if immutability and simplicity characterize the divine nature, the human nature is marked by the "nothingness of our origin," such that "mutability is the receptivity of the creature to being formed by God. It is also the distance between God and creation that allows creation to exist, and separates it from an essential relation to the immutable, eternal stability of divine existence."[10]

The mutability of human beings that marks who we are as image-bearers highlights the way in which humans have a unique relation to God as religious creatures. In the depths of one's soul, one encounters the very realities that one desires but cannot grasp: the eternal. Crucially, Rowan Williams then argues that the Augustinian sense of self is a "sign," for the self is "profoundly

---

that the image of God is found not in the body but rather in the soul or illuminated mind." Drever, *Image, Identity*, 24.

9. Augustine, *The Trinity*, 7.3.5.

10. Drever, *Image, Identity*, 61–62.

mysterious to us . . . and the locus of our deepest awareness of frustration."[11] The mystery of the self's depths and its longings for stability point to our need for humility, that recognition that we are at every moment dependent on God. Humanity is made in the *image* of God, after all, "a sign of its maker."[12] The soul, like the body, can tend further toward nonbeing and deformity by vice, or it can attend to God and thus acquire the thing signified by its own existence.[13] The two potential ends of the soul are further highlighted in relation to the soul's prelapsarian nature as analogous to both angelic and animalistic beings in *The City of God*:

> Man, on the other hand, whose nature was to be a mean between the angelic and bestial, He created in such sort, that if he remained in subjection to His Creator as his rightful Lord, and piously kept His commandments, he should pass into the company of the angels, and obtain, without the intervention of death, a blessed and endless immortality; but if he offended the Lord his God by a proud and disobedience use of his free will, he should become subject to death, and live as the beasts do—the slave of appetite, and doomed to eternal punishment after death.[14]

The mutability of the soul thus beckons the self to turn toward God, the source of its existence and the font of its well-being, and underlies that famous opening prayer of Augustine's *Confessions*: "You stir man to take pleasure in praising you, because you have made us for yourself, and our heart is restless until it rests in you."[15] As Cavadini shows, the self, or inner man, in Augustine is not some stable, rock-like, or self-referential substance but rather discloses a "reference that impels one not to concentrate on oneself, in the end, but on that to which one's self-awareness propels one, to God."[16] Drever shows that this metaphysical, relational, and ethical prompting of Augustine's doctrine of the image leads to a "paradoxical conclusion" that "the soul becomes most itself when it is least its own": "For Augustine, human identity is not forged *autos*. As I am created according to the image of another

11. Williams, *On Augustine*, 35.
12. Williams, *On Augustine*, 196.
13. Augustine, *Literal Meaning of Genesis*, 7.6.9.
14. Augustine, *City of God*, 12.21.
15. Augustine, *Confessions*, trans. Henry Chadwick (Oxford University Press, 2008), 1.1.
16. Cavadini, *Visioning Augustine*, 141.

(God), so I am most myself not when I am myself (i.e., imaging creation) but when I am according to another (i.e., imaging God)."[17]

This emphasis on the intellectual soul as the locus of the image of God leads Augustine to his psychological analogies of the Trinity, as located in the soul's memory, understanding, and will, in books IX–XI of *De Trinitate*.[18] The order of teaching is important—the exposition of the analogies of the Trinity in the soul is not an attempt at projection. Augustine is uninterested in projection—that is, going from the bottom-up, picturing what the Trinity must be like on the basis of the phenomenology and faculties of the soul observed by experience. Rather, Augustine is going top-down, from revelation of the Triune God to a reflection on the intellectual powers of the soul. The psychological analogies follow an exposition of the Trinity as faith seeks understanding, and Augustine is clear that "we have to avoid the sacrilegious mistake of saying anything about the trinity which does not belong to the creator but rather to the creature, or which is fabricated by vain imaginings."[19] Further, such a description of the powers of the soul is no mere exercise in introspection but prompts the soul to contemplate the divine Trinity: "For man's true honor is God's image and likeness in him, but it can only be preserved when facing him from whom its impression is received."[20] As the soul is deformed due to sin, it requires the grace of forgiveness and daily renewal "in the spirit of the mind in the recognition of God, not outwardly but inwardly day to day."[21] The soul, again, participates in God by way of intellectual contemplation of God.

BODY AND SOUL

This emphasis on the soul has led to some worries on whether Augustine's account is unduly dualistic or intellectualist, leading to a denigration of the body. While such an initial impression might be understandable (and later thinkers like Aquinas would indeed offer a more holistic perspective on the body-soul relation by deploying more Aristotelian resources), a closer

---

17. Drever, *Image, Identity*, 24.

18. Cf. Bonaventure, *Breviloquium*, 85–86.

19. Augustine, *The Trinity*, 9.prologue.1.

20. Augustine, *The Trinity*, 12.3.16. Cf. Herman Bavinck, *Philosophy of Revelation: A New Annotated Edition*, ed. Cory Brock and N. Gray Sutanto (Hendrickson, 2018), 55.

21. Augustine, *The Trinity*, 14.5.25.

reading of Augustine's texts shows that while his anthropology does posit a substantial soul distinct from the body, this is no "oppositional dualism."[22] The body remains essential to a proper account of human ontology and participates in the image of God in its own way, as we shall see. Moreover, Augustine's prioritization of the soul is not reflective of a kind of "substance metaphysics," if what we mean by this is that the soul is reduced to a kind of inert, static cube that remains fixed and unaffected through time and external realities. Rather, the soul's inherent mutability and dependence on God was already shown, and its relation to the body indicates an important feature of that psychic (soul-ish) pliability.[23]

Thus, it is important to note the ways in which Augustine understands the human body. I explore three interrelated aspects of Augustine's understanding of the body-soul relation: (a) the goodness of the body and the difference it makes for our identity, (b) the preservation of sexed difference in the resurrection, and (c) the social character of human beings.

First, then, Augustine defends the goodness of the body against some Neoplatonic concerns. Although Augustine does prefer Plato over the other philosophers, he never utilizes that philosophy uncritically and always subordinates it to Scripture's teachings. At the end of book 12 in *The City of God*, Augustine encounters the claim that bodies are prison-houses for the soul from which one should escape: "But since Porphyry maintains that if the soul is to be purified, all entanglement with a body must be escaped from; and at the same time agrees with Plato and the Platonists in thinking that those who have not spent a temperate and honourable life return to moral bodies as their punishment."[24] Such a claim presupposes the "oppositional dualism" that Augustine finds problematic and leads to the further claim that God could not be the direct creator of our material bodies. Augustine replies with the following line of reasoning:

> Let the Platonists, then, either cease menacing us with our bodies as the punishment of our souls, or exhort us by all means in our power to avoid

22. Drever, *Image, Identity*, 84.
23. Cavadini, *Visioning Augustine*, 141–42.
24. Augustine, *City of God*, 12.26. He has already anticipated this argument, as he notes in book 8 against the middle Platonist claim that there is no relation or overlap between the transcendent and the material.

> and escape from. But indeed, both opinions are quite false. It is false that souls return again to this life to be punished; and it is false that there is any other creator of anything in heaven or earth, than He who made the heaven and the earth. For if we live in a body only to expiate our sins, how says Plato in another place, that the world could not have been the most beautiful and good, had it not been filled with all kinds of creatures, mortal and immortal? But if our creation even as mortals be a divine benefit, how is it a punishment to be restored to a body, that is, to a divine benefit? And if God, as Plato continually maintains, embraced in His eternal intelligence the ideas both of the universe and of all the animals, then, should He not with His own hand make them all?[25]

It follows, therefore, that God is the creator of the body: "With good cause, therefore, does the true religion recognize and proclaim that the same God who created the universal cosmos, created also all the animals, souls, as well as bodies."[26] Augustine sees the body as *good* and as fitting for the indwelling of the soul: the body "which God formed of the dust, and to which a soul was given, that it might become a living body, that is, that man might become a living soul."[27] In book 13, Augustine shows his sensitivity to the biblical teachings of 1 Corinthians 15:44–55 on the distinctions between the earthly body and spiritual body, and the impact that the fall had on the body-soul relation in deformation and death.[28] As Fellipe do Vale has argued, "Augustine maintains that the features of the bodies we have are . . . *narratively-indexed* to the great story of what God is doing in Christ."[29] Thus, Augustine was not committed to a kind of "static" view of the soul that is untethered to bodily realities—while the soul is indeed a distinct substance, it is closely connected to the body, and the human person is itself impacted by the bodily changes in history: "Out of this nature, Augustine characterizes human identity formation according to a dynamic, relational process that opens to both divine (spiritual) and sociohistorical (embodied) dimensions."[30]

---

25. Augustine, *City of God*, 12.26. Cf. Bonaventure, *Breviloquium*, 89–93.
26. Augustine, *City of God*, 12.27.
27. Augustine, *City of God*, 13.24.
28. Augustine, *City of God*, 13.16–23.
29. Fellipe do Vale, "Cappadoccian or Augustinian? Adjudicating Debates on Gender in the Resurrection," *International Journal of Systematic Theology* 21, no. 2 (2019): 193.
30. Drever, *Forming of the Augustinian Soul*, 33.

Toward the end of *The City of God*, then, Augustine argues that the resurrection bodies will be conformed to Christ's own.[31] As he argues elsewhere, if the soul reflects the likeness of the Trinity, the body is promised to be like the Son in his resurrection and ascension:

> In this respect too we will be like God, but only like the Son, who alone in the triad took a body in which he died and rose again, carrying it up to the heavenly regions. This too can be called the image of the Son of God in which like him we shall have an immortal body, conformed in this respect not to the image of the Father or the Holy Spirit but only of the Son, because of whom alone do we read and receive on wholesome faith that *the Word became flesh* (John 1:14).[32]

Boersma's note on this passage on the importance of the resurrected body for Augustine is apt: "The fulfilment and perfection of the image of God, which is the ongoing perfection of the divine likeness, has as its archetype the embodied Son. This perfection will be fully realized only in the vision of God; as Christ, the image of the eternal God, reigns in his glorified body, so too the restored human image necessarily includes the resurrected body."[33] This motif will emerge again in the Reformed theologians: Though we are made in the image of our Triune Creator, the incarnate Son represents the norm of embodied human obedience.

Second, this affirmation of the goodness and resurrection of the body as conformed to the Son's leads Augustine to wonder about the resurrection of the sexes: Will our sexed differences (male and female) be preserved in the resurrection? Augustine argues for the affirmative: "For my part, they seem to be wiser who make no doubt that both sexes shall rise. . . . From these bodies, then, vice shall be withdrawn, while nature shall be preserved. And the sex of woman is not a vice, but nature . . . for it seemed fit that even Christ and His church should be foreshadowed in this event."[34] It is worth noting that Augustine is making a firm distinction between created and fallen natures. Confusion persists in our embodiment due to the vices that are tethered to

31. Augustine, *City of God*, 22.15.
32. Augustine, *The Trinity*, 14.5.24.
33. Boersma, *Augustine's Early Theology of Image*, 259.
34. Augustine, *City of God*, 22.17.

our bodies and which distract us from the highest good; these will be removed at the resurrection: "In the body's resurrected state, even internal organs and human genitalia, which have a particular use, will occasion the praise of God. . . . No longer will one look upon a woman's, or any person's body and feel lust, the desire to *use* another."[35]

The teachings of Christ in Matthew 22:29–30, then, refer to the cessation of marriage in the eschaton, but not of the sexes per se: "The Lord then denied that there would be in the resurrection, not women, but marriages." The distinction between the sexes is even affirmed in the passage itself, Augustine argued: "They neither marry" refers to "males," while "nor are given in marriage" "can only apply to females."[36]

Do Vale shows that Augustine's argument for the continuity of the sexes here rests on the narrative-logic of *The City of God*. The frame of creation and consummation envelops the logic of human identity. If the male-female relation was good but then corrupted through vice in the fall, the resurrection removes those vices and consummates the goodness God intended through that sexed distinction. "The only response to social misery, it seems, is a thoroughly social eschatology for which the pilgrims of the heavenly city now hope. This includes our gendered misery—all of the socially constructed misery experienced by women and men on account of their genders. We imagine gendered hope in the resurrection, where loss is restored and tears are wiped away."[37] The resurrected body harkens humanity back to creation; indeed, it is not merely created nature restored but consummated. There, Augustine insists that we will finally see God rule all things—including material reality—with our own bodily eyes.[38]

Finally, the social nature of human beings communicates their embodied character: "For there is nothing so social by nature, so unsocial by its

35. Douglas Finn, "Soul, Body, and the Miraculous Excess of the Human Being: Augustine's Theological Anthropology," in *T&T Clark Handbook to Theological Anthropology*, ed. Mary Ann Hinsdale and Stephen Okey (Bloomsbury T&T Clark, 2021), 170.

36. Augustine, *City of God*, 22.17. For a survey of readings on Matthew 22:29–30, see Danielle Treweek, *The Meaning of Singleness: Retrieving an Eschatological Vision for the Contemporary Church* (IVP Academic, 2023), 131–43.

37. Do Vale, "Adjudicating Debates on Gender in the Resurrection," 197. This is not to say that there are no complications with Augustine's views on gender. See E. Ann Matter, "Christ, God and Woman in the Thought of St. Augustine," in *Augustine and His Critics*, ed. Robert Dodaro and George Lawless (Routledge, 2000), 164–76.

38. Augustine, *City of God*, 22.29.

corruption, as this race."[39] Two points in the Genesis narrative indicate humanity's social condition: their creation from one man and the marriage between Adam and Eve. The former testifies to the social unity humans were meant to enjoy, while the latter indicates the "dear bond between man and wife"—a relational harmony between the sexes that will be consummated in heaven, as the sexes are purged from vice and the reality of Christ and the church is recognized.[40]

From the creation of the first man and this marriage would be birthed "these two cities or societies, so far as regards the human race."[41] The cities referred to here are the cities of God and the city of man, and what determines citizenship in one or another is the ordering of one's loves. These cities are identifiable not with any one temporal manifestation of a particular human culture of society but by that which lies underneath and informs their moral and teleological ends. The city of God is creational, as human beings were meant to gather together into a social culture that points to God as their love and peace, whereas the city of man was the product of the fall of Adam, "that by it the human nature was altered for the worse, and was transmitted also to their posterity, liable to sin and subject to death."[42] The two cities are thus marked by conformity to the flesh or spirit, and despite the differing customs of the nations, all humanity is boiled down to "no more than two kinds of human society, which we may justly call two cities, according to the language of our Scriptures."[43]

The two cities of Augustine, then, do not map onto the contemporary distinction between church and state, or private and public spheres. Rather, the two cities refer to two differing trajectories of the orientation of the self toward God, and those common loves unite selves into particular cultures. Love of God animates those who are citizens of the city of God, reformed by the grace of God, and such love animates all of their lives. Love of self, however, animates those who are of the city of man, and that love in turn animates all of their earthly dwelling.

Augustine's social description of humanity forms a precedent for the later neo-Calvinistic teachings on the antithesis between those who are federally

39. Augustine, *City of God*, 12.27.
40. Augustine, *City of God*, 12.27.
41. Augustine, *City of God*, 12.27.
42. Augustine, *City of God*, 14.1.
43. Augustine, *City of God*, 14.1.

represented by Adam or Christ, which animates the trajectories of godly or godless cultures. Further, Bavinck will extend this Augustinian insight and suggest that the image of God does not refer merely to the individual person (much less the soul) but also to humanity as a whole. The image will thus develop as humans multiply across space and time and as they form distinct cultures.

HUMANITY AS CREATED, FALLEN, REFORMED, AND CONSUMMATED: ON THE WILL

Augustine tethers his theological anthropology to the narrative of human history. When considering the condition of the person, we should ask if that person is understood in terms of their createdness, fallenness, or whether they have been refashioned or glorified by grace. The will, therefore, could not be considered in the abstract but in its concrete existence within that same narrative. "What the human will can *do* depends on what the human will *is* in relation to God—what it is in light of its creation ex nihilo in the image of God, its plight due to sin, its re-creation in Christ, and its future glorification."[44] In innocence, the human will can refrain from sin; after the fall, it can only sin; as redeemed, the will can sin or not sin; and as glorified, the human will never again choose to sin.[45] This tethering of the will to humanity's fourfold state will inform the later Reformed tradition. It is appropriate, therefore, to sketch Augustine's views of the will in creation, fall, redemption, and consummation, while noting the ways in which he developed such views in opposition to both the Manicheans and the Pelagians.

The Manicheans believed in an eternal opposition between spirit and matter, and as such were "dualists" who denied "the goodness of matter and therefore, since they saw man as a compound of matter and spirit, it logically followed that he must inevitably sin because of the material element in his nature."[46] Augustine countered Manicheanism by drawing from some Neoplatonist and scriptural teachings. From the former, he learned that evil cannot be a positive substance but a privation of goodness (which Augustine later

44. Komline, *Augustine on the Will*, 10.
45. Komline, *Augustine on the Will*, 11.
46. Gerald Bonner, "Pelagianism and Augustine," *Augustinian Studies* 23 (1992): 34.

confirms from Scripture), and from the latter, he learned that God is sovereign and has created all things, and because God is not the author of evil, sin must be an accident due to the perverse use of our created wills.[47] The created will, for Augustine, was a mutable good—it had the freedom to sin or not to sin, and to say that sin is inherent in our material nature is to claim that God is the author of sin.[48] The confession of God as the Creator and sovereign ruler of all things entails, therefore, that evil cannot be a "cosmic counterpart to God's goodness."[49] Human evil and the inclination toward vice are therefore the results of the fall, stemming from the abuse of Adam's will. Sin is an accident, not a substance, though it is a debilitating one that indwells us, forming in us vicious habits. As Augustine says: "The consequence of a distorted will is passion. By servitude to passion, habit is formed, and habit to which there is no resistance becomes necessity. By these links, as it were, connected one to another (hence my term a chain), a harsh bondage held me under restraint."[50]

The fallen will thus presupposes Augustine's doctrine of original sin. Two features of his mature understanding are pertinent here: our participation in Adam's primal sin and the inherited sin transmitted from Adam to his progeny. While humanity was created upright (Eccles. 7:29), Adam's sin "altered" their nature: "By [the first couple] so a great a sin was committed, that by it the human nature was altered for the worse, and was transmitted also to their posterity, liable to sin and subject to death."[51] The transmission of sin to Adam's progeny was due to the "seminal nature" that "was there from which we were to be propagated; and this being vitiated by sin, and bound by the chain of death, and justly condemned, man could not be born in any other state."[52] From the abuse of free will, the "whole train of evil" and its ensuring miseries follow, and only the grace of God can emancipate sinners from this corrupt condition.[53]

47. E.g., Augustine, *Confessions*, 7.7.

48. Komline, *Augustine on the Will*, 35.

49. McCall, *Against God and Nature: The Doctrine of Sin* (Crossway, 2019), 221. The Reformed tradition continues this emphasis on the contingency and liberty of the will (and secondary causes) and sees them as compatible with the predetermination of the divine decree. See, for instance, the Westminster Confession of Faith 3.1 and 9.1–2.

50. Augustine, *Confessions*, 8.10.

51. Augustine, *City of God*, 14.1.

52. Augustine, *City of God*, 13.14.

53. Augustine, *City of God*, 13.14.

This language of our participation in the "seminal nature" in Adam, or stemming from the same "corrupt root," forms the basis of a realist doctrine of original sin—which we will revisit in chapter 8. According to Augustine's realism, Adam's progeny inherits Adam's corrupt nature because they exist in some way, really, in Adam, and so his sin is their sin, his guilt is their guilt, and his corruption is their corruption. Realism is usually poised as an alternative to federalism, according to which Adam is divinely appointed to be the federal representative of the human race, and thus Adam's progeny inherit Adam's sin due to the personal imputation of his guilt and corruption by God to that progeny. Jesse Couenhoven is thus correct to observe that, "for Augustine, it is not our legal situation that makes us guilty—we are judged guilty because our seminal participation in Adam means that we actually participated, somehow, in the primal sin. Thus Adam's sin and ours are the same."[54]

As we shall see in chapter 8, though Augustine's understanding of the transmission of sin is not by way of legal representation, realism and federalism are not poised as mere contraries in the Reformed tradition, and federalism might address some weaknesses with realism. While emphasizing the federal representation of Adam was certainly prioritized in covenant theology, this usually includes the enfolding of some realist intuitions into that federalism (as seen, especially, in Herman Bavinck).

What about the corruption transmitted, then? Augustine observes that it is life after the "flesh," the "carnal" (not created) sense, that characterizes the misdirection of both the soul and body.[55] Though the word "concupiscence" can refer to desire in general, in this context it refers to the tendency to desire sin. Augustine's letter to Simplician signals to his maturing realization that the fallen will is incapable of doing good: "The fact that doing the good is not in our part is part of the deserts of the original sin."[56] Indeed, if the "created will, for Augustine, opens doors of possibility," the "fallen will imposes

54. Jesse Couenhoven, *Stricken by Sin, Cured by Christ: Agency, Necessity, and Culpability in Augustinian Theology* (Oxford University Press, 2013), 29–30.

55. Augustine, *City of God*, 14.2. Also: "These are indeed the crimes of wicked men, yet they spring from that root of error and misplaced love which is born with every son of Adam." *City of God*, 22.22. See also Couenhoven, *Stricken by Sin*, 32–33. Cf. Bonaventure, *Breviloquium*, 85.

56. Augustine, "Letter 37, to Simplician," in *Responses to Miscellaneous Questions*, ed. Raymond Canning and Boniface Ramsey (New City Press, 2008), 1.1.10. See Komline, *Augustine on the Will*, 94–107.

chains of necessity."[57] His letter to Simplician is an extended reflection of Paul's letters, especially Romans 9, leading him to conclude that "even faith itself is a gift of God rather than an exercise of human freedom."[58] Indeed, for Augustine, God's mercy allows us to will the good and is itself prior to our exercising that will: "For, since it is not a good will that precedes a call, but a call that precedes a good will, it is rightly ascribed to God who calls that we will what is good, but it cannot be ascribed to us that we are called."[59]

The Pelagians were concerned that such a radical doctrine of depravity would discourage obedience (for we are incapable of willing the good out of our own freedom) and, worse, bring back the Manichean error that evil is an intrinsic part of our being.[60] The distinctive mark of Pelagian doctrine is thus the denial of original sin, which implies the further denial that grace precedes faith (or, to state it positively, that we "somehow initiate and cause our own salvation by exercising our faith and performing good works").[61] The grace that precedes faith also allows Christians to obey God, even in this embodied life. This obedience, then, anticipates life in the hereafter, in resurrected, spiritual bodies. Love of God will be fixed in our vision, both spiritual and bodily: "How great shall be that felicity, which shall be tainted with no evil, which slack lack no good, and which shall afford leisure for the praises of God, who shall be all in all!"[62]

THOMAS AQUINAS AND HYLOMORPHISM

Before we move into retrieving a Reformed doctrine of theological anthropology, some comments on Aquinas are necessary. If Augustine modifies Plato's dualism with biblical revelation, which led him to prioritize the soul without denigrating its relation to the created body, Aquinas modifies Aristotelian hylomorphism with the biblical teachings on the distinctness and separability of the soul.

57. Komline, *Augustine on the Will*, 62.

58. Babcock, "Augustine's Interpretation of Romans," 66.

59. Augustine, "To Simplician," 1.2.12.

60. "Unless we keep this double concern in Pelagian theology in mind: to maintain right doctrine and to encourage men and women to live the Christian life in accordance with what they believed to be the teaching of the Gospel, we shall fail to understand the movement." Bonner, "Pelagianism and Augustine," 34.

61. McCall, *Against God and Nature*, 299 (see also page 289).

62. Augustine, *City of God*, 22.30.

Substance dualism is the view that the human being is a compound of two distinct substances—an immaterial soul and a material body—and it is usually accompanied by the further claim that the soul is the source of our identity.[63] Hylomorphism, however (which etymologically stems from the Greek words *hylos* [matter] and *morphe* [form]), argues that the soul is just the life of the body, which gives the body its "shape" and form. According to hylomorphism: "The body is the material cause (the 'stuff' of the human) and the soul is the formal cause (What makes that stuff into a human rather than some other kind of creature). Rather than seeing the soul and body as distinct substances, then, hylomorphism presents the soul and the body as distinguishable but equally necessary aspects of a human person."[64]

If substance dualists need to account for the scriptural teachings on the goodness of the body, the hylomorphist has to account for the teachings on the separability and distinctness of the soul. Much of the Christian tradition has emphasized a highly integrated view of the body-soul relation, with varying degrees on the prioritization of the soul.[65] As such, much of the tradition presents a Christian anthropological model that lies somewhere within the substance-dualism and hylomorphism spectrum. While presupposing the Augustinian teachings on the indexing of the person along the lines of creation, fall, reformation, and consummation, representatives of the Reformed tradition, as we shall see, took up a view of human ontology that was somewhere in between Augustine's dualism and Thomas's modified hylomorphism, while also taking "a fuller account of the infection of the reason itself by sin."[66] This last section thus briefly sketches Thomas's teachings on the image of God and the body-soul relation from the *Summa Theologiae*.

First, Thomas follows Augustine in noting that the first person plural of Genesis 1:26–28 refers to the creation of humanity after the image of the

63. "For Augustine, bodies may form and perhaps morph into other kinds of bodies, and the soul may change in its own moral and intellectual manner. But developments in the material sphere do not direct or ground fundamental developments in the intellectual sphere." Drever, *Forming of the Augustinian Soul*, 82.

64. Marc Cortez and Michael P. Jensen, "Human Ontology," in *T&T Clark Reader in Theological Anthropology*, ed. Marc Cortez and Michael P. Jensen (Bloomsbury T&T Clark, 2018), 130.

65. Helm, *Human Nature*, 4.

66. Helm, *Human Nature*, 24.

Trinity, and not the Son alone.[67] He provides at least two reasons for this claim, each of which follows Augustine. The first is a theological reason from the singular substance of the Father and Son: "Because as the Son is like to the Father by a likeness of essence, it would follow of necessity if man were made in likeness to the Son, that he is made to the likeness of the Father."[68] This is virtually a restatement of Augustine's reasoning, for "whatever is made to the likeness of the Son must also be made to the likeness of the Father."[69] The second is an exegetical point: If the Father created humanity after the image of the Son, the text would have said, "Let us make man in *your* image," rather than the first person plural "our"; so "the Divine Trinity made man to Its image, that is, of the whole Trinity."[70] This, too, is a restatement from Augustine: "If the Father did not make man to his own image but to the Son's, why did he not say 'Let us make man to your image and likeness' instead of saying 'our'?"[71]

Second, Aquinas follows Augustine in following the promptings of Ephesians 4:24 and Colossians 3:10 to locate the image of God in the intellect or mind and its faculties.[72] With the revelation of the Trinity in hand, Aquinas continues to observe that the mind not only distinguishes "rational creatures" over other creatures, but it also displays an analog of the Trinity. In the "procession of the word in the intellect, and a procession of the love in the will, there exists an image of the uncreated Trinity, by a certain representation of the species."[73] While creatures in general might reflect "traces" of God (as he is their Creator), only human beings are made in the image and likeness of God.

That human beings are called image-bearers by virtue of their intellectual nature, therefore, has ontological, relational, and ethical implications—our intellectual nature resembles God's, and we are called to understand and love God:

> Since man is said to be the image of God by reason of his intellectual nature, he is the most perfectly like God according to that in which he can best

67. Thomas Aquinas, *Summa Theologiae*, trans. Fathers of the Dominican Province (1920), I, q. 93, a. 5, ad. 4.
68. Aquinas, *Summa Theologiae*, I, q. 93, a. 5, ad. 4.
69. Augustine, *The Trinity*, 12.2.7.
70. Aquinas, *Summa Theologiae*, I, q. 93, a. 5, ad. 4.
71. Augustine, *The Trinity*, 12.2.7.
72. Aquinas, *Summa Theologiae*, I, q. 93, a. 6, s. c.
73. Aquinas, *Summa Theologiae*, I, q. 93, a. 6, co.

> imitate God in his intellectual nature. Now the intellectual nature imitates God chiefly in this, that God understands and loves Himself. Wherefore we see that the image of God is in man . . . inasmuch as man possesses a natural aptitude for understanding and loving God; and this aptitude consists in the very nature of the mind, which is common to all men.[74]

Much like Augustine, then, Aquinas argues that image-bearers have a "natural desire for its exemplar," as image-bearers have a reference point outside of themselves.[75]

Third, for Aquinas, the soul is "the first principle of life . . . the act of a body," and further "it belongs to the notion of a soul to be the form of a body."[76] A couple of claims follow from these two convictions. The first is the following: If the soul is the principle of life and the act of a body, then the soul has particular operations that are connected to the body (though the rational soul can act on its own). Following Aristotle, these powers of the soul are tiered, from lowest to highest, as determined by their object.[77] The lowest operation of the soul is the vegetative, which has only the body as its object; then there is the sensitive, which has as its object all external bodies; and finally there is the rational power, "which regards a still more universal object—namely, not only the sensible body, but all being in universal."[78] This rational soul "far exceeds the corporeal nature that it is not even performed by any corporeal organ."[79] While in human beings the three (vegetative, sensitive,

74. Aquinas, *Summa Theologiae*, I, q. 93, a. 4, co.

75. Dominic Doyle, "From Image to Indwelling: Aquinas' Theological Anthropology," in *T&T Clark Handbook to Theological Anthropology*, ed. Mary Ann Hinsdale and Stephen Okey (Bloomsbury T&T Clark, 2021), 176. I'm aware that there is a lively debate on the issue of the natural desire for God and the nature/grace relation in Aquinas that we cannot adjudicate here. See, e.g., Laurence Feingold, *The Natural Desire to See God according to St. Thomas Aquinas and His Interpreters*, 2nd ed. (Sapientia, 2010); and David Grumett, "De Lubac, Grace, and the Pure Nature Debate," *Modern Theology* 31 (2015): 123–46.

76. Aquinas, *Summa Theologiae*, I, q. 78, a. 1, co.; a. 5, co., respectively.

77. Aquinas, *Summa Theologiae*, I, q. 78, a. 1, co.

78. Aquinas, *Summa Theologiae*, I, q. 78, a. 1, co. So, Lapine: "The more imperfect and receptive the powers are, the more they are conjoined with the body. The intellective soul is not even exercised by means of a corporeal organ, since it must receive universal forms in its knowing (I. 78.1)." *The Logic of the Body: Retrieving Theological Psychology* (Lexham, 2020), 44.

79. Aquinas, *Summa Theologiae*, I, q. 78, a. 1, co. Note Wood's comment, however: "Their incorporeality does not, however, extend so far as to preclude any sort of correlation whatsoever with bodily parts, states, and processes. Indeed . . . Aquinas thinks that intellectual operations depend in normal cases on the brain." Adam Wood, *Thomas Aquinas on the Immateriality of the*

and rational) refer to numerically the same soul, some life-forms have only the vegetative (as in plants), and others the vegetative and sensitive (as in animals). If, however, humans have a rational soul that exercises its powers "without the mediation of any bodily organ . . . then it has an act of being on its own," and further it "must also be capable of existing by [itself] apart from the body as the subject of such incorporeal powers and operations."[80]

The second implication complicates this picture somewhat, since, for Thomas, the human person is not the soul alone, or the body, but rather the whole soul-body composite. Aquinas details the consequences of this in ways that would take us beyond the scope of the present chapter, but two points are worth considering. The first is that this hylomorphic view of the human person is a much more integralist and holistic account of the body-soul relation than offered in substance dualism.[81] The second, however, is that such a view raises questions about the continuity of the person after death. If the body is essential to the human person, then what are disembodied souls in heaven? Are they not personal? Aquinas wrestled with this question and defended the biblical account of the separability of souls, and as such he substantially modified the Aristotelian view:

> Aristotle had no conception of a resurrection, and so his hylomorphism was initially developed as an account with mortalist assumptions. But Aquinas not surprisingly developed an account of the soul which survived death but did so in an incomplete state because it became bodiless at death, awaiting the resurrection of the dead. So Aquinas introduced the idea of a *substantial* unity of soul and body. So the soul surviving death lacked its body and was incomplete without it, for in death it came to lack a substantial part, this anamoly being rectified in resurrection. . . . What this shows is that the doctrinal contours of Scripture, and particularly of the New Testament,

---

Intellect (Catholic University of America Press, 2020), 4. As we will see, Bavinck will press on this aspect of Christian-Aristotelian anthropology.

80. Wood, *On the Immateriality of the Human Intellect*, 95–96. Cf. Bonaventure, *Breviloquium*, 87.

81. This has implications for the question of sex in the afterlife: "On the Thomistic model, I am essentially my soul that informs some matter. Arguably, my soul is essentially gendered as male or female. The descriptive content of what makes one male or female is a natural property essentially instantiated by each individual. . . . The bodily sex type is a manifestation of a deeper fact about the person." Joshua Ryan Farris, *An Introduction to Theological Anthropology: Humans, Both Creaturely and Divine* (Baker Academic, 2020), 224.

> were respected. When the data of revelation required it, they invariably trumped the original pagan outlook of Aristotle.[82]

There are still ongoing debates, however, on the tenability of Aquinas's view of the disembodied soul, as seen in the exchanges between survivalists and corruptionists. Survivalists argue that the human person survives death and the separation of the soul from body, because the soul just is a person, while corruptionists argue that although the separated soul survives the separation from the body, the person does not. On this latter view, the soul is not a person. While typically substance dualists prefer the former view, and Thomists the latter, there are mediating voices who try to retain their Thomist credentials while preferring survivalism, and there are those who want to offer a third way in arguing that the disembodied soul in heaven is an "incomplete person."[83] Reformed theologians were aware of this issue but do not seem to have lingered on it for long—instead, many of them, including the Leiden Synopsis, Petrus van Mastricht, and Herman Bavinck, would continue to speak in strikingly hylomorphic ways (in varying degrees) and thus emphasize that death unnaturally severs the essential body away from the soul, even while we do retain our identity in heaven as we await resurrection.

CONCLUSION

This chapter has surveyed Augustine's views on the image of God, the body-soul relation, and the tethering of human nature to its fourfold state in creation, fall, redemption, and consummation. Along the way, we see the scriptural teachings on the body-soul relation and the image (explored in chap. 1) exert pressure on Augustine's theological account—that we are *image-bearers* means that the soul is most itself when it chooses conformity with God, and that the soul is embodied means that what we do with our bodies impacts the soul, and that our sexed bodies will be resurrected in glory. The biblical

82. Helm, *Human Nature*, 240.

83. See Daniel D. De Haan and Brandon Dahm, "After Survivalism and Corruptionism: Separated Souls as Incomplete Persons," *Quaestiones Disputatae* 10 (2020): 161–76; and Mark Spencer, "Survivalist, Platonist, Thomistic Hylomorphism: A Reply to Daniel De Haan and Brandon Dahm," *Quaestiones Disputatae* 10 (2020): 177–84.

narrative of creation, fall, redemption, and consummation also prompts Augustine's reflections on the will.

These Augustinian moorings form the precedent for the later Reformed tradition. I have also surveyed briefly Thomas Aquinas's views on the image of God and the body-soul relation; while Thomas follows a broadly Augustinian tradition, his preference for a modified hylomorphism to speak of the body-soul relation will also prove significant for the Reformed tradition. Despite their holistic construal of the soul-body relation, however, there are lingering questions on whether these thinkers were right in locating the image specifically in the intellectual soul rather than seeing the intellectual capacity of man as merely one aspect of imaging God and on whether one can exclude the body from the *imago Dei*.[84] The Reformed tradition would continue to wrestle with such questions, and a diversity of positions would be offered.

FURTHER READING

Drever, Matthew. *Image, Identity, and the Forming of the Augustinian Soul*. Oxford University Press, 2013. A wonderful and thorough exposition of Augustine's account of the image of God and embodied soul.

Couenhoven, Jesse. *Stricken by Sin, Cured by Christ: Agency, Necessity, and Culpability in Augustinian Theology*. Oxford University Press, 2013. An analytically informed exposition and application of Augustine's account of original sin and moral responsibility.

Komline, Han-Luen Kantzer. *Augustine on the Will: A Theological Account*. Oxford University Press, 2020. A readable and trustworthy narration of Augustine's account of the will.

Williams, Rowan. *On Augustine*. Bloomsbury, 2016. A collection of essays on Augustine's theology, including chapters on the image of God and identity, that also highlights the pastoral implications of his work.

Wood, Adam. *Thomas Aquinas on the Immateriality of the Intellect*. Catholic University of America Press, 2020. Aquinas's conception of the rational soul is complex, and Adam Wood's exposition is a lucid help to navigate the primary sources.

---

84. Ryan S. Peterson, *The Imago Dei as Human Identity: A Theological Interpretation* (Eisenbrauns, 2016), 34–36.

5

HUMANS, BODY AND SOUL: WITNESSES FROM THE REFORMED TRADITION

With the precedents from Augustine and Thomas in view, this chapter sketches a theological account of the image of God and created human ontology that draws from the Reformed tradition in the periods of high orthodoxy and late modernity. Along the way, we shall see that the Reformed tradition inherits the questions and prompts from that Augustinian tradition. They wrestled with questions like: How do the body and soul relate to each other? What does it mean to be image-bearers of God? And how should we think about the differences between the created, fallen, and redeemed human?

Indeed, many of the catholic themes are adumbrated in the Reformed tradition—the image of God both refers to an ontological and ethical reality and positions humanity in close proximity to God and in positive relation with him (original righteousness), and humanity straddles the angelic and animal spheres of creation. The body and soul are thus closely related, though we shall see some diversity in Reformed thought on how to articulate that close relation, with some emphasizing a more dualistic perspective and others a hylomorphic one (while still affirming the separability of the soul from the body). By modifying dualism and hylomorphism, the Reformed tradition seeks to do justice to the biblical teachings on the holistic character of the body-soul relation (as seen in texts like Gen. 2:7 and Ps. 139, the sense of נפש, as we saw in earlier chapters) and the unnaturalness of their separation at death. As we shall see in the chapters that follow, the Reformed tradition continues to be sensitive to the way in which human nature is modified by the fourfold states of innocence, fall, redemption, and consummation. It is in a deeper reflection on the tethering of the human to these states of the biblical plotline that we see these Reformed thinkers develop their account of the image, which at certain points includes resisting what would become Roman Catholic accents on anthropology. As John Calvin (1509–1564), the magisterial Reformer, argued, the knowledge of ourselves "is twofold: namely, to know what we were like when we were first created and what our condition became after the fall of Adam."[1] While the Reformed tradition does have much in common with the broader Catholic accounts of the body-soul relation, then, its accents on original righteousness, the bondage of the will, and the totality of corruption do mark out a distinct trajectory (though, one that retrieves an Augustinian line).

Reformed teaching on human nature is rich but rarely discussed in the contemporary literature, in part because of the "relational turn" to theological anthropology and its suspicion of ontological description. In much of twentieth-century anthropology, there has been a decisive shift among theologians to locate the image of God on the relationships that humans can have, with the concomitant judgment that metaphysical descriptions of what it means to be human are a speculative distraction from the retrieval of human relationality.[2] In my estimation, this turn away from metaphysics toward an isolated focus on human relations is unnecessary, for relationality presupposes metaphysics. Thus, this chapter presents the contours of a Reformed account of human nature and shows that such accounts never leave behind relational or vocational concerns. After sketching some parameters from the confessional witnesses, I survey the views of Francis Turretin, Petrus van Mastricht, and the Leiden Synopsis on the locus of the image of God and the

1. John Calvin, *Institutes of the Christian Religion*, trans. Ford Lewis Battles, ed. John T. McNeill (Westminster, 1960), 1.15.1.

2. For a narration of this "relational turn" and critiques, see Joanna Leidenhag, "The Challenge of Autism for Relational Approaches to Theological Anthropology," *International Journal of Systematic Theology* 23 (2021): 109–34; and Harriett A. Harris, "Should We Say That Personhood Is Relational?," *Scottish Journal of Theology* 51 (1998): 214–38.

body-soul relation. As I mentioned in chapter 4, these seventeenth-century thinkers represent the Reformed tradition in its mature state, taking the writings of the magisterial Reformers (like Luther and Calvin) and codifying them in an institutionalized setting. If the magisterial authors were writing more occasional and pastoral texts at the beginning of the Protestant Reformation, these Reformed scholastic thinkers represent the crystallization of the Protestant Reformation in a codified form.[3]

The point here is not to go into exhaustive detail over every aspect of their treatments, but to show that the Reformed tradition was sensitive to matters of theological anthropology, concerned as they were to produce a holistic account of the image of God and the body-soul relation. Some aspects are merely introduced here, like the interest in faculty psychology. Others are picked up in later chapters, especially the sin that inheres in us and the restoration brought about by Christ. Indeed, the material on the image of God and human nature should be presupposed as one moves into discussions of sin, corruption, and restoration, for sin involves a misdirection of created nature, and grace restores nature.

With the survey of these representative authors in Reformed orthodoxy in hand, the chapter then turns to a presentation of Herman Bavinck's contributions to theological anthropology, showing that this tradition continues to be developed through the period of late modernity. I show that he stands on and yet develops the doctrine of humanity found in the period of Reformed orthodoxy. We shall see that his contribution lies in the holistic way in which he described the image of God, his emphasis in including the body in the image, and the identification of personality and corporate humanity as essential features of the image of God as well.[4] As I hope to keep emphasizing, the Reformed orthodox thinkers surveyed here and Herman Bavinck felt no need to choose between identifying the image with the structure of the human being or in our unique vocations or in the way in which we can relate

3. For an introduction to Reformed scholasticism, see Willem J. van Asselt, T. Theo J. Pleizier, and Pieter L. Rouwendal, *Introduction to Reformed Scholasticism*, trans. Albert Gootjes (Reformation Heritage Books, 2011); and Richard A. Muller, *Post-Reformation Reformed Dogmatics*, 4 vols. (Baker Academic, 2003).

4. For a deeper treatment of Herman Bavinck on theological anthropology, see especially N. Gray Sutanto, *God and Humanity: Herman Bavinck and Theological Anthropology* (Bloomsbury T&T Clark, 2024).

to God and others. They offered metaphysical sketches of human nature and the image of God that refused to isolate merely one capacity, but the metaphysical sketch served to demonstrate the importance of humanity's obedience to their calling to the cultural mandate, to love their neighbor, and to have fellowship with God.

In a final section, I then discuss the debate between creationism and traducianism on the origins of the human soul and make a case for a creationist view. This presentation of Reformed thought on humanity thus sets up the six theses on human nature and the image of God in the next chapter.

CONFESSIONAL WITNESSES

To get a sense of what the Reformed tradition says about human nature, it is wise to begin with some statements from the Reformed confessions. The confessional witness outlines that we are made in God's image, originally righteous, and comprising of body and soul, and it outlines some of the implications of these affirmations without filling in all of the metaphysical details.

The Second Helvetic Confession (1566) describes the image of God in the chapter on creation and denotes that humanity was made with original goodness according to the image of God, providing a terse entryway. In following God, humanity exercises faithful dominion over all things. Humanity is also created as male and female, and human beings are composed of the "two different substances" of soul and body; the soul is separated from the body at death (due to the curse of sin) but will be reunited in the final resurrection:

> Scripture says that in the beginning he was made good according to the image and likeness of God; that God placed him in paradise and made all thing subject to him (Gen chp 2). This is what David magnificently sets forth in Psalm 8. Moreover, God gave him a wife and blessed them. We also affirm that man consists of two different substances in one person: an immortal soul which, when separate from the body, neither sleeps nor dies, and a mortal body which will nevertheless be raised up from the dead at the last judgement, in order that then the whole man, either in life or in death, abide forever.

In the next chapter of this confession, which is on the fall of humanity, the image of God is associated particularly with the Adamic pre-fall original righteousness, which was then lost after the fall: "In the beginning, man was made according to the image of God, in righteousness and true holiness, good and upright. But when at the instigation of the serpent and by his own fault he abandoned goodness and righteousness, he became subject to sin, death and various calamities." This sense of the original uprightness of created humanity is an important emphasis of the Reformed tradition—we are not created neutrally, but *good*.

As we are going to see, the confessional witness relates the image of God not only with the metaphysics of who human beings are—created with dignity and honor because we are image-bearers of *God*, and yet humble and dependent because we are *image* and not God—but also with a task and calling.[5] Humanity is to live in fellowship with God, characterized by righteousness, holiness, and knowledge (Eph. 4:24; Col. 3:10), and to represent God in loving cultivation of creation. In other words, humans are ensouled bodies, created with the original righteousness that allows us to have positive fellowship with God and cultivate creation properly, which is lost in Adam and restored in Christ. Calvin in particular argues that Ephesians 4:24 and Colossians 3:10 show us a fuller definition of "image," which refers to "the restoration of [Adam's] corrupted nature." Ephesians 4:24 and Colossians 3:10 thus not only refer to the way in which humans are sanctified unto righteousness but also denote the original Adamic righteousness *to which* we are restored: "Consequently, the beginning of our recovery of salvation is in that restoration which we obtain through Christ, who also is called the Second Adam for the reason that restores us to true and complete integrity."[6] Grace, therefore, restores nature. The image of God refers to both what we are and what we are supposed to be, in conformity to God in righteousness, holiness, and knowledge.

The Canons of Dordt (1618–1619), part of the "Three Forms of Unity" for the Dutch Reformed churches, emphasize this latter sense of the image as

5. "Humanity is like God, but unlike God we have limits. We are derived copies, not the original. We possess an exalted status as reflections of the very Creator of the universe but also a humble status as merely derived copies of the original." Richard Lints, *Uncommon Unity: Wisdom for the Church in an Age of Division* (Lexham, 2022), 112.

6. Calvin, *Institutes*, 1.15.4.

original righteousness under article one of the third and fourth points of the doctrine on human corruption and conversion:

> Human beings were originally created in the image of God and were furnished in mind with a true and sound knowledge of the Creator and things spiritual, in will and heart with righteousness, and in all emotions with purity; indeed, the whole human being was holy. However, rebelling against God at the devil's instigation and by their own free will, they deprived themselves of these outstanding gifts. Rather, in their place they brought upon themselves blindness, terrible darkness, futility, and distortion of judgment in their minds; perversity, defiance, and hardness in their hearts and wills; and finally impurity in all their emotions.[7]

The Westminster Confession of Faith 4.2., likewise, highlights both ontological and ethical components, mentioning the imbuing of humanity with "immortal and reasonable" souls, the mutability of the will, and original righteousness and dominion over creatures, along with the imprinting of the moral law of God in human hearts:

> 2. After God had made all other creatures, he created man, male and female, with reasonable and immortal souls, endued with knowledge, righteousness, and true holiness, after his own image, having the law of God written in their hearts, and power to fulfil it; and yet under a possibility of transgressing, being left to the liberty of their own will, which was subject unto change. Beside this law written in their hearts, they received a command not to eat of the tree of the knowledge of good and evil; which while they kept they were happy in their communion with God, and had dominion over the creature.[8]

Chapter 6, on the fall, however, mentions the loss of "original righteousness and communion with God," which emphasizes that pre-fall humanity was not created neutrally or with any natural tendency away from God. Rather, again, humanity was created in positive fellowship with God and was living

7. Cf. Heidelberg Catechism, Q&A 6.

8. Cf. Westminster Larger Catechism, Q&A 17, 21. The Westminster Divines specify that it is the soul that is the locus of the image of God, though other Reformed theologians would include the body as well while maintaining that God himself is spirit without body. See Westminster Assembly, *Annotations*, Gen. 1:26.

in conformity with the divine will. Indeed, as later Reformed theologians (like Bavinck) would emphasize, the fall does not change the ontological fact that humans are made in God's image, but we have lost the proper knowledge (wisdom), righteousness, and holiness that characterized humanity in the state of innocence. It is the sanctifying work of the Spirit, in the language of the Larger Catechism, Q&A 75, that renews "the whole man after the image of God."

In sum, ontological, vocational, and ethical components are present in the confessional witness, such that there is no need to pit an ontological (or substantial) account of the *imago Dei* against ethical and vocational ones. Human beings are created as inherently religious creatures, knowing God in true righteousness and holiness, and despite the loss of that knowledge and original righteousness, human beings continue to be creatures with ensouled bodies in God's image, imbued with dignity, honor, and delegated dominion over creation. With these parameters in view, I turn now to some representative texts of Reformed orthodoxy to introduce their emphases on the locus of the image of God, before turning to the body-soul relation.

FRANCIS TURRETIN, PETRUS VAN MASTRICHT, AND THE LEIDEN SYNOPSIS ON THE IMAGE OF GOD AND THE BODY-SOUL RELATION

Francis Turretin's *Institutes of Elenctic Theology*, Petrus van Mastricht's *Theoretical-Practical Theology*, and the Leiden Synopsis display a representative sampling of Reformed orthodoxy on the locus of the image of God and the body-soul relation. Francis Turretin (1623–1687) was a Genevan Reformed scholastic who taught at the Academy of Geneva. Petrus van Mastricht (1630–1706) was a high orthodox Reformed scholastic theologian who taught at the universities of Duisburg and Utrecht. The Leiden Synopsis is a collection of disputations that codifies Reformed orthodoxy, written by leading Reformed theologians at the University of Leiden: Antonius Thysius (1565–1640), Johannes Polyander (1568–1646), Andreas Rivetus (1572–1651), and Antonius Waleus (1573–1639). Each of these seventeenth-century texts thus forms an authoritative and mature representation of the Reformed tradition, bringing into greater clarity the Reformational developments initiated by the magisterial or second-generation Reformers of the sixteenth century.

All three texts show a keen desire to uphold the important connection between the body and soul. However, while Turretin emphasizes that the locus of the image is still more properly the rational soul and original righteousness, Van Mastricht and the Synopsis include the body as part of the image of God.[9]

Francis Turretin

Turretin denies understanding the image of God in two ways before identifying three aspects in which the image consists: in the soul, original righteousness, and the dominion of humanity over creatures. The two denials consist in, first, understanding the image as a "participation of the divine essence," for only the divine Son is properly the image of the invisible God (Col. 1:15), and, second, identifying the human body as the image of God. Concerning the latter, Turretin clarifies that though the body participates in the immortality of the soul and evinces a beautiful structure, symmetry, and majesty over other creatures, it is still not to be identified with the image proper: "If human members are attributed to God in the Scriptures, it does not therefore follow that the image is to be placed properly in these, since they are ascribed to him after the manner of men (*anthropopathos*) and must be understood in a manner becoming God (*theoprepos*) not formally and properly, but figuratively and analogically."[10] The image is not shown on the body formally, but rather consequently and effectively as the soul inhabits the body. The soul, then, is the "proper seat" of the image of God. The bodily language by which the Scriptures speak of God are applied to God anthropomorphically, after all. Turretin speaks of the image of God as antecedently in the soul, formally in original righteousness, then consequently in dominion and immortality.

9. Helm's description that the Reformed orthodox adopted varying degrees of modified hylomorphism to describe the body-soul relation is apt. See Paul Helm, *Human Nature from Calvin to Edwards* (Reformation Heritage Books, 2019), 55–78.

10. Francis Turretin, *Institutes of Elenctic Theology*, vol. 1, *First Through Tenth Topics*, ed. James T. Dennison, trans. George Musgrave Giger (P&R, 1992), 465–66. Cf. Peter Martyr Vermigli, *Philosophical Works: On the Relation of Philosophy to Theology*, ed. and trans. Joseph C. McLelland (Davenant, 2018), 40–44.

First, then, the soul is the seat of the image of God because of its spiritual, simple, and incorruptible nature. Immortality properly belongs to the soul "intrinsically and as to its faculties, viz., the intellect and will and the liberty arising from both."[11] It is on this basis that human life is imbued with dignity, as indicated by the texts that prohibit killing human beings, even after sin (Gen. 9:6; James 3:9). Souls continue to exist despite the death of the body, proceeding to eternal life or punishment, subsisting apart from the body in the intermediate state, while waiting for the resurrection.[12]

Second, Turretin argues that original righteousness belongs properly to the image.[13] Original righteousness characterizes the direction of the soul and thus the right exercise of its faculties: "embracing wisdom in the mind, holiness in the will, and rectitude and good order . . . in the affections."[14] This distinction between the soul itself and the original righteousness that characterizes the soul sets up Bavinck's distinction between the broad and narrow senses of the image of God. Original righteousness is lost at the fall, as Adam's will, upright as it was, was still mutable.[15] It is this feature of the image of God that is restored upon regeneration, per Colossians 3:10, Ephesians 4:24, and Romans 12:2.[16] Original righteousness thus emphasizes the proper orientation of image-bearers, to be in fellowship with God and thus to steward God's creation.[17]

Turretin juxtaposes his understanding of original righteousness as a feature of humanity's proper natural state from a Roman Catholic view:

---

11. Turretin, *Institutes of Elenctic Theology*, 1:466.

12. Turretin, *Institutes of Elenctic Theology*, 1:484–88.

13. For explorations of original righteousness in the Reformed tradition, see Hans Madueme, *Defending Sin: A Response to the Challenges of Evolution and the Natural Sciences* (Baker Academic, 2025), 153–99; Harrison Perkins, *Righteous by Design: Covenantal Merit and Adam's Original Integrity* (Christian Focus, 2024); and Brian Mattson, *Restored to Our Destiny: Eschatology and the Image of God in Herman Bavinck's Reformed Dogmatics* (Brill, 2011).

14. Turretin, *Institutes of Elenctic Theology*, 1:466.

15. Cf. Herman Bavinck, *Reformed Dogmatics*, vol. 2, *God and Creation*, ed. John Bolt, trans. John Vriend (Baker Academic, 2004), 550 (hereafter *RD*). Turretin notes that Adam's will enjoyed a fourfold liberty: "(a) from coaction; (b) from physical necessity; (c) from sin; (d) from misery." Turretin, *Institutes of Elenctic Theology*, 1:466.

16. Turretin, *Institutes of Elenctic Theology*, 1:467.

17. Turretin, *Institutes of Elenctic Theology*, 1:468. So, Vermigli: "For, when he was fashioned, man was made right and, as Scripture says, in the image of God. Therefore, Adam's appetite for agreeable and preserving things, when first he was created, was not raging out of control to the point that he was averse to right reason and the Word of God." Peter Martyr Vermigli, *On Original Sin*, trans. Kirk Summers (Davenant, 2019), 28.

> The Romanists hold original righteousness to be a supernatural gift, superadded to the native gifts and powers of the entire man. Bellarmine explains the reason why they determine this to be so. There was in man naturally a contest between the flesh and the spirit, the reason and the appetite, from which flowed a certain disease and languor of nature, arising from the condition of the material. Therefore God added original righteousness as a "golden bridle," to repress that conflict and to cover like a precious garment their nakedness, and as a remedy to heal that weakness. . . . This is the more common opinion among them, although the Jansenists and others exclaim loudly against it. Whence arose this expression of the Scholastics: "Naturals remained untouched, but the supernaturals only were lost."[18]

A Roman Catholic anthropology would characterize original righteousness as a sort of supernatural bridle that constrains the natural fleshly appetites (concupiscence) of natural humanity even before the fall. As Abigail Favale puts it, citing the Catechism of the Catholic Church: "The fall is not a plunge from our natural state into a more, corrupt, unnatural state: it is a fall from what the Catechism calls 'the grace of original holiness,' a reversion to our mortal condition.'"[19] The fall, therefore, did not result in a loss of the natural righteousness proper to human nature, but rather merely of that supernatural bridle, and as a result, humanity is back in its natural state. By way of contrast, for Turretin, that original righteousness was not a gift of supernature but was, like health, a gift appropriate to Adam's original and created human nature.

Third, then, the image consists in humanity's "dominion" over other creatures. While Turretin's language might seem latent with potential misuse and hubris to modern ears, mentioning as he does that other creatures "are bound to serve [humanity] as their master and to minister to his use," Turretin qualifies this dominion significantly, mentioning that "whatever that dominion was even before the fall, it differed infinitely from the dominion of God, which is independent, natural, absolute and unlimited. However man's, on the other hand, is dependent, precarious and circumscribed within its own

---

18. Turretin, *Institutes of Elenctic Theology*, 1:471.

19. Abigale Favale, *Genesis of Gender: A Christian Theory* (Ignatius, 2022), 45, citing *The Catechism of the Catholic Church*, no. 399.

limits."[20] Hence, in the section on original righteousness properly belonging to humanity as created, Turretin argues that "exercising dominion over the other creatures" would be impossible "without original righteousness": "For how could he either wisely and justly hold dominion over creatures or serve God, if not endued with wisdom and holiness?"[21] This is the natural righteousness of Adam, and that which would have been "propagated to posterity if man had remained innocent."[22]

Turretin's emphasis on the dominion of humanity over other creatures indicates that the bodily character of humanity remains important to him, though the "proper seat" is located elsewhere.[23] The soul may be able to subsist without the body, but the soul remains dependent on the body "as an object and occasion" of at least some of the soul's functions.[24] This is seen in two ways. First, due to "union with the body, the soul does not work through the intellect without first working through the phantasy, so that by an operation through the phantasy and at the presence of phantasms, it is excited to work through the intellect."[25] Phantasms are the sensible images or ideas received through the body's senses of sensible things, upon which the intellect works.[26] The dependence of the reception of phantasy on the body is reiterated when Turretin argues that those of older age (a second childhood) have little to no access to phantasms: "What survive are obscurely presented to the intellect" in those instances. Immaterial things like God and the angels are known independently of phantasms, but human beings know sensible things by way of phantasms "with respect to external sensible things and singulars." Second, Turretin argues that "fury and madness" can be incurred on the soul "on the part of an injured organ."[27] Specifically, the vitiated brain

20. Turretin, *Institutes of Elenctic Theology*, 1:469.

21. Turretin, *Institutes of Elenctic Theology*, 1:468.

22. Turretin, *Institutes of Elenctic Theology*, 1:471. Turretin here is polemizing against the "Romanists" who argued that original righteousness was a supernatural gift, which relieved humanity of the natural "contest between the flesh and the spirit"—original righteousness was thus a superadded "golden bridle" in that view.

23. Helm's description of Turretin's treatment as showing "some of the signs of hylomorphism, but not of all," mixed with some preferences for "Platonic dualism," is thus quite apt. *Human Nature from Calvin to Edwards*, 71, 73. Missing in Turretin are references to the vegetative functions of the soul.

24. Turretin, *Institutes of Elenctic Theology*, 1:486.

25. Turretin, *Institutes of Elenctic Theology*, 1:486.

26. Cf. Helm, *Human Nature from Calvin to Edwards*, 72.

27. Turretin, *Institutes of Elenctic Theology*, 1:486.

can cause misleading apprehensions of sense and phantasy, and such cases need to be treated with physical remedies. Further, as human beings age, no change occurs with regard to the soul but with the body, and yet the intellectual capacities of the soul are markedly affected.[28]

Petrus van Mastricht

Van Mastricht's *Theoretical-Practical Theology* discusses the creation of humanity as a body-soul unity first, prior to the discussion on the image of God, but for symmetry's sake we will treat the latter before the former. Van Mastricht's treatment, along with the Leiden Synopsis and Herman Bavinck, displays a disposition toward a holistic treatment of the image of God, refusing partitive definitions of the image.

Like Turretin, Van Mastricht first qualifies what the image of God is not before offering positive definitions: (1) The image of God does not belong to the structure or figures of the body, for God is Spirit; (2) the image does not refer to the human nature of Christ, for Scripture attests that we are made "according to the image of God, not of Christ, and that Christ in his incarnation was made like us in all things except for sin"; (3) we do not bear the perfect image of God, which belongs properly to the divine nature of the Son alone.[29]

Rather, the image of God consists in the "conformity" of humanity "whereby he in measure reflects the highest perfection of God."[30] The sense of conformity here has both metaphysical and ethical connotations: Humanity images God essentially and is called to imitate God in obedience. This conformity consists in five aspects: (1) the essence of humanity, (2) the faculties of the soul, (3) original righteousness (or what Van Mastricht calls "natural perfection"), (4) immortality, and (5) dominion. This emphasis on conformity brings into view both ontological and normative aspects of the image of God—human beings are image-bearers and ought to conform to God and his will.

---

28. For an engagement with a theology of the body in dialogue with more contemporary material, e.g., affect theory and the cognitive science of religion from a Reformed perspective, see Sutanto, *God and Humanity*, esp. chaps. 3 and 4.
29. Van Mastricht, *TPT*, 3:285.
30. Van Mastricht, *TPT*, 3:285.

With regard to the first, Van Mastricht emphasizes the inclusion of the body in the definition of the image of God: "The first conformity is in the very essence of man, and that in its entirety, in body and soul. Hence throughout Scripture the image of God is attributed to the whole man (Gen. 1:26–27; 1 Thess. 5:23)."[31] The inclusion of the body is the reason for which God forbids murder (Gen. 9:6), and the body too will be restored according to the image of God. Van Mastricht anticipates the objection that the body is excluded from the image because God himself is immaterial. His response: "Certainly not in the material crassness of our members, but in their formal perfection, for when all imperfection has been removed . . . our members, or rather the virtues of our members, belong to God, certainly not formally, but eminently."[32] What Van Mastricht means by this is that the body is fitting to be used in service of God, so much so that God is often described anthropomorphically as having hands, eyes, or ears. Although Van Mastricht does not elaborate on this here, Bavinck would later take this line of reasoning to argue that the incarnation itself is proof that the body is made in the image of God, for its members are "fitting" for God to assume. Thus, the body is fitted for God, not "zoomed in," as it were, as if our bodily parts somehow refer univocally to the being of God; rather, the whole body "eminently" signifies its Maker, making it, as a whole, a proper sign and means of divine representation.

Second, however, Van Mastricht argues that the image of God is "much more perfectly" observed "in the essence of the soul," because of the soul's "spirituality, simplicity, invisibility, and immortality," though God has these in a much higher and different way.[33] The soul and its faculties do not merely image God generally, but the Triune God specifically: "The second conformity of the divine image is in the faculties of the soul, the intellect and will, as they are acknowledged by all in both, in man as well as God. And also, the variety of the faculties appears to adumbrate (not demonstrate) the plurality of divine persons in one essence."[34] Van Mastricht elaborates on the way in which the psychological faculties modestly image (adumbrate) the Trinity in the "practical" exposition on the doctrine, arguing that the image of God

31. Van Mastricht, *TPT*, 3:285.

32. Van Mastricht, *TPT*, 3:285.

33. Van Mastricht, *TPT*, 3:286. This is not meant to exclude the body from the image, as we've seen.

34. Van Mastricht, *TPT*, 3:286.

in us leads to the knowledge of God's subsistence. The sense here is that we cannot prove or come to know the Triune God without Scripture, "yet with revelation presupposed, we are able to some small extent to declare them from man created in the image of God, that is, to the extent that we may perceive from there, if not the existence, at least the possibility of three persons in one essence."[35] The modesty that marks Van Mastricht's description of the soul's Trinitarian reflection has clear Augustinian echoes:

> And as the intellect differs from the will in the same soul, so the Son and the Holy Spirit differ, the Son being begotten of the Father as through an act of the intellect, for which reason he is called in the Scriptures the image of the Father par excellence, and likewise the Word and wisdom of God, but the Holy Spirit through an act of the will or of love, for which reason he is called through appropriation the Spirit.[36]

An adumbration is not an a priori demonstration, and when considered through the lens of special revelation, one could see a modest reflection of the Trinity in the human soul and its faculties. This means that the internal life of the soul itself is a sign of God, and if all creation manifests the glory of God (Ps. 19:1), this must include ourselves as image-bearers.

The third conformity is the "chief conformity of the divine image," which is in the "gifts, or the natural perfection of those [psychological] faculties," located in the intellect, will, and affections.[37] It was a "gift" precisely because Adam's ability to conform himself to the divine will was itself a result of his positive communion with God, and yet this gift was "natural," that is, concreated within him: "It was the natural perfection, of those faculties."[38] The intellect is imbued with wisdom, such that upright humanity had the ability to name the animals according to their natures, and humanity was thus able to exercise proper "governance" over other creatures.

The right conformity of intellect, will, and affection is that which leads to original righteousness, referring to Adam's public "conformity of his whole

35. Van Mastricht, *TPT*, 3:299.
36. Van Mastricht, *TPT*, 3:299.
37. Van Mastricht, *TPT*, 3:286.
38. Van Mastricht, *TPT*, 3:286.

person to God and his law."[39] The sense of "original" here therefore referred to his representational function as humanity's federal head, "since his righteousness was the origin of all the righteousness of the whole human race that would follow."[40] This righteousness is not a substance but a quality that "diffused through the entire substance, and thus common to body and soul, and likewise to the mind, will, and affections."[41] In other words, if Adam had remained upright, properly ordering his faculties, he would be able to pass down his virtues to his progeny.

Van Mastricht continues to defend this Reformed view from what he considers the "opinion of the papists," according to which "concupiscence" is inherent in natural humanity and that this state of nature remains intact after the fall.[42] Original righteousness would thus be a superadded gift, given to humanity to control the natural "discord of flesh and spirit."[43] As Daniel Hill has shown, for Van Mastricht, "sin and salvation" are "moral and covenantal terms," such that whatever "soteriology seeks to resolve, the problem lies in humanity's accidental corruption and not any lack of being on the creature's part."[44]

Concupiscence is, for the Reformed tradition, itself sinful, a product of our corruption rather than of our natural state. In the Roman Catholic view, however, concupiscence is natural and that which is kept in check by way of the supernatural grace of God. Hence, when Van Mastricht turns to the violation of the covenant of works (or nature), he responds to the question of how a person endowed with *natural* original righteousness could have fallen into sin. He argues that Adam was endowed indeed, but mutably so that he was still "able to sin," and that Adam sinned out of his own freedom of the will.[45] This answer is against "the Pelagians, Jesuits, and Remonstrants," according to whom Adam was created with a "wrestling of the flesh and Spirit." To the contrary, "The concupiscence of the flesh against the spirit is, as God (Exod. 20:17) and the apostle (Rom. 7:7) declare, without doubt sin," and thus

39. Van Mastricht, *TPT*, 3:287.
40. Van Mastricht, *TPT*, 3:287.
41. Van Mastricht, *TPT*, 3:287.
42. Van Mastricht, *TPT*, 3:296.
43. Van Mastricht, *TPT*, 3:296.
44. Daniel J. Hill, "Union, Distinction and Creaturely Perfections: Petrus van Mastricht's Rejection of Deification," *Scottish Journal of Theology* 78 (2025): 200.
45. Van Mastricht, *TPT*, 3:417, see also 424–25.

cannot be considered inherent in created humanity, lest God be charged as being the author of sin.[46] This is an important point to which we will refer in chapter 9, on the corruption of humanity.

The sense of original righteousness as a "gift" is thus not meant to indicate that this was a superadded extra on top of human nature—it was a righteousness that was fitting for human nature, *concreated*, as it were, like health is to the human body. Hence, the fall did not consist in the loss of a superadded gift, but it consists in the distortion of created human nature itself and the loss of communion with God.[47] Van Mastricht, like Turretin, juxtaposes his position over against a Roman Catholic position: "The papists certainly acknowledge an original righteousness, but one which was not natural to man, but a supernatural gift, like a certain golden bridle, conferred upon natural man to restrain the conflict between the flesh and the spirit."[48] The claim that original righteousness is inherent to created human nature is important for at least two reasons then: (1) Created human nature is *good*, positively inclined toward God, such that concupiscence does not inflict humanity in the state of innocence; and (2) the fall into sin does not lead to a mere privation of some superadded bridle that was meant to constrain an inherently concupiscent human nature, but it leads to a corruption of nature itself.

The fourth and fifth conformities refer to immortality and the dominion of humanity over creation. The immortality Van Mastricht has in mind here is the created immortality before sin, emphasizing that human death came because of sin and that before sin there were neither internal nor external causes for sin. Humanity would have been confirmed unto perfect life had perfect obedience been offered to God. Human dominion is exemplified by the natural ability of created humanity to tame the rest of the creatures, by virtue of his nature (James 3:7), created as he is a little lower than the angels. Yet, like Turretin, Van Mastricht emphasizes that this dominion is so "under God, who conferred that dominion (cf. 1 Cor. 15:27–8)."[49]

Van Mastricht's discussion of the body-soul relation is congruent with his treatment of the image of God, as he emphasizes the unity between body and

46. Van Mastricht, *TPT*, 3:416–17. Of course, Van Mastricht affirms that the fall was still not outside the eternal decree of God (*TPT*, 3:418–19, 424–25).

47. Van Mastricht, *TPT*, 3:464.

48. Van Mastricht, *TPT*, 3:463–64.

49. Van Mastricht, *TPT*, 3:289.

soul.[50] The body is made fittingly to reflect humanity's stature over creation and its heavenly end, and the soul is a discrete substance, which, though subsisting by itself when separated from the body at death, is "incomplete" without the body.[51] The immateriality of the soul means that it can perceive immaterial things in an immaterial way, but it is an "incomplete substance, ordered to composition with a body, through which it is recognized to differ from the angelic essence."[52] Van Mastricht then adopts the Aristotelian depiction of the soul's vegetative, sensitive, and rational life, which, as we saw in chapter 4, refers to the operations of the soul tied to the unconscious workings of the body (vegetative), the senses (sensitive), and the abstract (rational).[53] The rational life consists of two faculties, the intellect and will, and though these witness to the immateriality of the soul, they remain connected to the body, as seen in the faculty of speaking. Van Mastricht understands affections as nothing but "acts of the will, although they also greatly depend upon the temperament of the humors, of bile, blood, and so forth, as well as upon the sensitive appetite."[54] Though, of course, he was relying on an outdated biology, these comments show that he was sensitive to the ways in which the body and soul impact each other.

Van Mastricht argues that the intimate union of body and soul, as depicted in the Scriptures, represents a view that contradicts the followers of Plato and Rene Descartes (1596–1650). Against Plato, the soul is not "the assisting form, like the captain of a ship . . . but the informing form, through which man is placed in and among this species of things."[55] Nor is the soul operative on just one specific part of the body, but rather "the whole soul is in each of its parts, because, since it is spiritual and invisible, it touches each of its parts."[56] Against Descartes, the soul is not a mere thinking thing over against the extended body. The soul rather animates the entire body. The body-soul relation is thus most intimate, more akin to light and air rather than a ghost

50. See also his discussion in Petrus van Mastricht, *Novitatum Cartesianum Gangrena* (Jansson-Waesburg, 1677), 419–25. This is against the Cartesian view, according to which the body simply refers to "extension" and soul refers to "thought."

51. Van Mastricht, *TPT*, 3:256.

52. Van Mastricht, *TPT*, 3:256.

53. Van Mastricht, *TPT*, 3:257.

54. Van Mastricht, *TPT*, 3:258.

55. Van Mastricht, *TPT*, 3:260.

56. Van Mastricht, *TPT*, 3:260.

in a machine, and yet their close relation does not negate that the soul was breathed by God into the body (Gen. 2:7) and is thus a distinct substance.[57]

Van Mastricht's section on the practical implications of humanity as created in God's image helpfully draws out the ethical imperatives that flow from this teaching and the redemptive-historical dimensions of considering humanity. The image calls forth three duties: (1) that we ought to love God in gratitude with our whole selves, (2) that we are mindful of ourselves that we should be imaging God and not some other standard, and (3) that we should love our neighbor with a love proper to who they are as image-bearers.[58]

Further, we should be mindful of our created dignity, deplore the loss of the qualities of image-bearing after the fall, and zealously seek our restoration. How might that restoration take place? Van Mastricht points to God as not merely the "primary efficient cause, according to his promises . . . and not only the efficient cause, but also the exemplary cause (Matt. 5:48)."[59] It is here that Van Mastricht is attentive to the importance that Christology plays for our doctrine of the image of God. While Van Mastricht has denied that humanity was made after the human nature of Christ ontologically speaking (as we have explored in chap. 1 as well), the Son remains the "archetype as well as the exemplar of this restoration" because he "is by his nature the most perfect photograph of the Father (Col. 1:15; Heb. 1:3)."[60] We receive the restoration that God offers when we pursue saving faith, by which we "receive and put on the essential and most perfect image of God, which is Christ (Gal. 3:27), and with him, as with the head, the trunk, the vine, and so forth, we are united, so that he dwells in us (Eph. 3:17), lives in us (Gal. 2:20), makes us like himself in his death and resurrection."[61] Believers ought thus to attend to Christ and his character: "We should look, I say, upon his virtues, his obedience (Phil. 2:8), his love (Eph. 5:2), his gentleness (1 Pet. 2:21, 23), and we should look upon them in such a way that we imitate them (Matt. 11:29)."[62]

For Van Mastricht, Christology is the restorative principle, norm, and exemplar for the qualities of the image of God, rather than the ontological

57. Van Mastricht, *TPT*, 3:260.
58. Van Mastricht, *TPT*, 3:303–4.
59. Van Mastricht, *TPT*, 3:306.
60. Van Mastricht, *TPT*, 3:306.
61. Van Mastricht, *TPT*, 3:306.
62. Van Mastricht, *TPT*, 3:306–7.

ground of the image. Christ was made to be like us in our human nature so that he might show us the qualities of righteous humanity. As I elaborate later, I suggest therefore that we were made after the image of the Triune God, and we are to live according to the norm of the incarnate Son of God, who himself showed perfect obedience to the moral law.[63]

Synopsis of a Purer Theology

A briefer witness from Reformed orthodoxy rounds off this chapter's survey. The Leiden Synopsis's discussion of the image of God and body-soul unity in disputation thirteen also includes the body in its definition of the image of God: "The whole man in both body and soul is 'created in the image of God and according to his likeness.'"[64] The disputation begins with a description of humanity as the sum "of everything and the bond that links earthly and heavenly things."[65] It then emphasizes: "By that we do not mean the body and the soul separately but something that is composed from both, that is from the rational soul and the body which a very tight and close bond binds together into one nature, united in one person."[66]

As the Synopsis describes humanity's dignity as the crown of all creation, it attends to the divine consultation prior to the fashioning of humanity in Genesis 1:26, taking the first person plural there as a reference to the Triune God: "The three persons of the Godhead are brought on to act together, since God says, 'Let us make man in our own image, according to our likeness.' This obviously indicates the plurality of the divine persons (Prov. 8:22–30; John 1:3; Job 33:4; Psalm 104:30)."[67] Thus humanity is a "close copy" of the Triune God himself.[68]

The disputation then attends to the creation of the body before the soul—it notes that the material of the earth (the dust) in itself could not form a body,

63. Cf. Bavinck, *RD*, 2:554–55.

64. *Synopsis of a Purer Theology: Latin Text and English Translation*, vol. 1, *Disputations 1–23*, ed. Dolf te Velde, trans. Riemer A. Faber (Brill, 2014), 329.

65. *Synopsis of a Purer Theology*, 1:315. The editors rightly note that this is alluding to the idea of humanity as a "microcosm," which made its way from Aristotle to Christian theology and will also appear in Bavinck.

66. *Synopsis of a Purer Theology*, 1:315.

67. *Synopsis of a Purer Theology*, 1:317.

68. *Synopsis of a Purer Theology*, 1:317.

but rather it was the power of God and his fashioning that produced a body fitting for a soul. The body's earthly material and the immediate fashioning of God testified to the simultaneous humility and dignity of human nature.[69] The soul, then, is breathed by God into the body as an efficient cause, showing itself to be a distinct, spiritual substance, and can persist without the body at death. Despite being of a distinct spiritual nature, the soul differs from the angelic beings as it "tends by nature to have a body."[70] Indeed, "without the body the soul is not entirely blessed, but it is fully happy only when it is united with the body. This is proof that the resurrection of the body is necessary for mankind's blessedness."[71]

Nevertheless, the disputation continues to emphasize the natural immortality of the soul, arguing that at least four reasons attest to its immortality: (1) that the soul directly comes from God and bears his image, (2) that the soul is simple and hence cannot be broken apart, (3) that the soul naturally knows God in an "implanted" way and is thus able to discern between good and evil, tending toward God as the soul's blessedness, and finally (4) that nearly all cultures attest to the belief in the soul's immortality.[72]

The Synopsis also offers a modest faculty psychology. The "seat" of the soul is what the Scriptures have called the "heart," in line with the "Peripatetics [Aristotelians] and Stoics."[73] The heart is the center of the soul and that which drives the two psychological faculties of the intellect and will; the soul "exercises its powers within the body, and in fact by means of its appropriate instruments, just as understanding is conducted through the brain. In essence, then, it is located in this specific part, but its workings are throughout the entire body."[74]

Created humanity was upright and good, displaying an "inner integrity" in "the soul, the body, the affections and actions and in the immortality of the whole man."[75] It had outstanding knowledge, and the will was free not only from coercion but also from the "necessity of sinning," aligned as it was with the will of God.[76] The disputation also seemed to presuppose the

69. *Synopsis of a Purer Theology*, 1:319.
70. *Synopsis of a Purer Theology*, 1:321.
71. *Synopsis of a Purer Theology*, 1:325.
72. *Synopsis of a Purer Theology*, 1:325–27.
73. *Synopsis of a Purer Theology*, 1:323.
74. *Synopsis of a Purer Theology*, 1:323.
75. *Synopsis of a Purer Theology*, 1:329.
76. *Synopsis of a Purer Theology*, 1:329.

distinction between the sensitive and rational appetite, and it mentions the proper aligning of the affections (being a function of the sensitive life of the soul) with the intellect and will (functions of the rational life of the soul).

Original righteousness consisted in this "harmony and consensual action of all the parts of the created man," gifted to the species in a manner that paralleled its "opposite"—that is, original sin.[77] It is from this conformity of the whole self to God that humanity was able to exercise proper dominion over the whole earth, and it is this righteousness, holiness, and knowledge that is restored to redeemed humanity by the Spirit.[78]

HERMAN BAVINCK ON THE IMAGE OF GOD

In this section, I expound Herman Bavinck's views on human nature and the image of God. I suggest that Bavinck's position synthesizes and clarifies the tradition that he receives and produces a holistic picture of the image of God and human ontology. As we shall see, he does this by observing that Scripture prompts readers to consider humanity organically, rather than mechanically. In an organism, he would argue, one observes a unity that animates the distinct parts of the whole—and Bavinck observes that humanity is organic in multiple dimensions. Humanity is organic in terms of the structure of its being (the body-soul relation), in terms of its proper function (original righteousness), and in terms of its corporate identity.

Bavinck's position, despite occasionally lacking some of the scholastic subtleties of the previous thinkers surveyed, presents several strengths in terms of synthesis and clarity. We have seen that the Reformed tradition sought to articulate a holistic account of the image of God, but Bavinck begins his sketch by indicating that human beings simply *are* image-bearers: "We must highlight, in accordance with Scripture and the Reformed confession, the idea that a human being does not *bear* or *have* the image of God but that he or she *is* the image of God."[79] Again: "The whole being, therefore, and not *something in man* but *man himself*, is the image of God."[80]

77. *Synopsis of a Purer Theology*, 1:331.
78. *Synopsis of a Purer Theology*, 1:331.
79. Bavinck, *RD*, 2:554 (emphasis original).
80. Bavinck, *RD*, 2:554 (emphasis original).

Two affirmations follow from the fact that human beings are image-bearers of God: that we are made in the image of the whole Triune God, and that the whole person is made in the image of God. With regard to the former, Bavinck notes that we image not one perfection or merely one person of the Triune God but rather the whole Godhead: "It is not something in God—one virtue or perfection or another to the exclusion of still others, nor one person—say, the Son to the exclusion of the Father and the Spirit—but that God himself, the entire deity, is the archetype of man."[81] Like Van Mastricht, Bavinck self-consciously denies making the incarnate Christ the ontological ground of the image of God in humanity, appealing to texts like Romans 8:3, Philippians 2:7–8, and Hebrews 2:14: "It has frequently been taught that man has specifically been made in the image of the Son or of the incarnate Christ, but there is nothing in Scripture that supports this notion."[82] The incarnate Son is thus the ethical norm, not the metaphysical foundation, for humanity.

Human beings are made in the image of the Triune God, and Christ is God made in human likeness.[83] If the Trinity is the archetype of humanity's ectypal shape, then, as we shall see, humanity has to be considered organically—the absolute unity-in-diversity in God analogically manifests itself in the human individual and as a corporate unity. As the archetype, God is the font, origin, and foundation for creation, and as the pinnacle of creation, humanity is related to God as an ectype or imprint of the divine being. Individual humans are organic unities, possessing bodies and souls, faculties, and ethical responsibilities driven by a united personality. Corporately, the entire human race is a single organism, together manifesting the image of God, united by a single federal head in Adam or Christ.[84]

Second, then, Bavinck emphasizes that nothing in a human being is excluded from the image. The caution with which Bavinck speaks about the "psychological exploration" of the image is a function of this affirmation.

---

81. Bavinck, *RD*, 2:554.

82. Bavinck, *RD*, 2:554–55. Recall Aquinas: "First, because as the Son is like to the Father by a likeness of essence, it would follow of necessity if man were made in likeness to the Son, that he is made to the likeness of the Father." Aquinas, *Summa Theologiae* I, q. 93, a. 5.

83. Bavinck, *RD*, 2:554–55.

84. As I show elsewhere, the claim that the organism of humanity is an ectype of the Triune God does not compromise but rather depends on classical affirmations of divine simplicity. See N. Gray Sutanto, *God and Knowledge: Herman Bavinck's Theological Epistemology* (Bloomsbury T&T Clark, 2020), chap. 2.

To identify strictly a capacity, function, or aspect of humanity as that which adumbrates (to use Van Mastricht's term) the Trinity is to risk excluding some group of human beings who might lack the presence or exercise of such capacities or functions. Prior to the cautious explorations of those adumbrations, then, Bavinck again reiterates pointing to humans as such, in a concrete sense and "in all conditions and relations," as made in the image of God:

> It follows from the doctrine of human creation in the image of God that this image extends to the whole person. Nothing in a human being is excluded from the image of God. While all creatures display *vestiges* of God, only a human being is the *image* of God. And he is such totally, in soul and body, in all his faculties and powers, in all conditions and relations. Man is the image of God because and insofar as he is truly human, and he is truly and essentially human because, and to the extent that, he is the image of God. Naturally, just as the cosmos is an organism and reveals God's attributes more clearly in some than in other creatures, so also in man as an organism the image of God comes out more clearly in one part than another, more in the soul than in the body, more in the ethical virtues than in the physical powers. None of this, however, detracts in the least from the truth that the whole person is the image of God. Scripture could not and should not speak of God in a human manner and transfer all human attributes to God, as if God had not first made totally in his own image. And it is the task of Christian theology to point out this image of God in man's being in its entirety.[85]

It is worth noticing that in Bavinck's description, the soul is not a "proper seat" of the image of God over against the body. Rather, Bavinck is implicitly utilizing a distinction between epistemology and metaphysics here—although the soul might display the image of God more clearly or most immediately, the body, no less than the soul, is metaphysically made in the image of God as well. The language of "organism" is also deployed to explain the place of the soul without denigrating the body. In Bavinck's theology, creation is organic precisely because it comes from a Triune God—if God is an absolute unity-in-diversity, three persons subsisting in one simple substance, then

85. Bavinck, *RD*, 2:555.

creation will fittingly reflect that unity-in-diversity in an analogical manner. An organism exhibits that ectypal unity-in-diversity, as organisms are made up of discrete parts that are animated by a single orienting life.[86] Consider a human body—one might pick out the heart or the brain in order to indicate an animating core, so to speak, of the whole, but it would not follow that the lungs or stomach are less a part of the body. So it is with the soul and the ethical virtues; we might point to these to indicate humanity's orientation toward God most immediately, but the body is still included in the image of God. God himself is described anthropomorphically and fittingly by way of the parts of the human body, the human soul tends toward a body, and the person, the soul's direction, is manifested in the body.

With these initial orienting comments in view, Bavinck then goes on to posit five features of created human ontology and the image of God.

The Human Soul

First, the image of God is indicated by way of the human soul. God breathed life into humanity such that it would become a living soul (Gen. 2:7). Bavinck reiterates that "soul" and "spirit" in Scripture are used interchangeably and are not meant to indicate a tripartite human being, divided between body, soul, and spirit. The words "soul" and "spirit," however, do highlight different aspects of the same substance: As spirit, humanity receives its life directly from God (unlike the animals), such that humanity could survive a separation from the body. Yet, as soul, that "spiritual component in him (unlike that of the angels) is adapted to and organized for a body and is bound, also for his intellectual and spiritual life, to the sensory and external faculties."[87] As such, the rational faculties are accessible, as it were, by way of and as connected to the sensory "because he is a sentient and material being and as such is related to the animals."[88] Like the Leiden Synopsis, Bavinck thus describes humanity as a sort of microcosm, a connecting link between the heavenly and the earthly: "He unites and reconciles

86. For more on the organic motif, see James Eglinton, *Trinity and Organism: Toward a New Reading of Herman Bavinck's Organic Motif* (Bloomsbury T&T Clark, 2010); Sutanto, *God and Knowledge*.

87. Bavinck, *RD*, 2:556.

88. Bavinck, *RD*, 2:556.

within himself both heaven and earth, things both invisible and visible."[89] As a spiritual being, humanity images God as the soul of man is immaterial, invisible, simple, one, and immortal, but as an embodied soul, he is connected to the earth. Nonetheless, the psychic and somatic aspects of humanity are made fitted for the spiritual, such that God himself becomes incarnate, and Scripture applies humanity's many psychosomatic functions to describe God.[90]

The Faculties of the Soul

Second, the structure and presence of the faculties of the soul reflect God: "In all these psychic capacities and activities of human beings we can see features of the image of God as well."[91] Bavinck offers a modest faculty psychology here (that he expands in the *Foundations of Psychology* and the *Triumph of the Soul*), which involves identifying the heart as the center of human personality, with two faculties: the intellect and will.[92] The heart, he argued, is "the *organ* of man's life. It is, first, the center of physical life but then also, in a metaphorical sense, the seat and fountain of man's entire psychic life, of emotions and passions, of desire and will, even of thinking and knowing."[93] Bavinck also refers to Augustine: "In the heart, mind, and will (*memoria, intellectus, voluntas*) Augustine even saw an analogy of the triune being of God."[94] But in a broader way than Augustine, Bavinck is suggesting that the unity of the faculties itself reflects the unity-in-diversity of the Triune God.

---

89. Bavinck, *RD*, 2:556. Again, on page 562: "Thus man forms a unity of the material and spiritual world, a mirror of the universe, a connecting link, compendium, the epitome of all of nature, a microcosm, and, precisely on that account, also the image and likeness of God."

90. In a later text, Bavinck signals his retrieval of Augustine's emphasis on the soul's proximity to God and doctrine of illumination: "He found there even, in the triad of *memoria, intellectus*, and *voluntas*, a reflection (*afdruk*) of the triune being of God. Augustine was the philosopher of self-examination, and in self-consciousness he discovered the starting-point of a new metaphysics." Bavinck, *Philosophy of Revelation*, 55. Bavinck argues that "The mind of man is indeed no *tabula rasa*, no empty form, but a totality of life from the very first moment of its existence. And when it becomes conscious of itself, this self-consciousness is not a mere formal apprehension of existence but always includes within it an apprehension of a peculiar nature, a particular quality of mind." *Philosophy of Revelation*, 55.

91. Bavinck, *RD*, 2:557.

92. For a further analysis of Bavinck's faculty psychology, see Sutanto, *God and Knowledge*, chap. 7; and Sutanto, *God and Humanity*, chap. 2.

93. Bavinck, *RD*, 2:556–57.

94. Bavinck, *RD*, 2:557.

Further, while the Reformed tradition displays diversity on the primacy of the will or intellect, Bavinck refused to identify one faculty of the soul as having primacy.[95] It follows, therefore, that the heart—or, as he would call it, the *personality*—animates the exercise of both the intellect and the will, which explains why each person is distinct from others.

Original Righteousness and the Image of God as Broad and Narrow

Third, Bavinck emphasizes the original righteousness of humanity, which refers to the proper exercise of the faculties of the soul, appealing to the language of Ephesians 4:24 and Colossians 3:10: "Man was not created as a neutral being with morally indifferent powers and potentialities, but immediately made physically and ethically mature, with knowledge in the mind, righteousness in the will, and holiness in the heart."[96] Created humanity was thus obedient toward God, despite being short of consummation and glory. As such, humanity was receptive of the communion and gifts of the Holy Spirit before the fall, which is the precondition of humanity's goodness. Indeed, that goodness is not "for a second conceivable without communion with God."[97] Bavinck clarifies that this pre-fall communion with the Spirit is distinct from the sort of indwelling that restored believers would come to have in Christ: "In the case of Adam, therefore, this indwelling was entirely natural. No truly good and perfect human being is even conceivable apart from the Holy Spirit."[98]

The communion of the Spirit envisioned here is thus also distinct from what Bavinck considers to be the mistake of Roman Catholic nature/supernature dualism, according to which original righteousness was a gift of supernature (*donum superadditum*) in order to constrain natural concupiscence—a "golden bridle," recall from the sections on Turretin and Van Mastricht. The conformity to God that Adam exhibited is humanity's natural state, and that conformity was concomitant to the indwelling and fellowship of the Spirit

95. See the 1921 work, which marks his mature position: Herman Bavinck, "The Primacy of the Intellect or the Will," in *Essays on Religion, Science, and Society*, ed. John Bolt, trans. Harry Boonstra and Gerrit Sheeres (Baker Academic, 2008), 199–204.

96. Bavinck, *RD*, 2:557–58.

97. Bavinck, *RD*, 2:558.

98. Bavinck, *RD*, 2:558.

that Adam was gifted by virtue of being created in the image of God. Adam was created in a positive relation to God, and there was no inherent tendency away from God in Adam's created nature.

It is in this context that Bavinck's discussion of the broad and narrow senses of the image of God should be understood. The broad sense of the image of God refers to the ontological makeup or structure of humanity, and the narrow sense refers to the proper orientation of the same. Prior to the fall, humanity possessed both the broad and narrow senses, but the narrow sense in a mutable way. After the fall, humanity retained the broad but lost the narrow. In restoration, then, humanity would regain the narrow sense, and in consummation, the narrow sense will be confirmed and perfected. In Bavinck's understanding, this distinction between the broad and narrow images is formed for two reasons: to do justice to Scripture and to counter the supernatural dualism of Rome. Concerning the first reason, Bavinck observes that Scripture continues to call humanity image-bearers, and thus all humans should be treated with dignity and respect (Gen. 5:1; 9:6; Acts 17:28; 1 Cor. 11:7; James 3:9), and yet the ethical direction and content of that image has been lost but is restored in Christ alone (Eph. 4:24; Col. 3:10). The language of broad and narrow is meant to account for that double way, of preservation and loss, in which Scripture speaks concerning humanity's image-bearing.

Concerning the second reason, Bavinck observes that righteousness is proper and integral for human nature as such: "The dispute concerned the question of whether that original righteousness was *natural* or, at least in part, *supernatural*. Reformed theologians asserted the former."[99] By way of contrast, "In Rome's view, a human being can lose the 'supernatural righteousness' and still be a good, true, complete, sinless human, with a natural justice that in its kind is without any defect."[100] The Reformed tradition, he clarifies, does not deny that original righteousness could be described as a gift, but it was a gift that was proper to the created natures of humanity. For instance, our health is a gift of God, but we would be sick, incapable of properly functioning, without it. Hence, like the loss of health, the loss of original righteousness results in a corrupted nature rather than a reversion to a natural state with an original propensity toward fleshliness. Indeed, the

99. Bavinck, *RD*, 2:551.
100. Bavinck, *RD*, 2:551.

post-fall human is "an abnormal, a sick, a spiritually dead human being, a sinner."[101] Bavinck would thus often charge that this Romanist dualistic anthropology is mechanical rather than organic. It was a mechanical anthropology because it depicts the loss of righteousness as a loss of an external reality, rather than the privation of something integral to human nature. Rather than the language of nature and super-nature, Bavinck preferred the distinction between the broad and the narrow to communicate the original righteousness of innocent humanity and the corruption that ensues from that loss.

Later on, Bavinck would argue that any rendering of fallen humanity that affirmed its capacity to do natural good without common grace and only denied that it had the capacity to discern supernatural good is still mired in dualistic thought: "The supernaturalist view is still at work here, the image of God stands alongside nature, is detached from it, and is above it. The loss of the image, which renders man totally deaf and blind in spiritual matters, still enables him in earthly matters to do much good and in a sense renders him independent from the grace of God in Christ."[102] By way of contrast, Reformed theology insists that sin has corrupted the whole man, including his natural capacities, so that redemptive grace would have significance not only for the sinner's access to supernatural goods but also for enabling proper functioning in the natural spheres: "The grace of God in Christ restores the whole person, and is of the greatest significance for his or her whole life and labor, also in the family, science, society, the state, art, science, and so forth."[103]

As we shall see later in chapters 7–9, what accounts for humanity's ability to do good in natural affairs, then, is not a stable natural state left intact after the fall but rather *common grace*. Bavinck's organic account of humanity's ontology and quality is one of his most enduring insights for a Reformed anthropology. Humanity was made to have fellowship with God, and man had this communion naturally in the state of innocence because he was made in the image of God. "Thus, also before the fall, a human being was the dwelling place of the entire holy Trinity, a most splendid temple of the Holy Spirit."[104]

101. Bavinck, *RD*, 2:551.
102. Bavinck, *RD*, 2:554.
103. Bavinck, *RD*, 2:554.
104. Bavinck, *RD*, 2:559.

Original righteousness, which sustains one's fellowship with God, is a natural, concreated gift, without which humans are corrupted, damaged, and broken.

The Body

"In the fourth place," Bavinck writes, "the human body belongs integrally to the image of God."[105] The starting point for his discussion of the body is yet again another resistance to dualism: "A philosophy that either does not know or rejects divine revelation always lapses into empiricism or rationalism, material or spiritualism. But Scripture reconciles the two."[106] Humanity's spirit is "psychically organized and must, by virtue of its nature, inhabit a body. It is of the essence of humanity to be corporeal and sentient."[107] Bavinck points to the fashioning of the body from the dust in Genesis 2:7 as having logical priority over the breath of life, for it was molded in order to be animated by that breath. As such, the body is not a prison, but a marvelous piece of art from the hand of God almighty, and just as constitutive for the essence of humanity as the soul.[108] Further, it is through the body that we serve God, and the body discloses the direction of the soul: "It is always the same soul that peers through the eyes, thinks through the brain, grasps with the hands, and walks with the feet. . . . It is one and the same life that flows throughout the body but operates and manifests itself in every organ in a manner peculiar to that organ."[109]

Bavinck sees this emphasis on the intimate union between soul and body, and the concomitant close connection between psychology and physiology, as marking an improvement from the past Christian deployments of Aristotelian anthropology for our doctrine of humanity. He makes this clear in his *Foundations of Psychology*: While he argues that analyzing the soul in terms of its rational, sensitive, and vegetative operations (as per chap. 4) does

105. Bavinck, *RD*, 2:559. On Bavinck and the body and the image of God, see also Isaac Whitney, "The Body and the Image of God in Bavinck and the Reformed Orthodox," *Scottish Journal of Theology* (2024): 1–12; and Jessica Joustra, "An Embodied *Imago Dei*: How Herman Bavinck's Understanding of the Image of God Can Help Inform Conversations on Race," *Journal of Reformed Theology* 11 (2017): 9–23.

106. Bavinck, *RD*, 2:559. This thought would serve well as a thesis for Bavinck's *Christian Worldview* (ed. and trans. N. Gray Sutanto, James Eglinton, and Cory Brock [Crossway, 2019]).

107. Bavinck, *RD*, 2:559.

108. Bavinck, *RD*, 2:559.

109. Bavinck, *RD*, 2:559.

connect the life of the soul with the body, and is to be preferred over other models offered in the nineteenth century, "the connection of soul and body and the bond between physiology and psychology are frequently absent."[110] In other words, Bavinck wants a fuller integration between body and soul and is unwilling to suggest that the rational soul is detached from the workings of organs of the body, which, in his perspective (whether rightly or wrongly), is characteristic of a Christianized Aristotelian hylomorphism: "The notions of a vegetative soul and a sensitive soul definitely take the body into account. But with the rational soul the body completely fades into the background."[111]

By way of contrast, then, Bavinck emphasizes that the soul's intellectual functions are never independent of the body and are in fact dependent on the brain as the soul's "bearer and organ."[112] Bavinck also gives due consideration to the phenomenon of the "unconscious," a marker of the intertwining of body and soul, which Helm agrees had not been recognized by the Reformed scholastics.[113] The connection of the rational soul with the brain prompts contemporary questions about the continuity of identity in the intermediate state, when the soul is separated from the body. For, if the operation of the rational soul is tethered to the brain as well, how would the rational soul survive the death of the body? While I do treat this question in a later chapter, Helm's observation that the tradition was not "too troubled with these particular problems of loss and continuing identity, having confidence in the power and purpose of God 'who raises the dead'" holds true, largely, for Bavinck as well.[114]

If one objects to the idea that the image includes the body due to the fact that God is incorporeal, Bavinck argues that Christian theology has always affirmed that the material world itself is considered a revelation of God, as God is its Creator. Further, the revelation of God is intensified and climactically disclosed in the incarnation of Jesus Christ—that God can assume

110. Herman Bavinck, "Foundations of Psychology," ed. John Bolt, trans. Jack Vanden Born, Nelson Kloosterman, John Bolt, *The Bavinck Review* 9 (2018): 26.

111. Bavinck, "Foundations of Psychology," 26 (emphasis added).

112. Bavinck, *RD*, 4:616.

113. See, e.g., Herman Bavinck, *Over het onbewuste: Wetenschappelijke samenkomst op 7 juli 1915* (Kirchner, 1915). An English translation is available at Herman Bavinck, "The Unconscious," in *Essays on Religion, Science, and Society*, ed. John Bolt, trans. Harry Boonstra and Gerrit Sheeres (Baker Academic, 2008), 175–98. Helm, *Human Nature*, 171.

114. Helm, *Human Nature*, 16.

human flesh is a decisive proof that the human body is essential to the image of God. "From the beginning creation was so arranged and human nature was immediately so created that it was amenable to and fit for the highest degree of conformity to God and for the most intimate indwelling of God."[115]

Implicit in Bavinck's discussion here is a denial that God could just assume any created thing unto himself—it is not fitting for God to assume trees or ants to himself, but it is proper for God to assume human nature in the incarnation. These other aspects of creation manifest vestiges of God (or, to use Aquinas's term, traces of God), but only human nature is the image of God.[116] "God could not have been able to become man if he had not first made man in his own image."[117] The body was teleologically oriented toward immortality in its innocent state, and it was only sin that tore asunder the organic union between soul and body.

Finally, Bavinck argues that the embodied human has several strengths over the disembodied angels. Humans are connected to the earth and to one another by blood and ethical relations in a way that angels cannot be, and thus humans can be united together under a federal representative, such that they can be redeemed by that representative after they have fallen. For Bavinck, human physicality is not a detrimental weakness of our nature that makes us inferior to the angels but actually enriches human existence with a complex web of relations of which angels know little. Furthermore, because humans are the recipients of God's redemption, angels do not experience the full range of benefits from God.[118]

Paradise and Representation

Fifth, Bavinck argues (albeit in merely a single paragraph) that humanity's habitation in paradise is indicative of image-bearing. Blessedness and holiness go together, and so do the spiritual and the physical. The actions of humanity impact its environment, which explains why fallen humanity

---

115. Bavinck, *RD*, 2:560.

116. Though we cannot develop this point here, I suggest that Bavinck's discussion would complement the older discussions on specific obediential potency and the image of God. See Steven A. Long "*Creation ad Imaginem Dei:* The Obediential Potency of the Human Person to Grace and Glory," *Nova et Vetera* 14 (2016): 1175–92.

117. Bavinck, *RD*, 2:560.

118. Bavinck, *RD*, 2:461–63.

dwells on a cursed earth.[119] If humanity is the link between heaven and earth, and is a microcosm of the whole of nature, then it represents nature in all of its being and actions. As the "micro-divine-being," humanity represents God as prophet, priest, and king over creation, and its actions affect and are affected by its environment. Bavinck draws from the language of Genesis 3:17 and Romans 8:19–20. The sin of humanity leads to a cursed ground, and the redemption of humanity is tied to the redemption of the cosmos. No other creature is imbued with such representative responsibility, and that representative function is another indication of humanity's identity as image-bearers.

Humanity's Organic Shape: Corporate and Covenantal

Drawing from the older tradition on the necessity of the diversity of creation in order to reflect the glory of an infinite God, Bavinck argues that the creation of humankind had a teleological orientation. If humanity is made in the image of an infinite God, the infinite perfections of God could be imaged (however faintly) only by way of a multitude of human beings, glorifying God side by side. This explains why it was not good for Adam to be alone, and so the woman was created, and why they were called to be fruitful and to multiply:

> The creation of humankind in God's image was only completed on the sixth day, when God created both man and woman in union with each other . . . in his image. Still, even this creation in God's image of man and woman in conjunction is not the end but the beginning of God's journey with mankind. It is not good that the man should be alone (Gen. 2:18); nor is it good that the man and woman should be alone. Upon the two of them God immediately pronounced the blessing of multiplication (Gen. 1:28). Not the man alone, nor the man and woman together, but only the whole of humanity is the fully developed image of God, his children, his offspring. The image of God is much too rich for it to be fully realized in a single human being, however richly gifted that human being may be. It can only be somewhat unfolded in its depth and riches in a humanity counting billions of members.[120]

119. Bavinck, *RD*, 2:561.
120. Bavinck, *RD*, 2:577.

The next chapter will tease out more fully the rich implications of this important paragraph, especially as it relates to the call of dominion and the cultural mandate. For now, notice that the image of God refers not merely to the individual human being but also corporately to all of humanity considered together. Interpreted in this way, the social nature of humanity therefore stems from its triune makeup. As humankind multiplies, so does the image of God develop. Here, Bavinck applies the language of organism to humanity considered as that corporate whole—each member of humanity plays a vital part of the whole organism: "So also that humanity in turn is to be conceived as an organism that, precisely as such, is finally the fully developed image of God."[121]

Recall that an organism requires not merely a diversity of members but also a united center. The election of a federal head, who represents the whole, is thus required for the organism to be considered *as* a single entity, a unity-in-diversity: "Only humanity in its entirety—as one complete organism, summed up under a single head, spread out over the whole earth, as prophet proclaiming the truth of God, as priest dedicating itself to God, as ruler controlling the earth and the whole of creation—only it is the fully finished image, the most telling and striking likeness of God."[122]

The election of Adam as the federal representative of the human race, therefore, was no mere or arbitrary legal fiction, but it was fitting, given humanity's organic and triune shape. If human beings are made in the image of the Triune God, then Adam's federal headship is the ethical center of humanity's corporate and organic unity. "Humanity cannot be conceived as a completed organism unless it is united and epitomized in one head. In the covenant of grace Christ has that position, and he is the head of the church; in the covenant of works, that position is occupied by Adam."[123] The ties that bind together the organism are not merely physical then (for humans, like other animals, are tied together by blood), but ethical. In other words, animals are tied by blood but are not ethical. Angels are ethical beings but are not tied together (such that when an angel falls into sin, no other angel is implicated in that fall). Ethical relations are constitutive for human ontology.

121. Bavinck, *RD*, 2:577.
122. Bavinck, *RD*, 2:577.
123. Bavinck, *RD*, 2:578.

Personality

That humanity is an organism indicates, however, that each human being is still a distinct individual, not enveloped into that corporate whole as a drop of water into an ocean. The importance of the individuality of each human being emerges in the language of "personality," which shows up in a key way in Bavinck's argument for creationism over traducianism (a debate that we will explore further below). To provide a rough definition for now, creationism argues that God creates an immortal soul directly as each human being comes to existence at the moment of conception, whereas traducianism argues that the soul is propagated naturally from the parents to the child.

The presence of a soul is that which distinguishes a human being personally: "The moment an immortal spiritual soul dwells in an organism, there exists a human being, an individual, a personality, be it only germinally."[124] Bavinck, as we shall see, preferred creationism over traducianism, because the former respects the mystery of personality while maintaining humanity's physical connection to the entire race. If humanity is a single organism, each individual is still a concrete person, and the individual's personality is not elided by the connection with the whole. Creationism "upholds the unity of humanity and at the same time it respects the mystery of the individual personality. Every human being, while a member of the body of humanity as a whole, is at the same time a unique idea of God, with a significance and destiny that is eternal."[125]

When this discussion is put into the backdrop of the rest of Bavinck's writings, the importance of personality for the image of God becomes clearer. In his *Foundations of Psychology*, one of the critiques that Bavinck registers against the Christian-Aristotelian accounts of human nature that one might find in the older Reformed scholastics is that "the unity of psychic life and the mutual relationship of these three psychic activities [rational, sensitive, vegetative] are not adequately emphasized."[126] Later on, he argues that a presentation of the different faculties of the soul, of the intellect and will,

124. Bavinck, *RD*, 2:583.
125. Bavinck, *RD*, 2:587.
126. Bavinck, "Foundations of Psychology," 25.

would describe merely that which every human being has in common and would not yet pinpoint the distinctness of each individual: "There is therefore a subject that stands above all representations, all phenomena of feeling and willing, a subject that possesses all of them and that to a certain extent, governs them."[127]

These are generative comments indeed. A properly Trinitarian theological anthropology should thus do justice to the organic makeup of human nature and the organic unity of corporate humanity, but it should also consider the distinctness of each individual, as each displays a unique personality. A Christian theological anthropology holds together both the corporate and personal dimensions of human existence.

Let us take stock. Herman Bavinck draws from the traditioned discussions, as witnessed from our survey of the confessional material, Turretin, Van Mastricht, and the Leiden Synopsis. Like them, Bavinck affirmed an integral view of the body-soul unity and an attentiveness to faculty psychology, and he affirmed that original righteousness was inherent to humanity's creation as made in God's image. However, we also see some clarifying remarks. On the body-soul relation, Bavinck wants a more integrated unity, not merely including the body in the definition of the *imago Dei*, but he also develops and critiques Christian-Aristotelian faculty psychology for describing the rational life of the soul in ways that seem to detach it from the body. On original righteousness, Bavinck distinguishes between a broad and narrow sense of the image of God: Created humanity possessed both a broad (ontological) and narrow (qualitative) sense of the image but lost the narrow sense after the fall. This allows Bavinck to articulate clearly in what ways humanity had retained and lost the image of God due to sin, and how the grace of regeneration renews it. Crucially, Bavinck also argues that the *imago Dei* does not just have an individual referent, but it also refers to the whole of humanity considered organically together, which gives his theological anthropology an inherently covenantal and teleological orientation. The importance of personality then complements this corporate recognition to preserve the integrity of the individual as a distinct member of that organic whole.

127. Bavinck, "Foundations of Psychology," 98.

CREATIONISM AND TRADUCIANISM

Before moving on to some summative propositions, we should consider the debate between creationism and traducianism in more detail. Creationism refers to the view that God creates the soul at the moment of conception without any preexisting material, whereas traducianism refers to the view that the souls are propagated and transmitted from the parents to the child. The nature of propagation for the traducian view, Turretin clarifies, is not a mere physical one: "The soul is propagated by the soul, not by a decision and partition of the paternal soul, but in a spiritual manner, as light is kindled by light (so Balthasar Meisner and most Lutherans)."[128] Hence, Van Mastricht clarifies that the debate is about whether God creates each soul immediately or mediately. Furthermore, he emphasizes that, with respect to the creationist position, God is the efficient and not material cause of the soul—God does not create the soul out of his own substance.[129] If God were the material cause of the soul, then God would be divisible, mutable, and a part of him could be transferred over to humanity, making them human. Creationism holds, therefore, that God is the efficient cause of the soul in a direct sense.

Bavinck offers a bit more charity to traducianism than Van Mastricht, arguing that "in the strength of their arguments traducianism and creationism are almost equal," though, as we saw, he ultimately opted for creationism due to its ability to preserve the special care of God for each individual, the distinct character of the soul, and the soul's connection with the body along with the mystery of personality.[130] Further, Bavinck notes that "Eastern Orthodox, Roman Catholic, and Reformed theologians almost unanimously embraced the former view [Creationism], while the latter found acceptance only among the Lutherans."[131] Let me synthesize some common biblical-theological and philosophical reasons found in the Reformed tradition for creationism over traducianism.

First, Genesis 2:7 is taken as a "law of creation." What is stated there is not merely a historical recording of what took place for Adam's creation but

128. Francis Turretin, *Institutes of Elenctic Theology*, vol. 1, *First Through Tenth Topics*, ed. James T. Dennison, trans. George Musgrave Giger (P&R, 1992), 477.

129. Van Mastricht, *TPT*, 3:261.

130. Bavinck, *RD*, 2:581.

131. Bavinck, *RD*, 2:584.

is a type of the creation of each human individual. At conception, then, God breathes a new, immortal soul into each body. What is propagated, therefore, is not the soul from parent to child, but rather the body that is fitted for that soul. Hence, Genesis 2:24 records Adam proclaiming that Eve was flesh of his flesh, not soul of his soul.

Second, Scripture often nominates God as the one who is the giver of the soul. The Reformed theologians appeal to the following passages with regularity: "And the dust returns to the earth as it was, and the spirit returns to God who gave it" (Eccles. 12:7); "The oracle of the word of the LORD concerning Israel: Thus declares the LORD, who stretched out the heavens and founded the earth and formed the spirit of man within him" (Zech. 12:1). Indeed, God is referred to as the "Father of spirits/souls" (Num. 16:22; Job 38:28; Isa. 57:16; Heb. 12:9; 1 Pet. 4:19). Concomitant with this, the biblical passages utilized to refer to humanity's propagation from past generations (e.g., Gen. 2:23; 46:26; 1 Cor. 11:8; Heb. 7:9–10) refer to our bodies rather than our souls.

Third, the soul is immaterial and hence simple and indivisible, but traducianism seems to materialize the soul, making it diffusible, transferable, and divisible. If the souls of children are derived from their parents, one might ask the question: Is the whole soul transferred, or just a part? If the whole, then the parents would lose life; if a part, then the soul is divisible and hence material, and really no different substantially from the physical body.[132]

Bavinck thus argued that traducianism is thrown into a two-horned dilemma—it either falls back to materialism or leaps into creationism.[133] Traducianism lapses into materialism because it implies that the soul is a by-product of semen and egg, emerging out of purely physical material. How would we account for the essential difference, then, between the physical and the spiritual within the human being? On the other hand, it smuggles in creationism, because the semen and the egg form a fetus and "God gave to the sperm and the ovum the *capacity*, on being united, to produce a soul that neither of them had prior to the union but that is still spiritual and immortal, then we are actually dealing with another form of creationism."[134] If the soul

132. Turretin, *Institutes of Elenctic Theology*, 1:480.
133. Bavinck, *RD*, 2:583.
134. Bavinck, *RD*, 2:582 (emphasis original).

suddenly emerges mysteriously, in other words, upon the commingling of sperm and egg, then this is precisely the sort of mystery that creationism preserves.

Fourth, Van Mastricht observes that one of the most potent reasons in support of traducianism is the transmission of sin: "By the help of hereditary transmission, the propagation of original sin can be explained more easily. For it neither occurs through the body, nor can it occur through the soul, apart from hereditary transmission."[135] Bavinck, however, responds to this reason persuasively by arguing that such an explanation presupposes sin as a material substance, but this is a mistaken understanding of sin: "Traducianism cannot help resolve [the hereditary transmission of original sin] because sin is not material, not a substance, but a moral quality, moral guilt, and moral corruption."[136] It is true that the soul, after the fall, is created by God "not from above or outside, but under the conditions of, and amid, the sin-nexus that oppresses the human race," such that original sin and not original righteousness is now transmitted unto humanity. However, physical heredity alone cannot explain that transmission because what is transmitted is not a material substance.[137] The propagation of sin by way of imitation and physical influence are symptoms, rather than explanations, of the spread of original sin.

Finally, as Bavinck argued, creationism preserves the uniqueness of humanity and the individual while still tethering them to the rest of creation and the organic whole of the human race. It preserves the uniqueness of humanity as opposed to angels and the material world: Unlike angels, the immaterial soul is fitted for a body and we are bound by our bodily and blood-relations, and unlike the animals, human beings are imbued with the life-giving breath of God and made in his image (Gen. 2:7). Because God is the cause of each soul, creationism preserves the individual personality, even as each personality shares a relational bond with organic humanity.

135. Van Mastricht, *TPT*, 3:276.

136. Bavinck, *RD*, 2:581. Van Mastricht (like Bavinck) would not deny, however, that seminal transmission could physically incline a person "toward this or that actual sin." *TPT*, 3:475.

137. Bavinck, *RD*, 2:584. Original sin and the propagation of sin will be treated further in another chapter.

CONCLUSION

This chapter has offered a representative sampling of the Reformed tradition on human nature and the image of God. From Turretin, Van Mastricht, and the Leiden Synopsis, we have seen that the Reformed tradition was sensitive to the integral connection between the body and soul, humanity's original righteousness as concreated with Adam, and the vocational responsibilities of human beings as religious creatures before God. We have also seen that the late-modern theologian Herman Bavinck would take those insights and develop them into an organic anthropology, arguing that the image of God refers not just to human individuals as body-soul unities, but also to the corporate whole of the human race. Chapters 4 and 5 thus serve as a historical-theological presentation of a Reformed-catholic theological anthropology, and the next chapter offers a dogmatic synthesis that advances the implications of this anthropology in ways that anticipate chapters 7–9 on corporate humanity, original sin, corruption, and redemption.

FURTHER READING

Helm, Paul. *Human Nature from Calvin to Edwards*. Reformation Heritage Books, 2018. Though Helm's seemingly ad hoc selection of thinkers and topics in this book makes it less accessible than others, it is still worthwhile reading to get a sense of the range of debates on theological anthropology in the Reformed tradition between Calvin and Edwards.

Lapine, Matthew. *The Logic of the Body: Retrieving Theological Psychology*. Lexham, 2020. A good introduction to faculty psychology and the importance of seeing the connection of the body and the soul in the broader Catholic and Reformed traditions.

Sutanto, N. Gray. *God and Humanity: Herman Bavinck and Theological Epistemology*. Bloomsbury T&T Clark, 2024. This work was written for those seeking a deeper treatment of the contours and implications of Bavinck's theological anthropology, especially in relation to topics such as affect theory, the cognitive science of religion, race, and corporate humanity.

6

HUMAN NATURE AND THE IMAGE OF GOD

A DOGMATIC SYNTHESIS

WITH A HISTORICAL-THEOLOGICAL presentation of a Reformed-catholic account of theological anthropology in view, I suggest six dogmatic propositions that synthesize the insights of the last two chapters on human nature and the image of God. These, in turn, will inform the initial theses at the end of the book and the chapters that follow on corporate humanity, original sin, corruption, and redemption.

First, *all human beings are made in the image of the Triune God*. As witnessed in chapters 4 and 5, human beings are made in the image of the whole Triune God, and that image manifests itself in the properties and unity-in-diversity of the soul, the propriety of the body for the inhabiting of that soul, communion with God and incarnation, the unity-in-diversity of the human race, original righteousness, and personality. This does not mean that we cannot retain the insight from Herman Ridderbos that the Son of God is the archetypal image, but it does highlight that the Son is that archetypal image in his *divine* nature, whereas the Son's *human* nature was made in the likeness of our human nature (as we discussed in chaps. 1, 4, and 5).[1] As Augustine and

1. Herman Ridderbos, *Paul: An Outline of His Theology*, trans. John Richard De Witt (Eerdmans, 1997), 68–85.

Aquinas argued, recall, "Because as the Son is like to the Father by a likeness of essence, it would follow of necessity if man were made in likeness to the Son, that he is made to the likeness of the Father."[2] Human beings image the whole Triune God in both a corporate and individual sense. Further, and as we shall revisit when we treat the topic of sex and gender in chapter 10, we image the Triune God as we are creators and yet dependent, birthed, begetters, and receivers.

The distinction between personality as an individuating principle and a common human nature demonstrates the importance of affirming both corporate connectedness and individual uniqueness. In other words, describing the common human nature all persons have does not yet exhaust the individual, who has a unique personality. That personality inheres in our human nature, but each person is formed in conscious and unconscious ways by a myriad of unique features: physiological genetics, nurture and upbringing, cultural location and experiences, and the unique creation of God. Each individual is thus distinct, in possession of incommunicable properties that make them the kind of personality that they are. "If we say that someone is a person, we are saying that he or she is someone, a unique Individual; and this cannot be understood as the chance implication of one predicate, or even of an ensemble of predicates."[3] As Steven Duby has noted, a person is "the principle which acts," and a nature is that "by which" a person acts.[4] *Who* we are is delimited by *what* we are, though *what* we are does not exhaust *who* we are.

Bavinck applies this important principle on personality to the older theme of the imitation of Christ. Although each Christian is called to be an imitator and a disciple of Christ, that imitation does not take the shape of uniformity. Christ's person is too rich to be imitated in every way by any single Christian, and each apostle or disciple is represented in Scripture to follow Christ in distinct ways, each preserving their own personality. John remains personally distinct from Peter, and Peter from Paul, and Paul from

2. Thomas Aquinas, *Summa Theologiae*, trans. Fathers of the Dominican Province (1920), 1. q. 93 a 5.

3. Robert Spaemann, *Persons: The Difference Between "Someone" and "Something,"* trans. Oliver O' Donovan (Oxford University Press, 2017), 39.

4. Steven Duby, *Jesus and the God of Classical Theism* (Baker Academic, 2022), 86.

Barnabas.[5] Jesus does not call us to be like anyone else, and he calls us to obey him in our own distinct, personal ways.

It is important to emphasize Bavinck's insistence that human beings *as such*, concretely, are the image of God and possess all of these qualities and dignities. He refuses to isolate a capacity or to identify one particular human culture or behavior that exemplifies the image. Indeed, the Reformed tradition refuses to choose between substantial, vocational, and relational aspects of the image and argues that each should be considered holistically together under the image of God. If humans beings are made in the image, one cannot isolate one property of the human as the locus of the image: The whole person *is* made in the image of God. Such a claim is consistent with Ryan Peterson's argument that "the abilities and attributes of human existence are subordinate to human identity [as made in the image of God]."[6] While it is true that some in history have misused and abused the substantial or structural aspect of the image of God to denigrate one group or other, such prejudiced attitudes are in principle excluded by the doctrine. Indeed, the doctrine of the image of God indicates that all human beings share a dignified human nature that determines their intrinsic worth, and this nature remains stable regardless of the differences we see in the actualization of mental, physical, or relational capacities: "In other words, the contingencies of human existence and functioning are dependent on a stable image furnishing the worth of each individual human being."[7]

To say it another way, the fact and presence of the image of God is identified with every human being *as human*, despite the "contingencies" of each human being. We are not dignified because of some instrumental value that we bring to the table, nor is our dignity dependent on achievement or merit—human existence *in itself* is good. As noted in chapter 1, the Aristotelian distinction between potency and actuality is helpful here—each human being is birthed with the powers of the soul and body, fitted for righteousness and fellowship with God and each other, whether or not one actualizes or exercises those

5. For more on this, see N. Gray Sutanto, *God and Humanity: Herman Bavinck and Theological Anthropology* (Bloomsbury T&T Clark, 2024), esp. chap. 5.

6. Ryan S. Peterson, *The Imago Dei as Human Identity: A Theological Interpretation* (Eisenbrauns, 2016), 17, see also 36.

7. Joshua Ryan Farris, *An Introduction to Theological Anthropology: Humans, Both Creaturely and Divine* (Baker Academic, 2020), 86–87.

capacities, and is as such an image-bearer. Those capacities may not be actualized in the right way, and that actualization might well be hampered by physical and fallen conditions in the present life, but, as Harriet Harris puts it, "to be a person is to have certain capacities whether or not these are realized."[8] The Bible's description of our common origin as specially created by God is a foundational bedrock for the fundamental equality of each person. It follows, therefore, that people of all ethnicities, of varying cognitive actualities, and of both sexes are ontologically equal, dignified, created, and loved as image-bearers.

To identify human beings as image-bearers of God means that human beings are intrinsically religious creatures. We were created to glorify God and enjoy him forever (Westminster Shorter Catechism, Q&A 1). We are signs that point to our Maker, and we are created to worship (Eccles. 3:11). If we do not worship God, we will end up worshiping something else (Rom. 1:18–23), with disastrous consequences. True religion, therefore, is not about developing a particular set of habits or beliefs that are peripheral to what we are, but it is about aligning with the proper telos of our creation. To be a Christian, as Bavinck argues, is to become properly human as we seek to align ourselves with human nature's meaning and end.[9]

Second, *attending to the image of God includes affirming humanity's ontology, including the soul's immateriality, immortality, and faculties of intellect and will. An ontology of the embodied human soul is presupposed as the precondition for the self's ethical direction, function, and relationality*. All of the Reformed representatives surveyed above were attentive to the biblical-theological connotations of the image of God and were drawn precisely toward metaphysical considerations rather than away from them.

To say it another way, the Bible prompts us toward deep descriptions of what we are, not just what we are called to do.

Indeed, in contrast to the metaphysical skepticism emblematic of the "relational turn" discussed at the beginning of chapter 5, while Reformed theologians regularly issued warnings against excessive speculation on the metaphysics of the soul, they affirmed a modest and broad outline of a faculty

8. Harriett A. Harris, "Should We Say That Personhood Is Relational?," *Scottish Journal of Theology* 51 (1998): 234.

9. Herman Bavinck, *Christianity and Science*, trans. and ed. N. Gray Sutanto, James Eglinton, and Cory C. Brock (Crossway, 2023), 203.

psychology and the ontology of the soul and did not think that such considerations were hindrances but rather complementary to understanding humanity's relation to God and one another. This includes attending to the simplicity and immateriality of the soul, even while distinguishing that simplicity from the absolute (omni-modal) simplicity of God; the immortality of the soul, as seen in life everlasting, whether in damnation or blessedness, and in the hope of resurrection (which signifies an immortality that is shared with the body); and the relation of will and intellect (and unconscious affects), along with their unity in the heart.

As such, the contemporary tendency to bifurcate identity and ontology when discussing the image of God is quite alien to Bavinck and the earlier Reformed orthodox tradition.[10] There is little we can say about what human beings are called to do and the relationships we are called to have if we fail to have a good grasp on what we are.

Third, *the image of God includes the body, as shown in its created goodness, dependence, and fittingness for the soul such that it discloses our personality, in its fittingness for the incarnation, and in God's commitment to its resurrection*. This emphasis on the goodness of the body and the involvement of the body as disclosing who we are in God's image is worth emphasizing, given the modern tendency (in an almost gnostic fashion) to see the body as an impediment to human flourishing.

On one level, as we have seen, creation, incarnation, and resurrection are the threads that indicate the intrinsic *goodness* of the body. God considers human beings as psychosomatic unities, and this composition is *good*. There is no denigration of the material order, as the soul is fitting for the body and the Son himself becomes incarnate fittingly in a human body. Though we will explore this further in a later chapter, this also means that

10. Richard Lints's otherwise helpful work on a biblical theology of human identity still exemplifies that tendency: "The language of the *imago Dei* draws attention away from ontological accounts of human identity toward theological accounts. Human identity is in view rather than human nature." Richard Lints, *Identity and Idolatry: The Image of God and Its Inversion* (IVP Academic, 2015), 23. Likewise, I demur when Michael Horton juxtaposes "metaphysics" from the "narrative-ethical" when he says that "the image of God in humankind is itself official rather than essential; ethical rather than ontological; eschatological rather than metaphysical." Michael Horton, "Image and Office: Human Personhood and the Covenant," in *Personal Identity in Theological Perspective*, ed. Richard Lints, Michael S. Horton, and Mark R. Talbot (Eerdmans, 2006), as included in Marc Cortez and Michael P. Jensen, eds., *T&T Clark Reader in Theological Anthropology* (Bloomsbury T&T Clark, 2018), 127.

the sexual difference between male and female, and their inherent biological and personal complementarity, is *good*. "Sexual difference is not a mishap, but cause for celebration and wonder. The difference is *good*, our bodies are *good*."[11]

On another level, our bodies remind us of our intrinsic finitude: that we are *image* and not God himself, and hence we are dependent creatures and have a metaphysical and moral reference point outside of ourselves. Bodies require sleep, food, shelter, and care, and remind us that the Sabbath is made for humanity and not for God. Sabbath rest points us toward the God we need for our flourishing and ongoing existence, thus directing us away from ourselves. As Christa McKirland has indicated, humans have God as their constitutive need, but this is not a denigration of who we are but rather our dignity, for we are the sort of creatures—image-bearers—who are naturally opened up, as it were, for a second-personal relationship with God.[12] Morally, Philip Ziegler has pointed to Bavinck's embodied holism to remind us that what we do with our bodies, therefore, matters theologically:

> The inclusion of the *body* within the understanding of the *imago dei* . . . suggests that consideration of its form and use and modification is a matter of properly theological concern, and not something that could be adjudged to be simply *adiaphorous*. Reformed theology can never be indifferent to what is done and with the body as the body itself is at stake in the inalienable human vocation to bear out the image of God in creaturely life.[13]

What we do with our bodies is a *theological* and *moral* issue because God has called us to represent him *through* our bodies.

Furthermore, the close union between souls and bodies indicates that bodies disclose the *personhood* and that our relationships are mediated by bodies. As Favale has emphasized in the form of a principle drawn from John Paul II: "*The body reveals the person*."[14] Each person is incommunicable, and that uniqueness is disclosed by way of the body. Males and females point to one

11. Abigale Favale, *Genesis of Gender: A Christian Theory* (Ignatius, 2022), 40 (emphasis original).
12. Christa McKirland, *God's Provision, Humanity's Need: The Gift of Our Dependence* (Baker Academic, 2022).
13. Philip Ziegler, "'Those He Also Glorified': Some Reformed Perspectives on Human Nature and Destiny," *Studies in Christian Ethics* 32 (2019): 169 (emphasis original).
14. Favale, *Genesis of Gender*, 40 (emphasis original).

another in integral reciprocity, and relationships are strengthened by way of caring for one another's bodies in sharing food, drink, and shelter, and as we communicate with our words through mouths that speak and facial expressions without words. "Our bodies simultaneously proclaim our individual personhood and our capacity for relation."[15] Bodies and personality go together—we are persons in flesh and embodied persons.[16] If the body is not a prison-house of the soul but manifests who we are, when confronted with a living body, we are not just encountering a mass of flesh that is subject to our own interpretation, but rather we are encountering *someone* (signified by our recognition of the face) with a nature that was ordered by God himself.[17] We shall revisit this theme on the recognized meaning of our bodies in chapter 10, which addresses gender and sexuality.

The body's close relation to the soul thus also points to the importance of attending to the body in matters of sin and sanctification. The body (which includes the formation of the brain) impacts our cognitive and conscious lives, and sin often impacts us in ways that precede our conscious attention.[18] We are often much worse than our beliefs.[19] God sanctifies us as the Spirit disciplines our embodied habits. Simeon Zahl has shown by a theological deployment of affect theory that we become what our bodies attend to, as we are molded not just by the doctrine we believe or articulate but also by our social location and everyday existence.[20] Bodies mirror one another in entrainment, and so our communities shape who we become. Discipleship thus involves liturgical habituation as much as belief formation.

Our bodies thus inflect the virtues that humans are called to pursue. Wisdom, righteousness, and holiness are learned through our embodiment. Humans have blood and ethical bonds, and they are morally responsible for one

---

15. Favale, *Genesis of Gender*, 41.

16. J. Budziszewski, *On the Meaning of Sex* (Intercollegiate Studies Institute, 2014).

17. Julián Marías, *Metaphysical Anthropology: The Empirical Structure of Human Life*, trans. Francis M. López Morllias (Pennsylvania State University Press, 1971), 148.

18. See N. Gray Sutanto, *A Sense of the Divine: An Affective Model of General Revelation from the Reformed Tradition* (Cambridge University Press, 2025).

19. For more on the embodied and psychical affects of sin, see Sutanto, *God and Humanity*, chaps. 3–4.

20. Simeon Zahl, *The Holy Spirit and Christian Experience* (Oxford University Press, 2021).

another in ways that cannot be replicated by immaterial creatures, whether angels or artificial intelligence.[21]

Humans are thus also the beneficiaries of God's redemptive purposes, as they are able to be represented by Christ, who is incarnate in human nature. The incarnation and resurrection witness to the body's importance. As we saw in Herman Bavinck, God takes on *human flesh*, not an ant's or a rock's, as fitting to himself. Christ's resurrected human body also guarantees the resurrection of our bodies, as God is committed to consummate our human natures.

Fourth, *the result of Adam's first sin is the loss of original righteousness, and Christ's human nature is the exemplar for the restored and sanctified image of God.* Sin and the desire to sin are consequences of the fall, and they are ethical deformations of human nature rather than an inherent concupiscence within human nature as such. The fall, therefore, does not result in the mere loss of a *donum superadditum*—a superadded gift above nature that left human nature intact—but rather leads to the distortion of human nature itself and the loss of communion with God. That distortion, however, does not mean that human beings have lost the broad sense of the image of God (ontology) but rather the narrow sense of the image, desiring created things over God, ignoring the law of God, and thus acting contrary to right knowledge. Human beings continue to be image-bearers, just as a broken mirror is still a mirror or as a dying tree remains a tree. The fallen desires (concupiscence) that we have, therefore, are features of our corruption and are illicit rather than functions of an intact nature that lacks the bridle of supernatural gifts.

The place of Christology, and specifically of Christ's righteousness as exemplified in his embodied human character, is in pointing us to the norm of human living. The divine Son is the eternally begotten image of God, and his eternal Sonship means he fittingly assumed a human nature in our likeness as a son of Adam and lived that human life as the second Adam in perfect obedience to the law of God. He shows us the perfect human being who images God

21. While a full-orbed treatment of artificial intelligence and human nature must await another work (especially as AI continues to morph and develop), it is important to note that AI can only imitate personhood but never participate in it. AI cannot be said to embody wisdom, righteousness, or holiness—it cannot, for instance, pray, become morally accountable, or forgive and be forgiven. For some helpful initial theological work on AI, see Ximian Xu, *The Digitalised Image of God: Artificial Intelligence, Liturgy, and Ethics* (Routledge, 2025).

in knowledge, righteousness, and holiness (Col. 3:10; Eph. 4:24). As humans imitate Christ and follow the law by the Spirit, we are being conformed to that image once again. Sanctified and perfected human beings are therefore image-bearers not merely ontologically but also morally and consummately. The saints of the church triumphant in heaven live consistently with who they are.

Fifth, *the vocation of stewarding and cultivating creation is essential to who humans are as image-bearers of God.* Image-bearers are culture makers. As they are embedded within their natural environment and are time-bound creatures, humanity will cultivate nature in order to live. The commandment to be fruitful and multiply is thus not arbitrary but fitting given humanity's natural design, and thus culture was always meant to be God-directed, for humanity's culture-making was supposed to represent God's own creativity. This representation is analogical, for humanity is dependent on God's order and design and has to work according to the grain of nature in cultivating it. Humans work with preexisting nature, whose meaning is given to them by God, whereas God creates out of nothing and imbues all things with meaning. As we shall see in the next chapter, therefore, the so-called cultural mandate is not an added extra but merely the vocational dimension of what it means to be God's image-bearer. We are to exercise cultivation because humans *will*, de facto, represent God in their everyday lives, whether poorly or properly.

It was the fall that enabled the separation between culture and true religion. While humanity was supposed to have true religion as the animating principle behind all of its labor, fallen humanity erects a culture against God. The fall therefore inaugurated the antithesis between those who would create a culture that seeks to glorify God and those who seek a culture that is against God. The former culture will now be produced by way of the Spirit's work in regeneration through the church's witness, whereas the latter is a culture produced by nature alone. It is, as we shall see, the reality of common grace that suspends the culmination of the spiritual antithesis between those in Adam and those in Christ.

Finally, *the image of God refers to humanity as a single, corporate whole and thus has a teleological orientation.* As Bavinck has shown, because human beings are finite and the Triune God is infinite, only a diverse and manifold humanity can adequately image God. Humanity's dispersion and multiplication is thus the unfolding of the image of God, as each individual and community occupies a different time and place, representing God in their complementary ways across the globe. This corporate understanding of the image of God thus renders the cultural mandate fitting to who we are and has significant implications for understanding the relation between gender and race with the image (as we shall see in chaps. 10 and 11). The image thus has an eschatological dimension: The gospel restores image-bearers so that they can once again represent God well, and in the last day, consummate humanity will dwell with God bodily. The next chapter dives into this corporate account of the image in more detail as it considers the cultural mandate and the Great Commission in theological context.

CONCLUSION

Because all discussions of sin, grace, and ethics presuppose theological metaphysics, this chapter has sought to encapsulate a Reformed-catholic account of human nature and the image of God presented in chapters 4 and 5. I presuppose and advance these dogmatic propositions—on the meaning of image-bearing, the soul, the body, the loss of original righteousness, the normativity of Christ's obedience, the cultural mandate, and the corporate character and telos of humanity—in granular ways in the following chapters.

FURTHER READING

Van Mastricht, Petrus. *Theoretical-Practical Theology*, vol. 3, *The Works of God and the Fall of Man*. Reformation Heritage Books, 2021. This is the volume where Van Mastricht treats the subjects of human nature and the image of God, including discussions on the close (hylomorphic) relation of the body and soul, the meaning of the image of God, and the practical implications of these teachings. We are merely seeing the beginnings of the translation projects on the Reformed scholastics, and I suggest that Van Mastricht is the best starting point for beginning to read them as he covers the exegetical, dogmatic, and practical dimensions of each theological topic he treats.

Farris, Joshua Ryan. *An Introduction to Theological Anthropology: Humans, Both Creaturely and Divine*. Baker Academic, 2020. A thorough and systematic introduction to a broadly Reformed anthropology, though with more of a Cartesian accent in some chapters.

Webster, John. "The Human Person." In *The Cambridge Companion to Post-Modern Theology*, edited by Kevin Vanhoozer. Cambridge University Press, 2003. Webster argues in persuasive ways that a description of human ontology is necessary for a robust understanding of a human person, especially as a response to deconstructive postmodernism.

Bavinck, Herman. *Biblical and Religious Psychology*. Translated by Herman Hanko. Edited by Gregory Parker Jr. Reformed Free, 2023. Bavinck's mature yet accessible treatment of theological anthropology, covering not only the biblical material but also its empirical dimensions.

Cooper, John. *Biblical Anthropology and the Monism-Dualism Debate*. Eerdmans, 2000. One of the best defenses of a biblical dualist model of the body-soul relation. Cooper combines with biblical depth and historical-theological rigor.

7

THE CULTURAL MANDATE AND ORGANIC HUMANITY

HUMAN VOCATION IN CREATION, FALL, AND REDEMPTION

HUMANITY'S ORGANIC CHARACTER means that the whole individual is the image of God. But would a single individual suffice to image God? And how would that image-bearing function relate to the call to exercise proper dominion over creation? Bavinck describes the dogmatic logic:

> [The *imago Dei*] can only be somewhat unfolded in its depth and riches in a humanity counting billions of members. Just as the traces of God (*vestigia Dei*) are spread over many, many works, in both space and time, so also the image of God can only be displayed in all its dimensions and characteristic features in a humanity whose members exist both successively . . . and contemporaneously side by side.[1]

If God is infinite, then only a diversity of creatures can reflect his glory. If humanity is the image of God, therefore, then only humanity considered as a corporate whole can adequately reflect him.

An earlier version of this chapter was published in N. Gray Sutanto, "Cultural Mandate and the Image of God: Human Vocation Under Creation, Fall, and Redemption," *Themelios* 48 (2023): 592–604.

1. Bavinck, *RD*, 2:577.

The mandate given to humanity to be fruitful and multiply (Gen. 1:28), as we have seen in chapter 1, calls for humanity to spread out across the earth. A proper, God-given dominion is intrinsic to who humans are as image-bearers. As human beings disperse throughout the globe, God's image is represented throughout as well. The creation of humanity, then, invokes a telos—a diverse humanity dispersed yet united by a single representative, a federal head in Adam. Just as the Trinity comprises an absolute unity-in-diversity, humanity, too, will manifest an analogical and organic unity-in-diversity, not only in their individual makeup (in body and soul and original righteousness, as explored in the previous chapters) but also as a corporate whole. This chapter explores this vocation and calling to be "fruitful and multiply" and to "fill the earth and subdue it" from a theological perspective, addressing the relationship between creation and culture, as well as the cultural mandate after the fall and the gospel, while the next chapter more fully explores Adam's covenant headship, the ethical unity that undergirds humanity's organic character.

"FRUITFUL AND MULTIPLY"—CULTURAL MANDATE AND THE IMAGE OF GOD

There are two aspects to the cultural mandate in the state of innocence: the task of begetting and the organic multiplication of people, and the task of forming a diversity of cultures.[2] Embedded in the creation of humanity, therefore, is a teleological orientation—humanity was meant to spread and cultivate creation in obedience to their God, and no one community can possibly reflect the richness of the image: "The image of God is much too rich for it to be realized in a single race, ethnic group, or culture."[3]

The call of the cultural mandate therefore fittingly corresponds to the proper dominion that image-bearers of God are supposed to have over creation, and it is recognized by more contemporary thinkers as the "vocational" aspect of the image of God.[4] God gave the tasks of work and cultivation before

---

2. This is not to reduce marriage to procreation, and after the fall, the Great Commission is intrinsic for Christian obedience to the cultural mandate.

3. Irwyn Ince, *The Beautiful Community: Unity, Diversity, and the Church at Its Best* (InterVarsity, 2020), 57.

4. This aspect is recognized by the vocational perspective on the image of God in contemporary theology. Cf. Lucy Peppiatt, *Imago Dei: Humanity Made in the Image of God* (Cascade Books, 2022), 27–45.

the fall, showing the inherent goodness of human labor in culture-making. To be "fruitful and multiply" refers to the natural multiplication of human beings and the work that cultivates nature for their own good, in accordance with God's command.

As image-bearers labor in obedience to the mandate, William Edgar aptly describes this work as an exercise of "analogous power" that was given to human beings from God, including the "development of agriculture, the arts, economics, family dynamics, and everything that contributes to human flourishing."[5] These tasks are reflections of the calling to steward creation in ways that imitate God. Recall that Psalm 104:14–15 situates human work as parallel with and yet dependent on God's work. God causes the "livestock" and "plants" to grow so that humans might make "wine" and "bread" to gladden their hearts. To put it in theological terms: God creates *ex nihilo* while humans create *ex natura*. God speaks and nature comes to be, but humanity, in an analogous fashion, creates out of the preexisting natural material that God gives. Dominion, therefore, refers to this human cultivation of the natural world, going with the grain of God's design.

Human dominion is thus one of stewardship, displaying simultaneously both humanity's dignity and servitude before God. J. H. Bavinck says it this way:

> We, the human race, are predestined to fulfil a distinctive calling in that history; as humanity, we are assigned an exceptional place in the greater context of the kingdom from the very first. We are simultaneously *subjects* and to some extent *co-rulers*, viceroys over certain regions. Not everything is subjected to us: we are not given authority over the course of the stars and the planets or the tides of the never-resting seas. But the earth and its plants and animals have been assigned to us, given for us to rule over and to use for God's service, to fathom and understand creation's hidden powers, and so to bring to full development the innate possibilities of creation.

5. William Edgar, *Created and Creating: A Biblical Theology of Culture* (IVP Academic, 2016), 168. Bavinck says it this way: "And this dominion of the earth includes not only the most ancient callings of men, such as hunting and fishing, agriculture and stock-raising, but also the trade and commerce, finance and credit, the exploitation of mines and mountains, science and art." Herman Bavinck, *Wonderful Works of God*, trans. Henry Zylstra (Westminster Seminary Press, 2020), 189.

> That is the meaning of the cultural calling allotted to us immediately after creation (Gen. 1:28–29).[6]

This sense of culture-making as the interplay between nature and human cultivation, as humanity images God analogously, corresponds well with Henry Van Til's classic work *The Calvinistic Conception of Culture*. There, he defines culture as the "secondary environment" that humanity builds out of the primary environment of God's creation: "In this book I use the term ["culture"] to designate that activity of human, the image-bearer of God, by which he fulfills the creation mandate to cultivate the earth, to have dominion over it and to subdue it. The term is also applied to the result of that activity, namely, *the secondary environment which has been superimposed upon nature by man's creative effort*."[7]

To cultivate creation well therefore involves discerning God's design for creation—culture-making can easily deform into hubris and abuse when we determine for ourselves what we ought to make out of the natural world. Herman Bavinck thus warns that any fulfilling of the earthly vocation should be situated within the context of obedience to the word of God. This is signified by the conjunction of the command to be fruitful and multiply with the prohibition against eating of the tree of the knowledge of good and evil. The former denotes humanity's responsibility toward earth, and the latter toward heaven—but both together are needed for humanity to accomplish either task well. Both tasks, Bavinck argues, are really one, for "man can fulfill this calling over against the earth only if he does not break the bond of connection which unites him with heaven, only if he continues to believe God at his word and to obey his commandment. The twofold task is essentially therefore one task."[8] Our religious orientation animates and informs our horizontal acts of cultivation.

---

6. Johan Bavinck, *Between the Beginning and the End: A Radical Kingdom Vision*, trans. Bert Hielema (Eerdmans, 2014), 29–30.

7. Henry R. Van Til, *The Calvinistic Concept of Culture* (Presbyterian and Reformed, 1959), 7 (emphasis added).

8. Bavinck, *Wonderful Works*, 169. As Turretin tersely puts it: "Man was made by God to acknowledge and worship his Creator and to exercise dominion over the other creatures." Francis Turretin, *Institutes of Elenctic Theology*, vol. 1, *First Through Tenth Topics*, ed. James T. Dennison, trans. George Musgrave Giger (P&R, 1992), 1:468.

To put it another way, cultivating the earth is a great good, but without obedience to God's word, humans will not only abuse their proper vice-regency but also will lose the highest good, which is God himself. Proper earthly dominion requires and presupposes true religion. Earthly and heavenly vocations comprise a singular holistic calling: "Work and rest, rule and service, earthly and heavenly vocation, civilization and religion, culture and *cultus*, these pairs go together from the very beginning."[9] If religion should animate humanity's work, then the dominion that image-bearers have over creation is not merely kingly but priestly—the cultural mandate is at once also a heavenly mandate, as that vertical relation with God determines how humans represent God on earth. Our kingly work of cultivation thus presupposes that we are called as priests as well: "As priests of creation, humanity has the function and privilege to assist the creation to realize and evidence its rational order and beauty and thus to express God's beauty and being back to God."[10]

The obedience to the word of God and Adam's responsibility to convey that word to Eve and his progeny also testifies to humanity's prophetic role. Adam knew God's word, and it is by obedience to that word, communicating it and transmitting it, that humanity recognizes the meaning of creation.

CULTURAL MANDATE, THE FALL, AND COMMON GRACE

We shall consider the doctrine of original sin in greater detail in the next chapter. For now, it is important to recall that humanity did not remain in their original state of righteousness. Humanity sinned against God by listening to the temptations of the serpent and ate of the tree of the knowledge of good and evil. Because of this first sin, corruption and guilt now qualify human nature (Gen. 3:1–19). God, however, was gracious to humanity and did not leave them to decay in the gratification of the corrupted flesh, and we see God's mercies not only to Adam and Eve, supplying them with animal clothing, but also to the line of the murderous Cain, allowing them to develop culture (Gen. 4:17–26). This preservation of Cain shows that, despite the fall, God allows humanity

9. Bavinck, *Wonderful Works*, 169.

10. Joshua Ryan Farris, *An Introduction to Theological Anthropology: Humans, Both Creaturely and Divine* (Baker Academic, 2020), 196.

to continue to cultivate creation organically and by nature. However, the true religion that is meant to animate that work is no longer present. To use a neo-Calvinistic distinction, human structures continue to develop, but their directions are no longer for God.[11] Because human beings are made in the image of God, fallen image-bearers will continue unwittingly to represent him as they form families, farm, develop technology, raise shelter, inhabit cities, and so on. The fall, however, means that these earthly tasks are now divorced from the heavenly, and so we misuse and misunderstand our place in the created order and dwell in cultures that are in principle against God. Further, the created order now resists that work, such that human labor is often difficult, fatiguing, and even seemingly futile, as the book of Ecclesiastes indicates.

The presence and development of culture presupposes that fallen image-bearers continue to retain some relative virtue, as culture-making requires a measure of peace, truth-telling, cooperation, trust, and so on. As such, the production of culture in the post-fall order is indicative of the presence of God's common grace: his delayed judgment of sinners, his commitment to the goodness of creation and human work, and his refusal to give sinners over to their deepest impulses. Romans 1:24, 26, and 28, it is important to note, show that God *gives us over* to our sinful desires in wrath, which entails that, in his mercy, he restrains our vices. Common grace refers to his gifting of epistemic, moral, and life-giving goods to sinful creatures.

Bavinck refers to James 1:17 and describes the gifts of common grace as quite all-encompassing, including all human culture and the stability of the natural world. He specifically attributes to common grace the "continued existence of" the possibility of sinners seeing clearly God's general revelation (Rom. 1:19), "the labor of man and the fertility of the woman" (Gen. 3:19–20), the development of culture (Gen. 4:20–22), the Noachian covenant (Gen. 8:21–22), the faithfulness of the natural order, the forbidding of murder (Gen. 9:5–6), the dispersion of humanity after Babel (Gen. 11:8), the reaping of the fruits of our labor (Matt. 5:45; Acts 14:16–7), and ongoing morality.[12] "All these are due to

---

11. See Herman Bavinck, *Philosophy of Revelation: A New Annotated Edition*, ed. Cory Brock and N. Gray Sutanto (Hendrickson, 2018), 201; Al Wolters, *Creation Regained: Biblical Basics for a Reformational Worldview* (Eerdmans, 2005). See also Jonathan Chaplin, *Faith in Democracy: Framing Politics of Deep Diversity* (SCM, 2021).

12. Herman Bavinck, *Guidebook for Instruction in the Christian Religion*, ed. and trans. Gregory Parker Jr. and Cameron Clausing (Hendrickson, 2022), 46.

common grace in connection and in service of special grace. In a word, 'every good gift and perfect gift is from above, coming down from the Father of lights, with whom there is no variation or shadow due to change (James 1:17).'"[13] In sum, after the fall, common grace is the precondition for the stability of society, allowing for image-bearers to enjoy peace temporally with varying degrees, for them to perceive the moral order and the character of God that is requisite for that peace, for them to labor and make families that form the seeds of culture, and for some relative control over culture despite the consequences of the fall. Recall, also, the discussion in chapter 3 on God's preservation of the family line of Cain in Genesis 4 and 5 and the Tower of Babel narrative in Genesis 11. Despite the misuse of culture against God, God continues to remain committed to the dispersal and cultivation of human culture.

It helps, therefore, to see the cultural mandate not as some special command, an added extra that has little to do with human nature. Rather, the cultural mandate corresponds to the proper dominion given to humans as constitutive of who they are as image-bearers. In other words, despite the fall, because human beings remain ontologically image-bearers, they continue to form families, labor, and thus develop culture. What Herman Bavinck says in the context of the formation of higher learning is also relevant for the relation between human nature and culture as such: All of the "sciences rest especially on the inner intuition of the soul, on the deepest conviction, on the nobility of our human nature, on the majesty of the subject. . . . And only so can science, not in place of but alongside religion, be of benefit to humanity if it recognizes the human being's reasonable and moral nature and builds upon this in faith."[14] One fails to account for the possibility of culture without an appeal to God's good gifts.

As Augustine argued, unregenerate sinners thus form fallen civilizations: the earthly manifestation of the city of man. This is the default situation of every person after the fall: "When these two cities began to run their course by a series of deaths and births, the citizen of this world was the first-born, and after him the stranger in this world, the citizen of the city of God, predestinated by grace, elected by grace, by grace a stranger below,

13. Bavinck, *Guidebook*, 46.

14. Herman Bavinck, *Christianity and Science*, trans. and ed. N. Gray Sutanto, James Eglinton, and Cory C. Brock (Crossway, 2023), 150.

and by grace a citizen above."[15] In a way that anticipates our discussion of redemption in chapter 9, Augustine here is forming the conceptual basis for the later neo-Calvinist idea of the antithesis. Cultures will continue to exist, but now culture will be divided up into two—one that is animated by the love for man as primary, and the other that is animated by the love for God. The city of man, in the fallen order, comes first temporally, and out of that city, God regenerates some in order that they would become citizens of the city of God. Though the fulfillment of that city comes only in the resurrected order, the love for God animates those citizens such that they form a new kind of culture on earth.

The citizen of the city of God, therefore, who lives her earthly life and labors under the principle of her heavenly citizenship, is made such by grace:

> By grace, for so far as regards himself he is sprung from the same mass, all of which is condemned in its origin; but God, like a potter (for this comparison is introduced by the apostle judiciously, and not without thought), of the same lump made one vessel to honor, another to dishonor. But first the vessel to dishonor was made, and after it another to honor. For in each individual, as I have already said, there is first of all that which is reprobate, that from which we must begin, but in which we need not necessarily remain afterwards is that which is well approved, to which we may be advancing attain, and in which, when we have reached it, we may abide. Not indeed, that every wicked man shall be good, but that no one will be good who was not first of all wicked; but the sooner any one becomes a good man, the more speedily does he receive this title, and abolish the old name in the new.[16]

To put it in more Bavinckian parlance: By common grace, unregenerate culture is sustained, but by special grace—the proclamation of the gospel, the sanctifying work of the Spirit, and the communion of the church—the elect are regenerated unto a new culture and are thus animated by the vision of the kingdom of God.

15. Augustine, *City of God*, trans. Marcus Dods (Random House, 1993), 15.1.
16. Augustine, *City of God*, 15.1.

COMMON GRACE AND CULTURAL MANDATE: COMPLEMENTARY OR ALTERNATIVES?

At this point, we should pause and consider a potential objection from second-generation neo-Calvinist Klaas Schilder (1890–1952). Schilder is credited as the author who coined the term "cultural mandate" to refer to Adam's vocation in the garden.[17] Indeed, Schilder describes Adam as an office-bearer, "God's fellow-worker," whose cultural labors were so integrated with his worship of God that it could be "immediately and constantly be called 'liturgy,' i.e. ministry in and for the kingdom."[18] Like Herman and Johan Bavinck, Schilder also continues the emphasis that humans are to image God by rendering "productive the 'possibilities' that were put into the created world and that were later to be discovered by humanity and respected according to their 'kind'—they would take out of the world all that it has in it."[19] He connects this creational imperative to Jesus's parable of the talents (Matt. 25:14–30) and the responsibility of the laborers to steward them well.

As laborers are called in the covenant of works to fill and multiply, they are advancing creation toward its telos:

> When God created the world, this was God's wise intent. It did not please him to create the world ready-made. He only created it good. The world, then, as it came forth from God's hands, was a world-in-promise, a world-in-hope; and as long as it was good, this hope could not be called vain. . . . The world of Paradise was a beginning. And in the beginning was given, in principle, everything that had to be there potentially in order to let it develop into a completed world of perfect order, the *polis*, the *civitas*, the

---

17. Klaas Schilder, *Christ and Culture*, trans. Williem Helder and Albert H. Oosterhoff (Lucerna, 2016), 78. Although, as we saw, Herman Bavinck has already spoken of a "mandate" given to Adam in Genesis, to have dominion and to obtain heaven. In another place, Bavinck argued, "The Reformation restores to culture its freedom and independence. The right of cultures is expressed in the mandate [in Genesis 1:28]. . . . Culture exists because God bestowed on us the power to exercise rule over the earth." Bavinck, "The Kingdom of God, the Highest Good," trans. Nelson D. Kloosterman, *The Bavinck Review* 2 (2011): 161. For more on Schilder, see Marinus de Jong, "The Church Is the Means, the World Is the End: The Development of Klaas Schilder's Thought on the Relationship Between the Church and the World" (PhD thesis, Kampen Theological University, 2019).

18. Schilder, *Christ and Culture*, 59–60.

19. Schilder, *Christ and Culture*, 68, see also 77.

> "city" (state) of God, as it was paradisally designed and would later be built.[20]

This trajectory depicts a consummate world under the lordship of God, and as such, it would be a mistake to wedge a separation between "culture" and "religion." Like Bavinck, Schilder thus argues that the liturgical and the "secular" were one task.

The entrance of sin separates the work of culture from religion, and the trajectory of unity-in-diversity that would have characterized culture as humanity multiplies devolves into cacophony, as individuals are motivated not by love of God and neighbor but of self. While culture should preserve a natural multiformity, "Satan makes use of these distinctions to bring about separation."[21] The moral law might restrain human rebellion, but left to themselves, sinners would eradicate that law for the sake of autonomy.

Given all of these neo-Calvinistic and positive views on culture, then, it is perhaps surprising to see that Schilder explicitly rejects the doctrine of common grace, especially when one considers that common grace is usually *the* doctrine that Kuyper and Bavinck point to in order to ground an uncompromisingly theological engagement with culture post-fall.

Schilder objects to common grace for at least three reasons. First, he argues that theologians mistakenly attribute to common grace what should properly be attributed to nature. The restraint of sin and the enjoyment of culture and life-giving goods are intrinsic to nature and time. If humanity bears the image of God, and they are creatures of time, then they will naturally develop culture and enjoy its fruits: "Consequently, the fact that the gifts of creation blossom and expand is a matter not of grace but of nature."[22]

The fall, then, does not mean that humans would cease to form culture—for they are time-bound and naturally culture makers, and "continuation of time after the Fall . . . is not grace."[23] Rather, the fall merely produces cultures that are no longer considered "religious labor" but acts "of egoism, of self-preservation, of zest for living . . . not service to God but self-service."[24]

20. Schilder, *Christ and Culture*, 74–75.
21. Schilder, *Christ and Culture*, 82.
22. Schilder, *Christ and Culture*, 89.
23. Schilder, *Christ and Culture*, 90.
24. Schilder, *Christ and Culture*, 89.

Second, Schilder argues that describing the enjoyment of culture post-fall as "grace" is a misnomer because the postlapsarian situation also displays a common judgment, insofar as the grace of regeneration is not poured out without limit. So, if the postlapsarian situation in general is "grace," then it is as much "judgment": "Whoever calls the restraining of the curse 'grace' should at least call the 'restraining' of the blessing 'judgment.'"[25] As such, it is unhelpful to call the universal condition of life after the fall a matter of "grace" or "judgment," Schilder argues—they are uninformative at best and misleading at worst. It's better, instead, simply to argue that sinners will continue to build culture, but a culture that is divorced from service of God.

The natural development of culture is thus not a matter of grace or judgment but is the *precondition* of grace and judgment, the canvas on which the antithesis between regenerate and unregenerate is lived out, as it were. Grace refers to regeneration, and the regenerate will produce religious, God-directed culture. Judgment refers to the ungodly, as those under the curse who create culture against God. Schilder adjudicates tersely: "There is no universal (or general) grace for all people. Therefore Abraham Kuyper's construct was erroneous."[26]

Finally, Schilder distinguishes between common grace and the cultural mandate, preferring the latter over the former in order to motivate Christian cultural activity. In his judgment, "common grace" is an "anthropocentric" doctrine, for it focuses on what is *permissible* for Christians to partake in after the fall and also on the remnants of goodness after sin.[27] Instead, by focusing on a "common command" and a "common mandate," one takes the point of departure from God, focusing on his intention in creation itself prior to the fall, thus motivating Christian activity without bestowing undue optimism toward non-Christian culture.[28] In effect, Schilder is setting up the cultural mandate as an alternative to the doctrine of common grace.[29]

25. Schilder, *Christ and Culture*, 88.

26. Schilder, *Christ and Culture*, 92. Hence, Jochem Douma observes that for Schilder, "Only when something promotes eternal salvation can we truly speak of grace." *Common Grace in Kuyper, Schilder, and Calvin: Exposition, Composition, and Evaluation*, trans. Albert H. Oosterhoff, ed. William Helder (Lucerna, 2017), xi.

27. Schilder, *Christ and Culture*, 145.

28. Schilder, *Christ and Culture*, 145.

29. In a milder earlier treatment, Schilder posits the alternatives this way: "It is better to choose one's position, one's point of view in the discussion [of Christian engagement with

Schilder's *Christ and Culture* is a penetrating biblical theology of culture, but his critique of common grace is unpersuasive, for his three arguments here overlook certain questions that the doctrine of common grace seeks to address.

First, though we may grant that sinners will continue to build culture naturally, it is surely a matter of God's general benevolence that sinners would continue to enjoy the fruits of their labor, would not be successful in their attempts at eradicating the moral law known in their hearts, and would, even in their tendency toward egoist self-preservation, relatively enjoy friendships with their neighbor. So long as this is the time of God's patience (2 Pet. 3:9), which delays the final judgment, and so long as God is not in wrath giving us "over" to our natural desires (Rom. 1:24, 26, 28), we are enjoying God's active benevolence in his gifting us with moral, epistemic, and life-giving goods such that a temporal, relative peace can be enjoyed.[30] Common grace is thus juxtaposed not against nature but against sin: It is that which grounds and accounts for the relative access that sinful humanity has with the true, good, and beautiful. "From the fall onward, human life and humanity itself is not simply grounded in the order of creation. . . . The fruit of common grace—being allowed to retain something of what we by nature possessed by Adam, is a gift of grace."[31]

Second, though I agree that nature and culture form the backdrop for the antithesis, common grace addresses the question of why it is that, despite the antithesis, regenerate and unregenerate alike can still enjoy relative peace with one another. Surely, this is because the regenerate are not as sanctified as they could be (as we imperfectly obey God and still wrestle with the presence of sin), and it is because the unregenerate are not as evil as they could be and often still exhibit virtue (albeit by borrowed capital, for "the Holy Spirit is the author of life, of every power and virtue").[32] In the last day, the antithesis will

culture], *not in the idea of common grace, but in the Reformed idea of office.*" Klaas Schilder, "Culture and Common Grace," in *The Klaas Schilder Reader: The Essential Theological Writings*, ed. George Harinck, Marinus de Jong, and Richard Mouw, trans. Albert Gootjes and Albert Oosterhoff (Lexham, 2022), 151 (emphasis original).

30. For more on common grace in Kuyper and Bavinck, see Cory C. Brock and N. Gray Sutanto, *Neo-Calvinism: A Theological Introduction* (Lexham, 2023), chap. 8.

31. Herman Bavinck, *Reformed Ethics*, vol. 1, *Created, Fallen, and Converted Humanity*, ed. and trans. John Bolt (Baker Academic, 2019), 149.

32. Herman Bavinck, "Common Grace," trans. Raymond van Leeuwen, *Calvin Theological Journal* (1989): 41.

be eschatologically realized, such that the elect and non-elect will no longer inhabit the same culture together.[33] In other words, while we can concede that nature is the canvas for the antithesis, common grace explains why it is that the antithesis often exists merely in principle and not in practice. Schilder himself articulates these emphases using different terms—such as "common temperance" and *synousia*, "a being together"—that still characterize elect and non-elect alike in the present redemptive-historical order.[34] Hence, though he rejects "common grace" as a term, he still accepts it conceptually.

Far from downplaying the antithesis between belief and unbelief, then, common grace actually *presupposes* the antithesis and does not make sense without it. Without the antithesis, common grace is a superfluous doctrine, hanging in the air, as it were. As Kuyper argued, common grace corresponds to the Reformed emphasis on the radical doctrine of sin that Calvinism has taught:

> If we see in sin a cause of spiritual and physical weakening, but not a deadly quick-acting poison that if unrestrained immediately leads to spiritual, temporal, and eternal death, then there is certainly no restraining of sin—a conclusion to which Calvin was the first to point, and on which the entire doctrine of common grace is built. This is why the Reformed confession has continuously placed full emphasis on the deadly character of sin and has seriously combated any weakening of the concept of sin.[35]

Indeed, the doctrine of common grace allows Kuyper to (1) sketch a world-and-life view that pushes the church outward to participate within every sphere of life (2) without compromising the radical confession that the unregenerate world is totally depraved apart from grace.[36] Thus, I suggest that common grace and the cultural mandate ought to be seen not as alternatives but as complementary: Common grace is the ground for the possibility of the cultural mandate, and it is the reason why Christian and non-Christian culture can coexist relatively before the final judgment. Further, common

33. In an earlier essay, Schilder noted that he did not want to reject common grace in itself, but that, on the question of Christian engagement with culture, common grace was the wrong doctrine from which to "take our point of departure." "Culture and Common Grace," 152.

34. Schilder, *Christ and Culture*, 109–12.

35. Abraham Kuyper, *Common Grace*, vol. 1, *God's Gifts for a Fallen World*, trans. Nelson D. Kloosterman and Ed M. van der Maas, ed. Jordan Ballor (Lexham, 2015), 1:299–300.

36. This line is drawn from Brock and Sutanto, *Neo-Calvinism*, 25.

grace is not anthropocentric, nor does it give undue optimism toward non-Christian culture. Rather, given that common grace presupposes the antithesis and the radical depravity of the sinner, the doctrine highlights that unbelieving cultures always live on borrowed capital, as it is the Spirit of God himself who enables them to enjoy gifts, truth, and goodness—the very Spirit of God whom unbelieving cultures deny.

THE GOSPEL AND THE CULTURAL MANDATE

Schilder's warning recognizes that cultural activity in itself, if divorced from God, is not pleasing to God and thus could not be considered an end in itself. To love the world and worldly culture as an end is to misplace it as an idol. To have the right order of loves means that God must come first. "So this world is nowadays destroyed not by sports, the cinema, etc., but by their being isolated as goods in themselves."[37] Thus, Schilder recognizes that cultural engagement that matters must be *mediated* by the preaching of the gospel—that is, by the church's evangelism and obedience to the Great Commission. Two points are worth reflecting on here: (1) the centrality of the gospel as grace restores nature, and (2) the resurrection as a witness to the death and restoration of the cosmos, such that the consummation of creation after the fall requires not an incremental and linear advancement toward the eschaton by way of Christian labor but a judgment and apocalyptic act of God that resurrects and purifies creatures and creation.

First, then, as I shall argue further in chapter 9, sinners made alive in Jesus through the word of God are called to put on their new man, which is patterned after the image of God (Col. 3:10; Eph. 4:24). In other words, the Great Commission is the means by which the narrow image of God is restored to humanity, as sinners receive renewed knowledge, righteousness, and holiness. The grace of regeneration that accompanies the preaching of the gospel to sinners reconciles them to God as they place their faith in Jesus Christ. By justification, they can approach God as they are considered righteous, and by the sanctification of the Spirit, they are given the qualities necessary to

37. Schilder, *Christ and Culture*, 119.

redirect their culture-making efforts to God, as they, in principle, are now able to accept and act on the moral law.

Before the fall, the multiplying and dispersal of the image of God was a natural process by way of procreation and culture-making. After the fall, procreation multiplies the image of God in the broad sense, but the preaching of the gospel is necessary to multiply the image of God in the narrow sense. As the Leiden Synopsis pithily puts it: "It is not generation, but re-generation that makes Christians, and no one is cleansed from sins by being born but by being re-born."[38] The image of God in the narrow sense is precisely the qualities of right knowledge, righteousness, and holiness necessary for God-glorifying cultures to exist: cultures exhibited by godliness and submission to the kingship of Christ, love of neighbor, and proper cultivation of creation. Indeed, Christ comes as the second Adam so that post-fall humanity could once again "fulfill this original service of God and, by rights as well as in fact, to give back to God his world and his work-community" by appeasing the divine wrath, reconciling God's people back to God, giving them eternal life, and judging the world such that it would become consummate under his kingship.[39] Schilder's reference to the "work-community" also signals the importance of the institutional church for culture-making, as the church is the mother of all believers and is the means by which the Spirit disciples and nurtures God's children.

Bavinck argues that the second commandment entails a positive imperative to look to Christ and his image-bearers in creation and redemption. Indeed, we ought not raise and venerate images of God because we are created in his image, and as we imitate the humanity of Christ as the second Adam, we advance in conformity to the image of God:

> Therefore, God says: You will find no image of me in any creature; that would dishonor me. But if you want to image, take a look at Adam, at human beings, who are created in my likeness. Above all, look at the Son, the image of the Invisible God, God's One and Only Firstborn, God's other *I*, the expression of his self-sufficiency. Whoever sees him sees the Father. As Christ is,

38. *Synopsis of a Purer Theology: Latin Text and English Translation*, vol. 1, *Disputations 1–23*, ed. Dolf te Velde, trans. Riemer A. Faber (Brill, 2014), 367.

39. Schilder, *Christ and Culture*, 62.

> so is God. He is the perfect likeness, the adequate Image. Let us be satisfied with that. God may be venerated with no other image than the Son. Beholding him and venerating him, we are changed into his likeness (2 Cor. 3:18). God wants, as it were, to multiply images of himself, to see nothing but images, likenesses, portraits of himself. Human beings themselves must be God's image, and not make pieces of wood or stone into God's image. The new humanity in Christ, from all sides and everyone in their own way, reflects and mirrors God. God is mirrored in us; we are mirrored in God. "When [Christ] appears, we shall be like him [and like the Father] because we shall see him as he is" (1 John 3:2). God makes images of himself in us. But not we of God. God photographs himself.[40]

In short, we are not to form images of God, because we are the ones who are called to represent God on earth. Without the grace of sanctification that conforms us to Christ, however, that representation is distorted and broken, as we choose to worship idols and tend to resemble and image those idols instead of God. The Great Commission, therefore, does not negate the cultural mandate but rather is the necessary means by which we fulfill it.[41] Only as we are transformed by the gospel could we again image and represent God properly. The kingdom of God, therefore, is both a "pearl of great price" and a "leaven which permeates the whole meal."[42] It is *because* the gospel is about entrance to a spiritual kingdom that believers on earth can become positive influences on culture:

> The gospel gives us a standard by which we can judge phenomena and events; it is an absolute measure which enables us to determine the value of the present life; it is a guide to show us the way in the labyrinth of the present world; it raises us above time and teaches us to view all things from the standpoint of eternity . . . it is opposed to nothing that is pure and good and lovely. It condemns sin always and everywhere; but it cherishes

---

40. Herman Bavinck, *Reformed Ethics*, vol. 2, *The Duties of the Christian Life*, trans. and ed. John Bolt, Jessica Joustra, Nelson D. Kloosterman, Antoine Theron, and Dirk van Keulen (Baker Academic, 2022), 174–75. For Bavinck's christological doctrine of the beatific vision, see Nathaniel Gray Sutanto, "Herman Bavinck on the Beatific Vision," *International Journal of Systematic Theology* 26, no. 1 (2022): 1–17.

41. See the discussion in G. K. Beale and Mitchell Kim, *God Dwells Among Us: A Biblical Theology of Temple* (IVP Academic, 2021), 24–25.

42. Bavinck, *Philosophy of Revelation*, 211–12.

marriage and family, society and the state, nature and history, science and art.[43]

In Bavinck's view, then, the gospel itself is not about social change, liberation, or worldly transformation; it is about the forgiveness of sins and the sanctification of the whole person before God. But because the gospel impacts the whole *person* and discloses the values of *eternity*, believers cannot help but see all things in light of God and seek to witness to the creational and redeemed ends of each sphere of culture.

Second, however, our culture-making now does not advance the kingdom of God incrementally, as if that kingdom is established by human hands. Rather, because the whole world is living under the curse of God and is tainted by sin, the world needs to be created and consummated anew by God himself. The resurrection sets the pattern for the rest of the world: "For the creation was subjected to futility, not willingly, but because of him who subjected it, in hope that the creation itself will be set free from its bondage to corruption and obtain the freedom of the glory of the children of God" (Rom. 8:20–21). As death is the path toward glorified consummation, so would creation be consumed and purified by fire, only to emerge as a new, perfected cosmos (2 Pet. 3:11–13). That world is not a replacement of this world but is a consummation—a consummation by way of divine intervention, death and resurrection, not by way of progressive human advancement or Christian cultural cultivation. Bavinck sums this up well: "The resurrection is the fundamental restoration of all culture."[44]

Hence, because divine intervention alone, in the work of final judgment and re-creation, can bring about that new world, Christian culture-making today is not an advancement of the kingdom of God physically and temporally, for the kingdom of God is not of this world—that is, it is achieved not from the ground up but from the top down. As renewed image-bearers cultivate culture and love their neighbors, then, they are merely *witnessing* to the direction of the next world, and it is a veiled witness to a world that does not welcome it. We are promised not linear success but persecution and resistance. The neo-Calvinistic teachings on the cultural mandate that

---

43. Bavinck, *Philosophy of Revelation*, 211–12.
44. Bavinck, *Philosophy of Revelation*, 211.

I outlined above thus lead not to transformationalism with a triumphalist tinge but rather to a kind of *chastened transformational witness*, as Christianity leavens families and cultures just as grace restores nature.[45] As Kuyper himself argued, it is not as if our cultural efforts will survive the final judgment and be transposed to the new world in a univocal fashion; rather, all we can hope for is that our efforts would provide some seed, some faint witness, to the new world order.[46]

Herman Bavinck reminds Christians that this hope for the final consummation of culture ought not eclipse the Christian's ultimate hope and desire: to behold God and to dwell in his presence through Jesus Christ. Christ is not a mere restorer of culture, but he is the pinnacle of culture himself; as the federal head of all of renewed humanity, he brings it before the face of God: "He is Prophet and Priest but also King, who does not cease his work until he has delivered the kingdom perfect and complete to God the Father."[47] Christians are thus not to rest their identities on their work, as if the kingdom of God depends on us, but we are to come to Jesus in whom there is rest (Matt. 11:27–29).

CONCLUSION

This chapter has argued that the cultural mandate is the vocational aspect of the image of God. Humans are created to be fruitful and multiply. Embedded in that calling is a teleological dimension: We were created to disperse and cultivate creation, and as corporate humanity multiplies, so we image God more fully. The chapter has also shown that God is committed to the fulfillment of the cultural mandate despite the fall, and he preserves human cultures, even in all of their unbelief, in this present redemptive-historical order of common grace. The preservation of unbelieving culture forms the backdrop and serves the purposes of special grace, through which God calls for himself a people who would witness to the kingdom of a consummate

45. For the ways in which the entrance of Christianity in the second century leavened Greco-Roman culture, see Larry Hurtado, *Destroyer of the Gods: Early Christian Distinctiveness in the Roman World* (Baylor University Press, 2017).

46. See Brock and Sutanto, *Neo-Calvinism*, chap. 6.

47. Bavinck, *Philosophy of Revelation*, 241.

age. The next two chapters will zoom in on original sin, corruption, and redemption.

FURTHER READING

Edgar, William. *Created and Creating: A Biblical Theology of Culture*. IVP Academic, 2016. Edgar's book is a helpful primer on the debates on the relationship between Christianity and culture, and it forms a good introduction to a broadly neo-Calvinist account of the cultural mandate.

Schilder, Klaas. *Christ and Culture*. Translated by Williem Helder and Albert H. Oosterhoff. Lucerna, 2016. As I argued in this chapter, Schilder was mistaken to reject common grace. Yet, this work remains a seminal introduction to the biblical contours of the cultural mandate.

Bavinck, Herman. "Common Grace." Translated by Raymond C. van Leeuwen. *Calvin Theological Journal* 24 (1989): 38–65. An essential article from Bavinck. He details the redemptive-historical contours of common grace, along with the ways in which it is a distinct Reformed doctrine that avoids the dualisms that he identifies with Roman Catholic theology.

Bavinck, Herman. "The Catholicity of Christianity and the Church." Translated by John Bolt. *Calvin Theological Journal* 27 (1992): 220–51. Another essential Bavinck article. Here, he argues that Christianity is a universal religion because it is not tethered to one culture or location but can leaven any culture.

Brock, Cory, and N. Gray Sutanto. *Neo-Calvinism: A Theological Introduction*. Lexham, 2023. The chapters on the image of God and common grace detail Kuyper's and Bavinck's corporate accounts of human nature and the ways in which God gifts fallen creatures moral, epistemic, and life-giving goods.

8

ORIGINAL SIN AND FALLEN HUMANITY

GUILT AND DEPRAVITY

THIS CHAPTER PRESENTS a theological account of original sin and fallen humanity that draws from the Reformed tradition.[1] After briefly surveying the Reformed confessional witness on these matters, I explore the imputation of original sin in both guilt and corruption, and the connection of that imputation with the metaphysics of human nature. I then expound on the nature of fallen humanity and the relation of sin to human nature. This chapter is thus a dogmatic development of the biblical material surveyed in chapter 2. I also provide a defense of the federalist model of the transmission of original sin, according to which Adam's guilt and corruption is transmitted to his progeny because he was the appointed representative of humanity.

REFORMED CONFESSIONAL WITNESS

The sixth and seventh chapters of the Westminster Confession of Faith describe the fall of humanity in Adam and its consequences succinctly, and

1. For some historical studies, see Aaron Denlinger, *Omnes in Adam ex pacto Dei: Ambrogio Catarino's Doctrine of Covenantal Solidarity and Its Influence on Post-Reformation Reformed Theologians* (Vandenhoeck & Ruprecht, 2010); and Pierrick Hildebrand, *The Zurich Origins of Reformed Covenant Theology* (Oxford University Press, 2024).

for the sake of space we shall focus on this statement. While the confession does not address every detail (which we will attempt to fill out in the sections below), it does outline the main contours of the doctrine of original sin.

The confession observes that the fall of man occurred due to the success of Satan's temptation against Adam and Eve, and yet this first sin remains within the divine counsel, permitted and purposed within God's sovereign plan (6.1). This is an important point to make: The confession upholds together divine sovereignty and the freedom of humanity's choice in the garden. Indeed, created, innocent humanity had the freedom to sin or not sin. In the first two articles of chapter 9 on human free will, the confession speaks of humanity enjoying natural liberty, being "neither forced, nor, by any absolute necessity of nature, determined to good or evil" (9.1). Further, in the state of innocence, humanity had the "power to will and to do that which was good and well pleasing to God; but yet so mutably, so that he might fall from it" (9.2). In fact, the Leiden Synopsis describes the "internal cause of the fall" as the "free will of both our parents; better yet, it is the bending of the will that listened to Satan instead of God."[2] Innocent humanity was created good, but mutably so: "Both of our parents were created by God in such a way that they were able not to sin if they willed not to sin, and they were able to sin if they willed to."[3] The sovereignty of God and the unchangeable character of the divine decree do not compromise but rather establish the liberty and contingency of the creaturely will.

The Reformed tradition is self-conscious in its affirmation of what Muller has called an "almost paradoxical point": "that an eternal and all-powerful God can in fact predetermine that some events will occur as a result of contingent or free acts of creatures and can therefore foreknow such events according to his *scientia libera seu visionis* [free knowledge of vision]."[4] Reformed

2. *Synopsis of a Purer Theology: Latin Text and English Translation*, vol. 1, *Disputations 1–23*, ed. Dolf te Velde, trans. Riemer A. Faber (Brill, 2014), 347.

3. *Synopsis of a Purer Theology*, 1:347. As we shall see, sin is not a substance, and affirming that sin is substantial implies that God is the author of sin, since all that is not God owes its creation from God. Sin, rather, originated as a misdirecting of our human nature, resulting in an accidental defect that qualifies that nature.

4. Richard Muller, *God, Creation and Providence in the Thought of Jacob Arminius: Sources and Directions of Scholastic Protestantism in the Era of Early Orthodoxy* (Baker, 1991), 260–61. Hence, in a more recent work: "Choice is therefore free from coercion and physical necessity, but remains under the extrinsic necessity of a dependence on God and under the intrinsic determination by the intellect. . . . The spontaneity and willingness requisite to choice rest, therefore, not on

theologians who are committed to the ordination of all things by way of the divine counsel need not—and should not—be fearful about affirming the real freedom of creatures, especially in reference to this first sin. As the confession has already established, that God "ordains whatsoever comes to pass" does not, and cannot, be taken to imply that God is "the author of sin" or that "violence" was "offered to the will of the creature" (3.1). Reformed theologians, therefore, are not afraid of appealing to creaturely free will as the source of evil.

The next two articles of the sixth chapter outline the consequences of original sin and in that way define what makes this sin "original": "By this sin they fell from their original righteousness and communion with God, and so became dead in sin and wholly defiled in all the parts and faculties of soul and body" (6.2), and "They being the root of all mankind, the guilt of this sin was imputed; and the same death in sin, and corrupted nature, conveyed to all their posterity descending from them by ordinary generation" (6.3). Westminster Confession of Faith 6.2. refers back to the original righteousness that humanity had by nature before the fall, and the loss of that original righteousness did not leave their natures unaffected. Burgess is no exception in considering this point to be contrary to Romanist teaching:

> Now the Orthodox do maintain against Papists, *That that original righteousness was not a supernatural perfection concreated with him; For as Adam being made to glorifie God, was thereby to have a rational soul, so also such perfection in that soul, which might make him capable of his end, otherwise man would have been created in a more imperfect and ignoble condition than any creature.*[5]

For Burgess, original righteousness was a gift that was fitted for the proper functioning of Adam's nature, a debt of nature and a concreated perfection (a position consistent, as we saw, with Bavinck, Turretin, and Van Mastricht). This original and concreated positive direction and communion we had with God was lost, as the humans are now guilty and alienated from God. As a

an indifference in the will but on the rational judgment that is in all human beings." Richard Muller, *Divine Will and Human Choice: Freedom, Contingency, and Necessity in Early Modern Reformed Thought* (Baker Academic, 2017), 292. See Francis Turretin, *Institutes of Elenctic Theology*, vol. 1, *First Through Tenth Topics*, ed. James T. Dennison, trans. George Musgrave Giger (P&R, 1992), 513.

5. Anthony Burgess, *A Treatise on Original Sin: Proving That It Is, by Pregnant Texts of Scripture, and Vindicated from False Glosses* (Anchora Spei, 1658), 19 (emphasis original), see also 25 and 118.

result, every part of their being is now affected by the defilement of sin—indeed, fallen Adam is now dead in sin (Eph. 2:1–3). Physical and spiritual death is the just penalty for sin.

Westminster Confession of Faith 6.3 further clarifies that the sin of our parents did not affect just them. The alienation and guilt they received was "imputed" to us, and corruption is passed down to all who descend from them. In this sense Adam's sin was "original"—not just that it was the first human sin, but that it is the "origin" of our guilt and corruption. The alienation and guilt Adam and Eve received was "imputed" to us, and corruption is passed down to all who descend from them. To "impute" here means to "*lay the charge or credit* of any one as a ground of judicial punishment or justification."[6] The guilt imputed, therefore, is not moral pollution but a legal, judicial status. Adam's progeny is guilty because Adam acted as a representative.

We also receive an inherited corruption, for we have the same fallen human nature that is propagated from Adam. Westminster Confession of Faith 7.2 articulates the centrality of Adam's person: He disobeyed God not as a private person but rather as the federal head of humanity—that is, Adam was our representative in the covenant of works: "The first covenant made with man was a covenant of works, wherein life was promised to Adam; *and in him* to his posterity, upon condition of perfect and perpetual obedience."[7] The confession here is outlining what has come to be known as the *federalist* view of original sin: the doctrine according to which we are implicated by Adam's sin because he is appointed by God as our federal—that is, covenantal—representative, and his guilt becomes our guilt by imputation. We will be elaborating on and defending this federal view of the transmission of original sin later in this chapter.

One should observe the parity of "original sin" and "original righteousness." If Adam is our representative, whatever he does will implicate his people, for better or for worse. If Adam were to remain righteous in the garden, vanquish the serpent, defend the word of God, and guard the sanctity of the Edenic temple, then God would confirm and glorify Adam. Adam would then pass down that perfected nature to his posterity. Likewise, if Adam were to

6. Archibald A. Hodge, *A Commentary of the Confession of Faith: With Questions for Theological Students and Bible Classes* (Presbyterian Board of Education, 1869), 156 (emphasis original).

7. Emphasis added.

fall—which was the case—so would he pass down his guilt and corruption to those he represents.

The inherited corruption is the reason we were made incapable of all good and are now positively inclined toward all evil, as 6.4 indicates: "From this original corruption, whereby we are utterly indisposed, disabled, and made opposite to all good, and wholly inclined to all evil, do proceed all actual transgressions." In other words, the sin originated (corruption) creates the propensity in us toward committing acts of sin. The answer of the Westminster Larger Catechism to the question of what sin is as "any want of conformity unto, or transgression of, any law of God, given as a rule to the reasonable creature" (Q&A 24) should be situated within the broader account of original sin and corruption.

The grace of regeneration curbs this propensity to sin, but Christians continue to struggle with indwelling sin. Further, the confession goes on to emphasize that every sin, even "the motions thereof" (that is, the desires that do not consummate into action), is indeed illicit and sinful: "This corruption of nature, during this life, doth remain in those that are regenerated; and although it be, through Christ, pardoned and mortified; yet both itself, and all the motions thereof, are truly and properly sin" (6.5). As the ninth chapter, on freedom of the will, puts it, the fallen will "hath wholly lost all ability of will to any spiritual good accompanying salvation: so as, a natural man, being altogether averse from that good, and dead in sin, is not able, by his strength, to convert himself, or to prepare himself thereunto" (9.3) This article anticipates the importance of effectual calling and regeneration, which is the subject of chapter 10. The sinner does not and cannot do anything prior to regeneration to make himself or herself predisposed toward faith. Rather, regeneration precedes faith.

For committing these sins and for exhibiting the propensity toward sin due to our corruption, fallen humanity deserves punishment. Every sin is ultimately against God's law, which in turn is against God's will and glory. Indeed, our guilt stems not only from original sin (which is imputed) but also from our own sinful desires and actual sin: "Every sin, both original and actual, being a transgression of the righteous law of God, and contrary thereunto doth, in its own nature, bring guilt upon the sinner, whereby he is bound over to the wrath of God, and curse of the law, and so made subject to death, with all miseries, spiritual and temporal" (6.6).

THE SIN ORIGINATED: GUILT, CORRUPTION, OR BOTH?

The subject of original sin thus focuses not merely on the originating sin (the sin that Adam had committed) but on the sin originated (the consequences of originating sin that Adam's posterity inherit from Adam). The confessional affirmations above utilize two important terms: "guilt" and "corruption." Guilt, as Petrus van Mastricht puts it,

> follows sin, partly from sin's intrinsic nature and demerit, insofar as it is not an intermediate or indifferent thing, but a thing by its own nature evil and demanding punishment, which cannot be denied, except the nature of things be confused and every distinction between good and evil taken away; and partly from the sanction of the divine law.[8]

Guilt follows naturally from wrongdoing or transgression of God's law and will. Van Mastricht then goes on to distinguish between "potential guilt" and "actual guilt"—the former referring to the "intrinsic worthiness of punishment" that the sinner incurs upon himself or herself, and the latter referring to the "actual ordination of punishment," which can be taken away by God's grace.[9] The punishment that follows from such a guilt is death (Rom. 6:23), not only the death that humans will experience in this life physically, but also spiritual death, which is alienation from God and an inability to obey him, and eternal death at the final judgment.[10]

In other words, humanity inherits a twofold liability: the liability to guilt (*reatus culpae*) and the liability to punishment (*reatus poenae*).[11] In line with

8. Van Mastricht, *TPT*, 3:450.
9. Van Mastricht, *TPT*, 3:450.
10. See the discussion in McCall on the options of the scope of "death" that is the wages of our sin in McCall, *Against God and Nature: The Doctrine of Sin* (Crossway, 2019), 312–18. Sin results in (1) the entrance of death for any and all living organisms, (2) animal death and human death, (3) human death, and (4) a particular, fallen kind of death (the death of any and all living organisms, in this fourth view, is an intrinsic feature of creation). Though McCall prefers the third view, he rightly notes that the second and third views are in accord with reason and orthodoxy.
11. Charles Hodge's unlinking between guilt and punishment, such that the imputation of original sin, for him, refers only to the latter, is thus a minority report within this federal tradition. See Charles Hodge, *Systematic Theology*, vol. 2, *Anthropology* (Thomas Nelson and Sons, 1872), 194 (see also 476). See also Oliver D. Crisp, "Federalism vs Realism: Charles Hodge, Augustus Strong, and William Shedd on the Imputation of Sin," *International Journal of Systematic Theology* 8 (2006): 66; Oliver Crisp, *The Word Enfleshed: Exploring the Person and Work of Christ*

this distinction, the majority report of the federal position argued that image-bearers of Adam are guilty of Adam's sin and must be punished, for an inseparable logical connection binds guilt and punishment: One cannot bear a punishment if one is innocent, and likewise one cannot be held responsible to make a satisfaction for a violation if one is not the agent guilty of such a violation. God imputes the sin of Adam to them, and they are liable to punishment because of it.

Corruption, on the other hand, is the internal defilement of human nature. Because all human beings stem from Adam, Adam's corrupted human nature is propagated to his progeny (barring Christ), such that all are predisposed against good and positively toward evil. "There are as it were two essential parts of the corruption: an aversion from all moral good, especially spiritual and saving good, and an inclination to all moral evil (Jer. 2:13)."[12] We are thus in a body of death (Rom. 7:24), and it is this corrupted human nature that is described as the "flesh" or the "old man"—not that our natures are destroyed and then replaced, but rather that our nature is qualified with the propensity toward evil. Just as a rotten tree remains a tree, so are fallen human beings still human.

According to this Reformed-federal position of original sin, Adam's first sin resulted in a twofold curse upon humanity: original guilt and original pollution, with total depravity as an inherited result of his sin. God immediately imputed this curse on Adam's progeny on the basis of Adam's natural and representative bond with them. Francis Turretin's delineation of this was typical of this federalist view: "For the bond between Adam and his posterity is twofold (1) natural, as he is the father, and we are his children; (2) political and forensic, as he was the prince and representative head of the whole human race."[13] That is, God imputes the sin of Adam to his progeny because Adam was the first human being, and Adam represents them, as the actions of a prince represent his people.

God, therefore, does not reckon that only punishment should be meted out against Adam's progeny, but also the guilt of Adam's originating sin. This

(Baker Academic, 2016), 129n20. See also John Murray, *The Imputation of Adam's Sin* (Presbyterian and Reformed, 1959), 77; Annette G. Aubert, *The German Roots of Nineteenth-Century American Theology* (Oxford University Press), 194–219.

12. Van Mastricht, *TPT*, 3:454.

13. Turretin, *Institutes*, 616.

is no mere legal fiction, for our first parents are integrally connected to their posterity by the covenant.[14] As the Larger Catechism puts it, the "sinfulness of that estate whereinto man fell, consisteth in the *guilt* of Adam's first sin, the want of that righteousness wherein he was created, and the *corruption* of his nature, whereby is utterly indisposed . . . and made opposite unto all that is spiritually good, and wholly inclined to all evil, and that continually" (Q. 25). This view represents much of the Reformed tradition. As the Leiden Synopsis avers (though with a less developed covenant theology): "Just as all people sinned in both parents originally and were infected by this common ailment through the proliferation of that same damaged nature, so too they were counted guilty of the same crime and death (Rom. 5:12)."[15] Or, as Van Mastricht says: "The substance of this [original sin] includes two things, first the guilt which we have from Adam . . . from one man to condemnation, because we are all judged to have sinned in him, as the apostle says (Rom. 5:12, 16); then that stain and corruption itself that inheres in us. The first is customarily called imputed original sin, the latter inherent original sin."[16] Original sin thus has to do with both our *status* (guilt) and internal *defilement* (corruption). These affirmations have invited serious challenges, as we shall see, and later in the chapter I shall detail those objections and suggest some responses to them.

FEDERALISM AND REALISM

The Westminster Standards, then, upholds federalism. Adam is the federal head of humanity, and God imputes his guilt to his posterity and allows his corrupted nature to be propagated to them. Imputation in this federal context, as Caspar W. Hodge observes from passages like Leviticus 7:18, Psalm 32:2, Romans 4:8 and 11, 2 Corinthians 5:19, and James 2:23, refers to that divine act in which "God accounts such a one to be a sinner, and consequently guilty and liable to punishment. . . . In the same manner, when God is said to 'impute righteousness' to a person, the meaning is that He judicially accounts such

14. Van Masticht, *TPT*, 3:451.

15. *Synopsis of a Purer Theology*, 1:349.

16. Van Mastricht, *TPT*, 3:451. As Oliver Crisp notes, "The full-orbed doctrine of original sin [according to the Reformed orthodox tradition] comprises two aspects. There are original corruption and original guilt." Crisp, "Federalism vs Realism," 56.

a one to be righteous and entitled to all the rewards of a righteous person."[17] The foundation of such imputation is in the covenant of works (or nature) that God initiated with Adam: "the covenant which was contracted by God, not with our first parents alone, but with all their posterity . . . which also was violated by all . . . which accordingly involved their whole race in the same calamity with them."[18] Federalism thus holds an *immediate* transmission view of original sin, whereby God immediately imputes the sin of Adam to his posterity. The propagation of sin happens "through imputation or through merit, insofar as God judges that first covenant breaking of our first parents to have been committed by the whole human race (Rom. 5:12; 1 Cor. 15:21–22)."[19] The divine imputation explains transmission, as we saw in chapter 2.

Federalism is commonly juxtaposed against realism, though, as I shall suggest below, federalists can accommodate realist insights. Realism argues that the sin of Adam is transmitted to his posterity because they were *really* in him, as it were. Realists usually utilize the language of Adam's posterity as being in his loins or as being one with his nature before they were propagated as individuals. Augustine, recall, is usually credited as one early representative of this view:

> For we were in that one man, since we all were that one man who fell into sin by the woman who was made from him before the sin. For not yet was the particular form created and distributed to us, in which we as individuals were to live, but already the seminal nature was there from which we were to be propagated; and this being vitiated by sin, and bound by the chain of death, and thusly condemned, man could not be born of man in any other state.[20]

Realism goes in one or two directions with respect to guilt. The first is the immediate view, according to which all are found guilty in Adam because his sin is really their sin, for they were metaphysically one with him. There is thus no need for imputation due to covenant-breaking for Adam's guilt to be

17. Caspar W. Hodge, "Imputation," in *The International Standard Bible Encyclopedia*, ed. James Orr (Eerdmans, 1974), 1462.

18. Van Mastricht, *TPT*, 3:451.

19. Van Masticht, *TPT*, 3:455.

20. Augustine, *City of God*, trans. Marcus Dods (Random House, 1993), 13.14.

transmitted to his progeny. Corruption, of course, is immediately transmitted as well because our nature is one with Adam, and the emergence of our individuality presupposes that nature.

The second view is the mediate transmission of guilt.[21] We are not considered guilty for Adam's sin but receive corruption only from him. We are not culpable for Adam's sin or for inheriting this corruption. Inevitably, however, those who are corrupted commit acts of sin and thus become guilty by way of that sin. Vermigli articulates this mediate view well by way of an analogy of contracting a plague: "It is as if someone suffering from the plague infects others and those others die; we would say that each person died from his own sickness and not from that of someone else. But, if someone says those others died from the plague of that one from whom they contracted the contagion, this must be taken to mean that this person first came upon the plague and communicated it to them."[22] In Vermigli's perspective, then, we do not die because of Adam's disease, as it were, but we die due to having the disease ourselves—though the first person who contracted that disease was Adam. Hence, according to "the mediate view, humans are guilty for their own sin, which is a consequence of Adam's sin and our inheriting either sinful dispositions or a corrupted nature. In other words, according to the mediate view, humans are guilty for their own sinful actions or, even better, their own sinful dispositions."[23] Advocates of this view argue with regularity that its strengths consist in its denial of the imputation of original guilt. The imputation of original guilt seems unjust, after all, and it is implausible that God should count the sin of someone that I did not authorize, who lived generations before me, to be my own. For instance, as Crisp argues, drawing from Anselm and Zwingli: "[God] does not transmit Adam's guilt to me, so the condition in which I find myself (i.e., being born with the condition of original sin) is not one for which I am culpable, though it will lead to my death without the interposition of divine grace, just as some inherited conditions lead to death without medical

21. On the origins of the distinction between mediate and immediate imputation and the Saumur theologian Josua Placaeus (1569–1655), see J. V. Fesko, *Death in Adam, Life in Christ: The Doctrine of Imputation* (Christian Focus, 2016), 102–10.

22. Peter Martyr Vermigli, *On Original Sin*, trans. Kirk Summers (Davenant, 2019), 65.

23. Farris, *Introduction to Theological Anthropology*, 148.

intervention."[24] In a more recent iteration, Crisp clarifies that though we are not culpable for Adam's corruption, the possession of this corrupted nature does, indeed, lead one to "*death and separation from God irrespective of actual sin*."[25] By stating it this way, Crisp ensures that he is not affirming that this corrupted nature is somehow morally neutral, but rather that, just as the leprous are barred from engaging with the healthy, this corruption "renders them unfit for the presence of God."[26]

As noted above, federalism could make use of realist explanations. The Leiden Synopsis, for instance, affirmed that the efficient cause of originated sin was Adam's sin, which involved "the whole race of posterity which lay concealed in his loins and sinned along with him, in the same way as Levi paid tithes 'while he was in the loins of his father Abraham' (Hebrews 7:8–9). Similarly, the universal guilt or universal sin of the entire nature or species was to be passed on to all men by generation."[27] Individuals who emerge from that corrupted source are thus "infected with the vice of concupiscence . . . hostile to God."[28] Bavinck likewise argues: "Federalism certainly does not rule out the truth contained in realism; on the contrary it fully accepts it. It proceeds from it but does not confine itself to it. It recognizes a unity of nature on which the federal unity depends. In the human race, we encounter a variety of forms of community that are absolutely not based only, nor even principally, on physical descent but on another, a higher, *moral* unity."[29] I suggest that the issue, then, is not in whether we should consider ourselves as in some way metaphysically united to Adam. Both federalists and realists

---

24. Oliver Crisp, "Sin," in *Christian Dogmatics: Reformed Theology for the Church Catholic*, ed. Michael Allen and Scott R. Swain (Baker Academic, 2016), 213. Although he does not elaborate on this idea, Gijsbert van den Brink's attempt to reconcile the fall with evolutionary theory (esp. common descent) involves a gradualist account of the fall that seems to entail a mediated view of guilt's transmission: "This tendency [toward sin] was handed down through the generations not only (epi)genetically but also by social factors." Van den Brink, *Reformed Theology and Evolutionary Theory* (Eerdmans, 2020), 195, see also 192–94.

25. Oliver Crisp, *Participation and Atonement: An Analytic and Constructive Account* (Baker Academic, 2022), 165 (emphasis original). It should be noted that Crisp's iteration of the mechanism of the atonement in this book, a "representational union account" (p. 207), puts him quite close to the majority report of Reformed federalism.

26. Crisp, *Participation and Atonement*, 166.

27. *Synopsis of a Purer Theology*, 1:359.

28. *Synopsis of a Purer Theology*, 1:359.

29. Bavinck, *RD*, 3:104; Herman Bavinck, *Gereformeerde Dogmatiek*, 3rd ed., 4 vols. (Kok, 1918), 3:93.

would affirm that we share Adam's human nature and are integrally connected to him. Rather, federalists suggest that realism is not to serve as the account for the transmission of Adam's sin. It is not the mechanism that transmits guilt, though the unity of nature that humanity shares with Adam is one reason why the transmission of guilt is not unjust, as we shall see.

In what ways, then, is realism vulnerable to criticism?[30] First, realism as the main mechanism for the transmission of Adam's sin and guilt would prove too much.[31] If we are metaphysically one with Adam, why are we guilty only for the originating sin that Adam committed and not for every sin Adam does henceforth? As Bavinck remarked: "If Adam's trespass has been ours in this realistic sense, we would also be responsible for all the other sins of Adam, all the sins of Eve, even all the sins of our ancestors, for we were included in them as in Adam when he violated the probationary command."[32] Realism also implies traducianism, and there are good reasons to reject traducianism, as we explored in the previous chapter.[33]

Second, realism would render imputation unnecessary and thus compromises the covenantal character of Adam's representation. The reason that Adam's covenantal character is important is because of the parallel between he and Christ: Just as Adam's act of disobedience is imputed to his posterity, so is Christ's act of obedience imputed to his people. Justification is a remedy for the guilt of sin: Both are legal declarations that follow the merit or demerit of righteousness and sin. McCall described this logic: "As the righteousness of Christ is imputed to us in a legal or forensic sense, so also the sin of Adam was imputed to us in a legal or forensic sense."[34] Charles Hodge recognized, therefore, that when Christ became "sin" for us (2 Cor. 5:21), it is not that

30. Charles Hodge traces the "repudiated" doctrine of mediate imputation to Placaeus and collates testimonies from Andre Viret's collection on original sin and imputation in "Testimonies on the Doctrine of Imputation," *The Princeton Review* 4 (1839): 553–79. See also Charles Hodge, "Inquiries Respecting the Doctrine of Imputation," *The Biblical Repertory and Theological Review* 2 (1830): 448–49. However, Fesko's evaluation of Rivet's collation seems accurate: "Rivet's treatise seems to miss the mark because he cites multiple sources that do not directly address the question of immediate imputation." *Death in Adam*, 104.

31. Realism also risks reifying sin; see, in this regard, Andrew M. Leslie, "Retrieving a Mature Reformed Doctrine of Original Sin: A Conversation with Some Recent Proposals," *International Journal of Systematic Theology* 22 (2020): 340–45.

32. Bavinck, *RD*, 3:104. McCall rightly says that Bavinck's "concerns are illustrative of the common criticisms." McCall, *Against God and Nature*, 168.

33. As Bavinck argues, "A creationist cannot be a realist." *RD*, 3:105.

34. McCall, *Against God and Nature*, 164.

Christ himself *became* personally sinful. Similarly, when the Christian is rendered righteous, it is not "to mean that we personally performed the acts of his perfect obedience, and in person died upon the cross."[35]

Put another way, the covenant of grace is in parallel with the covenant of works, and because in the former God imputes the righteousness of Christ representatively, rather than physically, so too there must be a representative sense in which we are "comprehended" in Adam.[36] "A union of representation is not a union of identity."[37] Bavinck argues that the one who follows the logical ends of realism would conclude that "all imputation, both in the case of Adam and in that of Christ, would be unnecessary."[38] In short, realism cannot fully account for the transmission of original sin because the covenant of works and the covenant of grace stand and fall together.[39] The way Adam's sin is transmitted to his progeny parallels the way Christ's righteousness is transmitted to his people, and both are by way of imputation.

Third, the covenant idea and imputation show that sin is not physical but ethical and that human beings are morally connected. As we have seen in chapters 5 and 7, and we shall further explore below, the organism of humanity is tied together by ethical, rather than merely physical, relations: "Earlier already we remarked that the relations in which people stand to one another are distinct from those that are found in angels and animals. While related to both, humans are also different from both. They are creatures with a character of their own. For that reason, physical unity in their case is not enough; an ethical, a federal unity is added as well."[40] What makes humans different from animals is the ethical bonds that connect them, and the covenant idea is a recognition of this.

---

35. Hodge, "Inquiries," 437. For more on the imputation of sin to Christ, see G. A. van den Brink, *The Transfer of Sin: The Debate on Imputation in the English Antinomian Controversy (1690–1700) in Its International and Interconfessional Context* (Brill, 2025).

36. Bavinck, *RD*, 3:102.

37. Hodge, "Inquiries," 437.

38. Bavinck, *RD*, 3:102. For a creative treatment of a realistic account of penal substitution that has no need for imputation (coincidentally following somewhat Bavinck's presentation of realism's "logic" here), see Oliver D. Crisp, "Original Sin and Atonement," in *The Oxford Handbook of Philosophical Theology*, ed. Thomas P. Flint and Michael C. Rea (Oxford University Press, 2009), 441–43.

39. Bavinck, *RD*, 3:103.

40. Bavinck, *RD*, 3:103.

As McCall also observed, "Perhaps Bavinck's most important criticism concerns the moral responsibility of human persons as distinct agents."[41] Realism threatens to reduce humanity into a single physical entity and, in consequence, reify sin into a sort of physical substance, without recognizing that the sin of each is uniquely one's own and that each personality and individuality is unique. Adam's ethical representation shows that his sin is really his own—we are comprehended in him representatively, just as Christ's act of righteousness was his and we are considered righteous not because we really were righteous the way Christ was. Again, "with Adam: virtually, potentially, and seminally, we may have been comprehended in him; personally and actually, however, it was he who broke the probationary command, and not we. If realism were to reject this distinction and be totally consistent, all imputation, as we saw, would become unnecessary."[42] Realism reduces individuals into a singular metaphysical continuity.

Fourth, a corruption-only account fails to evade the very problem it was trying to avoid in the first place—namely, that the imputation of original guilt is unjust.[43] The observation that God could not transfer the guilt of Adam to his posterity, for Adam's progeny did not yet exist and do not approve of what he did, usually motivated a corruption-only account. Adam's posterity, therefore, are not guilty for Adam's sin but receive only inherited corruption from him. However, as Andrew Leslie and Hans Madueme have shown, this prompts two further queries.[44] If it was unjust for God to impute the guilt of Adam to his posterity, why would it be just for God to allow Adam's corruption to spread to his posterity, especially if that corruption would lead the entire human race to its own condemnation? As Hodge puts it, is it not unjust for God to determine "out of mere sovereignty, to call them into existence depraved, and then condemned them for this depravity?"[45] In fact, in Scripture we see that God gives us over to our corruption as a punishment (Rom. 1:24, 26, 28; Eph. 2:1–3). The transmission of corruption is explained

41. McCall, *Against God and Nature*, 169.

42. Bavinck, *RD*, 3:102.

43. On the compatibility of Ezek. 18:20, Exod. 34:7, and Jer. 32:18, see Hodge, "Inquiries," 457–59.

44. Leslie, "Retrieving a Mature Reformed Doctrine," 346–47; Hans Madueme, "Mea Culpa: An Apology for Original Guilt," *Mid-America Journal of Theology* 32 (2021): 13–14.

45. Hodge, "Inquiries," 466.

by the imputation of Adam's sin and guilt. When realism denies that Adam's guilt is transmitted to us, it implies that the penalty of sin (corruption) can be transmitted to Adam's progeny without the transmission of guilt, but the imposition of a penalty without guilt is unjust.

Realism is thus caught at the horns of a dilemma. An appeal to realism to justify that divine decision to transmit Adam's corruption to his posterity would render one vulnerable to the objections against realism stated above. On the other hand, to justify why Adam's corruption is justly transmitted to his progeny, realism falls back to federalism: Adam's corruption is justly spread to humanity because he was, in some way, appointed a federal representative of the whole.[46] Hodge, then, predicts that those who reject immediate imputation would also reject the transmission of corruption, for the same objections against the former could be applied to the latter.[47]

The second query follows through with this logic concerning the corruption transmitted: If I am not guilty for Adam's sin, and I am not at fault for the corrupted nature that he transmitted to me, then how can God hold me accountable for the sins that I will inevitably commit? These sins, after all, spring forth from a nature that was passed down to me without my consent and from someone whose actions I disapprove of.[48] Crisp, for instance, appeals to the example of an alcohol-addicted mother who passes on that addiction to her unborn child, who inherited that addiction through no fault of her own.[49] In such cases, however, it is arguable that the child should be treated through therapy and rehabilitation and not be punished for his or her bouts of drinking. Corruption-only models, therefore, seem to move the problem one step back, and Hodge was perceptive when he observed that every attempt to explain the "ascription" of Adam's sin to his progeny presupposes some doctrine of imputation.[50]

---

46. Without the federalist principle, the transmission of sin seems to "perpetuate itself in some quasi-deistic fashion as mere collateral damage from one man's act." Leslie, "Retrieving a Mature Reformed Doctrine," 355.

47. Hodge, "Inquiries," 471.

48. "By its own logic, if the fall caused original corruption, for which we bear no guilt, then we should bear no guilt for any actual sins, which, as the theory goes, necessarily arise from that corruption." Madueme, "Mea Culpa," 13.

49. Crisp, *Participation and Atonement*, 157.

50. Hodge, "Inquiries," 439.

So, it appears that not only can federalism accommodate realist explanations, but realism is in *need* of federalism for its account of the transmission of sin. Federalism preserves the covenantal relations that tie together humanity and the gospel. What do we make, then, of the common objections against federalism? I turn to those objections and formulate a response next.

RESPONSE TO OBJECTIONS AGAINST FEDERALISM: A TRINITARIAN THEOLOGICAL ANTHROPOLOGY

When one turns to some discussions in contemporary theology, it appears that federalism has fallen on hard times. As McCall has put it, "According to federalism, we are considered guilty for something that we did not do and over which we had no control. To say that this view is counterintuitive is to put it mildly."[51] Blocher admits that federalism "sits uneasily with our sense of personal responsibility, not only modern, but in a biblically formed sense."[52] Or, as Farris observes, the problems are "obvious," and he sums up some of the most important problems in this way:

> The challenges are quite obvious. There is the fairness concern, first. It is hard to reconcile how it is fair that all humans could be held liable for the sin of one man. Second, there is the concern that humans did not have the choice to endorse Adam as their federal representative, as with so many leaders in our time. . . . Third, the doctrine appears to be a legal fiction, and, at least, in some cases it is not possible to impute the sins of one individual to another individual (e.g., in the case of murder).[53]

Farris's objections track well with three objections that Crisp has put forth in an earlier essay:[54] Federalism needs to tackle (1) *the divine will objection*, whereby it seems unfair (and arbitrary) that it is God's voluntary will alone that puts Adam in this arrangement as a federal head; (2) *the authorization objection*, which refers to the fact that Adam's inflicted progeny have not

51. McCall, *Against God and Nature*, 162.

52. Henri Blocher, *Original Sin: Illumining a Riddle* (IVP Academic, 1997), 74.

53. Joshua Ryan Farris, *An Introduction to Theological Anthropology: Humans, Both Creaturely and Divine* (Baker Academic, 2020), 146.

54. He would reiterate these objections in Oliver D. Crisp, "On Original Sin," *International Journal of Systematic Theology* 17 (2015): 257.

consented for Adam to act on their behalf; and (3) *the fiction objection*, according to which it seems that God is holding Adam's progeny responsible and thus guilty of Adam's sin purely by way of some legal fiction, for they did not, in fact, commit that first sin.[55] As McCall sums up, it appears that despite "its roots within historic Protestant theology (both Reformed and Wesleyan) and its widespread popularity within evangelicalism, the federalist position seems to face the stiffest challenges with respect to moral responsibility."[56] What shall a proponent of federalism say to these charges?[57]

To begin with, it is important to recognize the metaphysics of the image of God and humanity as the backdrop for God's covenantal arrangement with Adam. Bavinck's observation is pivotal: A Trinitarian theological anthropology implies that ethical relations are ontologically constitutive. Indeed, Bavinck develops Reformed theological anthropology in important ways. Though I have sketched this in earlier chapters, let me highlight some points most relevant to these objections against federalism.

Recall that Bavinck held that the *imago Dei* referred not merely to human individuals but to the entirety of the human race. Indeed, the human individual is thus a "compendium, the epitome of all of nature, a microcosm, and, precisely on that account, also the image and likeness of God, his son and heir, a micro-divine-being (*mikrotheos*)."[58] Human beings are connected to one another in such a manner that the individual is not comprehensible without the whole, and the whole is illumined by the individual.

For Bavinck, the unity of the image of God in the human race explains why sin inflicts the entirety of Adam's race—the parts are affected because they are comprehended in the whole, and the diversity of individuals is vitiated by sin because Adam is the head of humanity. Underneath this claim is Bavinck's provocative understanding that creation, and humankind in particular, is

55. Crisp, "Sin," 201–5. Or, as McCall has put it: "The worry here is that the federalist position simply cannot account for the apparently brazen miscarriage of justice that it proposes." *Against God and Nature*, 165.

56. McCall, *Against God and Nature*, 199.

57. For other recent and substantial defenses of the imputation of guilt, see Leslie, "Retrieving a Mature Reformed Doctrine"; and Madueme, "Mea Culpa," 7–34.

58. Bavinck, *RD*, 2:562. Here one can't help but hear an echo of Schleiermacher. Recall, above, "You are a compendium of humanity. In a certain sense your single nature embraces all human nature." Friedrich Schleiermacher, *On Religion: Speeches to Its Cultured Despisers*, 3rd ed., trans. John Oman (Paul, Trench, Trubner, 1893), 79.

patterned after the Trinity. Because the Triune Creator is an absolute unity-in-diversity, his creation is marked by unities-in-diversities, and all the more clearly so for the image-bearers of God.[59]

Family relations, national representations, and cultures all exemplify in analogical and concentric ways the way in which the human race is ethically connected. Each generation propagates its own distinct characteristics to the next, and as each family has its own distinct culture, so are some families inclined toward a particular sin or other, and the descents are impacted by those acts. As mothers, daughters, sons, or fathers sin, their sins ripple to the other members, and as participants of a society act in a certain way, so that corporate whole is impacted. We have distinct personalities, but we are not radically individuals.[60]

An atomistic and individualistic understanding of the human person is a mark of Enlightenment, revolutionary thought, and Bavinck recognizes that such a picture is a Western illusion.

Hence, the covenant of works, in which God considers Adam as the representative head of the human race, is a *fitting* arrangement that corresponds to humanity's organic shape—it is a special act of God that comports with the organic makeup of the human race as a unity-in-diversity. The imputation of Adam's sin, in other words, respects the ethical connectedness and the ontology of the human race: "The image of God in mankind in its entirety stands or falls with the covenant of works."[61] More broadly, the relational, legal, and ethical bond that connects humanity to two federal heads (in Adam or in Christ) reflects the organic makeup of an ectypal humanity created by a Trinitarian God. In a word, the unity and solidarity brought about by the headship of Adam or Christ "constitutes the organism of humanity."[62] If an organism is connected together by a unity and, in the case of corporate

59. I explicate the logic, textual evidences, and fruits of this claim (especially against the common charges that federalism renders God arbitrary and imputes merely legal fictions) in Nathaniel Gray Sutanto, "Herman Bavinck on the Image of God and Original Sin," *International Journal of Systematic Theology* 18 (2016): 174–90.

60. As Henri Blocher recognized, "Not only does Scripture stress the unity of the race, based on a common origin (Acts 17:26; cf. Gen. 3:20), but it conceives of groups, and ultimately of humankind, as organic wholes under representative 'heads.' Communities are more than aggregates of individuals; they have an identity of their own, which is expressed in the person of the leader. . . . Contrary to animal species, the human race is one in some spiritual way, as well as genetically; it is furnished with a 'head.'" Blocher, *Original Sin*, 96–97.

61. Bavinck, *RD*, 2:572.

62. Bavinck, *RD*, 3:106.

humanity (as distinct from the animal kingdom), that unity is found in an ethical and moral center, then it is fitting that the acts of Adam or Christ would implicate the whole: "The covenant of works and the covenant of grace are the forms by which the organism of humanity is maintained also in a religious and an ethical sense. Because God is interested, not in a handful of individuals, *but in humanity as his image and likeness*, it *had* to fall and be raised up again in one person."[63]

The sense of it "had to fall" here should not be taken in the sense of absolute necessity, as if God were constrained to create humanity in this way. Rather, we should take it as a sort of fittingness—just as it was fitting for God to create a creation with all of its lavishness and diversity, so would it be fitting for his image-bearers to be made to reflect his unity-in-diversity. The covenantal arrangement reflects this.[64] Bavinck grounded Adam's representative status not merely on his being a "*first* in a series" but on the organic (and Trinitarian) makeup of humanity, just as Christ is the unity that undergirds the diversity of renewed humanity.[65]

Hence, I demur to McCall when he argues that "where realist theories can offer ostensible explanations about how it is that we are 'in' or 'with' Adam, federalists cannot make such claims at all and are forced to fall back on purely forensic or legal categories."[66] As we have seen, federalists are quite happy to draw from realist moves, and Bavinck is no exception by offering this Trinitarian logic for conceiving human ontology. To repeat, we are one not substantially, but ethically, and that ethical connectedness is ontologically grounded. The ethical relations that bind us are part and parcel of what it means to be human.

Finally, I respond to Farris's and Crisp's three objections more directly. Against the (1) *divine will objection*, then, I argue that God's will here is not

63. Bavinck, *RD*, 3:106; *Gereformeerde Dogmatiek*, 3:96 (emphasis added). The sense that humanity "had to fall and be raised up again in one person" invokes a fittingness relation, rather than that of absolute necessity.

64. Ian McFarland's critique of Herman Bavinck, to the effect that Bavinck failed to provide a "rationale" by which "*Adam* can be described" as a federal head, then, does not take into sufficient account the Trinitarian and realist underpinnings of Bavinck's theological anthropology. Ian McFarland, *In Adam's Fall: A Meditation on the Christian Doctrine of Original Sin* (Blackwell, 2010), 153 (emphasis original).

65. McFarland, *In Adam's Fall*, 153.

66. McCall, *Against God and Nature*, 199.

arbitrary at all, but rather he acts in comportment with who he is. It is fitting, in other words, that he should create his image-bearers in such a way where their ontological makeup analogically reflects who he is. If God is a unity-in-diversity (as a simple Triune God) archetypally, then his image-bearers will conform to an organic unity-in-diversity, with Adam as the federal head of that unity. This flows straightforwardly into (2) the *authorization objection*—to not accept Adam's federal representation is beside the point, for it would be tantamount to rejecting our very human nature. As Bavinck often argued, we are not merely individuals but ethically connected people, and these connections are mere analogs to the ontological solidarity that we have with Adam. Our connection to Adam depends not on our authorization but on human nature itself. In the same way, (3) the *legal fiction* objection becomes rather immaterial, for the covenantal arrangement is fitting, given humanity's organic shape. Further, the transference of guilt, though typified in the imputation of Adam's sin most clearly, is also manifested in the sacrificial system of the old covenant, where sin offerings depict the transference of guilt from humans to sacrificial animals (Lev. 4:1–35; 5:14–17; 16), and, as we saw, in occasions like the sins of Achan and David (Josh. 7; 2 Sam. 24:10–15).[67] To refuel any of these objections also requires critiquing Bavinck's Trinitarian anthropology. Specifically, one would have to raise the objection that it is implausible, or unfitting, that humanity should reflect this organic, ectypal triune shape.

CONCLUSION: ORIGINAL SIN'S EXPLANATORY POWER

In this chapter, I presented a Reformed federalist position with regard to original sin and the fall. In so doing, I argued that original sin involved the imputation of Adam's guilt and the propagation of a corrupt human nature. This imputation and transmission of sin's guilt and corruption is due to the covenantal arrangement that God initiated with Adam, as Adam is humanity's federal head. Along the way, I juxtaposed federalism against realism, while showing that federalism can accommodate realist instincts. Finally, I

---

67. Mark Boda, *A Severe Mercy: Sin and Its Remedy in the Old Testament* (Eisenbrauns, 2009), 59–60; Hodge, "Imputation," 1463–64; Fesko, *Death in Adam*, 175–96.

responded to some common objections against federalism by appealing to Bavinck's Trinitarian theological anthropology.

In the next chapter, I shall outline the main contours of fallen human nature and the saving benefits of regeneration, sanctification, and glorification.

Before moving on, however, let us pause to consider how this revealed doctrine of original sin explains the plight of humanity. Though, at first glance, the doctrine of original sin presents us with a dark picture of the human condition, we should not lose sight of its illuminating work. It is to be believed not merely because God has revealed it: It explains human life.

Henri Blocher's searching and probing exploration of this doctrine led him to consider how original sin provides a more satisfactory account of the human condition than alternative philosophies that sought to do the same. Appealing to "Neo-Calvinist philosophers and apologists," he argues that a departure from God leads to a mangled perception of creation that tends to absolutize one aspect of creation over against another, as opposed to the Christian worldview (or social imaginary) that would rather see the polar ends of a perceived dichotomy as constitutive of a much larger, harmonious whole: "As soon as the foundational reference to God is erased, each of the two terms comes to stand on its own; being absolutized, they can no longer recognize each other, but only their opposition. The idol at one end calls for the counter idol at the other end."[68]

Blocher then observes that the Christian doctrine of original sin brings a more transcendent worldview than the limiting visions of human reason without revelation.[69] Exposed to the experience of sinfulness, humans encounter the simultaneity of "misery and royal descent," "shared inheritance and individual decision," and "necessity and responsibility."[70] We tend to pit these against one another: Humans have been described as miserable animals,

68. Blocher, *Original Sin*, 122–23.

69. Throughout this book, I am presupposing the use of worldview in line with Herman Bavinck's *Christian Worldview*, ed. and trans. N. Gray Sutanto, James Eglinton, and Cory Brock (Crossway, 2019), and the distinction between world vision and worldview in Johan Bavinck's *Personality and Worldview*, trans. James Eglinton (Crossway, 2023). Readers who are less acquainted with Bavinck's discussion and are suspicious of uses of "worldview" can simply read in "social imaginary," per Charles Taylor's use in place of the word. I am suggesting that if the word "worldview" is not used, some other word will inevitably be deployed to get at the metaconcept—whether "worlds," "social imagination," "framework," "philosophy of reality," etc.

70. Blocher, *Original Sin*, 83–104. Blocher is thus recognizing the neo-Calvinist analytic of what Christopher Watkin has termed "diagonalization." See Christopher Watkin, *Biblical Critical Theory: How the Bible's Unfolding Story Makes Sense of Modern Life and Culture* (Zondervan, 2022).

pitiable in our depravity and laughable in our misery, on the one hand, but we are also royal, meant to outlast our mortal coils, and called to project a manifest destiny beyond this earth. While we are all responsible for our own decisions and are called to work harder for moral improvement, we also recognize that we are the product of our past and ancestors, and that our present dispositions are the results of socioeconomic and generational factors beyond our control. We are held culpable for our own decisions, but we find in ourselves and before us a propensity toward actions of which we disapprove. Humankind is indeed a riddle, and the temptation is to solve the riddle by absolutizing one side of the phenomenon and providing a simplistic world vision.

Original sin, Blocher argues, is thus a key to explaining these artificial binaries. Human beings were created good, even royal, but we are image-bearers that have chosen to imitate creatures rather than the Creator. We have fallen a great height, and the fall is all the greater, the sin all the more depraved, *because of* the heavenly ends for which we were designed. We retain individual personalities, but we have a common nature that was inherited from Adam and we were corrupted due to his sin. Particular sins are perpetuated through families, cultures, and nations that form the sorts of actual sins toward which one may gravitate. Sin is before us, such that the whole world really does present us with the powers of the evil one (1 John 5:19), and yet we each sin in our own way and salvation can be one's own by faith. The Christian doctrine of sin, then, is part and parcel of a much larger, cosmic worldview that cannot be domesticated by the human imagination.

FURTHER READING

Watkin, Christopher. *Biblical Critical Theory: How the Bible's Unfolding Story Makes Sense of Modern Life and Culture*. Zondervan, 2022. Watkin unfolds the explanatory power of original sin in three brilliant chapters (chaps. 4–6) in an overall excellent overview of the necessity of the Christian faith to explain modern culture and life.

Johnson, Keith L., and David Lauber, eds. *T&T Clark Companion to the Doctrine of Sin*. Bloomsbury T&T Clark, 2016. A reliable handbook that surveys the biblical foundations, major theologians, and dogmatic issues to the doctrine of sin.

Blocher, Henri. *Original Sin: Illumining the Riddle*. IVP Academic, 1997. Though Blocher objects to the imputation of Adam's guilt, this older work of biblical theology is still exemplary in treating the explanatory powers of the doctrine of original sin.

Bavinck, Herman. *Reformed Dogmatics*, vol. 3, *Sin and Salvation in Christ*. Baker Academic, 2006. The opening chapters on the doctrine of sin advance a defense of federalism that makes use of realist intuitions and develops an account of organic, corporate humanity that coincides with covenant theology.

9

THE HOPE OF SALVATION

CORRUPTION, GRACE, AND CONSUMMATION

THE PREVIOUS CHAPTER introduced the doctrine of original sin and its two consequences, original guilt and original corruption, while focusing primarily on the former. This chapter explores the extent of and remedy for the latter: What are the implications of the transmission of corruption? In what ways are our natures now defiled or, as Paul puts it, by nature "dead in trespasses and sins" (Eph. 2:1–3)? What is the hope and solution for corrupted sinners? As we shall see, sinfulness has qualified the whole of our nature, and this biblical teaching forms what modern theologians would call the doctrine of "total depravity." Our state is so deprived of the capacity to will the good that God restrains our corruption by his common grace, and only a divine intervention in effectual calling and regeneration can reform and redirect sinners toward faith in Christ. After canvassing Reformed teaching on human corruption, then, I shall outline the ways in which common grace and our sinfulness relate, and I will offer an exposition of different kinds of actual sins. Finally, I will outline the ways in which the grace of regeneration, sanctification, and consummation correspond to the restoration and perfection of human nature after the fall.

ORIGINAL CORRUPTION: THE FALLEN HUMAN NATURE AND TOTAL DEPRAVITY

The created human nature is vitiated by sin. As Adam was the font of the human race, when he fell into sin, his nature was corrupted, losing original righteousness. Thus, as we saw in the previous chapter, sinful human beings are now bereft of all good and positively inclined toward evil, lawlessness, and autonomy. Question 25 of the Westminster Larger Catechism reiterates what we read in the confession, as it says that due to Adam's originating sin, Adam's nature was corrupted: "Whereby he is utterly indisposed, disabled, and made opposite unto all that is spiritually good, and wholly inclined to all evil, and that continually; which is commonly called original sin, and from which do proceed all actual transgressions." Other Reformed formulas confirm this. As chapter 8 of the Second Helvetic Confession puts it:

> By sin we understand that innate corruption of man which has been derived or propagated in us all from our first parents, by which we, immersed in perverse desires and averse to all good, are inclined to all evil. Full of all wickedness, distrust, contempt and hatred of God, we are unable to do or even to think anything good of ourselves. Moreover, even as we grow older, so by wicked thoughts, words and deeds committed against God's law, we bring forth corrupt fruit of an evil tree.

It is worth noting that in this statement, the consequences of the corruption transmitted affect not merely our outward acts but also our internal lives: "unable to do or even to think anything good of ourselves." Or as the Canons of Dordt articulate in article one under the third point of doctrine on human corruption: "They brought upon themselves blindness, terrible darkness, futility, and distortion of judgment in their minds; perversity, defiance, and hardness in their hearts and wills; and finally impurity in all their emotions." The Heidelberg Catechism, Q&A 5, tersely says, therefore: "I have a natural tendency to hate God and my neighbour."

Francis Turretin, then, observes that unregenerate sinners are dead in sin: "The sinner is destitute of the life of grace and loses all spiritual sense and motion; so that he can neither know anything true nor do anything good, any more than a dead man can bring himself to life."[1] Every faculty of the human soul resists heavenly and spiritual realities: "For as to the intellect (the eye of the mind), not only is he called 'blind' and 'weakened' (Eph. 4:18), but also 'darkness itself.' . . . As to the will, not only is he said to have a 'depraved' and 'deceitful' heart to be corrected . . . which ought to be broken and taken away, rather than what is able to be softened and admit life."[2] There is nothing in the corrupted human that can prepare or predispose them toward faith or salvation. Regeneration and conversion, therefore, depend on God's power alone: "As, however, man can contribute nothing to his creation, resurrection, and regeneration, so neither can the sinner contribute anything to his conversion. He ought rather to ascribe it wholly to the grace of God."[3]

These holistic ways with which the Reformed tradition describes the corruption of sin led to the modern summation of the doctrine of "total depravity"—humanity is now totally depraved, corrupted, and directed by sin. Sin is thus not limited to specific acts (actual sin) but is a condition of the fallen human being.[4]

But in what sense is this depravity "total"? As an initial foray, Tom McCall provides needed clarity, and while he focuses on what total depravity does not mean first before articulating what it means positively, we will flip his discussion. Total depravity means at least three things. First, it is "total" in the sense that it impacts "all members of the human race. All members of the human race—other than Christ, suffer from it."[5] Second, it means that "all parts or aspects of the human person are negatively impacted by it."[6] In the language of faculty psychology, it means not only the body but also the soul, the heart, the mind, the will, and affections are all affected by sin. We will what we know is wrong and we do not desire what is right; we deceive ourselves into not believing what is painfully obvious, and we also fail to

1. Francis Turretin, *Institutes of Elenctic Theology*, vol. 1, *First Through Tenth Topics*, ed. James T. Dennison, trans. George Musgrave Giger (P&R, 1992), 672.

2. Turretin, *Institutes of Elenctic Theology*, 1:673.

3. Turretin, *Institutes of Elenctic Theology*, 1:676.

4. Total depravity, like the acronym TULIP, of course, is a modern summation rather than a term provided by the Reformed orthodox sources (see Richard A. Muller, *Calvin and the Reformed Tradition: The Work of Christ and the Order of Salvation* [Baker Academic, 2003], 51–69). I am merely deploying it here as a useful heuristic tool.

5. Thomas McCall, *Against God and Nature: The Doctrine of Sin* (Crossway, 2019), 309.

6. McCall, *Against God and Nature*, 309.

communicate the truth, and so on. We can be more precise here as well: Total depravity means that our corruption is *radical*, in the sense of the Latin word *radix*—it gets to and comes from the center, so to speak, and roots of who we are. Our hearts are corrupted and evil, and because the faculties of the soul and the members of the body are directed by our hearts, our whole selves are sinful.

Bavinck describes this pervasiveness of sin by pointing to its mysteriousness and the unconscious ways in which we seem to run headlong to sin. Indeed, he argues that the psychological studies of his own day pointed to the depths of the soul and also to the corruption of sin: "The theory of the unconscious finds support in Holy Scripture insofar as it definitely takes the view that the soul is much richer and deeper than the consciousness (Ps. 44:21; Prov. 4:23; Jer. 17: 9–10; 1 Cor. 14:25; 1 Pet. 3:4; etc.), and it posits this thought as basic to its doctrine of sin (Gen. 8:21; Pss. 19:12; 51:10; Jer. 17:9; Mark 7:21)."[7] In another place, he describes the radical effects of our total depravity in terms of the intransigence of the stubborn human heart, even when confronted with truth:

> The heart has its own logic and it yields no syllogism to the understanding. Whoever does not realize and acknowledge this must explain the tenacity of their opponents' stubbornness and their unwillingness to seek shelter. Intellectualism leads to intolerance and looks down on the foolish and reluctant crowd with contempt. But even without unwillingness or misunderstanding, it often happens that a man cannot surrender himself under an argument, because he cannot convince himself and his heart; because he is his heart, he keeps opposing, even though his intellect is at the end of all contradiction. And in such a case, he would prefer to comfort himself with his intellect than displease the heart [*gemoed*]. Peace with one's own heart is elevated by the peace of the head. The logical power of truth has always proved impotent by itself to convert the heart without any other help.[8]

7. Herman Bavinck, "The Unconscious," in *Essays on Religion, Science, and Society*, ed. John Bolt, trans. Harry Boonstra and Gerrit Sheeres (Baker Academic, 2008), 197.

8. Herman Bavinck, "Hoofd en Hart," in *Christophilus: Jaarboekje Nederlandsch Jongelings-Verbond* (1892): 74. English translation available at Herman Bavinck, "Head and Heart," trans. Gregory Parker Jr., *Modern Reformation* (2021): https://modernreformation.org/resource-library/articles/head-and-heart.

For Bavinck, it is insufficient, then, to speak of the "noetic" effects of sin or even of the fallen will. Sin has infected us in ways that precede our conscious attention and decision-making, such that we might speak of the *psychological* (soul) effects of sin. If the heart is deceitful beyond all things (Jer. 17:9), attending to our sinfulness is painstaking, difficult, and, in fact, impossible without the work of God.

Third, McCall clarifies that sin now characterizes "all that unsanctified sinners *do*."[9] As we will show below, even the formally good things that sinners do are not done for God; indeed, they often do these things against God and for an idol in place of God. Because of that, sin is a fatal and tragic condition that needs a remedy outside of ourselves.

But we cannot stop here. We should clarify what total depravity does *not* mean. And here McCall is helpful as well, and I shall show the ways in which the Reformed tradition provides some needed granularity.

First, he says, it does not mean that "every sin is equally bad."[10] Though every sin is mortal (indeed, the Reformed are critical of the Roman Catholic classification of sins as either mortal or venial), the consequences of sin are various, each fitting to the character of the sin committed, and some sins are indeed more heinous in the sight of God. The Westminster Larger Catechism treats this topic with precision and balance—on the one hand, as Q&A 152 puts it, every sin merits the wrath and curse of God (the curse of which refers to eternal death): "Every sin, even the least, being against the sovereignty, goodness, and holiness of God, and against his righteous law, deserve his wrath and curse, both in this life, and that which is to come; and cannot be expiated but by the blood of Christ."[11] Yet, on the other hand, sins are not "equally heinous in themselves, and in the sight of God," as Q&A 150 says: "But some sins in themselves, by reason of several aggravations, are more heinous in the sight of God than others." The next answer provides some reasons for this gradation: "(1) from the persons offending . . . (2) from

9. McCall, *Against God and Nature*, 310.
10. McCall, *Against God and Nature*, 308.
11. On each sin bringing the curse, which is death, Q&A 93 says: "Q: What is the moral law? A: The moral law is the declaration of the will of God to mankind, directing and binding every one to personal, perfect, and perpetual conformity and obedience thereunto, in the frame and disposition of the whole man, soul, and body, and in performance of all those duties of holiness and righteousness which he oweth to God and man: promising life upon the fulfilling, and threatening death upon the breach of it."

the parties offended . . . (3) from the nature and quality of the offense . . . (4) from circumstances of time and place" (Q&A 151). The Reformed tradition is thus sensitive to the distinction between God as the one whom all sins are ultimately against and the diverse modes of sin.

Second, "Total depravity does not mean that every person (or even every unregenerate person) is equally depraved by sin."[12] Or, to put it another way, total depravity does not mean that every person is as bad as they could be or is perpetually committing the most heinous of sins. Though, as we shall see, I argue that the reason total depravity is not *utter* depravity is due to God's intervening common grace, a typical way to speak about the apparent goodness that can still be exemplified by unregenerate sinners is an appeal to the remnants of the light of nature—remnants that continue to be held onto by sinners due to common grace. As the Canons of Dordt say, under article four of the third doctrine on the "inadequacy of the light of nature":

> There is, to be sure, a certain light of nature remaining in all people after the fall, by virtue of which they retain some notions about God, natural things, and the difference between what is moral and immoral, and demonstrate a certain eagerness for virtue and for good outward behavior. But this light of nature is far from enabling humans to come to a saving knowledge of God and conversion to him—so far, in fact, that they do not use it rightly even in matters of nature and society. Instead, in various ways they completely distort this light, whatever its precise character, and suppress it in unrighteousness. In doing so all people render themselves without excuse before God.

The "light of nature" refers to the result of what has been termed by Bavinck as "general revelation": that work of God of revealing himself to all of creation, as described by Psalm 19 and Romans 1:18–23. Because of general revelation, fallen creatures continue to know God (e.g., his divine nature, eternal power, and wrath, per Rom. 1) and thus know the difference as well between right and wrong. Hence, this article specifies that, with regard to the *saving* knowledge of God specifically, the human is radically incapable of obtaining or even of preparing oneself to obtain it. Further, it is worth

12. McCall, *Against God and Nature*, 308.

noting that, according to the Canons of Dordt, even with regard to *natural* matters, despite possessing some knowledge, sinners still do not use that knowledge "in matters of nature and society" properly. They "suppress the truth in righteousness" (e.g., Rom. 1:18), and hence they "completely distort this light," as the article continues to say.

How do they distort this light, and how do they misuse the knowledge of natural matters in "nature and society"? Much can be said about the phenomenology of self-deception, unbelief, and their ideological or social consequences. As seen in the exegetical section, humans tend to substitute worship of the real God with a lesser idol, a god of their own imaginations, because those gods are less sovereign and judge less severely than the real God (Rom. 1:18–32). Further, idols are controllable and contained by human hands, serving ends that we have determined for them. Worship of idols is thus subservient to and useful for human aims, whereas the absolute God of the Bible is self-contained and our only hope in escaping divine judgment is by his own sovereign freedom and mercy.[13] When we substitute *that* God with creaturely idols, we idolize some aspect of nature or culture as an ultimate rather than a penultimate end, thus putting a weight on those aspects that they cannot sustain.[14]

What is of concern here, however, is the sense of "total" depravity. Total depravity means, at the very least, that the fallen human is totally incapable of saving knowledge and good—that is, they are naturally and morally unwilling to desire Christ and to exercise saving faith in him. Only regeneration can bring that about. Further, total depravity also means that, despite natural morality and natural knowledge, they continue to "distort" and misuse such knowledge with regard to natural affairs ("nature and society"). As I argue below, however, with regard to these natural affairs, those who suffer from total depravity can still do some good and access truth because common grace intervenes and suspends that distortion from becoming final.

The sense of nature and society here has to do with penultimate life: matters of common culture. As Van Mastricht elaborates, one can distinguish between different kinds of good: "(1) natural good, walking, reasoning; (2)

13. Cf. John Cavadini, *Visioning Augustine* (Wiley-Blackwell, 2019), 144.
14. See David Koyzis, *Political Visions and Illusions: A Survey and Christian Critique of Contemporary Ideologies*, 2nd ed. (IVP Academic, 2019).

moral good, the exercise of some sort of civil virtue; (3) ecclesiastical good, to which sort belongs the duties of external divine worship; and (4) a spiritual and saving good, which accompanies salvation."[15] Those in the state of sin could do "natural, moral, and ecclesiastical good, but absolutely none for spiritual and saving good."[16]

As we shall see, however, the tendency of the Reformed is not to attribute these remnants of the reception of the light of nature to the strength of human nature *qua* nature, but rather to God's grace: "God willed all these bits of his own image to survive in us from the fall, first so that they may be witnesses of his most undeserved goodness toward us; then so that they may be like seeds from which the divine image through the grace of restoration might afterward begin to bloom again."[17]

SINS, BLINDNESS, AND COMMON GRACE

The question remains: How do people distort natural knowledge and morality in matters of nature and society? Two distinctions provide more clarity. The first is commonplace in Reformed scholasticism, which is the distinction between sins *per se* and sins *per accidens*, and the second is the distinction between the common and the normative.

The distinction between sins *per se* and sins *per accidens* illumines that actual sins are diverse. We are all corrupted by sin, but we all sin distinctly and in various ways. Sins *per se* are those sins that are by their very nature "repugnant to the law, such as idolatry, blasphemy, homicide."[18] On the other hand, sins *per accidens* refer to acts that, considered in themselves, may not be formally evil but "through the circumstances, from the efficient cause, the end, the manner, and other things, vice is added from elsewhere to an act that is good *per se*."[19] The Leiden Synopsis argues that this distinction is useful but should be clarified, for even sins *per accidens* are judged no less severely

15. Van Mastricht, *TPT*, 3:463.
16. Van Mastricht, *TPT*, 3:463.
17. Van Mastricht, *TPT*, 3:291.
18. Van Mastricht, *TPT*, 3:493.
19. Van Mastricht, *TPT*, 3:493–94.

than sins *per se*.[20] Further, to illustrate sins *per accidens*, the Synopsis points to a few examples. An act might be right but not from the right principle of the heart, as in 1 Timothy 1:5, which commands that acts should be done out of purity of heart. An act might be sinful when it is done for the wrong end, as "the Pharisees fast, pray, and give alms, in order to obtain glory from men (Matthew 6:1)."[21] Finally, an action might be evil because of "sinful circumstances," as seen in the examples of the sons of Aaron offering strange fire (Lev. 10:1), when Uzzah touched the ark to keep it from falling (2 Sam. 6:6), and when believers wrongly exercise Christian liberty and cause stumbling (Rom. 14:20).[22]

Overall, though, this distinction also illumines how an unregenerate society can continue with relative peace and not devolve into utter chaos. In other words, although total depravity does say that everyone has been corrupted, we do not all exercise sins *per se* (for thus peace would be impossible) but sins *per accidens*. As Paul says, even the gentiles continue to do the law, despite being in their sin (Rom. 2:14). One way to illumine why sins *per se* and *per accidens* are both punishable sins is to attend to Bavinck's articulation of egocentricity as the ultimate principle of all actual sins: He argues that the "organizing principle of sin is self-glorification, self-divination; stated more broadly, self-love or ego-centricity."[23]

Recall, as well, the earlier chapter on dominion and the cultural mandate. As Bavinck argues, there is no neutrality in culture. Either true religion or unbelief will "animate" our cultural efforts, and true religion lines up our cultural mandate under the "heavenly" mandate of obedience to God for the sake of fellowship with him. Thus, the "sins *per accidens*" might be "splendid vices" insofar as they are formally good works, though not done for the proper end—namely, the glory of God. When those works are set not to God but to an idol, we end up working for a deified object that cannot deliver. Or, to say it another way, when good ends become ultimate ends, they cannot satisfy the human heart and instead substitute God with a creature, the giver with

20. *Synopsis of a Purer Theology: Latin Text and English Translation*, vol. 1, *Disputations 1–23*, ed. Dolf te Velde, trans. Riemer A. Faber (Brill, 2014), 391.

21. *Synopsis of a Purer Theology*, 1:391.

22. *Synopsis of a Purer Theology*, 1:391.

23. Herman Bavinck, *Reformed Ethics*, vol. 1, *Created, Fallen, and Converted Humanity*, ed. and trans. John Bolt (Baker Academic, 2019), 105.

the gift. Formally good deeds done for wrong ends explains the possibility of an unbelieving culture and society to persist temporally, in this order of God's patience and common grace.

The second way in which we might distort natural morality and society is by confusing the common (even universal) from what is natural, essential, or normative. Sin blinds and darkens the mind, the Scriptures often repeat, and causes us to confuse the truth. We "suppress the truth" in unrighteousness (Rom. 1:18) and thus substitute what we know of God for creaturely idols and standards. Because sin is now a ubiquitous human experience, we confuse abnormal acts with the norm. If everyone errs, surely, then to err is human, we have often heard it said. But to err (in the sinful sense) is not human, and originally human nature was made with righteousness and holiness.

As Jake Meador shows, the ancient Greco-Roman world, for instance, confused the seemingly boundless male desire for sex with the natural state of affairs. As the logic goes: If this sexual desire is so natural (we are born this way), then it is proper to give in to it as much as possible. "The classical world assumed that male sexual energy was basically boundless and that the stability of the city relied on finding ways to direct and discipline that energy. This meant that for men any number of sexual acts were admissible—anything from marital sex to keeping a female mistress to keeping a few young boys around to rape."[24] In this context, then, the Christian sexual ethic (as expressed, say, in 1 Cor. 6–7 or Eph. 5:21–33) is not only counterintuitive but also unnatural. In fact, it seems to suppress the universal human experience and desire for immediate sexual gratification. Indeed, unregenerate and regenerate reason dispute not merely the authority and claims of Scripture but also what is regarded as natural or unnatural.

Christian theology has long insisted that the Christian view of marriage and sexuality, for instance, just *is* a description of the normative, natural order of things, and it is sin that has caused us, universally but in diverse ways, to deviate from the norm. To draw from Plato's allegory of the cave, if everyone else is happily satisfied when looking at shadows and chained to a wall in a cavern, the philosopher who tells them that there is a world outside of the cave to be enjoyed is looked upon with deep suspicion. Cornelius

24. Jake Meador, *What Are Christians Good For? Life Together at the End of the World* (InterVarsity, 2022), 71.

Van Til articulates this distinction between the common and the normative vividly by way of his own modification of Plato's allegory:

> If the God of Christianity does exist, the evidence for Him must be plain. And the reason, therefore, why "everybody" does not believe in Him must be that "everybody" is blinded by sin. Everybody wears colored glasses. You have heard the story of the valley of the blind. A young man who was out hunting fell over a precipice into the valley of the blind. There was no escape. The blind men did not understand him when he spoke of seeing the sun and the colors of the rainbow, but a fine young lady did understand him when he spoke the language of love. The father of the girl would not consent to the marriage of his daughter to a lunatic who spoke so often of things that did not exist. But the great psychologists of the blind men's university offered to cure him of his lunacy by sewing up his eyelids. Then, they assured him, he would be normal like "everybody" else. But the simple seer went on protesting that he did see the sun.[25]

Sin is indeed empirically verifiable, but it is empirically verifiable *through* illumination, lest we confuse the sinful condition with the essential or normative.[26] As the Catechism of the Roman Catholic Church articulates well, then, revelation is needed to perceive rightly the realities of sin and the fallen condition of the human race: "Without the knowledge Revelation gives of God we cannot recognize sin clearly and are tempted to explain it as merely a developmental flaw, a psychological weakness, a mistake, or the necessary consequence of an inadequate social structure, etc. Only in the knowledge of God's plan for man can we grasp that sin is an abuse of the freedom that God gives to created persons so that they are capable of loving him and loving one another."[27]

This situation is dire indeed. While special revelation presupposes the natural order, the knowledge of that natural order is so suppressed in principle by the unregenerate mind that they have substituted it with some other standard, determining the knowledge of good and evil for itself. But God

25. Cornelius Van Til, "Why I Believe in God," Reformed.org, 1996, https://reformed.org/apologetics/why-i-believe-in-god-by-cornelius-van-til.

26. Henri Blocher, *Original Sin: Illumining a Riddle* (IVP Academic, 1997), 84–85.

27. Catechism of the Catholic Church, section 2, chapter 1, article 1, paragraph 7 (388), https://www.vatican.va/archive/ENG0015/__P1C.HTM.

did not leave us to our own devices; between the fallen human being and the grace of regeneration is common grace, by which God restrains sin and gifts unregenerate sinners with life-giving, moral, and epistemic gifts. We suppress the truth, but not totally and finally in this life, due to the present redemptive-historical order of common grace.[28]

Petrus van Mastricht affirms this "inward" grace that curbs sin but does not redeem. He argues that God so "tempers the severity of this spiritual slavery" in many ways, allowing us to retain shards of original righteousness and "wisdom in the intellect," such that in general humanity might still acknowledge that God ought to be worshiped and that we should treat our neighbors with Jesus's golden rule. He then argues that there is "internally" a "restraining grace, by which sin itself is not removed or diminished, but its action is so curbed so that it would not burst its restraint, a grace also by which the more upright at least abhor more atrocious sins (1 Cor. 5:1)," and, alongside that internal grace, an external grace, "through certain political, ecclesiastical, economic, and academic remedies, by which in some measure the license of sin is restrained, and indeed there is added a stimulus to perform upright deeds."[29]

The reason why total depravity is not utter depravity is due to God's internal and external graces. Internally, God restrains sin, curbing it within us, and externally, God allows society to temper our sinfulness through its laws and order. Vermigli likewise speaks of God as "sometimes present and illumines [sinners] with excellent, heroic virtues that restrain original sin, keeping States and governments held together in at least some civil order . . . these good qualities were restraints on original sin and a depraved nature, lest everything be in upheaval, good laws come to ruin, and the light of nature, in a way, be extinguished."[30] Common grace is far from a nineteenth-century neo-Calvinistic invention; conceptually, it has always been there in the Reformed tradition, rooted in a reading of the Scriptures. Notice, then, that this "restraining grace" for Van Mastricht is not reducible to the external restraints of the law, mediated by political, churchly, economic, and academic means. Common grace is inward as well, as God does not leave us

28. Blocher, *Original Sin*, 89.
29. Van Mastricht, *TPT*, 3:528.
30. Martyr Vermigli, *On Original Sin*, 54.

without a witness and restrains the sinful heart from running headlong into destruction. As Schilder argues forcefully, the language of the "remnants of natural light" that we might see in the Reformed tradition should not lead us to praise fallen humanity as such but to worship God: "Will someone now turn to sing the praises of that natural light? Or the praises of the remnants? Or the praises of the conscience? Let them rather sing the praises of God, who preserves the 'nature' of his creatures, regardless of how fiercely they struggle against."[31] The remaining light of nature is a witness, therefore, to the grace of God and not to the goodness of humanity *simpliciter*.

Christians recognizing common grace therefore should cultivate two virtues that usually do not go together. When confronted with the unbeliever, they should lament that the unbeliever is rejecting Christ and should be fueled with evangelical zeal for the unbeliever, and yet the Christian should also be prompted to give thanks to God, for the unbeliever continues to manifest external gifts that were given to them by the Spirit of God. The latter without the former leads to a kind of naivete that waters down the need to call unbelief toward repentance, but the former without the latter leads to an over-realized understanding of the antithesis, causing us to view unbelievers with total suspicion, as if they are not made in God's image and are not benefactors of the Spirit's generosity.

SIN AND SUBSTANCE: A CLARIFICATION

We have said much about the fact and consequences of corruption. But what is this sinful corruption exactly? That is, what is this corruption and sin metaphysically? Is sin a substance that now coinheres with our human nature? The broad Reformed and catholic tradition has offered a rather unanimous answer to this question. Sin is not a substance, for if it were, then God would be the author of sin. All of existence can be categorized under two headings: Creator or creature. God alone is Creator, as he does not exist in a class—he is sui generis and is not composed between genus and species, for none is like him (Exod. 15:11). Everything else that exists does so as creatures of God

31. Klaas Schilder, "'No' to Natural Theology (1939)," in *The Klaas Schilder Reader: Essential Writings*, ed. George Harinck, Marinus de Jong, and Richard Mouw, trans. Albert Gootjes and Albert Oosterhoff (Lexham, 2022), 209.

(John 1:1–4; Col. 1:15–17). Sin, therefore, according to the tradition's dogmatic logic, cannot have existence—it is not a substance but rather a privation. For, if it exists substantially, then it was directly created by God, and God is not an author of sin:

> For sin is not a thing of essence that has its own existence, but it is concomitant, dwelling among us, easily ensnaring us (Rom. 7:20, 21; Heb. 12:1). It is something that inheres in human beings as an accident in the subject. Although these things [essence and sin] cannot be separated within corrupt man, yet we do assert that they should be distinguished. For God is the creator of all substances; yet sin neither was created by God, nor is it a creating thing or an essence.[32]

Further, to assert that sin has its own substantial existence is to fall into the error of Manicheanism, according to which there are two opposing forces of good and evil that vie for power, which would compromise not only the assurance that good will be victorious over evil ultimately but also the sovereignty and omnipotence of God.

Hence, sin is a "corruption of [Adam's] nature" (Westminster Larger Catechism, Q&A 25) rather than a nature of its own. As Van Mastricht says, it "certainly presupposes something positive, in which it is present as in its subject, yet it is not itself something positive or real, for then it would require the first cause as its author, for it cannot occur that something would be positive or real that would not depend necessarily upon the first cause."[33] If there is a sense in which God is the "cause of sin," Van Mastricht argues, it is only so because God is the primary cause of sin's "material nature or substrate" (human nature), which is corruptible and corrupted by sin.[34] The language of sin and evil as "privation," therefore, should not eclipse its debilitating and evil quality. It is not merely a lack of health but a sickness, not merely blindness but distortion. It is a corruption of the good, a debasing of reason, and not a mere "nothing"; it is parasitic on creatures with the potency for reason and obedience, in angels and humanity, and directs their wills against a law that they know. Hence, the Westminster Larger Catechism (Q&A 24) defines sin as

32. *Synopsis of a Purer Theology*, 1:369.
33. Van Mastricht, *TPT*, 3:448.
34. Van Mastricht, *TPT*, 3:449.

"any want of conformity unto, or transgression of, any law of God, given as a rule to the reasonable creature." Again, Van Mastricht says: Sin "is not something purely negative; for thus it also would not be evil, or punishable by God . . . the subject in which that privation exists, is only rational creatures, angels and men, to whom alone a law has been prescribed which they can understand and transgress; and furthermore, in these beings the subject is their faculties, habits, and actions, inasmuch as they can depart from the law."[35] Privation is thus not about mere absence but the absence of a quality that is natural to a particular form. A tree with the lack of sight is not called blind, for sight was never part of its nature to begin with. A human who lacks wisdom, however, is foolish, and the human who lacks righteousness is wicked.

Sin corrupts the whole being by directing the will against God and for a purported good that sinners have determined for themselves—a counterfeit good. The language of sin as a privation, then, should not lead to the false conclusion that it merely weakens creatures, but, as David Kelsey has noted, "may focus and intensify their powers in dangerous ways."[36] Because humanity was created for the highest good, which is God, and sin directs us away from God, corrupting our nature, sin has been classically considered as being both against God *and* nature. Much like the deformed palate that prefers and is accustomed to the flavor of a sweet poison over the food that is fitting for the body, sin is folly and against nature. Turretin puts it tersely: "The orthodox constantly maintain that sin is to be distinguished from the substance itself, as an accident and vicious quality from its subject."[37] Sin is a perversion of nature, a pollution, a corrupting influence. As McCall argues, sin is a parasite; sin is "something parasitic on goodness, something that is a deprivation that leads to depravity," and sin is thus "*unnatural*."[38]

ON NATURE AND CONCUPISCENCE

If sin is unnatural, then, the corruption as a result of the fall does not leave human nature intact. Sin is a vicious quality, as we saw, that adheres to the

35. Van Mastricht, *TPT*, 3:448.

36. David Kelsey, *Eccentric Existence: A Theological Anthropology*, vol. 1 (Westminster John Knox, 2009), 407.

37. Turretin, *Institutes of Elenctic Theology*, 1:636.

38. McCall, *Against God and Nature*, 232–33 (emphasis original).

human subject. Corrupted humans are thus defiled by concupiscence, an internal tendency to desire to sin.

As we saw in earlier chapters, the loss of original righteousness is not the loss of a supernatural addition to an otherwise untouched human nature. Such a view was expressed by the Roman Catholic dictum that the "naturals remained untouched, but the supernaturals only were lost."[39] Bavinck refers to this view as the "supernaturalist" position because original righteousness was conceived as a supernatural bridle that restrains the natural tendency toward the flesh in the natural man. With regard to natural affairs, then, though humanity might have a natural concupiscence, "the loss of the image, which renders man totally deaf and blind in spiritual matters, still enables him in earthly matters to do much good and in a sense renders him independent from the grace of God in Christ."[40] By way of contrast, recall, Bavinck argues that the loss of original righteousness and the corruption of the fall lead us to lose the narrow sense of the image of God, though we retain the broad sense. The loss of that narrow sense (the proper function and direction of the image in righteousness, holiness, and knowledge), however, so affects the broader sense that we can say we are wholly corrupted in the sense of total depravity outlined above.[41]

What, then, shall we make of "concupiscence"—that is, of the inclination toward evil in the "natural" man? Van Mastricht elucidates the issue and distinguishes three categories: (1) primary-first motion concupiscence, which lacks all consent of the will; (2) secondary-first motion, which enjoys some consent; and (3) second motions, which is the perpetrating of the sin with full consent.[42] The primary-first motion is thus the spontaneous appearance of some inclination toward sin and is not yet contemplated with consent or enjoyment by our consciousness. The question is whether "actual concupiscence toward evil with respect to its primary-first motion, is sin."[43] Van Mastricht then observes that due to the desire to preserve the possibility of

39. Turretin, *Institutes of Elenctic Theology*, 1:471.

40. Bavinck, *RD*, 2:554.

41. So, the Leiden Synopsis: "Even Adam, after the fall into sin, kept the same essence of his own nature that he had previously, and he remained the same man. Our essence indeed does not change into another essence either by sin or grace, even though it is spoiled by evil or made perfect by good." *Synopsis of a Purer Theology*, 1:369.

42. Van Mastricht, *TPT*, 3:505.

43. Van Mastricht, *TPT*, 3:505.

perfection in the regenerate, "papists" deny that this primary-first motion is sin. As the Catechism of the Catholic Church continues to say:

> Etymologically, "concupiscence" can refer to any intense form of human desire. Christian theology has given it a particular meaning: the movement of the sensitive appetite contrary to the operation of the human reason. The apostle St. Paul identifies it with the rebellion of the "flesh" against the "spirit." Concupiscence stems from the disobedience of the first sin. It unsettles man's moral faculties and, without being in itself an offense, inclines man to commit sins.[44]

The rebellion of the "flesh," in this view, is not "itself an offense," and it refers to the movement of the sensitive appetite (in the body) contrary to the rational appetite. Original justice (or righteousness) was the bridle that kept that innate conflict between flesh and spirit in check, but the fall means the loss of that original justice such that we are now characterized by this inner tension.

Van Mastricht argues that the "Reformed . . . state that all acts of concupiscence, even the primary-first, are sins," due to texts such as Romans 7:7, Exodus 20:17, and Matthew 22:37. If, as James 1:14–15 says, this concupiscence is the source of actual transgressions, then how can the cause of sin itself not be sinful? "Accordingly, it is not valid to say . . . it begets sin, therefore it is not sin."[45] In contemporary times, this discussion of concupiscence has implications on recent debates on homosexuality and identity. From a Reformed Protestant perspective, same-sex attraction that is not acted upon is still a feature of corruption and concupiscence (Rom. 1:18–31) and is thus illicit as a primary-first motion sin.[46] So Vermigli states: "Therefore, since all these lusts incite us to disobeying and rebelling against the Word of God, they are transgression and should be called sins."[47] Bavinck concurs: "The Reformation spoke out against that [Roman] position, asserting that also the impure thoughts and desires that arose in us prior to and apart from our will are

---

44. Catechism of the Catholic Church, part 3, section 2, chapter 2, article 9 (2515), https://www.vatican.va/archive/ENG0015/__P8P.HTM.

45. Van Mastricht, *TPT*, 3:506.

46. On this topic, see Matthew Roberts, *Pride: Identity and the Worship of Self* (Christian Focus, 2023).

47. Vermigli, *On Original Sin*, 17.

sin."[48] Indeed, the presence of the inclination of sin is not a mark of created nature but of fallen natures, and concupiscence remains in the regenerate as what some have called "indwelling sin."

REGENERATION AND CONSUMMATION

Given the condition of defiled humanity, then, God alone can be the source and cause of our salvation. This brings us to a discussion of the divine work of effectual calling and regeneration. If we are fallen, it is impossible to acquire salvation progressively by incremental steps of moral action. What is needed is a miraculous divine work that changes us from the inside out, causing us to be born again to new life (Eph. 2:4–10). This doctrine of regeneration, with the doctrine of original sin as its correlate, is a distinctive feature of Christianity over against, say, an Islamic view of salvation and sin. As Mona Siddiqui shows, it is, in fact, a fundamental difference between the two traditions. In Christianity, sin is not reducible to an act but is a condition that must be healed by grace; in Islam, however, sin is an act and not a condition, and thus guidance is sufficient to lead us back to God:

> Herein lies a fundamental difference between Christianity and Islam, in that the very nature of sin means that guidance alone cannot redeem or restore that which humankind has lost. Sin is not a human act, but a human condition in which people are weak and need grace. If prophecy is not enough, then neither is guidance, Scripture or otherwise, it is divine grace which must be seen to be active in human life which redeems. From the Muslim perspective, guidance and grace work together, not to transform our sinful condition, but to lead us to God.[49]

Indeed, one's theology of grace is connected to a doctrine of sin because the solution corresponds to the problem, and the magnitude of the grace of God in Christ shows us the depth of one's sinful condition. In Islamic theology, there is no parallel doctrine of original sin as there is in Christian faith. Hence, it follows that sin is not a condition from which acts flow, but rather the view of sin is focused in the acts themselves. If sin merely refers to acts, and not to

---

48. Bavinck, *RD*, 3:143.
49. Mona Siddiqui, *Christians, Muslims, and Jesus* (Yale University Press, 2013), 197–98.

a corrupted nature, then it is sufficient for God to send reminders, guidance, and signposts by way of the messengers in order for humans to return and walk on the straight path (Sura 1.6). Grace, therefore, refers to those signs and revelations that in turn guide humanity.

According to Christian teaching, however, original sin has precipitated a debilitating condition, and it would be a mistake of the Pelagian heresy to deny that we have inherited this original sin from Adam. We sin not merely due to imitation but because of propagation and imputation. For God to give teachers and guidance is thus not enough—we need a penal substitutionary atonement by way of a second Adam, a second federal head, who would represent sinners. Jesus Christ's life, death, resurrection, and ascension are an indication of the love and grace of God, and surely this was redemption accomplished.[50]

But were this work to remain outside of us, we would not have benefited from it. Redemption is not merely accomplished but also applied to sinners.[51] We receive that redemption, therefore, by Spirit-wrought faith, which puts us in union with Christ. In union with him, believers receive the benefits of justification (which imputes Christ's righteousness to us, dealing with our guilt), sanctification (which restores and transforms us to be more like Christ, dealing with our corruption), adoption (which enfolds us into the kingdom of God, our Father, as children of God, dealing with our alienation), and glorification (which consummates the work that was begun in us, dealing with death and the very presence of sin).

The question, however, is how corrupt sinners can will to put their faith in Christ. How might those who are depraved desire Christ as their treasure? In the state of sin, after all, the Westminster Confession of Faith says that humanity is "altogether averse from that good" and thus "not able, by his own strength, to convert himself, or to prepare himself thereunto" (9.3). A Reformed answer here lies in the doctrines of effectual calling and regeneration,

---

50. This is not to limit Christology to matters of redemption, though it does place the incarnation within the fitting order of God's saving economy. Cf. John Webster, "The Place of Christology in Systematic Theology," in *The Oxford Handbook of Christology*, ed. Francesca Murphy (Oxford University Press, 2015), 611–27; Justus H. Hunter, *If Adam Had Not Sinned: The Reasons for the Incarnation from Anselm to Scotus* (Catholic University of America Press, 2020); and N. Gray Sutanto, "Consummation Anyway: A Reformed Proposal," *Journal of Analytic Theology* 9 (2021): 223–37.

51. John Murray, *Redemption Accomplished and Applied* (Eerdmans, 2015).

which renew our fallen natures and enable us to trust and follow Christ. Westminster Confession of Faith 10.1 says it this way:

> All those whom God hath predestinated unto life, and those only, He is pleased, in His appointed and accepted time, effectually to call, by His Word and Spirit, out of that state of sin and death in which they are by nature, to grace and salvation by Jesus Christ: enlightening their minds, spiritually and savingly, to understand the things of God, taking away their heart of stone, and giving unto them an heart of flesh; renewing their wills, and by His almighty power determining them to that which is good; and effectually drawing them to Jesus Christ; yet so as they come most freely, being made willing by His grace.

The doctrine of effectual calling refers to the power of God's word and Spirit to regenerate fallen sinners in God's appointed time. The work of regeneration renews the hearts of elect sinners so that they might know, trust, and embrace Christ as revealed in the word of God. As the confession states, regeneration restores every aspect of our being—"enlightening" minds, transforming hearts, "renewing" wills—so that we might be drawn to Christ as proclaimed in the gospel. We would thus come most "freely," while being "made willing by his grace."[52] Regeneration results in us seeing the beauty of Christ, and subsequently we would desire him freely and decisively. This restoration is not adding a new substance into us but mitigates the vitiating powers of sin: "So the Christian is nothing other than a reborn, renewed, and hence, a truly human person."[53]

This does not mean that there are no longer residual influences of sin in the regenerate Christian's heart, but it does mean that this sin no longer enslaves them. In the state of grace, Christians are able to choose that which is spiritually good but continue to wrestle with indwelling sin: "When God converts a sinner and translates Him into the state of grace, He freeth him from his natural bondage under sin, and, by His grace alone, enables him

52. As our wills act on the rational consent of our understanding, our wills are thus never indifferent but yet free from coercion. In other words, we enjoy the freedom of spontaneity but not the freedom of indifference. See Turretin, *Institutes of Elenctic Theology*, 1:665–66; and James Anderson and Paul Manata, "Determined to Come Most Freely: Some Challenges for Libertarian Calvinism," *Journal of Reformed Theology* 11 (2017): 272–97.

53. Bavinck, *RD*, 4:436.

freely to will and to do that which is spiritually good; yet so as that, by reason of his remaining corruption, he doth not perfectly, nor only, will that which is good, but doth also will that which is evil" (WCF 9.4).

Bavinck argues that this state of grace allows us to forge bonds of love that rebind humanity together, as manifested in the community of the visible church. Indeed, his discussion of the spiritual life corresponds to the sinful life that the Spirit renews. Fittingly, regeneration produces a reuniting of one's self into a harmonious whole and a renewal of one's fellowship with God and others—it produces a life force that redeems the self and necessarily turns us *toward* others, restoring the spheres of state, science, art, culture, and family. The human individual is filled with gaps and disharmony—our wills conflict with our minds, our deeds with our consciences, and so on—but the spiritual life gives us a new, organizing principle of life: "Love of God gives stature and form to the spiritual life; it organizes and inspires it, turning it into one beautiful organic whole which functions as the foundational *life-force*."[54]

If sin loosens and atomizes, then the Spirit renews and rebinds. This life force, crucially, is an outward-looking one. It drives oneself into fellowship with others and thus reverses the atomizing powers of egocentricity (recall the principle of actual sin). The spiritual life manifests itself precisely in the new bonds that are re-created with fellow believers as believers are drawn toward God: "Because love for God is its foundation, spiritual life itself consists of fellowship with God, with Christ, and with fellow believers. Love strives after and *is* fellowship, a fellowship that is only possible through and in love. Hatred separates; love binds."[55]

When Christians reconcile and bind ourselves in ethical ties with one another, we are not only obeying God's commands—we are becoming more *whole*. Indeed, we are witnessing to the work of God that renews and reconnects the organism of humanity. Love binds the organism of redeemed

54. Bavinck, *Reformed Ethics*, 1:248.

55. Bavinck, *Reformed Ethics*, 1:248. As Philip Ziegler also notes, fellowship with God and fellowship with other believers go together: "Reformed sources will regularly speak in related terms of a 'glorious and perfected *fellowship*' of believers with God and one another: when this tradition comments on the eschatological *state* of human being it does so chiefly with affective terms befitting this relational scenario, speaking of joy, blessedness, glory, and a 'full and pleasant sense of God's favor.'" Ziegler, "'Those He Also Glorified': Some Reformed Perspectives on Human Nature and Destiny," *Studies in Christian Ethics* 32 (2019), 173.

humanity together, uniting all of redeemed humanity under a single head and maturing them toward a final end. This brings us to a discussion of human nature as perfected and glorified.

GLORIFICATION

What is that final end of human nature, then? It is important to note that the work of regeneration points us back to human nature as it was supposed to be. Sin is, again, an accidental quality that parasitically distorts human nature, and grace restores that nature. Regeneration, however, points not merely to a reversal of sin but also to the consummation and perfection of nature. Regeneration is the inauguration of a total renewal, bringing us back to the telos of Adam in the garden: consummate perfection. There, as Westminster Confession of Faith 9.5 articulates, "The will of man is made perfectly and immutably free to good alone, in the state of glory only." Indwelling sin will be no more, and sanctified sinners are immutably transformed to be perfected saints.

This state of glory has two stages, both of which we have intimated in chapter 3: the intermediate state (of heaven), where the souls of the saints await their resurrected bodies, and the resurrection itself—but both have the beatific vision as the central object of the Christian's joy.[56] Entering into glory presupposes the path of death and resurrection, as a sin-cursed cosmos necessitates purification. While Christians will die "once" (Heb. 9:27), their souls will be immediately taken up into heaven and await their resurrection at the new creation. The Westminster Larger Catechism Q&A 86 affirms that after death, the souls are "made perfect in holiness, and received into the highest heavens, where they behold the face of God in light and glory." Answer 90 further adds that the soul will be resurrected, where we are "made perfectly holy and happy both in body and soul."

Bavinck counsels us to be modest when it comes to the doctrine of the intermediate state, where the souls are awaiting their resurrected bodies.

56. There is, of course, some debate on the nature of the beatific vision in the intermediate state, with some in the tradition (like Calvin) arguing that the body is necessary for the fullness of the enjoyment of the vision, such that the intermediate state itself cannot be considered glory proper. See Steven Tyra, *"Neither the Spirit Without the Flesh": John Calvin on the Beatific Vision* (Bloomsbury T&T Clark, 2023).

Indeed, he comments that the "history of the doctrine of the intermediate state shows that it is hard for theologians and people in general to stay within the limits of Scripture and not attempt to be wiser than they can be."[57] We do well to heed this warning and merely point to one important facet of theological anthropology here: The intermediate state is not the final destination of the dead, for, if the image of God refers to the body-soul unity, then souls without bodies are incomplete. As we saw especially in the Leiden Synopsis, Van Mastricht, and Bavinck, what distinguishes the human soul from angels is that the former is fitted for a body and is that which shapes the body. The soul without the body is thus incomplete. The "I" is the self that animates the whole soul-body composite, rather than identified merely with the soul, in keeping with the "aspectival" distinction that we saw between the inner man and the outer man (2 Cor. 4:16). The Leiden Synopsis (while not going into as much detail as, say, Aquinas[58]) articulates this logic well: "For since God struck that covenant not with souls but with persons, and the names Abraham, Isaac and Jacob stand for whole persons, life must of necessity be related to whole persons, and not only to some of their parts. Therefore, life relates not only to the immortality of souls, but also to the resurrection of bodies."[59]

Bavinck echoes the logic of the Leiden Synopsis and argues against an oppositional dualism that pits the soul over against the body:

> [The doctrine of the resurrection of the body is] diametrically opposed to all dualistic theories according to which the body is merely an incidental dwelling place or prison of the soul. The essence of a human being consists above all in the most intimate union of soul and body in a single personality. The soul by nature belongs to the body, and the body by nature belongs to the soul. Although the soul does not itself create the body, it nevertheless has its own body. The continuity of the individual human being is maintained as much in the identity of the body as in the identity of the soul.[60]

57. Bavinck, *RD*, 4:614. For more on Bavinck and the beatific vision, see N. Gray Sutanto, *God and Humanity: Herman Bavinck and Theological Anthropology* (Bloomsbury T&T Clark, 2024), chap. 9.

58. See Aquinas, *Summa Theologiae*, Ia. Q. 75–76, 84–89; see also Adam Wood, *Thomas Aquinas on the Immateriality of the Intellect* (Catholic University of America Press, 2020), chaps. 5 and 6.

59. *Synopsis of a Purer Theology*, 3:521.

60. Bavinck, *RD*, 4:694. There are certain questions to be asked about the continuity of our identity in the intermediate state given that our selves refer to the body-soul composite rather than

The whole person is constituted by the close relation of the body and soul. The Westminster Confession of Faith reminds us that this state of glory and the perfection of our selves is not just for the obtaining of some "abstract" righteousness but a conformity to the will of God and for the purposes of living as a psychosomatic unity in the presence of God: "The souls of the righteous, being then made perfect in holiness, are received into the highest heavens, where they behold the face of God in light and glory, waiting for the full redemption of their bodies" (WCF 32.1).

As such, that resurrection, too, is a resurrection that conforms to Christ's resurrection, who is the firstfruit: We are "made conformable to His own glorious body" (WCF 32.3). To say it another way, our resurrected and consummate natures are not ends in themselves but are for the *sake of* fellowshipping with God in Christ, the Christian's ultimate longing and joy. As Boersma has recently argued, the Scriptures and the broad Christian tradition uphold a transformative account of the resurrected body such that all of its "physical and intellectual capacities" will "be healed and transfigured," and that those capacities will obtain "powers of contemplation" that no heart can imagine now (1 Cor. 2:9).[61] Those contemplative powers are focused on God in and through Christ, and the whole self is transfigured progressively through eternity as it beholds God in Christ. Indeed: "For then shall the righteous go into everlasting life, and receive that fullness of joy and refreshing which shall come from the presence of the Lord" (WCF 33.2).

CONCLUSION

This chapter rounds off this book's second part. Chapters 4–9 present a historical and dogmatic sketch of human nature through the states of creation, fall, and redemption. This chapter has focused on human nature in its corruption and redemption—I have clarified that sin has affected our whole selves,

---

just the soul that could not be fully explored here. Perhaps we can say that we are a mere fragment (an incomplete person) there—but it's still *my* soul that's awaiting my body, and perhaps God, too, sustains our identity in a supernatural way. See Daniel D. De Haan and Brandon Dahm, "After Survivalism and Corruptionism: Separated Souls as Incomplete Persons," *Quaestiones Disputatae* 10 (2020): 161–76; and Jordan Steffaniak, "Retrieving Reformed Philosophy of Mind: Herman Bavinck's Eclectic Harmonism as Gateway to Neo-Aristotelianism," *Evangelical Quarterly* 94 (2023): 26–50.

61. Hans Boersma, *Seeing God: The Beatific Vision in Christian Tradition* (Eerdmans, 2018), 429. Cf. Sutanto, *God and Humanity*, chaps. 8–9.

that sin is nonetheless not a substance but a vicious quality that modifies human nature, that actual sins are diverse, and that common grace is that which restrains this corruption from becoming absolute. I also have shown that the depth of our defilement entails that only God alone can transform and regenerate our natures. Salvation belongs to the Lord (Jon. 2:9), and God saves to the utmost, causing us to be not only sanctified but also glorified unto fellowship with Christ in our resurrected bodies.

With this dogmatic presentation of a Reformed theological anthropology in view, we turn to the book's final section, the application of anthropology on two difficult topics: sex and gender on the one hand, and race on the other.

FURTHER READING

Gaffin, Richard B. *In the Fullness of Time: An Introduction to the Biblical Theology of Acts and Paul*. Crossway, 2022. While technically a work of exegetical theology, the book shows the profound ways in which God applies Christ's saving work on humans.

Tyra, Steven. *"Neither the Spirit Without the Flesh": John Calvin on the Beatific Vision*. Bloomsbury T&T Clark, 2023. A readable monograph on the traditioned debates on the mode of the beatific vision in the intermediate state and the resurrection.

McFadyen, Alistair. *Abuse, Holocaust, and the Christian Doctrine of Sin*. Cambridge University Press, 2009. A penetrating treatment on the psychological, social, and empirical depth of sin, as witnessed in cases of child abuse and the Holocaust. McFadyen shows that the Christian doctrine of sin is not a mere dogmatic treatment but has explanatory power for these real atrocities.

10

HUMAN SEXUALITY

MALE AND FEMALE

One of the most pressing issues in contemporary times concerns the nature of sex and gender. A variety of questions arise when one brings up the subject of sex, concerning whether, for instance, there is a distinction between sex and gender, what it means to be embodied beings, the proper place of marriage and singleness in Christian theology, and the relationship between our biological selves and the cultural norms one associates with our sexed bodies. It is thus imperative to discuss the nature of sex in a theological perspective, in order then to draw some pastoral and ethical reflections on these fraught issues.

Previous chapters have addressed sex from various angles. Chapter 1 notes the created goodness of our sexed existence and embodiment. Chapter 4 lays some of the groundwork for an Augustinian account of sexuality from the perspectives of creation and consummation. Chapters 5 and 6 show the ways in which the Reformed tradition has incorporated the body into a highly holistic account of the human being and the image of God, and chapter 7 indicates that procreation and culture-making are important components of the cultural mandate, as implications of the corporate account of the image of God.

This chapter sustains attention on this topic and lays some parameters for thinking theologically of sex and gender that build on the previous threads and address some contemporary concerns. It moves in five steps. The first section returns to Genesis to observe the good creation of the complementary relation between male and female. The second shows how to think responsibly about marriage as a sign to Christ. The third wrestles with the current proposals to revise our traditional accounts of gender in an attempt to include biological males or females as "trans women" or "trans men," respectively. The fourth section then investigates the distinction between nature and custom and the different social roles that men and women might occupy from a biblical and theological perspective. Finally, I end this chapter by considering the way in which Bavinck's account of corporate and consummate humanity might chasten our investigations into the meaning and enactment of masculinity or femininity.

BACK TO GENESIS: THE MALE-FEMALE RELATION IN GENESIS 1:27–28; 2:15–25

Let us return to Genesis and consider the equality-in-difference that characterizes the male-female relation. Genesis 1:27 establishes the fundamental ontological equality between male and female. Moreover, verse 28 also gives them both a common blessing and a common mandate. Eve was not made a helper for Adam's own ends, but rather both require the other to fulfill a common command from God, and both sin and suffer the consequences of the fall.[1]

The significance of the two sexes is shown not merely in their common dignity and calling, however, but also in their mutual dependence, difference, and non-interchangeability—what John Kleinig calls a "dynamic polarity,"[2] or as Prudence Allen describes it, an "integral complementarity,"[3] and what J. Budziszewski terms "polaric complementarity."[4] "Men and women aren't just

1. Abigale Favale, *Genesis of Gender: A Christian Theory* (Ignatius, 2022), 48 (emphasis original).
2. John Kleinig, *Wonderfully Made: A Protestant Theology of the Body* (Lexham, 2021), 34.
3. Prudence Allen, *The Concept of Woman*, vol. 3, *The Search for Communion of Persons, 1500–2015* (Eerdmans, 2016), 467. See also Julián Marías, *Metaphysical Anthropology: The Empirical Structure of Human Life*, trans. Frances M. López-Morillas (Pennsylvania State University Press, 1971), 133–42.
4. J. Budziszewski, *On the Meaning of Sex* (Intercollegiate Studies Institute, 2014), 41.

different, but different in corresponding ways . . . different in ways that make them natural partners."[5] Allen is emphatic that this integral complementarity is the opposite of both, on the one hand, a "hierarchical complementarity" of the woman's "systematic" subordination to the man—which happens only in light of the fall—and, on the other hand, an "egalitarian complementarity," where the ministerial roles of the two sexes become interchangeable.[6] Males and females are two wholes that come together in complementary communion, rather than two parts that need each other for wholeness. This is seen in the text in two ways.

The first is the command "to be fruitful and multiply" in Genesis 1:28, right after the poetic declaration that God has created his image-bearers as male and female. Both, together, are required to produce life, and this command means that procreation, the result of sexual union, is a natural result of their embodied complementarity. Males or females alone cannot give life. Both must come together as "one flesh" (Gen. 2:24). We are not reducible to our biology, but it is a necessary aspect of what makes males and females distinct. The language of act and potency (explored in chap. 1) is particularly useful here as it signifies the total orientation of male and female bodies as distinct from one another: "This *potentiality* that belongs to femaleness is always present, even if there is some kind of condition, such as age and disease, that prevents that potential from being actualized. The very category of 'infertility' does not undermine this definition, but affirms it. A male who cannot get pregnant is not deemed 'infertile,' because he never had that potential in the first place."[7] The reason why marriage is between man and woman is because of the potential generativity of this union, and it is only the entrance of recent technology that has veiled (though it can never eradicate) the natural design (cf. 1 Cor. 11:3, 11–12).[8]

The second way the Genesis account shows the communion that males and females have is in the sense of their complementary relationship and

5. Budziszewski, *On the Meaning of Sex*, 41.

6. Allen, *Concept of Woman*, 3:474 and 3:482, respectively.

7. Favale, *Genesis of Gender*, 121. Regarding the point concerning the category of "infertility," cf. Vern Poythress, *Making Sense of Man: Using Biblical Perspectives to Develop a Theology of Humanity* (P&R, 2024), 479.

8. Poythress, *Making Sense of Man*, 488–89.

companionship.[9] In glory, we retain our sexed bodies and yet will not express them by a marital relation. This indicates that our sexed bodies have a fundamental significance that precedes the marital union. We can express our maleness and femaleness in our relationships more broadly considered in several social roles. Here, Bavinck is eloquent: Male and female were created as equally accountable to God, yet they have a reciprocal relation with each other and are not reducible to the other. He writes:

> The woman is not merely created *alongside of* him but *out of* him (1 Cor. 11:8). . . . She is out of Adam and yet is another than Adam. She is related to him and yet is different from him. She belongs to the same kind and yet in that kind she occupies her own unique position. She is dependent and yet she is free. She is *after* Adam and *out of* Adam, but owes her existence to God alone. And so she serves to help the man, to make his vocation of subduing the earth possible. She is his helper, not as mistress and much less as slave, but as an individual, independent, and free being, who received her existence not from the man but from God, who is responsible to God, and who was added to man as a free and unearned gift.[10]

While we should be cautious in elaborating on the specific differences between the male and female that go beyond biology (as I shall further investigate below), the Bible does affirm that *there is* a difference between the two, and that this difference is good. This complementary polarity between male and female indicates that, even though each individually is an image-bearer of God, precisely in their "relationship and fellowship with each other" the image is disclosed in a richer way: Not "in the man alone, nor in the woman alone, but in both together, and in each in a special way, the image of God is expressed."[11] Bavinck is not saying that there is a univocal or one-to-one relationship between each person of the Trinity with one sex or gender (as if the Father is like the husband and the Son is like the wife). Nor would

9. Allen suggests that there are four features of complementarity: ontological (human nature has both male and female forms), physical and biological, psychological, and spiritual. *Concept of Woman*, 3:469.

10. Herman Bavinck, *Wonderful Works of God*, trans. Henry Zylstra (Westminster Seminary Press, 2020), 171. See the parallel passage in Herman Bavinck, *Guidebook for Instruction in the Christian Religion*, ed. and trans. Gregory Parker Jr. and Cameron Clausing (Hendrickson, 2022), 82.

11. Bavinck, *Wonderful Works*, 188.

Bavinck entertain the idea that the Father is eternally in authority whereas the Son is eternally in submission (which is both a Trinitarian error and an overextension of the husband-wife relation to characterize all males and females).[12] Earlier chapters have already indicated that the whole Deity is the archetype of humanity.[13] Rather, Bavinck's point is that the unity-in-diversity of the male-female relation is itself a microcosm of the broader, corporate account of the image of God, as humans are intrinsically socially and relationally connected. Each individual, relation, family, and culture images God in its own way as humanity multiplies, and the male-female relationship "and fellowship" itself contributes to that broader dynamic. As Amy Peeler observes: "When humanity reflects the image of God, it does so in interdependence between men and women."[14]

This recognition of the dignity and equality of women with men resources Bavinck's conviction that "the progress of civilization finds its measuring rod in the position which the woman finds herself among the people," either by "exaggeration" or by "deficiency"—that is, either by exalting her above all or by falsely denigrating her.[15] It is the Christian faith, he argues, that has recognized her dignity and rightful place as opposed to the older orders that tend toward her oppression.

The complementary character of male and female is, secondly, further denoted in Genesis 2. Note the prompts for the creation of the woman in Genesis 2:18–25. Adam sees the woman with a "sigh of recognition," after naming all the animals and not finding a partner suitable for himself.[16] God recognizes that it is not good for man to be alone and thus fashions the woman from his side, equal to him yet different from him, and to be commissioned alongside him to fill and cultivate the earth. Herein is a basic insight from John Paul II: The body itself reveals personhood, reciprocity, and theological

12. Cf. Scott Swain, *The Trinity: An Introduction* (Crossway, 2020); N. Gray Sutanto, "Herman Bavinck on the Image of God and Original Sin," *International Journal of Systematic Theology* 18 (2016), 177–90.

13. In this way, the oblique and brief passages from Herman Bavinck's *The Christian Family* (Christian's Library Press, 2012), 3, 7–8, should be read in light of what he has said clearly in the *Reformed Dogmatics* and *De Vrouw in de Hedendaagsche Maatschappij* (Kok, 1918).

14. Amy Peeler, "Imaging Glory: 1 Corinthians 11, Gender, and Bodies at Worship," in *Beauty, Order, and Mystery: A Christian Vision of Human Sexuality*, ed. Gerald Hiestand and Todd Wilson (IVP Academic, 2017), 158.

15. Bavinck, *De Vrouw in de Hedendaagsche Maatschappij*, 77.

16. R. R. Reno, *Genesis* (Brazos, 2017), 75.

significance. He writes, "Man and woman constitute, so to speak, two diverse ways of 'being a body' that are proper to human nature in the unity of this image."[17] As Danielle Treweek observes, this significance of the male-female relation is eschatologically fecund: "The eschatological virginal life will be one in which sexual duality remains significant, both for the purposes of mature personal subjectivity *and* perfected interpersonal relationship."[18]

Favale also comments on Adam's "sigh of recognition" in the "silent declaration" of Eve's body. Adam recognizes "that she is both like him—more like him than any other earthly creature—and not like him. Their difference is complementary, but asymmetrical; this is not a mirror image or polar opposite. She resembles him in their shared humanity—'bone of my bones and flesh of my flesh'—but differs in the feminine form of her humanity."[19] Their ontological equality is irreducible to interchangeability or uniformity, and the fall mars this delicate creational balance.

Finally, it should be noted that the New Testament refers back to the creation of male and female. Jesus appeals to Genesis 1:27 and 2:24 as a basis against the naturalness of divorce. The intrinsic goodness of the male-female relation, then, is affirmed throughout the Scriptures as a fundamental natural reality. Indeed, Jesus's gendered resurrection body and his teaching that marriage will be no more, while maintaining that there remains a distinction between those who marry and those who would be given in marriage (Matt. 22:30), indicates that we will continue to be male and female in the resurrection, as Augustine argued. This is fitting, given that grace restores nature and the created order determines the trajectory of consummation.[20] Paul, likewise, appeals to "nature" to warn against the sins of homosexuality (Rom. 1:18–32).[21] The rooting of the male-female relation, marriage, and procreation in the creation order indicates that these

17. John Paul II, *Man and Woman He Created Them: A Theology of the Body*, trans. Michael Waldstein (Pauline Books & Media, 2006), 178.

18. Danielle Treweek, *The Meaning of Singleness: Retrieving an Eschatological Vision for the Contemporary Church* (IVP Academic, 2023), 196.

19. Favale, *Genesis of Gender*, 39.

20. See Brian Mattson, *Restored to Our Destiny: Eschatology and the Image of God in Herman Bavinck's Reformed Dogmatics* (Brill, 2011); Anthony Thiselton, *1 Corinthians* (Eerdmans, 2006), 1264.

21. Cf. Matthew Levering, "Thomas Aquinas on Sexual Ethics," in *Beauty, Order, and Mystery: A Christian Vision of Human Sexuality*, ed. Gerald Hiestand and Todd Wilson (IVP Academic, 2017), 165–80; Allen, *Concept of Woman*, 3:467–68.

matters are not reducible to social convention or pragmatic utility. They are rooted in God's design.

MARRIAGE AS A SIGN TO THE CHRIST-CHURCH RELATION AND SINGLENESS

Along with the creational accounts of male and female, Paul appeals to marriage as a mystery that points to Christ and his church (Eph. 5:29–33). In that text, Paul offers a christological interpretation of Genesis 2:24. While the marriage of Adam and Eve was first historically, Christ and the church is first logically. God imbued this marriage with a teleological significance: "The leaving and cleaving of a man to his wife signals the way in which the eternal Son has sought out and united himself to his bride, the church."[22] This christological gloss forms the basis for the ethical injunctions Paul supplies in Ephesians 5:33 for the husband to love his wife "as himself," and for the wife to respect her own husband, as well as to submit to him as her head (Eph. 5:22–24).[23] Elsewhere, Paul recognizes that if Christ is the head of his church, then the church is his body (1 Cor. 12:12–31).

A few comments are in order. First, the Christ-church grounding for the relation of husbands and wives is specific to that husband-wife relation. We should be on guard on overextension here, as Michael Allen warns: "Submission does not come as a blanket posture that marks all female relationships to all men. . . . The passage does not root this command in some generic or global hierarchy of the sexes. The text does call for a respect of one's own husband as husband, however, which takes the form of submission to authority in that singular, specific, relational context."[24] Authority and submission do not identify the relationship between all women and all men but refer in particular to the husband-wife relation.

Second, the Christ-church grounding gives a specific meaning to the husband's authority and the wife's submission. This text clearly demarcates a proper, benevolent, and sacrificial authority predicated on Christ's example

22. Michael Allen, *Ephesians*, BTCB (Brazos, 2022), 165–81.

23. Because the calls for submission in Ephesians 5:22–24 are ways to obey "The Lord," which relativizes all human authority, I agree with Allen that there is "no signal that 5:22–6:9 comprises anything other than some illustrations of the principle taught in 5:21." Allen, *Ephesians*, 134.

24. Allen, *Ephesians*, 134.

of sacrificing himself for the good of the church, from a malformed authority predicated on domination and abuse. In this regard, it is worth considering Lynn Cohick's suggestion that the language of the husband as the "head" of the wife refers not merely to his preeminence or authority *simpliciter* but to his position as the "source" of the wife, as the woman was taken out of the man (1 Cor. 11:3, 11–12), and as the husband is the "patron" that "provides a benefit to her client, which the client reciprocates through honouring his patron."[25] Reading Ephesians 5:22–24 in light of 1 Corinthians 11:3 and 11:11–12 is instructive, for the Father is the "head" of Christ not as if the Father is superior to Christ (that way lies subordinationism), but because he is the one who eternally generates the Son in Christ's divine nature and because he is the creator of the Son's human nature.[26] This use of "headship" to refer to the calling of the husband to sacrifice himself for the body as Christ did for the church is contrary to a typical Greco-Roman usage, according to which the body is expected to die for the head in military and political contexts. Cohick is thus correct in her argument that the husband's calling to sacrifice "undermines the [Greco-Roman] gender hierarchy by ceding honor to the wife as worthy of the husband's self-sacrifice."[27] Recognizing that headship includes both authority and source means that the *manner* of the husband's authority here is specific: It is a sacrificial, self-giving authority. Hence, this reading, in my view, does not contradict but complements the traditioned teachings on the husband as the authority over the family.

Gerald Hiestand has provided a fruitful theological reflection on the (physical) power dynamics indicated in this passage, especially related to the husband's calling to sacrifice himself for his wife. Drawing from Camille Paglia and John Paul II, Hiestand argues that the Christ-church relation parallels the power difference of male and female physicality. More specifically, Hiestand is reflecting on why it is that God has allowed males to possess more raw physical strength than females when such strength could and has often been used toward unjust ends: "The New Testament does not so much insist that husbands *should* be in the power position . . .

25. Lynn Cohick, *The Letter to the Ephesians*, NICNT (Eerdmans, 2020), 357.

26. Cohick, *Letter to the Ephesians*, 355–57, who draws from Cyril of Alexandria and John Chrysostom on reading head as "source." In my view, there is no need to juxtapose "source" with authority—headship language signifies both source and authority. Cf. Allen, *Ephesians*, 135.

27. Cohick, *Letter to the Ephesians*, 352.

but rather it simply acknowledges that husbands are, and then gives instruction about how men are to use their greater [physical] power."[28] The Christ-church analogy informs him here: "Christ's divine nature gives him a native strength that the church does not inherently possess. And indeed, this inequality of power is central to the entire narrative of Christ and the church, for it is precisely because the church occupies a position of vulnerability that Christ comes as her suitor. If the church possessed by nature the same power and strength that Christ possessed, there would be no gospel story."[29] How does Christ use his power for his own body? He puts it "in the service of sacrificial love . . . rather than using the endless power at his disposal to seek his own safety, he used his power to secure the safety of his bride."[30] The bride of the church, then, embraces this use of Christ's power as she entrusts herself to his sacrificial authority. As Rebecca McLaughlin summarizes well: "It's love across difference."[31] The church, however, is no mere passive recipient. As a result of Christ's sacrifice, the church is co-heir with Christ, participating with him, and will reign with him (cf. 2 Cor. 6:1; Rev. 21–22).

Third, we should note with care that while the husband is called to imitate Christ in his sacrificial love, the husband, too, is a member of the church of Christ and is thus in need of redemption and sanctification. In other words, the husband's imitation of Christ should not lead one to conclude that the husband *is* taking the place of Christ: "The husband nowhere fits the mold of Christ."[32] He, too, needs to be sanctified by Christ's blood. This explains why Paul does not call the wife to submit on the basis of the *husband's* Christ-likeness but "as to the Lord" (Eph. 5:22), just as the husband, too, is called to obey Christ and follow his example in sacrificial leadership. Both husband and wife, in other words, are accountable primarily to Christ for their relation with each other (which explains Paul's counsel that both ought to submit

28. Gerald Hiestand, "Put Pain Like That Beyond My Power: A Christocentric Theodicy with Respect to the Inequality of Male and Female Power," in *Beauty, Order, and Mystery: A Christian Vision of Human Sexuality*, ed. Gerald Hiestand and Todd Wilson (IVP Academic, 2017), 115 (emphasis original). My thanks to Rachel Gilson for bringing this essay to my attention.

29. Hiestand, "Put Pain Like That Beyond My Power," 112.

30. Hiestand, "Put Pain Like That Beyond My Power," 113.

31. Rebecca McLaughlin, *Secular Creed: Engaging Five Contemporary Claims* (The Gospel Coalition, 2021), 31.

32. Allen, *Ephesians*, 135.

to the other, Eph. 5:21).[33] Marriage is thus a *sign*—it points to a higher transcendent reality and as such there can be no horizontalized, univocal sense in which the husband is just the Christ and the wife is just the church. That would flatten the sign-substance distinction and would unduly divorce Ephesians 5 from 1 Corinthians 12 and other texts on the believer's union to the body of Christ, the church. John Cavadini draws from Augustine to warn against such flattened readings of Ephesians 5, arguing that the analogy that the wife is a *receiver* and the husband is a *giver* should not be overemphasized, lest one forgets that the husband *too* is a receiver and the wife is never passive (cf. 1 Cor. 7:3–4; 11:11–12): "Both husband and wife are members of the one body, the bride of Christ; both are profoundly receivers before they are anything else. It is in the first place as members of the church, bound to all others in charity, that they are configured to Christ's transforming and purifying love. Members of the church are not, in the first place, souls in individual relation with the Word of God, but rather members of each other in the flesh that the Word 'married' in the Incarnation."[34] It is not the case that the wife's spiritual standing depends on the husband—both are accountable to the word of God.

This accountability of each individual directly before God and the sign-nature of marriage are why the marital relation will no longer be extant in the resurrection order. Though we retain our sexed bodies (for the eschaton consummates our created telos), marriage's substance will be realized: "For the marriage of the Lamb has come and his Bride has made herself ready" (Rev. 19:7). The Christian teaching of marriage thus does not denigrate the joy and beauty of singleness. If marriage depicts the intimacy and sacrifice of Christ for the church, singleness points to his sufficiency as the groom for the church and points directly to this new order. As Dani Treweek has argued, singleness is "eschatologically instructive"; faithful marriage and singleness are "equally valuable and yet distinctly challenging forms of discipleship now."[35] Whether married or single, the body of the Christian is the Lord's. It is thus fitting that Paul would warn against sexual immorality, for our body is now the temple of the Spirit of Christ and we ought to honor him with

33. Cf. Cohick, *Letter to the Ephesians*, 353.

34. John Cavadini, *Visioning Augustine* (Wiley-Blackwell, 2019), 174. So Treweek, *The Meaning of Singleness*, 196.

35. Treweek, *The Meaning of Singleness*, 264.

it (1 Cor. 6:16–20). Faithful singleness, therefore, is a "vocation, a gift from God" (Matt. 19:11; 1 Cor. 7:7).[36] This is not just in the sense of a self-consciously chosen life of celibacy. Rather, singleness is per se and in itself, "while still being receptive to the possibility of marriage," "eschatologically significant."[37]

To further flesh out the sense of our sexed complementarity without marital relations, consider the way in which the Westminster Larger Catechism expounds on the fifth commandment:

> **Q. 123.** Which is the fifth commandment?
> **A.** The fifth commandment is, Honor thy father and thy mother: that thy days may be long upon the land which the Lord thy God giveth thee.
>
> **Q. 124.** Who are meant by father and mother in the fifth commandment?
> **A.** By father and mother, in the fifth commandment, are meant, not only natural parents, but all superiors in age and gifts; and especially such as, by God's ordinance, are over us in place of authority, whether in family, church, or commonwealth.
>
> **Q. 125.** Why are superiors styled father and mother?
> **A.** Superiors are styled father and mother, both to teach them in all duties towards their inferiors, like natural parents, to express love and tenderness to them, according to their several relations; and to work inferiors to a greater willingness and cheerfulness in performing their duties to their superiors, as to their parents.

Notice that the understanding of the divines here indicates that though parenting and biological fatherhood and motherhood are indeed important features of what it means to be male and female, the significance of these terms go much beyond biological parenting. All "superiors" (or authorities) are in view here in the various relations of family, church, or government. The catechism resists, therefore, universalizing the husband-wife relation, as if that is the only paradigm through which to see the male-female relation. Males are fathers, sons, brothers, and husbands; females are mothers, daughters, sisters, and wives. One could be a father to many without himself

36. Kleinig, *Wonderfully Made*, 189.
37. Treweek, *The Meaning of Singleness*, 199.

being a biological father; one could be a mother to many without herself being a biological mother. The claims of the catechism thus incorporate not merely family relations but also those who live in singleness in all of their various relations, and not all of the roles of authority are gender specific. In this sense, then, Deborah is a mother to Israel (Judg. 5:7), Paul is a father to Timothy (2 Tim. 1:2), and John calls the recipients of his letters "children" (e.g., 1 John 2:1). Recipients of Paul's letters, too, are often called "brothers" or "sisters." Scott Swain summarizes these observations: "In both civil and ecclesiastical contexts, we may be fathers and sons, brothers and sisters to those who are not members of our natural family."[38]

Amy Peeler's comment on 1 Corinthians 7 is consistent with and expands on Swain's observations:

> The man and woman unable to bear physical children still give a visual picture of the glory of God's ability to create life. . . . [Paul's] vigorous argument there . . . bars any contemporary diminishment of the nonfertile Christian. In nature and the church, men and women are dependent upon one another because all things naturally and spiritually find their source in God, who is Creator of all and the Father of the household of the Lord's followers. If all things come from God, then women and men, married and single, childbearing or no, can visually demonstrate in their bodies the full creative power of God.[39]

Such observations bear directly on the single person. The faithful single person is still a sibling or parent to many, and in obedience is himself or herself a pointer to the future order of consummate interpersonal relations without conjugal expressions (1 Cor. 7:25–31).

THE SEX/GENDER DISTINCTION?

With these biblical-theological observations in hand, then, it is no wonder that Westminster Confession of Faith reiterates that humanity was made "male and female" (WCF 4.1) and emphasizes that "marriage is to be between

38. Scott Swain, "Thoughts on Theological Anthropology: Man as Male and Female," *Reformed Faith and Practice* 5 (2020): 59.

39. Peeler, "Imaging Glory," 163.

one man and one woman: neither is it lawful for any man to have more than one wife, nor for any woman to have more than one husband at the same time" (WCF 24.1).

Contemporary thinkers, however, suggest that there should be a distinction, even a separation, between one's biological sex and one's gender. Now, there are various ways to describe this difference. Some theologians concede, while retaining traditional accounts of sex, that "sex" refers to the basic biological makeup of males and females, whereas "gender" refers to the *norms* that we associate with each sex.[40] In this case, then, "sex" refers to our biological constitution as males or females (defined by the capacity to produce large or small gametes), whereas "gender" has to do with masculinity or femininity, which are tethered to males and females, respectively. An even more common account (until very recently) is to say that "gender" is another way of referring to "sex"; that is, they are virtually synonymous. "Male" and "female" denote sex, while "man" and "woman" denote gender; to be a man is be an adult human *male*, and to be a woman is to be an adult human *female*.[41]

Later on, I suggest that we should reject the sex/gender distinction altogether (or at least preserve a natural conceptual link between them), but this does not mean that our sex entails a certain set of easily identified norms by which we need to abide. We should take care in distinguishing between nature and custom.[42] In this case, then, we would have one's sex and gender on the one hand, and the *norms* that we associate with one's sex and gender on the other. In contemporary times, however, the sex/gender distinction is pushed much further: Gender is now often considered untethered from our embodiment altogether. If "sex" refers to our biological makeup, "gender" refers to something different entirely, and various thinkers have imported

40. Matthew Mason, "The Authority of the Body: Discovering Natural Manhood and Womanhood," *Bulletin of Ecclesial Theology* 4 (2017): 43.

41. An original definition of gender identity links it closely to one's sex, as the awareness of one's belonging to a particular sex. As Byrne has shown, however, this "original clear definition . . . has now been lost." See Alex Byrne, "The Origin of 'Gender Identity,'" *Archives of Sexual Behavior* (2023): 2.

42. The distinction between nature and custom does not, however, imply that we have access to nature *without* custom or cultural mediation. As Marías argues: "Since man is not Adam (or Eve), but the inheritor of a tradition, composed of historical and social substance, so is his body, and of course his sexuality. Any regression to mere biology among naked physical things is just that, a regression from reality to a hypothetical intellectual construction." Marías, *Metaphysical Anthropology*, 141.

numerous definitions to this term: Perhaps it is an innate sense, or a self-chosen identity, or a set of norms that one takes to be relevant to one's self (the literature is not altogether consistent). This separation between gender and sex is often motivated so that one is enabled, say, to argue that biological males can and should be considered real "women" as their gender if they see themselves as women (and are thus trans women).

This is a difficult topic indeed, and a few comments should be made by way of prolegomena. First, the goal in this section is modest. Since the subject matter of this book is on human nature, this section focuses on critiquing models of sex and gender that untether the latter from the former. There are other works that one can point to that trace the genealogy and logic of the current trans-inclusive accounts of manhood or womanhood, and that is not the focus here.[43]

Second, much of the motivation behind these new ideological trends is a desire to care for those who are struggling with gender dysphoria, which refers to "experiences of gender identity in which a person's psychological and emotional sense of themselves does not match or align with their birth sex."[44] We should share this motivation. The disagreement is not that such persons ought to be loved and cared for, but rather on how exactly such care is defined. A Christian account would include the body as intrinsic to who and what we are, and not something malleable or changeable on the basis of our desires.[45] Further, the gospel communicates that we do not have to alter our bodies or who we are in order to receive unconditional love.

Third, by addressing this issue, one should not overstate its universality. In my judgment, transgender ideology, along with a social constructivist view of gender, is a particularly Western phenomenon and influence, and by

---

43. E.g., Carl Trueman, *Rise and Triumph of the Modern Self: Cultural Amnesia, Expressive Individualism, and the Road to Sexual Revolution* (Crossway, 2019); Abigail Shrier, *Irreversible Damage: The Transgender Craze Seducing Our Daughters* (Regenery, 2020); Favale, *Genesis of Gender*. See also the summative remarks by Rebecca McLaughlin, *Secular Creed*, 83–104.

44. Mark Yarhouse, *Understanding Gender Dysphoria: Navigating Transgender Issues in a Changing Culture* (IVP Academic, 2015), 19.

45. For two competing accounts on how gender dysphoria might be treated by the eschaton, compare Matthew Mason, "The Wounded It Heals: Gender Dysphoria and the Resurrection of the Body," in *Beauty, Order, and Mystery: A Christian Vision of Human Sexuality*, ed. Gerald Hiestand and Todd Wilson (IVP Academic, 2017); and Blake Hereth, "The Shape of Trans Afterlife Justice," in *Voices from the Edge: Centering Marginalized Perspectives in Analytic Theology*, ed. Michelle Panchuk and Michael Rea (Oxford University Press, 2020), 185–205.

and large it is unshared by the majority world. That is not to say that gender dysphoria does not exist in the majority context. However, the prioritization of psychological fulfillment, of sexual expression and desire as determinative manifestations of one's identity, and the importance of authenticity as markers of a Western world vision have made it such that transgender ideology has gained traction there in ways that it has not in, say, Indonesia.[46] In that regard, it has always struck me as confusing when someone from the United States objects to Christianity on the basis of the perception that Christianity is a Western or "white" religion; to the contexts at which I ministered in Indonesia, it was precisely transgender ideology and secularism's promiscuity that were the Western imports, not Christianity. Indeed, Christianity's sexual ethic has many points of contact with Islam and Confucianism in a way that transgender ideology or affirmations of promiscuity simply do not.

Fourth, God's decision, not ours, fundamentally determines human identity. This means that our creation in God's image and redemption in Christ are decisive about who we are; our sexual performance or feelings are not. "If some people substitute an alternative identity for their God-given identity, then they are either unaware of their identity or mistaken or both."[47] This means that our self-perception and feelings could be misaligned with our fundamental identity: We can be wrong about who we are. I suggest, therefore, that to be most authentic with who we are is to live in conformity with the will of God, in keeping with the orders of creation and redemption.

What, then, shall we say by way of response to this separation of sex and gender? It is impossible to be exhaustive here. In a series of essays, Tomás Bogardus has helpfully collected current revisionary accounts of gender and has advanced persuasive criticisms of each of these proposals. For the sake of space, I shall highlight his most salient arguments to the effect that untethering gender from sex leads to either unintelligible circularity or a reduction of gender to stereotypes.[48] Then, I shall discuss some worldview issues that undergird this debate.

---

46. On the distinction between world visions and worldviews, see J. H. Bavinck, *Personality and Worldview*, ed. and trans. James Eglinton (Crossway, 2023).

47. Ryan S. Peterson, *The Imago Dei as Human Identity: A Theological Interpretation* (Eisenbrauns, 2016), 57.

48. For this section, I am summarizing the arguments from Tomás Bogardus, "Some Internal Problems With Revisionary Gender Concepts," *Philosophia* (2019): 1–21; "Evaluating Arguments

Again, Bogardus has helpfully collected and summarized some of the revisionary accounts of gender on offer: (1) From Judith Butler, "to be a woman is to repeatedly perform as a woman, i.e., to regularly and for the most part behave in line with feminine gender norms"; (2) from Sally Haslanger, to be a woman is "to be systematically subordinated along some dimension (economic, political, legal, social, etc.)"; (3) for Katherine Jenkins, "womanhood is a matter of norm-relevancy: to be a woman is to take (enough) norms of femininity to be *relevant* to oneself (even if one does not, ultimately, abide by these norms)"; and (4) for Talia Mae Bettcher, being a woman is about sincere self-identification with womanhood.[49]

As Bogardus goes on to show, Sally Haslanger's definition meets immediate problems. On her account, if society eliminates all systematic subordination, then women would no longer exist. Further, on her account, the queens of nations would not count as women, for queens can hardly be considered subordinated in any systematic sense.[50] One is then left with the definitions offered by Butler, Jenkins, and Bettcher—each of which identifies women as taking certain norms to be relevant to one's self and thus is enacted by repeating actions that line up to those norms.

Each of these definitions ends up quite circular. Consider Butler's definition: In her words, gender is "created through sustained social performances," "gender cannot be understood as a *role* which either expresses or disguises an interior 'self.'"[51] So gender is not expressive of anything behind it, and gender is a repetition of acts that conform to certain social expectations.

---

for the Sex/Gender Distinction," *Philosophia* (2020): 1–20; "Why the Trans Inclusion Problem Cannot Be Solved," *Philosophia* (2022): 1–26. See also Bogardus, *The Nature of the Sexes: Why Biology Matters* (Routledge, 2026).

49. Bogardus, "Evaluating the Sex/Gender Distinction," 4–5. Bogardus is referring to Judith Butler, "Performative Acts and Gender Constitution: An Essay in Phenomenology and Feminist Theory," *Theater Journal* 40 (1988): 519–31; *Gender Trouble*, 2nd ed. (Routledge, 1999); Elinor Burkett, "What Makes a Woman?," *New York Times*, June 6, 2015, https://www.nytimes.com/2015/06/07/opinion/sunday/what-makes-a-woman.html (Burkett's definition is deployed for the purposes of trans-exclusion, it should be noted); Sally Haslanger, "Gender and Race: (What) Are They? (What) Do We Want Them to Be?," *Noûs* 34 (2000): 31–55; Katherine Jenkins, "Amelioration and Inclusion: Gender Identity and the Concept of *Woman*," *Ethics* 126 (2016): 394–421; Talia Mae Bettcher, "Through the Looking Glass: Trans Theory Meets Feminist Philosophy," in *Routledge Companion to Feminist Philosophy*, ed. Ann Garry, Serene Khader, and Alison Stone (Routledge, 2017), 393–405.

50. Bogardus, "Some Internal Problems," 3.

51. Butler, "Performative Acts and Gender Constitution," 528 (emphasis original).

Jenkins's offered revision here seems to be consistent with Butler's: To be a woman, in the sense of gender identity, is to have "an inner map that is formed to guide someone classed as a woman through the social and material realities of someone who is so classed."[52] Again: "Having a female gender identity . . . is that one takes those norms to be relevant to oneself."[53]

The issue of circularity in both of these accounts can be made clear by asking the following question: If to be a woman is to enact social performances repetitively that conform to the expectations about femininity, who exactly are those expectations of femininity about? The answer, typically, is that they are about women: But women are those who act repeatedly in a way that conforms to the social expectations of women—who in turn are the ones who repeatedly act in a way that conforms to the social expectations of women, and so on ad infinitum. You get the idea. Or to take Jenkins's language: If to have a female gender identity is to take the norms about women to be relevant to one's self, how should we define "women"—that is, the subset of people that those norms are about? Bogardus puts it well:

> According to Jenkins, to be a woman (by identity) is to take a sufficient number of "norms of femininity" to be relevant to oneself, to apply to oneself, to be *about* or *for* oneself. Now, social norms are about (types of) people. And a problem emerges when we ask *who these norms of femininity are norms about*, who these norms are *for*. Norms of the medical profession are norms about doctors, nurses, etc.; that's who the norms are for. Academic norms are norms about professors, students, etc. Now, what about Jenkins' "norms of femininity"? Who are these norms for? Presumably, these norms that play a role in determining womanhood are norms about women, they are norms for women, they are statements of how women ought to behave. In that case, substituting talk of internal maps for equivalent talk of gender norms, Jenkins' definition of womanhood amounts to this: Someone is a woman if and only if she takes (a sufficient number of) norms about women to be relevant to herself, i.e. to be about herself. And now the problem becomes obvious: we've used "women" in a definition of womanhood.[54]

52. Jenkins, "Amelioration and Inclusion," 421.
53. Jenkins, "Amelioration and Inclusion," 411.
54. Bogardus, "Some Internal Problems," 9.

If one defines women as the class of "the adult human female," more problems emerge.[55] Such a definition would be trans-exclusive because then trans women are males who take norms about women (i.e., adult human females) to be about one's self, but they are not adult human females (hence, not women), so they would be taking norms that are about another class of persons to be about them. So a dilemma emerges: If to be a woman is to take the norms about women to be about one's self, and a woman is defined as someone who takes the norms about women to be about one's self, then one is left with a circular and unintelligible definition. But if womanhood is defined in the traditional sense of an adult human female, then it is trans-exclusionary, for it excludes those trans women who don't consider themselves to be adult human females or it includes trans woman by admitting that they are mistaking themselves to be adult human females, taking the norms about that class of people for themselves. Bogardus goes further and contends that a trans-inclusionary definition of man or woman is impossible in principle because "*no matter what it means to be a woman*, it's one thing to *be* a woman, and another thing to *identify* as a woman. This follows from a more general principle: it's one thing to be some way, another thing to identify as being that way."[56]

Suppose we grant, however, that to be a man or a woman is not about being adult human males or females but to act in a way that takes the norms of masculinity or femininity to be about one's self. Notice that in such a definition, manhood and womanhood are defined entirely by a society's norms—that is, by cultural stereotypes and expectations. Rebecca McLaughlin identifies the problems with this move: "If we take biological sex out of the definition of a woman, we swing a wrecking ball at the building itself. We have cultural paintings to hang, but no walls. For decades,

55. "Jenkins' definition excludes trans women who don't think of themselves as biologically female, i.e., the many trans women who believe their gender does not match their (male) biological sex. They do not take themselves to be biological females—hence, in many cases, the desire to be female, and to transition physically—and so they do not take norms about biological females to be about them. But then Jenkins' definition says they are not women. . . . Moreover, *if* medical technology cannot really change a person's biological sex then on this alternative Jenkins is committed to saying that literally any trans woman would be *mistaken* to think of herself as a woman: to be women, biologically male trans women must (mis)take norms about biological females to be about them." Bogardus, "Some Internal Problems," 10.

56. Bogardus, "Why the Trans-Inclusion Problem Cannot be Solved," 24.

feminists have been differentiating biological sex from cultural stereotypes, creating space for women to live *as* women in different ways. But if our bodies are removed from the equation, those stereotypes are all we have left."[57] As Holly Lawford-Smith puts it, from a gender-critical feminist perspective there is "no understanding gender without sex."[58] It is by recognizing that these social norms are *about* women that one can begin to evaluate such norms and resist them when they serve toward the unjust or unnatural subordination of one sex to another. When these norms of gender are "unmoored from the body altogether, gender is defined by the very cultural stereotypes that feminism sought to undo. In other words, when a girl recognizes that she does not fit the stereotypes of girlhood, she is now invited to question her sex rather than the stereotype."[59] Such a redefinition of manhood or womanhood as identified with idealized social norms results in a confusion concerning intersex people: Instead of recognizing them as men and women with nontypical sexual development, intersex individuals are dehumanized "by insisting that any deviations from idealized norms are not 'really' male or female, but 'other.'"[60] On the contrary: "There are two sexes, male and female, and intersex conditions do not undermine this."[61] Intersex conditions presuppose, rather than provide counterevidence for, the sex binary.

A few points are worth making that touch on the worldview issues that undergird this debate. From a Christian perspective, the body is not a meaningless clump of matter that exerts no moral pressure on us. Rather, because creation manifests God's design, the body itself is *intrinsically* meaningful, and it presses its meaning upon us. This link between embodiment and teleology is that which is denied by proponents of the revisionary paradigms: "Gender is not passively scripted on the body, and neither is it determined by nature, language, the symbolic, or the overwhelming history of patriarchy."[62] Consider, for instance, Robin Dembroff's reasoning in an oft-quoted essay:

57. McLaughlin, *Secular Creed*, 86.
58. Holly Lawford-Smith, *Gender-Critical Feminism* (Oxford University Press, 2022), x.
59. Favale, *Genesis of Gender*, 158.
60. Favale, *Genesis of Gender*, 131.
61. Lawford-Smith, *Gender-Critical Feminism*, x.
62. Butler, "Performative Acts and Gender Constitution," 531.

> If gender is just reproductive features and nothing more, it makes no more sense to insist that people must look, love or act in particular ways on the basis of gender than it would to demand that people modify their behavior on the basis of eye colour or height. Even if reproductive traits are correlated to personality, physical capabilities or social interests, such correlations don't equate to norms. As David Hume has taught us, it doesn't make ought. Having feet is correlated with walking, but I can walk on my hands if I want to. Having a tongue is correlated with experiencing taste, but who cares if I decide to drink Soylent every day?[63]

The reasoning here is that if gender is synonymous with the sexed body, then nothing can be inferred about norms that we ought to live by, for bodies do not imply any oughts.

From a Christian (and theologically realist) perspective, however, bodies *do* in fact entail norms. As Alexander Pruss argues: "It just is a basic truth that minds are for knowing, eyes are for seeing, and human front teeth are for cutting while the rear ones are for grinding. Teleological properties, the directness of things toward an objective purpose—a *telos*—are properties just as basic as mass and electric charge are."[64] Such observations are particularly potent on the grounds of theism: "The theist can say that divine wisdom caused such a correlation," and theism further grounds the precondition of the truth-detecting capacities of human reasoning.[65] Bogardus also registers the same criticism:

> Here's another way to put it: if all you know of a thing is that he is an adult human male, you are in a position to know various normative facts about him; those normative facts are knowable solely by reflection upon one's concepts. You're not left wondering, for example, whether this adult human male ought to be enslaved; you're in a position to know he shouldn't be, given only the information that he's an adult male human. And likewise with females. This shows that there are a priori entailment relations between our concepts of adult human females and males, on the one hand, and

---

63. Robin Dembroff, "Why Be Non-Binary?," *Aeon* (2018): 5; available at https://philarchive.org/archive/DEMWBNv1.

64. Alexander Pruss, *One Body: An Essay in Christian Sexual Ethics* (University of Notre Dame Press, 2013), 105.

65. Pruss, *One Body*, 105–6. See also Bavinck, *Christian Worldview*.

> our moral concepts, on the other, presumably because there are entailment relations between the relevant mind-independent properties, and we're tracking these with our concepts. . . . So, it seems as though we do in fact "build in the *oughts* to categories like *adult male human* and *adult female human*," using Dembroff's terminology.[66]

The body is thus an epistemological authority, and the interior sense of how one feels ought not be isolated from other judgments from nature, reason, and revelation.[67] We may go even further: Without a stable, indeed, essential definition of "male" or "female," it would be impossible to evaluate the unjust social norms that become tethered to the sexes because the possibility of such an evaluation presupposes that there *are* just norms about *this* sex or another, and we have fallen short of identifying and following those norms.

To zoom out a bit further, then, one should note the inextricable link between theism and nature.[68] Reality is meaningful independent of the human mind, because creation is the external outworking of the eternal counsel of divine wisdom. Though our perception of reality is often clouded by our own finitude and sin, truth is in principle discoverable by one's cognitive faculties precisely because *God* has spoken, and it was his word that formed reality: "Yes, language does shape reality, but it is not our language that does so. Yes, there is a language that perfectly describes what there is, a language that when it is spoken, things are so, but that is not our language either. Creation is language-shaped from the beginning, but we and our tongues are not the shapers."[69] This is why, from a Christian-theistic perspective, disagreements and debate are not reducible to a mere power play: Your agreement with me or vice versa is not reducible to an act of power where one party submits to another, and "truth" is not reducible to the opinion of the one exerting authority.

66. Bogardus, "Evaluating the Sex/Gender Distinction," 13 (emphasis original).

67. "The present scenario of gender dysphoria depends on a private solipsist account of gender. While there are some truths about persons that are directly accessible only from one's own private access, it is not clear that this is the case with gender. As we consider the scriptural and traditional data, we see that both are predicated on a public account that is biologically determinate and not solely privately accessible by one's own internal states." Joshua Ryan Farris, *An Introduction to Theological Anthropology: Humans, Both Creaturely and Divine* (Baker Academic, 2020), 228.

68. See John Webster, "The Human Person," in *The Cambridge Companion to Postmodern Theology*, ed. Kevin J. Vanhoozer (Cambridge University Press, 2006), 219–34.

69. Christopher Watkin, *Biblical Critical Theory: How the Bible's Unfolding Story Makes Sense of Modern Life and Culture* (Zondervan, 2022), 69. See also Matthew Roberts, *Pride: Identity and the Worship of Self* (Christian Focus, 2023).

These debates presuppose that there is an objective standpoint that precedes the parties of the debate and that we have epistemic access to that objective reality as image-bearers. From a naturalistic perspective, however, claims concerning absolute truth or rationality are problematized.[70] A materialist might interpret a claim to reality as a veiled assertion of one's willpower over another, or merely a futile exercise of shooting arrows upward into the sky. The current revisionist accounts, therefore, cannot be understood without taking into account their naturalist presuppositions. These revisionist programs vindicate that atheism is not merely a subtraction of beliefs about God that leaves other beliefs intact. Deny God and nature itself will follow.

To return to the topic at hand: The attempt to separate sex and gender is dependent on the assumption that the body itself is not intrinsically meaningful. Furthermore, the separation of sex and gender has proved too vulnerable to logical problems that produce circular definitions of manhood or womanhood, and gender itself becomes reducible to cultural stereotypes. According to Christian theology, however, the body is *good*—it is created with dignity though it has been marred by the fall. The body is an intrinsic part of who we are, and we recognize our agency, personhood, and dignity by way of our bodies. What we do with our bodies is thus not theologically adiaphorous; the body is that through which we image God.

NATURE AND CUSTOM (OR TWO CHEERS FOR NATURAL LAW REASONING IN A POST-FALL ORDER)

Now that the sex/gender separation is rejected, then, I argue that gender is connected to sex and the body—in fact, I'd suggest that gender terms ("manhood" and "womanhood") and sex terms ("males" and "females") are synonyms. If we want to talk about the norms that are tethered to each sex, then we can do just that—refer to them as *norms* about the sexes; there is no need to refer to them as "genders." Does this mean, however, that *all* the norms that are associated with each sex are intrinsically natural or easily distinguishable from mere convention? It is one thing to affirm that males

70. For a powerful argument to this effect, see Plantinga's evolutionary argument against naturalism in Alvin Plantinga, *Where the Conflict Really Lies: Science, Religion, and Naturalism* (Oxford University Press, 2012), chap. 10.

and manhood and females and womanhood are connected; it is another to identify exactly how males ought to be *masculine* or females *feminine*. This latter task requires much care lest we fall into stereotyping or universalizing one set of customs as natural.

The notion that gender is a consequence or is identical with one's sex is often referred to as "gender essentialism." The opposing viewpoint is *constructivism*—the position that gender refers to something other than one's biological sex (as seen above), which also usually assumes that the norms one tethers to each sex are social constructs and have normative force only because of social conditions contingent on potentially authoritarian relations of power.[71]

If one rejects the sex/gender separation, however, then one is de facto a gender essentialist, if only in the sense that gender terms are now tethered to one's biological sex. Does this mean, however, that one automatically must subscribe to the view that the norms that are associated with each gender are not only natural but epistemically easy to determine? Not necessarily.[72] For clarity's sake, I suggest that one should distinguish between gender essentialism and *biological determinism*; the former refers to the tethering of gender terms to one's sexed body, and the latter is about whether one's sexed body *determines* that one should behave in accordance with certain norms, usually accompanied by the further claim that those norms about masculinity and femininity are rather easily identified.[73] In other words, if the sex/gender separation is rejected, then the question is: Does one's biological sex/gender *determine* that one would tend toward exemplifying certain norms or ought to be masculine or feminine in precise ways? Notice the question

71. E.g., Marc Cortez, *Theological Anthropology: A Guide for the Perplexed* (Bloomsbury T&T Clark, 2010), 47–53; Michelle Panchuk, "Gender and Justice: Human and Divine Gender in Analytic Theology," in *T&T Clark Handbook of Analytic Theology*, ed. James Arcadi and James T. Turner Jr. (Bloomsbury T&T Clark, 2021), 388–91. Cf. Mari Mikkola, "Gender Essentialism and Anti-Essentialism," in *Routledge Companion to Feminist Philosophy*, ed. Ann Garry, Serene Khader, and Alison Stone (Routledge, 2017), 393–405. See also Serene Jones, *Feminist Theory and Christian Theology: Cartographies of Grace* (Fortress, 2000).

72. For a similar argument that rejecting constructivism does not entail endorsing biological determinism, see, e.g., Fellipe Do Vale, *Gender as Love: A Theological Account of Human Identity, Embodied Desire, and Our Social Worlds* (Baker Academic, 2023), chap. 2.

73. Bogardus, "Evaluating Arguments for the Sex/Gender Distinction," 6–9. Bogardus is responding to Mari Mikkola's usage in "Feminist Perspectives on Sex and Gender," *Standard Encyclopedia of Philosophy*, May 12, 2008, updated January 18, 2022, https://plato.stanford.edu/entries/feminism-gender/#BioDet.

is no longer about the natural definitions of one's gendered body (e.g., the potency of childbearing), but rather about the status of the social norms or personality features that one associates with each sex.

Once the question is framed in this respect, then, I think essentialists about human nature can affirm that at least some (or most?) norms that we associate with each sex do, in fact, stem from social and cultural forces. This is not to say that all norms are merely social conventions—the Bible is filled with metaphors taken from the world of embodied and gendered experience as prescriptions for theological reflection and faithful obedience. Indeed, the norms that are most explicitly connected to our embodiment are on surer footing in this regard. Isaiah 49:15 compares God's love for his people with a mother who could not forget her child. God is like a comforting mother (Isa. 66:13). Creation groans for its renewal as a mother who is experiencing labor pains, waiting for the birth of her child (Rom. 8:22). These texts indicate something about motherhood that is unique to the female experience, which in turn teaches us something about God's relation to creation. Likewise, because men are physically stronger than women biologically (1 Pet. 3:7), the Bible particularly calls men to steward that strength appropriately (e.g., 1 Kings 2:1–2; 1 Cor. 16:13).[74]

Both men and women, of course, are to learn from each other—men should learn from the mother's compassion for her children, and women, too, are called to be courageous (cf. 1 Thess. 2:7, 11). Men, however, are called to emulate the mother's compassion *because* that compassion is inflected by her experience in a natural and normative way. These examples connect a particular trait with the embodiment of the female or male existence. The diversity of custom does not provide a reason to doubt that there is a natural order but just the reverse: That there are so many customs tied to sex and gender across every culture is "testimony that sexuality matters to just about every society. And the simplest explanation why it matters to so many is that it matters objectively and everyone knows this."[75] Nature impinges itself on

74. Hence, as Bavinck writes: "For this reason the Lord compares himself not only to a Father who takes pity on his children (Ps. 103:13), but also to a mother who cannot forget her nursing child (Isa. 49:15). He chastens like a father (Heb. 12:6), but also comforts like a mother (Isa. 66:13), and replenishes for the loss of both (Ps. 27:10)." *The Christian Family*, 3.

75. Pruss, *One Body*, 66.

our cultures, and this is why the cultural norms associated with gender are (rightly) held so highly.[76]

The distinction between nature and custom, however, does not mean that we should begin carelessly to form lists of traits that make up what it means to be masculine or feminine, because so much of our perception of nature is filtered through our own cultural experience and social conventions. We should be chastened in forming judgments about what it means, naturally, to be masculine or feminine, especially beyond embodied and biblical bounds, and we should carefully discern between unjust and just social norms.[77] And even while speaking about the Scriptures, we should be attentive to contexts and the distinction between a historical narration and an ontological description.[78]

To turn to contemporary times, there is nothing ontological, say, about the association of blue with males and pink with females. At best, some of these socially constructed norms might be good, reflective of the natural differences of male and female, or they might be harmless (like the blue and pink associations), but at worst, they might reflect mere stereotypes that can (or even should) be challenged. The norms that one associates with men in Indonesia, for instance, are markedly different from those in the United States. Anecdotally, and from my own experience, boys who grew up in Jakarta were not encouraged to embrace living with nature but were told to remain indoors and to work on a particular musical instrument or academic discipline like math. One was given a calculator for a birthday, not a fishing rod, and camping trips were nonexistent. Nature reminded our parents of the harsh conditions from which we came, and now that we have homes, why spend the time outside when you could invest in your education so that you could

76. If there is a distinction to be made between gender and sex that maintains their integral connection, then Do Vale provides a useful definition: "Gender is about the appropriation of social goods that pertain to our biologically sexed bodies, an appropriation that enables sexed bodies to acquire social meaning." Do Vale, *Gender as Love*, 104.

77. As Matthew Mason wisely notes, "It is better to begin not with personality traits, nor with athletic performance, but with the natural form of the human body, which exists in two natural forms: male and female." Mason, "The Authority of the Body," 48.

78. For one example, Nelson notes the mistake of identifying the mistake of Eve with an essentialized trait: "Yet when reexaminations of the fall stories in Genesis lead to an essentialization of supposedly 'feminine' characteristics, or when the aim of such examinations becomes the transference of blame from one character to another, we know that we have gone off track." Derek R. Nelson, *Sin: A Guide for the Perplexed* (Bloomsbury T&T Clark, 2011), 50.

become a lawyer, medical doctor, or business tycoon? As Jake Meador reminds us, even the common assumption that men should be the workers away from home and women the domestic nurturers is a result of the industrial revolution that changed working conditions: "Industry had broken the bonds that tied men to the household."[79] Favale rightly argues, therefore, that to observe that males and females are naturally different is not to infer that "these differences can be easily summarized in a list of contrasting traits that characterize each sex (for example, women are inherently more emotional, while men are inherently more rational)."[80] Especially when one considers that what is common is not identifiable with what is natural, epistemic modesty should be the norm for addressing whether this or that trait is natural to a particular gender.[81]

Consider the case of Herman Bavinck. In 1908, he wrote a treatise titled *The Christian Family*. This work defended the natural distinction and goodness between men and women but also associated certain cultural stereotypes with both sexes, which he had reconsidered by the time he wrote *The Woman in Contemporary Society* in 1918.[82] Considering the conditions of the looming world war and industrialization, which led women to occupy jobs and labor that were usually reserved for men, along with newer technologies that aided with domestic work, women's roles in society became markedly different. Older assumptions that women were incapable of certain work or of participating in public discourse were proven wrong. In light of this, Bavinck argued that women should be admitted into higher education and aimed for universal suffrage (though, mind you, as a nineteenth-century man he still believed that there should be separated classes between men and women).[83] While Bavinck still believed in the created goodness of the sex binary and

79. Jake Meador, *What Are Christians Good For? Life Together at the End of the World* (InterVarsity, 2022), 69. Hence, I'm less than confident in Budziszewski's detailed prescriptions of masculinity and femininity, though I agree with his overall grounding of the male-female distinction in nature, in *On the Meaning of Sex*, 60–61.

80. Favale, *Genesis of Gender*, 147–48. Hence, I believe Allen is right when she notes that "femininity was simply a woman's way of acting in the world, and masculinity simply a man's way of acting in the world." Allen, *Concept of Woman*, 3.469.

81. Do Vale, *Gender as Love*, 32–33.

82. Herman Bavinck, *De vrouw in hedendaagsche maatschappij* (Kampen, 1918). A portion of this work on Bavinck's argument for universal suffrage is translated in English for the first time in Gayle Doornbos and N. Gray Sutanto, eds., *The Essential Herman Bavinck: A Reader and Commentary* (Baker Academic, 2026), 522–30.

83. See also James Eglinton, *Bavinck: A Critical Biography* (Baker Academic, 2020), 279.

their attending complementary relation, he was aware that the norms one's culture might associate with the sexes/genders could be situationally contingent and deeply mistaken. As Bolt rightly stated then, Bavinck was after "true distinctions" without "stereotypes."[84] We do well to keep his sensitivity in view, even while recognizing that he was still a product of his own time.

Bavinck's resistance to stereotypes and his desire to uncover the truer distinctions between male and female remind us of the way in which the Christian faith corrected the distorted "natural" visions of the Greco-Roman world and transformed its sexual ethics. As noted in a previous chapter, on the basis of the perceived "natural virility" of the male sex, "the classical world assumed that male sexual energy was basically boundless and that the stability of the city relied on finding ways to direct and discipline that energy. This meant that for men any number of sexual acts were admissible—anything from marital sex to keeping a female mistress to keeping a few young boys around to rape."[85] The perceived differences between men and women led to a "double standard," therefore, with regard to sexual ethics, with fidelity to one partner deemed to be a natural characteristic of women but sexual liberty as natural to men. Against these distorted perceptions of nature, Christianity argued that *men*, too, must be loyal to their wives (e.g., 1 Cor. 7:3; 1 Tim. 3): "We see that the decisive step in early Christian sexual teaching was to bring males under the same sort of behavioral requirements that in the larger cultural setting was expected of 'honorable' women."[86] Far from seeking to perpetuate gender stereotypes, then, the entrance of Christianity into the Roman world led to a reconsideration of such stereotypes for the sake of a truer norm.

I suggest, therefore, that one can affirm essentialism with respect to sex/gender but reject a strong version of biological or gender determinism, according to which the sexes entail certain easily identifiable and universal norms. This does not mean that we ought to reject some of the implications of our embodiment that we considered above or the empirical data that suggests, for example, that men and women generally tend to prefer different activities or jobs, but it does mean that we are chastened and self-critical

84. John Bolt, *Bavinck on the Christian Life* (Crossway, 2015), 154.
85. Meador, *What Are Christians For?*, 71.
86. Larry Hurtado, *Destroyer of the Gods: Early Christian Distinctiveness in the Roman World* (Baylor University Press, 2017), 166.

when we make normative judgments about what it means to be masculine or feminine.[87] In other words, essentialism about sex should be accepted, but the stereotypes and judgments about the genders should indeed be carefully and theologically evaluated. Cortez's warning against essentializing our cultural preferences is worth heeding: "Human sexuality, then, is a natural and essential aspect of humanity. This does not mean, however, that any particular expression of, or interpretation of, human sexuality must be viewed as natural and essential. We must be ever mindful of our sinful proclivities for idealizing our preferences and experiences as expressions of something necessary and essential about humanity."[88]

These necessary cautions are why this section is subtitled "Two Cheers for Natural Law Reasoning in a Post-Fall Order"—affirming a natural order and the authority of our created bodies is necessary for a proper Christian theological anthropology. We should be quite chastened, however, because our perceptions of nature are mediated by our finitude, our cultural and temporal location, and our own sinful inclination to mistake our own preferences with the natural order.

ESCHATOLOGY AND THE CORPORATE IMAGE

As Bavinck completes a section on the creation of the male and female in his *Wonderful Works of God*, he reminds readers that our embodied difference points back to the corporate sense of the image of God and its consummation: "The way in which woman is created in Genesis 2 is the way along which she receives the image of God as well as the man (Gen. 1:27). In this is contained the further truth that the image of God rests in a number of people, with differentiation of race, talent, and powers—in short—in mankind, and further that this image will achieve its full unfolding in the new humanity which is the church of Christ."[89] God is interested not in bare particulars or uniform individuals but in complementary agents and relations. When discussing the male-female relation, one walks upon a tightrope. Christian revelation embraces many polarities that tend to be torn apart when left to our own

87. Cf. Mason, "The Authority of the Body," 46–48; Budziszewski, *On the Meaning of Sex*, 38–39.
88. Cortez, *Theological Anthropology*, 49.
89. Bavinck, *Wonderful Works*, 188.

devices: the created goodness of the difference between male and female along with the uniqueness and dignity of each sex, their life-giving possibility in fellowship and procreation along with the goodness of singleness, the need to account for traits and norms rooted in our embodiedness along with a resistance to distortions that lead to harmful stereotypes and abuse.

Bavinck's pointer to the corporate image and its consummation is helpful here. What if the individual is not to be pressured to express or identify every aspect of masculinity or femininity because only the corporate image of God, in the last day, could fully do justice to these expressions? And what if we need not be pressured to identify every aspect of masculinity or femininity because human history and culture is still unfolding, and the sanctifying work of the Spirit is not yet completed now? Eschatology thus allows us to chasten but not jeopardize a vision of human nature. It allows us to admit a distinction between nature and custom and yet do so with a sense of humility because we cannot fully identify where the boundaries are between the two. It also allows us to embrace the beauty of the ways in which nature is expressed through many different cultures, without unduly imposing a uniform expectation of what it means to be male or female that could so easily be confused with one historical-cultural expression. It also gives hope to those who might struggle with feeling at home with our bodies, as God heals whatever alienation we might feel with ourselves when he resurrects us.[90]

TRUTH FOR WORSHIP, LIFE, AND MISSION

This chapter has expounded on the scriptural grounds on the goodness of our embodiment as it implicates our understanding of sex and gender. I have shown that our creation as sexed creatures is *good* and identified some ways in which we may speak responsibly about the marital relation and singleness as pointers to Christ and the church. Our bodies witness to the complementary relation between males and females; men are called to use their strength in responsible ways as fathers and brothers in the various social roles in which they find themselves; women are generative and are called to be sisters and mothers in the various roles they find themselves in as well. There is thus

90. Mason, "The Wounded It Heals," 144–45.

no untethering of our gender terms from our sexed embodiment, and the norms related to the sexes are on surer footing when they are anchored in bodily realities.

Let me expound on more implications for worship, life, and mission. First, and perhaps most importantly, we ought to give thanks to God for the created diversity of humanity as male and female. We have seen that the image of God is more clearly seen not in an individual, nor in a uniform humanity, but on humanity in all of its uniqueness and its interdependence, not least from the interdependence we see between male and female (1 Cor. 11:11–12). The difference between male and female is good and became a source of conflict only due to sin. This interdependent goodness is seen not just in the marital union but also in the various social roles in which we find ourselves as brothers, sisters, mothers, and fathers.

Second, we should recognize that our primary identity is given to us, rather than achieved by us, in a twofold way: We are all created in the image of God, and Christians are in union with Jesus Christ. We live out who we are as image-bearers and as Christians *through* our embodiment, rather than defining ourselves by way of our sexual desires, orientation, societal norms, or inner psychological sense. John Kleinig rightly shows that it is "misleading and unhelpful to identify a person as either homosexual or heterosexual. We are sexual people who can engage in heterosexual or homosexual acts or even in both kinds. But that does not determine who we are."[91] If God has given us our bodies, we should seek to glorify God with them, living in ways that please him, for our own good. We can act in ways that are *consistent* with who we are as image-bearers and as united to Christ, or we can act in ways that are inconsistent with those basic realities.

Third, same-sex attraction and intercourse are sins against God and nature. I have argued or alluded to this in numerous ways throughout the book, but this is worth repeating and making explicit. This is not to say that we should be focused myopically on these sins—Paul, after all, argues that all people are equally unrighteous before God (Rom. 3:19–20). We should also emphasize that there are many other sins that Paul lists in Romans 1:18–32. Nonetheless, we should note Paul's emphases that these sins are against

91. Kleinig, *Wonderfully Made*, 204.

nature (Rom. 1:26–27). Stated positively, sexual union is ordered toward the generation of life. Paul also situates same-sex attraction as idolatrous, as one way in which we worship the creature over the Creator. Like fornication, these sexual sins affect the body (1 Cor. 6:18–20), manifested in the enslavement of the mind and will to our disordered passions and instincts.

Fourth, as an implication of points two and three, nonetheless, when we repent, these sexual sins do not bar us from the kingdom of God: "And such were some of you. But you were washed, you were sanctified, you were justified in the name of the Lord Jesus Christ and by the Spirit of our God" (1 Cor. 6:11). Those who are born again are born into a new life, no longer walking in the sins of our old ways. We are born as new creatures (2 Cor. 5:16–17), and Christians should treat one another as such—pure and chaste as the bride of Christ (2 Cor. 11:2). This is the gospel that we should proclaim to sinners in sin, whether sexual or otherwise—a gospel that drives all of our mission work: Believe in Jesus and purity is yours, by status immediately (justification) and in life progressively (sanctification).

Fifth, we should nurture and direct our hope in the resurrection of the body. Gender dysphoria and the problems that have to do with our bodies now, including aging, decay, suffering, and the conflict between the sexes, are features of the fall; we long for the day when we are perfected, glorified, and one with our consummate bodies. As Matthew Mason argues, "For those who experience gender dysphoria but cling to Christ for mercy and hope, surely one of the glories of the new creation will be to receive back the body they were originally given, transformed and glorified, to inhabit that body as their Creator and Redeemer's loving gift, and finally to be at rest."[92] In the last day, we will exist in harmony with all that God has intended us to be. The gospel is good news, not just because in it we see the forgiveness of our sins, but through it we also see the hope of resurrection, the consummation of our existence.

Finally, both marriage and singleness point us to Christ, though in distinct ways. Marriage testifies to Christ's sacrificial love and the church's sanctified submission. Singleness testifies to the sufficiency of Christ as our true bridegroom. As we saw in this chapter, that singleness is a gift should not

92. Mason, "The Wounded it Heals," 149.

be misunderstood as the claim that those with the "gift" of singleness would find it easy or have no desire for a marital relation. Singleness is a gift per se because it has eschatological significance—we will not be given in marriage in the last day, for the substance has come. The church, therefore, should be a welcoming community for both married families and singles, for the church is the body of Christ in which each have their place, and those who do not have children may, too, have children in the Lord and participate as brothers and sisters in the community of Christ.

CONCLUSION

This chapter has sought to give a biblical and theological account of sex, to challenge contemporary attempts to wedge gender from our sexed bodies, and to navigate through the difference between nature and custom on this issue. It is impossible to cover all the relevant ethical issues that may flow from these theological reflections on sex and human ontology, and the sketch I provided here is merely a starting point for further study and exploration. The eschatological and corporate note that Bavinck rings aids in advancing such conversations by providing a chastened yet firm position. In the next chapter, I turn to another difficult and important topic in theological anthropology, that of race.

FURTHER READING

Kleinig, John. *Wonderfully Made: A Protestant Theology of the Body*. Lexham, 2021. A wonderful exposition of the biblical teachings on the body, including discussions of sexuality and gender. Perhaps the best contemporary entryway text on this topic.

Favale, Abigail. *The Genesis of Gender: A Christian Theory*. Ignatius, 2022. The best accessible defense of a Roman Catholic account of the theology of the body and sexuality. Favale also responds persuasively to alternative ideologies of gender. There is much in this text with which Protestants can agree.

Pruss, Alexander. *One Body: An Essay in Christian Sexual Ethics*. University of Notre Dame Press, 2013. A thorough and penetrating natural law account of sexual ethics.

Do Vale, Fellipe. *Gender as Love: A Theological Account of Human Identity, Embodied Desire, and Social Worlds*. Baker Academic, 2023. Do Vale presents a constructive and broadly Protestant theology of gender in ways that take into account the current debates within gender studies.

11

HUMANITY AND CULTURAL DIVERSITY

ON RACE AND THE KINGDOM OF GOD

WHAT SHALL WE SAY on the subject of race? This topic has been fraught with complicated debates given where we are in history after the modern emergence of race-consciousness, which ontologizes race and locates people groups in a hierarchical schema—an act of "racialization." Race, however, is a social construct, as there are no ontological differences between human beings, though there are differences in culture. Racialization has allowed for the possibility of the subjugation of one people group through another and has made us prone to mistake cultural differences with cultural superiority. While much current literature on this fraught issue identifies and articulates the problems well, it is often less successful at suggesting peacemaking and reconciliatory solutions. I suggest that a Christian account of human nature and cultural diversity is necessary to gesture toward a path forward.

This book has introduced the corporate dimension of the image of God. Past chapters have described the way in which only humanity in its entirety, across space and time, could adequately image an infinite and Triune God. The cultural mandate and the Great Commission both emphasize the spreading of the image of God through different languages, cultures, and nations, such that God's glory might be represented through all the earth. Consistent with Willie James Jennings's argument that the diverse peoples develop along the lines of "geographically sustained identities," Bavinck envisions human beings as made for diversity across place and time, such that the kingdom of God is irreducible to a single culture. Consummate human culture is not uniform, but pluriform.[1] As Vincent Bacote observes: "The differentiation expressed in texts such as Acts 17:26 is based on geography and what we would today call ethnic/cultural identity."[2] Augustine, then, commenting on the unity of humanity, remarks that one should be mindful of our common creation so that we might cultivate stronger bonds of relations: "God created only one single man, not, certainly, that he might be a solitary bereft of all society, but that by this means the unity of society and the bond of concord might be more effectually commended to him, men being bound together not only by similarity of nature, but by family affection."[3] Racialization is the mistake of conflating cultural differences with natural differences, forgetful as it is of our common nature and origin.

Racialization is dehumanization. The positing of "race," however, is still a true "myth" malforming our imaginations as we live in a post-fall and post-colonial reality that has pushed differences toward division, pride, and racism.[4] Luke Powery says it another way: "While race is neither biologically nor ontologically real, it is *socially* real."[5] Contemporary existence presupposes the past "racialization" of the peoples, such that it shapes our world visions; the rhetoric of race categorizes the peoples as "other" and posits a hierarchy of higher and lower, a logic birthed out of certain colonial efforts.[6] As such, no contemporary introduction to theological anthropology can bypass the

1. Willie James Jennings, *The Christian Imagination: Theology and the Origins of Race* (Yale University Press, 2010), 63. See also Elizabeth Sung, "'Racial Realism' in Biblical Interpretation and Theological Anthropology: A Systematic-Theological Evaluation of Recent Accounts," *Ex Auditu* 31 (2015): 3–21.

2. Vincent Bacote, "Erasing Race: Racial Identity and Theological Anthropology," in *Black Scholars in White Space: New Vistas in African American Studies from the Christian Academy*, ed. Anthony Bradley (Pickwick, 2015), 134.

3. Augustine, *City of God*, trans. Marcus Dods (Random House, 1993), 12.21.

4. Bacote, "Erasing Race," 125.

5. Luke A. Powery, *Becoming Human: The Holy Spirit and the Rhetoric of Race* (Westminster John Knox, 2022), 4 (see also 45).

6. Powery, *Becoming Human*, 37.

topic of race. This chapter is divided into two: The first half sketches the fallen conditions that led to the emergence of a "gradation of existence" from which our "race-consciousness" emerged; the second draws from Herman Bavinck to draw a positive vision of human diversity through creation, fall, redemption, and consummation. Reintroducing Bavinck on this topic here indicates that Reformed theology has internal resources that might prove generative for a theological consideration of race.[7] Finally, I shall turn to a concluding section to expound on some implications of Bavinck's view for worship, life, and mission.

THE GRADATION OF EXISTENCE AND RACE-CONSCIOUSNESS

The emergence of modern race-consciousness and its "racialization" of the peoples, along with the concomitant "gradation of existence" between the races, is complex, and for the present purposes I shall introduce three strands: (1) a social-evolutionary and developmental view of human history and civilization, (2) the naturalization of race and culture, and (3) the conflation of "the kingdom of God" with one particular culture.[8]

First, then, consider Matthew Engelke's observations on the term "civilization" and its use in nineteenth-century romantic and colonialist discourse: "One of the most important things to keep in mind about 'civilization' is that it's a relational term. It really only makes sense if you have other conditions of life and outlooks to contrast with it. In the nineteenth century, the two most important were barbarism and savagery. Civilization itself was of fairly new

---

7. For an elaboration of Herman Bavinck's views on race and critiques of German nationalism, see N. Gray Sutanto, *God and Humanity: Herman Bavinck and Theological Anthropology* (Bloomsbury T&T Clark, 2024), chaps. 6–7.

8. Of course, with the caveat that the tendency to see one's own people as superior to another is as old as sin itself: "Though racism in the modern sense of whites as superior to all other ethnic groups emerged out of the various racial projects of European and Euro-American colonization over the past five hundred years, the practice of creating legal categories to distinguish those of one ethnic group over another for privileges of divvying out socioeconomic and political privileges is as old as sin itself. Biblical examples include the enslavement of the Israelites in Egypt, as well as the case studies of the Babylonian, Persian, Greek, and Roman Empires, which all aimed for the military, economic, and cultural conquest of the Jewish people." Robert Chao Romero and Jeff Liou, *Christianity and Critical Race Theory: A Faithful and Constructive Conversation* (Baker Academic, 2023), 50.

coinage (it's often traced to the eighteenth century)."[9] Under the influence of social Darwinism, this nineteenth-century discourse on civilization, exemplified by works like Edward B. Tylor's *Primitive Culture*, then went on to position European cultures as civilized and others as backward and barbaric.[10] It was not so much that so-called barbaric nations were incapable of achieving the civilization of the West, as it were, for they putatively shared the same mental capacities as the Europeans, but they were depicted as significantly underdeveloped and far less advanced than their European counterparts. Entering into these foreign lands, then, was often described as akin to entering a time capsule that disclosed past conditions out of which Europeans had evolved: "They were us-as-before. Children, more like, who might become us some day but still had a long way to go."[11] Bacote thus observed aptly that "the modern approach to race is linked to formation of society."[12] The language of aiding the other nations toward their own civilized maturity justified the colonialist project, and the differences between cultures implied to the colonialist a gradation of lesser to greater. Against such a project, Bavinck argues that this Eurocentrism and social Darwinism are making two basic mistakes: The language of "evolution" cannot be transferred from biological realities to social ones, and the so-called developments in European cultures can easily be found in other cultures. Further, European culture can itself be considered "behind," as it is often marked by particular sins of its own. Both of these mistakes stem from departing from divine revelation as the norm by which we should adjudicate every culture, including one's own, rather than raising one's own culture as the standard for every other.[13] As Robert Chao Romero and Jeff Liou argue: "How do we distinguish between the 'glory and honor' [of the nations, per Rev. 21:22–27] and cultural sin? That is why Scripture is paramount as our cultural sieve and plumb line. As Christ enters our lives, he sanctifies us—both personally and culturally—based on the truth of God's Word (John 17:17)."[14]

---

9. Matthew Engelke, *How to Think Like an Anthropologist* (Princeton University Press, 2018), 60.

10. Engelke, *How to Think Like an Anthropologist*, 62–63; Edward Tylor, *Primitive Culture: Researches into the Early History of Mankind and the Development of Civilization* (John Murray, 1865).

11. Engelke, *How to Think Like an Anthropologist*, 66.

12. Bacote, "Erasing Race," 130.

13. See especially Herman Bavinck, *Philosophy of Revelation: A New Annotated Edition*, ed. Cory Brock and N. Gray Sutanto (Hendrickson, 2018), chaps. 5 and 6.

14. Romero and Liou, *Christianity and Critical Race Theory*, 45.

Alongside this social-developmental view of human history is the phenomenon of ascribing cultural differences to natural, biological differences.[15] Or, as Bacote says, "Such clarifications can lead us to almost regard the various 'races' as different species given the level of distinctions."[16] Luke Powery traces this "race-based" science to the Swedish taxonomist Carolus Linnaeus (1707–1778), whose work informed nineteenth-century anthropologists. These "anthropologists who study both physical and cultural aspects of human beings began to measure, identify, and classify the so-called races. They accumulated data from all over the world on variables such as height, weight, skin color, brain size, and head shape, and produced a taxonomy."[17] The taxonomy conveniently placed Aryan Europeans at the top and, as such, "racism preceded race. . . . Science maintained the social order of the day."[18] Abraham Kuyper, despite sharing Bavinck's account of corporate humanity and the image of God, tragically perpetuated this mistake, as seen in this oft-quoted passage:

> The perception of difference the very source of our human consciousness, the causative principles of all that exists and grows and develops, in short the mainspring of all life and thought. . . . To put it concretely, if you were a plant you would rather be a rose than mushroom; if insect, butterfly rather than spider; if bird, eagle rather than owl; if a higher vertebrate, lion rather than hyena; and again, being man, richer than poor, talented rather than dull-minded, of the Aryan race rather than Hottentot or Kaffir. Between all these there is differentiation, wide differentiation.[19]

Problematic passages like these have led Kuyperian scholars like Vincent Bacote and Richard Mouw to construct a "neo-Kuyperian" project that seeks to correct Kuyper on the basis of neo-Calvinism's internal resources.[20] Indeed, Kuyper's strong doctrines of the corporate image of God and common grace

15. Powery, *Becoming Human*, 17.
16. Bacote, "Erasing Race," 136.
17. Powery, *Becoming Human*, 39.
18. Powery, *Becoming Human*, 40.
19. Abraham Kuyper, *Lectures on Calvinism* (1931; repr., Eerdmans, 1999), 195–96.
20. See Richard Mouw, *Abraham Kuyper: A Short and Personal Introduction* (Eerdmans, 2011), 80–85. See also George Harinck, "'Wipe Out Lines of Division (Not Distinctions)': Bennie Keet, Neo-Calvinism and the Struggle Against Apartheid," *Journal of Reformed Theology* 11 (2017): 81–98.

elsewhere (which led Bavinck to denounce racism in ways that Kuyper unfortunately did not) stand in sharp contrast to these comments that reflect Kuyper's imbibing of a nineteenth-century *zeitgeist*. Kuyper's comments here reflect his beliefs in a myth. As Bacote concludes: "We should prune Kuyper's troublesome views on race from his legacy and consider how to make his legacy blossom anew from within as well as considering ways to update and develop this living tradition."[21]

Finally, Romero and Liou also show that the entrance of modern race-consciousness in the European and expansionist colonial project of the early modern period often conflated Christianity or the kingdom of God with their own European culture.

> They alone held the institutional and theological keys to the kingdom of God, and that justified their colonial expansion over Africa, Asia, the Americas, and the Near East. According to the Doctrine of Discovery, Europeans could violently seize the lands of non-Christian ethnic groups for purposes of religious conversion. Indeed, people of color throughout the globe were considered "fortunate" to receive the salvation of their souls in exchange for the small price of their lands and enslavement.[22]

Such a move not only conflated Christianity with one's own cultural expression but also often traded in the historic, Jewish Christ with a projected Aryan one: "One interesting dimension of how this occurs is by cleaving the Jewish ethnic particularity from Jesus and reconceiving him as the ultimate rational and moral autonomous figure. This creation and, if you will, 'baptism' of whiteness as the pinnacle of humanity is then woven into the fabric of the modern world."[23] As J. Kameron Carter puts it: "At the genealogical taproot of modern racial reasoning is the process by which Christ was abstracted from Jesus, and thus from his Jewish body, thereby severing Christianity from its Jewish roots. . . . In making Christ non-Jewish in this moment, he was made a figure of the Occident. He became white, even if Jesus as

---

21. Vincent Bacote, "Kuyper and Race," in *Calvinism for a Secular Age: A Twenty-First Century Reading of Kuyper's Stone Lectures*, ed. Jessica and Robert Joustra (IVP Academic, 2022), 158.
22. Romero and Liou, *Christianity and Critical Race Theory*, 11.
23. Bacote, "Erasing Race," 128.

a historical figure remained Jewish or racially a figure of the orient."[24] Willie James Jennings thus challenges Christians to consider different pathways of responding to Christianity's past complicity with the history of colonialism. He categorizes three ways of responding. If the first way rejects Christianity altogether, a second way uses Christianity to reconstruct one's own native religion, while a third approach accepts Christianity. This third approach is further divided into two. Three-A refers to those who accepted Christianity and its colonialist expressions, whereas Three-B "accept[s] Christianity but did not accept its colonial configuration. . . . The biblical story was [seen to be] the way one entered God's world and life with God that was not a world controlled by white Christianity and certainly not slave-holding society or colonial operations."[25]

Two reflections flow from the genealogical account of race-consciousness I reproduced above. The challenge to reimagine a post-colonial theology and study of the cultures is important but more difficult than often imagined. It is important because one culture ought not to be raised as the norm or standard by which we should adjudicate another culture. Such a move precludes understanding other cultures on their own terms before assessing them with the word of God, and it risks projecting one's own people as the bearer or source of truth itself. However, a post-colonialist project is difficult because understanding difference and upholding diversity without uniformity are themselves *particular cultural values*, ones that are often unshared by other indigenous cultures. I suggest, of course, that the openness to natural (rather than sinful) cultural difference and the preservation of cultural diversity *are Christian values* and as such are not a product of the human imagination but rather disclosed by divine revelation. Scripture and Christian theology, I suggest, are foundations for appreciating cultural plurality that is not reducible to colonialism or relativism. A pitfall of the recent search for a post-colonial theology in contemporary academia is the implicit assumption that if we were to read the "indigenous" cultures or theologies well enough, we would find there the same (usually recent Western) values of the researcher, when the reality is that we would rather

24. J. Kameron Carter, *Race: A Theological Account* (Oxford University Press, 2008), 6–7.

25. Willie James Jennings, "Black Theology," in *The New Cambridge Companion to Christian Doctrine*, ed. Michael Allen (Cambridge University Press, 2022), 271.

often discover something far more different and category-eluding. Often, too, what we would find is a view that is far less "open" or "tolerant" than one might be willing to accept. The commitment to diversity found in non-Christian Western contexts thrives, after all, on borrowed capital from a Christian past. The search for diversity, in other words, needs to be funded from a position of faith in a divine revelation, such that the recognition of truth and falsehood becomes irreducible to the claim of cultural superiority. Divine revelation also helps the researcher become less brittle, as one can now anticipate and confront real differences without perceiving them as a challenge to one's own identity, for one is no longer seeing oneself as the source or arbiter of truth. To state it negatively: Failure to stand on divine revelation will indeed reduce claims of truth and falsehood to claims of cultural superiority. If there is no truth outside of one's culture, then there is no way of grounding the claim that the preservation and recognition of cultural diversity are goods to cultivate.

Further, if race and racialization are dehumanizing social fictions, and an alternative, more accurate way of describing the differences between people groups is by their geographically sustained identities and cultures, then cultural differences and human diversity are best understood in terms of geography, language, and values. An Indonesian who has grown up in the United States or London, for example, will have a fundamentally different outlook than an Indonesian who grew up in Jakarta or Surabaya. In other words, it is more helpful to understand human diversity in terms of localities. I am not here advocating for a kind of naive "color-blindness." We do well to identify when dehumanizing racial brackets are being imposed, for we live in an era of post-racialization, and we should be mindful of the ways in which such racialization has impacted our current contexts and reject the dehumanizing powers. We should also recognize that racialization is not indicative of reality, and it is thus unhelpful to appeal to race to define or gain a more accurate analysis of human diversity when other lenses, like class, language, culture, and localities, are more informative.

The path ahead is perilous indeed, and one way to begin an articulation of a positive vision of human diversity is to learn from the past. Bacote and Mouw sought to go deeper into their own Reformed and Kuyperian traditions to challenge Kuyper's own thoughts internally, and it is in that spirit that the next section reintroduces Herman Bavinck's positive account of human diversity.[26]

"HUMANITY IN ITS ENTIRETY": HERMAN BAVINCK ON HUMAN DIVERSITY IN CREATION, FALL, REDEMPTION, AND CONSUMMATION

Herman Bavinck has been pointed to by other scholars as a better alternative to Kuyper's flawed perspective on race. It is in that attempt to develop this tradition that Herman Bavinck appears within the neo-Kuyperian literature on race, not least because Bavinck resisted apartheid and "racial segregation" as early as the 1910s in response to white South African PhD students at the Free University of Amsterdam.[27] "Herman Bavinck points Kuyperians in a fruitful direction," writes Mouw, as Bavinck articulates that corporate humanity unfolds itself "in the rich diversity of humankind spread over many places and times."[28] This creational unfolding of humanity achieves its aim in redemption and consummation, as the many "redeemed *peoples*" are "gathered into the New Jerusalem from many tribes and tongues."[29] Jeff Liou, likewise, points to Bavinck's more nuanced discussion of the differences among the peoples. Despite "employing the scientific reasoning of his day and finding support from Darwin for his theological convictions regarding the unity of humanity . . . Bavinck lists those naturalists and racial theorists whom he thinks either under- or overestimate the significance of races."[30] Liou goes on: "In other words, however racial lines were drawn and however dully or brightly putative racial boundaries could be articulated, Bavinck considers the unity of humanity to be indissoluble."[31] George Harinck has also noted that Bavinck (unlike Kuyper) is "critical of the notion of defining

26. See also Andrew Ong, "World Christianity," in *T&T Clark Handbook of Neo-Calvinism*, ed. Nathaniel Gray Sutanto and Cory Brock (Bloomsbury T&T Clark, 2024), 426–38.

27. Harinck, "'Wipe Out Lines of Division (Not Distinctions),'" 84.

28. Mouw, *Abraham Kuyper*, 84.

29. Mouw, *Abraham Kuyper*, 84.

30. Jeff Liou, "Taking Up #blacklivesmatter: A Neo-Kuyperian Engagement with Critical Race Theory," *Journal of Reformed Theology* 11 (2017): 113. Liou is commenting on Bavinck, *RD*, 2:526.

31. Liou, "Taking Up #blacklivesmatter," 113.

racial differences."[32] Finally, Liou points to Bavinck's "eschatological humanity" as a resource.

> By extension, when Bavinck speaks of the image of God in collectivistic terms, he does so because of the covenant of works. Additionally, if the *vestigia Dei* are distributed over space and time, then the *imago Dei* likewise transgresses space and time. Thus the "universal" (if the word can be taken to include both unity and diversity) human family throughout history and geography *is* the image of God. . . . The innumerable, diverse multitude of Revelation 7:9 is the "restoration-plus" of the covenants: a single family that yet includes discernable nations, tribes, peoples, and languages, however those delineations were determined.[33]

Indeed, Bavinck rejects, in a much clearer way than Kuyper, understanding "race" as an essentialist reality, as if the different people groups differ according to nature or some biological feature; "race" is used rather to speak about the localized peoples in their geographical dispersion as the image of God spreads across the globe. An important recent contribution on Bavinck's viewpoint is James Eglinton's biography on Bavinck, which briefly surveys the historical material of Bavinck's occasional commentary on matters related to race, especially in relation to his second visit to America in 1908.[34] Drawing from Bavinck's public lectures and *dagboek* entries during his visit, Eglinton notes that Bavinck speaks in "apocalyptic tones of the unfolding disaster that was racialized hatred in America."[35] Bavinck predicts that America will be mired in the struggle between black and white citizens and is "struck by the segregated reality of American church attendance."[36] In Bavinck's judgment, "Unless it also underwent a profound transformation, the American church could not offer a solution

32. Harinck, "'Wipe Out Lines of Division (Not Distinctions),'" 83.
33. Liou, "Taking Up #blacklivesmatter," 115.
34. James Eglinton, *Bavinck: A Critical Biography* (Baker Academic, 2020), 244–49. Eglinton develops some of his claims there in his "'Indignation Would Arise Within You': Herman Bavinck on Racial Injustice in Europe and North America," in *Social Christianity in Scotland and Beyond, 1800-2000: Essays in Honour of Stewart J. Brown*, ed. Andrew Kloes and Laura M. Mair (Edinburgh University Press, 2024), 187–99. See also his "Planting Tulips in Rainforests: Herman and Johan Bavinck on Christianity in East and West," *Journal of Biblical and Theological Studies* 6 (2021): 277–92.
35. Eglinton, *Bavinck*, 248.
36. Eglinton, *Bavinck*, 248.

to the problem of race."[37] What, then, is Bavinck's positive vision of humanity and culture?

Creation

Bavinck begins his discussion of the unity of the human race in the *Dogmatics* in a way that anticipates his later reflections on the origins of racism surveyed above. "The unity of the human race," he writes, "is a certainty in holy Scripture (Gen. 1:26; 6:3; 10:32; Matt. 19:4; Acts 17:26; Rom. 5:12ff.; 1 Cor. 15:21f., 45f.) but has almost never been acknowledged by the peoples who lived outside the circle of [special] revelation."[38] The scriptural texts cited indicate the common creation of humanity and thus a common human nature as image-bearers. Bavinck went on to chronicle the construction of divisions by various philosophies throughout history—from the Greeks who "looked down on 'Barbarians,'" to the Indian caste system, to the idea of social evolution, and to the "defense of slavery" by many in the eighteenth century—upon the increased knowledge of the peoples of the world.[39] The apparent differences between the peoples had led to forgetfulness concerning human unity.

Bavinck acknowledges that the "existence of various peoples and races within humanity is most certainly an important issue" bringing into view real differences between ideas, customs, and religion.[40] The differences between the races are not understood in essentialist terms (as if the different peoples and their cultures were predetermined by some natural or biological reason that distinguished one people group from another). Rather, the differences are the result of geographical and linguistic dispersion. The Tower of Babel narrative of Genesis 11 indicates for Bavinck that these differences stem from a former unity, and God himself is the one who introduced the differences through "a single act . . . by which he intervened in the development of humanity."[41] Again, the origins of difference lie in the geographical dispersion of humanity, as the "more people live in isolation, the more language differences increase. The confusion of languages is the result of confusion in ideas, in mind, and in

37. Eglinton, *Bavinck*, 248.
38. Bavinck, *RD*, 2:523.
39. Bavinck, *RD*, 2:523–24.
40. Bavinck, *RD*, 2:525.
41. Bavinck, *RD*, 2:525.

life."[42] In the fourth volume of the *Dogmatics* (to be explored below), Bavinck would return to the Babel narrative to show that this introduction of these human differences cannot be reduced to a mere curse, but rather it is a blessing designed to further the mandate to be fruitful and multiply. In this section on human origins, however, Bavinck merely makes the point that the unity of the human race remains preserved after Babel: "For, however great the difference between the races may be, upon deeper investigation the unity and kinship of all people nevertheless emerges all the more clearly."[43] While Bavinck betrays the nineteenth-century preoccupation with the biological features of the different races, he still concludes that the physical differences among the peoples are rather superficial and, importantly, he insists that the aptitude of humanity for culture and religion remains stable across the cultures:

> Finally, in intellectual, religious, moral, social, and political respects, human beings have a wide range of things in common: language, intellect, reason, memory, knowledge of God, conscience, sense of sin, repentance, sacrifice, fasting, prayer, traditions about a golden age, a flood, and so forth. The unity of the human race, as Scripture teaches, is powerfully confirmed by all this. It is finally, not a matter of indifference, as is sometimes claimed but on the contrary of the utmost importance: it is the presupposition of religion and morality.[44]

If nature precedes grace, and grace restores nature, then it is the common human nature that is presupposed by the Christian teachings on the "atonement in Christ, the universality of the kingdom of God, the catholicity of the church, and the love of neighbor—these all are grounded in the unity of humankind."[45] In other words, the catholicity and pluriformity of the church are not mechanical appendages or forced additions to an otherwise uniform or cacophonous humanity, but rather they restore and elevate humanity to its original telos and design.

It is in the section on human destiny, then, that Bavinck returns to the telos of humanity, harkening back to the observations in previous chapters

---

42. Bavinck, *RD*, 2:525.
43. Bavinck, *RD*, 2:526.
44. Bavinck, *RD*, 2:526.
45. Bavinck, *RD*, 2:526.

on the organism of humanity and the covenantal makeup of human beings. If human beings constitute an organic whole, then the destiny of a fully developed organism is in view:

> Not as a heap of souls on a tract of land, not as a loose aggregate of individuals, but as having been created out of one blood; as one household and one family, humanity is the image and likeness of God. Belonging to that humanity is also its developments, its history, its ever-expanding dominion over the earth, its progress in science and arts, its subjugation of all creatures. All these things as well constitute the unfolding of the image and likeness of God in keeping with which humanity was created. Just as God did not reveal himself all at once at the creation, but continues and expands that revelation from day to day and from age to age, so also the image of God is not a static entity but extends and unfolds itself in the forms of space and time. It is both a gift (*Gabe*) and a mandate (*Aufgabe*).[46]

Hence, Bavinck speaks about "humanity in its entirety—as one complete organism" spreading across the whole earth, imaging God as earth's prophet, priest, and king.[47] The mutability of human development and the consummate end for which it is created reflect the Triune God's infinite richness, as human beings disperse throughout space and time. Human sin may distort the harmonious unity-in-diversity for which God had created humanity, "but by the last Adam, and his re-creating grace they are all the more resplendently restored to their destiny. The state of integrity—either through the fall or apart from the fall—is a preparation of the state of glory in which God will impart his glory to all he creates and be 'all in all' [1 Cor. 15:28]."[48]

Sin—Individual and Social

In volume 3 of the *Dogmatics*, then, Bavinck speaks of sin's effects on that original unity. If the image of God refers not merely to individuals but also to the development of corporate humanity, then actual sin takes not only individual but also social forms. As individuals act sinfully, habits of sin are

46. Bavinck, *RD*, 2:577. The language of gift and mandate again connects Bavinck conceptually to the *Bildung* tradition of conceiving human formation as a collective task.

47. Bavinck, *RD*, 2:577.

48. Bavinck, *RD*, 2:588.

perpetuated; and as each individual's habits develop, others are impacted and corrupted. "Just as sinful deed, when repeated over and over, fosters a habitual propensity . . . so sinful mores and habits can also reinforce an innate depravity in a family, among relatives in a family line, or among a people and develop it in a certain direction."[49]

Sin is too complex to be reduced to isolated acts, and Bavinck's corporate account of the image of God produces a more granular picture of sin's perpetuation and effects. Bavinck likens sin's effects to that of the spread of a disease—from individuals, to the family, to the nations, and from generation to generation. Sin ought not be spoken of merely in the abstract, but it has concrete manifestations in each "line." In a key passage, Bavinck argues that our depravity forms individuals, and those individuals form families, from one generation to the next: "Human beings are not individuals in an absolute sense. . . . A human being is born from the matrix of a community and from that very moment lives in a certain circle, situation, and period." From the microcosm of the family we see a culture in a miniature form; each family has its own distinct culture and thus has a pattern of life mired up in both sin and goodness, distinct to itself. When one zooms out even further, different families come together to form a society and, further on, a nation, a "spirit of the age," and "all of them together impact the individual person and modify his or her innate moral depravity." It follows that, just as each individual sins in distinct ways, so do families and cultures sin in distinct ways: "Sin, therefore, though it is indeed always essentially the same, manifests itself in differing ways and forms in different persons, families, classes, and nations and in different states and times." Sin can thus take a corporate and organic shape: "Sins in the East differ from those in the West, in tropical zones from temperate zones, in rural areas from cities, in civilized states from uncivilized ones, in the twentieth century from earlier centuries. There are family sins, societal sins, and national sins. . . . Aside from what we call 'original sin,' there is also 'corporate guilt' and the corporate action of sin."[50]

49. Bavinck, *RD*, 3:175.

50. Bavinck, *RD*, 3:175. On systemic sin in the Bible, see D. T. Everhart, "Communal Reconciliation: Corporate Responsibility and Opposition to Systemic Sin," *International Journal of Systematic Theology* 25, no. 1 (2023): 134–56. Cf. Herman Bavinck, *Guidebook for Instruction in the Christian Religion*, ed. and trans. Gregory Parker Jr. and Cameron Clausing (Hendrickson, 2022), 90–92.

The upshot of this, for Bavinck, is that sin is not reducible to individual acts because humans are always connected corporately: "As people are interconnected, so also are their sinful inclinations and deeds. Penetrating the infinite riches of all creation, sin also forms a realm that, animated by a single life principle, organizes itself in multiple forms and appearances."[51] Crucially, Bavinck cites Schleiermacher's *Christian Faith* §§71–72 at this juncture.[52] Bavinck has in view Schleiermacher's account of how individuals are corrupted by originated sin, which informs Bavinck's social account of sin's effects. After his presentation of this organic account of the imputation of Adam's sin, Bavinck is keen to maintain the balance between communal guilt—which acknowledges the reality of inherited sin as a law and reality—and the individual guilt that accrues from actual sin. Here, Bavinck appeals to Schleiermacher after a prefatory comment, agreeing that humanity is caught up in one another's guilt:

> It is . . . completely true that we can never with complete accuracy indicate the boundaries that separate personal guilt from communal guilt. What Schleiermacher says of original sin is something very different from what Scripture and the church say concerning it, but by itself is completely true of sin in general that it is the collective deed and collective guilt of the human race as a whole. In other words, the sinful state and sinful deeds of each individual are, on the one hand, conditioned by those of the previous generation, and, on the other, they in turn condition the sinful state and acts of later descendants. Sin is "in each the work of all and in all the work of each."[53]

---

51. Bavinck, *RD*, 3:175–76.

52. Friedrich Schleiermacher, *Christian Faith: A New Translation and Critical Edition*, ed. Catherine L. Kelsey and Terrence N. Tice, trans. Terrence N. Tice, Catherine L. Kelsey, and Edwina Lawler (Westminster John Knox, 2016), §§71–72. See also Derek R. Nelson, *What's Wrong With Sin: Sin in Individual and Social Perspective from Schleiermacher to Theologies of Liberation* (T&T Clark, 2009).

53. Bavinck, *RD*, 3:116, quoting Schleiermacher, *Christian Faith*, §71.1. On Bavinck's critical appreciation for Schleiermacher in general, see Cory C. Brock, *Orthodox Yet Modern: Herman Bavinck's Use of Schleiermacher* (Lexham, 2020); on Bavinck's critique of Schleiermacher's account of sin (in comparison with Charles Hodge), see N. Gray Sutanto, "Original Sin in Modern Theology: Charles Hodge and Herman Bavinck on Friedrich Schleiermacher," in *Ruined Sinners to Reclaim: Sin in Historical, Biblical, Theological, and Pastoral Perspective*, ed. David Gibson and Jonathan Gibson (Crossway, 2024), 699–724.

As he signals in that passage, while Bavinck does not, for instance, accept Schleiermacher's rejection of a historical fall, Bavinck does accept an account of systemic sin and allows for an analysis of concrete manifestations of systemic sins in families, nations, and across time.[54] The pluriform diversity of the peoples, meant to signify analogically the infinite riches of God's being, becomes a cacophony of sinful patterns in conflicting directions. Scripture itself, as indicated in earlier chapters, presents the sins of God's people as impacting the whole of Israel, and the sins of Babylon, Egypt, Sodom, and so on are not depicted uniformly. This corporate manifestation of sin also bestows sin with a cosmic sense. Sin is mysterious and ever-present, leading philosophers like Schelling to conclude that "the irrational, the darkness, the chaotic" is that which is "fundamental to everything."[55] As each locus in space and time bears a distinct sinful pattern, so does suffering take on particularities: "A stream of spiritual and physical misery in individual persons, families, generations, and nations, in state, church, society, science, and art has its origin in sin."[56]

It follows, then, that the division and misery that stem from cultural conflict are due to the entrance of sin. In creation's original trajectory, humanity was to disperse and organically multiply into different localities and cultures, each of which would complement the other to manifest something of the glory of God. This side of the fall, however, those differences are now sources of conflict and subjugation. But God is not content to leave humanity to its own devices; committed to the flourishing of humanity as a whole, God instills another principle through special grace to produce a kingdom of God that consummates creation's original trajectory.

54. So Romero and Liou: "Just as sin infects us as individuals, it also perverts our larger ethnic cultures. . . . Each culture contains distinct ethnic sin." *Christianity and Critical Race Theory*, 45.

55. Bavinck, *RD*, 3:177.

56. Bavinck, *RD*, 3:179. These moves inform Johan Bavinck's reflections on corporate guilt and responsibility: "In our sinning we do not stand isolated from one another: almost every sin we commit happens in community. Numerous sins are inherently of that nature. The sins of adultery and of quarrelling and dispute, for example, are communally based. But also those sins that are individually committed still happen in the greater context of society, and society as such has been the provocation behind them. That is the reason why, when a crime is committed, we can hardly make one person totally responsible for the act. Our judicial systems, which as a rule punish an offender in isolation, are always more or less one-sided because they do not take into account the role played by the parents, teachers, or friends of that person. All sin carries with it a degree of communality, as it finds its roots in society. We do not sin as individuals, but as members of our greater social environment." Johan Herman Bavinck, *Between the Beginning and the End: A Radical Kingdom Vision*, trans. Bert Hielema (Eerdmans, 2014), 60.

Redemption and Consummation

Redeemed humanity is restored natural humanity. Regeneration recreates new individuals, unites them to a new federal head in Christ, and thus forms a new humanity, the church. This church, too, is an organic unity developing across space and time. Bavinck expounds on these themes on the corporate and centrifugal account of the church across his earlier to his more mature works. I draw from his "Kingdom of God, the Highest Good" (1881), his "Catholicity of Christianity and the Church" (1888), his *Dogmatics*, then finally his *Guidebook on the Christian Religion* (1913).

The church points to the eschatological manifestation of the kingdom of God, where God's rule will be made manifest in the union of the new heavens and the new earth. This eschatological vision is the consummation of creation's original trajectory—originally, "the notion of a Kingdom of God that fosters the development of both individual and community, that is both the content and goal of world history, encompassing the whole earth and all nations" was the destiny of humanity, as it obeys God throughout the earth.[57] While the church is not synonymous with God's kingdom, it signals a future wherein God's rule is consummately realized in the parousia. "Apart from sin, the Kingdom of God would have existed among humanity from the very beginning and would have developed completely normally. Through sin, the Kingdom of God was disrupted, the various goods contained in the Kingdom were torn asunder," and so "the Kingdom of God is a Kingdom that does not yet exist fully but is coming into fuller existence."[58] It is the "unity, the inclusion, the totality of all moral goods, of earthly and heavenly, spiritual and physical, eternal and temporal goods," of which the church is one constituent part.[59] This unity-and-diversity motif of the kingdom signals its organic character: "The unity of an organism becomes the more harmonious, the more rich, and the more glorious to the degree that the multitude of parts increases."[60]

How do these motifs relate to the church consummately? "The Kingdom itself is also an organic personality whose head is Christ and whose subjects

57. Herman Bavinck, "The Kingdom of God, the Highest Good," trans. Nelson D. Kloosterman, *The Bavinck Review* 2 (2011), 136.

58. Bavinck, "The Kingdom of God, the Highest Good," 146.

59. Bavinck, "The Kingdom of God, the Highest Good," 141.

60. Bavinck, "The Kingdom of God, the Highest Good," 144.

constitute the body. Just as each personality has and must have an organism known as the body, so too the church is the body, the pure organism of Christ's divine-human personality, the pleroma, to use Paul's profound expression (Eph. 1:23) of him who fills all in all."[61] The church's geographic and temporal locations witness to the fullness of the church, finally manifested in glorified humanity:

> Viewing nothing human as foreign but as spiritual in nature, the Kingdom of God is universal, bound to no place or time, embracing the whole earth and everything human, independent of nation and country, of nationality and race, of language and culture. In Christ Jesus what is legitimate is only what has been created anew, with no exceptions. This is why the gospel of the Kingdom must be brought to all nations, to all creatures, not only to people but to the entire creation (Mark 16:15). The Kingdom of God extends as far as Christianity itself.[62]

That first clause on the kingdom of God "viewing nothing as foreign" foreshadows Bavinck's emphases in his 1888 address on catholicity. If the kingdom of God is only against sin, and not nature as such, then the entrance of Christianity into a particular culture or nation means that the particularities of that culture or nation would be preserved and uneradicated. Rather, each culture would be leavened by the transformative powers of the Spirit and would signal a final day in which cultural and national pluriformity would characterize the kingdom.[63] Consistent with Jennings's emphases, Bavinck depicts the influence of Christian faith as culture-preserving as the kingdom takes up the "cultural particularities" of each nation.[64]

Indeed, Bavinck's 1888 address included extensive discussions on the *leavening* power of Christianity as part of its catholicity. Indeed, true catholicity involves proclaiming the powers of the Christian religion to influence every sphere of culture. As such, Christianity, precisely because it is not tethered to a particular nation, culture, or perennial *Sitz im Leben*, has the capacity

61. Bavinck, "The Kingdom of God, the Highest Good," 145.
62. Bavinck, "The Kingdom of God, the Highest Good," 148.
63. "The history of the nations and of their states finds its principal idea and explanation to be the Kingdom of Heaven." Bavinck, "The Kingdom of God, the Highest Good," 163.
64. Jennings, *Christian Imagination*, 147.

to embrace and leaven any culture with which it comes into contact, thereby producing multiformity. In Bavinck's words, Christianity "can enter into all situations, can connect with all forms of natural life, is suitable to every time, and beneficial for all things, and is relevant in all circumstances. It is free and independent because it is in conflict only with sin and in the blood of the Cross there is purification for every sin."[65] In this last claim, Bavinck is echoing his oft-quoted axiom that Protestantism "traded the quantitative antithesis of the natural and the supernatural for the qualitative, ethical antithesis of sin and grace."[66] Christianity is only against sin, not against culture as such.

If this is the case, catholicity is most expressed not *in spite* of diversity but precisely *in* diversity. Catholicity consists not in mechanical uniformity but in a "richness," a "many-sidedness," and in "pluriformity."[67] Continuing on the claim that Christianity is a world religion and thus for every time and place, Bavinck argues for the inherent desirability of confessional and international diversity on distinctly Reformed grounds in this way: "That church is most catholic that most clearly expresses in its confession and applies in its practice this international and cosmopolitan character of the Christian religion. The Reformed had an eye for it when in various countries and churches they confessed the truth in an indigenous, free, and independent manner and at the Synod of Dort invited delegates from all over Reformed Christianity."[68] Reformed theology wishes for no uniformity, and the diverse confessions of the Reformed tradition witness to its catholic commitments.

This commitment to the catholicity of Christianity means that Christian theologians should not expect that the Christian expression of one culture should be replicated or repeated by another: American Christianity is not Dutch Christianity or German Christianity, and so on. As Harinck aptly

65. Bavinck, "The Catholicity of Christianity and the Church," trans. John Bolt, *Calvin Theological Journal* 27 (1992): 249. Bavinck's understanding of common grace and the universal character of the Christian vocation also grounds these claims. See especially his "Calvin and Common Grace," in *Calvin and the Reformation: Four Studies*, ed. William Park Armstrong (Revell, 1909), 99–130. "[Calvin's] ethics is diametrically opposed to all asceticism, it is catholic and universal in scope." "Calvin and Common Grace," 128.

66. Bavinck, *RD*, 4:410. Cf. James Eglinton, *Trinity and Organism: Toward a New Reading of Herman Bavinck's Organic Motif* (Bloomsbury T&T Clark, 2010), 40–41, 96.

67. Bavinck, "Catholicity of Christianity," 250.

68. Bavinck, *RD*, 4:323.

comments, Bavinck was committed to a kind of "cultural relativism," if only in the sense that Christianity can leaven any culture it finds because grace is only against sin and not nature or culture as such.[69] While Bavinck may not go as far as Jennings, who envisions a sort of pluriformity of the church that recognizes "various visions of orthodoxy," Bavinck certainly recognized the inevitability and goodness of various cultures expressing Christian faith according to their own language and customs.[70] Crucially, however, the focus on dispersion and geographically sustained identities shifts the emphasis away from skin color and toward localities and cultures.

The diversity of cultures and nations thus poses not a threat but rather an asset to the richness of the kingdom of God and will find their culmination in consummation: "Tribes, peoples, and nations will make their own particular contribution to the enrichment of life in the new Jerusalem. . . . The great diversity that exists in all sorts of ways is not destroyed in eternity but is cleansed from all that is sinful and made serviceable to fellowship with God and each other."[71] In a way that directly contradicts the monolingual vision of the eschaton in the Leiden Synopsis, Bavinck argues that multilingualism was the teleological intention of the cultural mandate and is thus restored and consummated in the final state.[72] Revisiting the Tower of Babel narrative in the fourth volume of the *Dogmatics*, Bavinck argues that diversity was the goal before the fall, was initiated again by God in Babel, and finally was reaffirmed at Pentecost and consummated in eternity:

> In unity God loves the diversity. Among all creatures there was diversity even when as yet there was no sin. As a result of sin that diversity has been

69. George Harinck, "Calvinism Isn't the Only Truth: Herman Bavinck's Impressions of the USA," in *The Sesquicentennial of Dutch Immigration: 150 Years of Ethnic Heritage; Proceedings of the 11th Biennial Conference of the Association for the Advancement of Dutch American Studies*, ed. Larry J. Wagenaar and Robert P. Swierenga (The Joint Archives of Holland, Hope College, 1998), 151–60, 154.

70. Jennings, *Christian Imagination*, 114. For more on Bavinck on cultural pluralism and catholicity, see Cory C. Brock and N. Gray Sutanto, *Neo-Calvinism: A Theological Introduction* (Lexham, 2023), chap. 3.

71. Bavinck, *RD*, 4:727.

72. "It is not as clear as to which language the blessed will use, although it is certain that the variety of languages—which is a consequence of sin—will cease there, according to the apostle (1 Cor. 13:18 [*sic*]). Hence some also draw the not improbable conclusion that the use of the Hebrew language will remain, because it is not a consequence of sin, and because Christ when he spoke to Paul from heaven even though the latter was originally Greek, used the Hebrew language, as the apostle explicitly observes in Acts 26:14." *Synopsis of a Purer Theology*, 3:609.

> perverted and corrupted, but diversity as such is good and important also for the church. Difference in sex and age, in character and disposition, in mind and heart, in gifts and goods, in time and place is to the advantage also of the truth that is in Christ. He takes all these differences into his service and adorns the church with them. Indeed, though the division of humanity into peoples and languages was occasioned by sin, it has something good in it, which is brought into the church and thus preserved for eternity. From many races and languages and peoples and nations Christ gathers his church on earth.[73]

Multilingualism is thus a creational good and indicates creation's trajectory that was complicated by sin but restored at Pentecost. Powery's comments on the gift of tongues at Pentecost concur: "The Spirit causes the mother tongues of those who are different to be on the tongues of the *other*. Their culture resides in the speech of those from another culture, creating a cross-cultural inhabitation. . . . At Pentecost, there is an integration of human beings through language in the Spirit, a gift of speech that comes with a purpose to be understood."[74] Pentecost reaffirms that God's judgment at the Tower of Babel was also a blessing—as humanity was dispersed and developed languages, they were enabled to proceed with the cultural mandate to be fruitful and multiply so that representatives of God could spread across the earth. The many languages of the dispersed peoples led to confusion only due to the occasion of sin, but they are redirected and redeemed at Pentecost, and ultimately preserved and consummated in eternity.

Finally, the *Guidebook on Christian Religion* crystallizes all these ideas succinctly, especially in Bavinck's chapters on the church and the consummation of the world. On the church, Bavinck argues that God gifts his Spirit so that "fellowship that unites believers together" emerges: "He does not hand [these blessings] out to a few isolated individuals but to a large number of

73. Bavinck, *RD*, 4:318. See also James Eglinton, "From Babel to Pentecost via Paris and Amsterdam: Multilingualism in Neo-Calvinist and Revolutionary Thought," in *Neo-Calvinism and the French Revolution*, ed. George Harinck and James Eglinton (Bloomsbury T&T Clark, 2014), 31–60. So Liou: "Scripture repeatedly uses the phrase 'wealth of nations' and related ideas. . . . The usages refer to material *and* cultural wealth of distinct cultures and nations beyond Israel. In Scripture, their diverse cultural productions are made pleasing to God." "Critical Race Theory," 246–47. Cf. Richard Bauckham, *The Theology of the Book of Revelation* (Cambridge University Press, 1993), 132–35.

74. Powery, *Becoming Human*, 58.

people, who from the beginning forms a historical continuity, an organic whole."[75] If there was a "close connection between ethnic unity and the religious community" in the old covenantal administration of Israel, Pentecost "freed [the church] from every national bond and organized them into their own community, independent from nation and country in the midst of the world."[76] This does not mean that cultural particularities were now rendered unimportant but that the gospel is "suitable and necessary for all people, in all times, in all circumstances, and in all situations."[77] Catholicity means that there is not merely "one denomination," but rather "the Christian congregation in which all churches together, in different degrees of purity, come to revelation."[78] This pluriformity of the church witnesses to the final manifestation of the kingdom of God: "The nations that are saved will walk in the light of the new Jerusalem, and the kings of the earth will bring their glory and honor into it (Rev. 21:24; 22:2). Although all share in the same salvation, the same eternal life, and the same fellowship with God, yet there will be all sorts of differences among them in rank and position, in gift and calling, in glory and radiance."[79] Bavinck's creational and eschatological affirmation of the good of ethnic and cultural diversity dovetails well with the "cultural wealth" thesis, recognized by theorists who seek to ameliorate racism today.[80] Revelation 21:22–27 affirms that the glory and honor of the nations will be brought into heaven: "We each possess community cultural wealth. This cultural treasure or 'glory' is a reflection of the glory of God in and through each of us as God's unique children."[81] As Romero and Liou observe, this involves at least both the tangible aspects of culture (such as food and literature) as well as the distinct perspectives that each ethnic group brings to the body of Christ—distinct perspectives that would be harmonious and united, rather than sources of division, in the last day.

This diversity does not eclipse true unity—the true end of humanity in its entirety, the vision of God: "For all will see God's face and be like him (Matt.

75. Bavinck, *Guidebook*, 161.
76. Bavinck, *Guidebook*, 161–62.
77. Bavinck, *Guidebook*, 166.
78. Bavinck, *Guidebook*, 166.
79. Bavinck, *Guidebook*, 193.
80. Romero and Liou, *Christianity and Critical Race Theory*, 42–44.
81. Romero and Liou, *Christianity and Critical Race Theory*, 43.

5:8; John 3:2; Rev. 22:4); all will know as they are known (1 Cor. 13:12); and all will be prophets, priests, and kings."[82]

TRUTH FOR WORSHIP, MISSION, AND LIFE

This chapter applies this book's Reformed theological anthropology to the difficult topic of race. After showing that "race" is ultimately a social construct, and that cultural and geographical differences account for the diversity of humanity, the chapter then sketched the way in which race-consciousness has emerged before turning to Herman Bavinck's positive account of human diversity through the redemptive-historical epochs of creation, fall, redemption, and consummation. It is hard to envision the preservation of cultural diversity without compromising an affirmation of enduring truths, but it is precisely what we see in the unity-in-diversity of the kingdom of God that will be realized in the eschaton.

To that end, this section will unfold some important implications for worship, life, and mission from the positive vision of corporate humanity and unity-in-diversity sketched by Bavinck above.

First, as I argued extensively in chapter 1 and observed again in this chapter, all human beings are equal, made, and loved as God's image-bearers. All human beings are thus persons with dignity, and racialization fails to carve nature at its joints. The differences we see among the various peoples are cultural rather than ontological. It follows that any beliefs concerning the superiority or inferiority of any one people group are not only false but sinful, failing to recognize the dignity and equality with which God has created every person.

Second, we should recognize that the church is catholic, and thus universal, not containable by one specific time or place. The church is a unity-and-diversity because humanity was created to be a unity-in-diversity. As we saw in chapters 7 and 8, we are united no longer with the first Adam but with the second, and the unity that binds the church is our union and confession of the Lord Jesus Christ. The church is one: "There is one body and one Spirit—just as you were called to the one hope that belongs to your call—one Lord,

82. Bavinck, *Guidebook*, 194.

one faith, one baptism, one God and Father of all, who is over all and through all and in all" (Eph. 4:4–6). Our spiritual unity and identity relativize the cultural boundaries in which we find ourselves. "There is neither Jew nor Greek, there is neither slave nor free, there is no male and female, for you are all one in Christ Jesus" (Gal. 3:28). The common confession that we have forms us as citizens of the kingdom of God.

Third, the creeds and confessions of the catholic church are thus of great value: They (e.g., Nicaea and Chalcedon) inform us of the essentials of the Christian faith and of what it is that distinguishes, say, Protestants from Roman Catholics, thus indicating to us matters of first importance. What is not contained in the creeds or confessions, therefore, is a matter of Christian liberty—creedal and confessional subscription do not impede but rather foster cultural pliability. There are, of course, certain things that will mark out each culture that has been shaped by Christian faith—worshiping on Sundays, for instance, or practicing forgiveness and repentance, the commitment to mercy and hospitality, and so on. But each culture will inflect these Christian practices with their own particularities.

Fourth, it follows that Christians should reject both cultural relativism and cultural uniformity. Because of the realities of human corruption, which impacts not merely individuals but families, societies, and cultures, there *are* fallen tendencies and dispositions that we ought to reject. The gospel transforms persons, and because of that, it will inevitably transform the communities of which those persons are a part. The gospel and the Bible challenge cultures characterized by greed, idolatry, polytheism, corruption in speech or act, sexual promiscuity, double-mindedness, racism, and selfishness, for the Spirit of Christ is the Spirit of holiness. The formation of the church is thus a formation of a new, spiritual culture: "Therefore, preparing your minds for action, and being sober-minded, set your hope fully on the grace that will be brought to you at the revelation of Jesus Christ. As obedient children, do not be conformed to the passions of your former ignorance, but as he who called you is holy, you also be holy in all your conduct, since it is written, 'You shall be holy, for I am holy'" (1 Pet. 1:13–16). All Christians are partakers of the new creation, and their lives are witnesses to that new world as ambassadors (2 Cor. 5:15–21). As Larry Hurtado and Tom Holland have shown, this is exactly the kind of transformation that happened when Christianity began to influence the Greco-Roman world.[83]

Yet, because the church in this present age is merely witnessing to the world to come (as we saw in chap. 7) and because the church is catholic, that is, universal, no one Christianized culture can claim to be *the* Christian culture or *the* kingdom of God made manifest *simpliciter*. The various Christian cultures all witness to the kingdom of God in their own distinctive ways, though there are spiritual fruits and confessions that bind them all together. As Bavinck himself recognized, we should not expect American Christianity, for instance, to look or sound the same as Dutch (or Indonesian, or Chinese, or British, etc.) Christianity.[84] Western Christendom is thus not coterminous with Christianity itself.

Fifth, we ought to recognize that we are finite creatures who need one another. We have personal and cultural blind spots, and God's revealed kingdom is far too capacious to be limited by our own limited horizons. It is wise, therefore, to be in close proximity with those who are culturally different from us so that we can be exposed to the subtle ways in which we have identified our own preferences with kingdom values. Christianity's catholic vision thus fosters a desire to learn more about what God is doing in cultures different from mine. Andrew Ong has made a persuasive case, showing that the catholicity of the Christian church directs us toward an engagement with "World Christianity."[85] This could be done not merely by traveling or engaging with the writings of the global church in an academic sense, but by engaging our neighbors, who, because of the globalized character of the world today, may well be from a different cultural background than us. That Christianity upholds a unity-in-diversity model of the cultures of the church means that, though we may have a natural and good love of the cultures in which we have found ourselves, we should recognize that the love of our own is a love with porous boundaries. The church, therefore, should strive toward *unity* when it finds itself in a context of cultural diversity.

---

83. Larry Hurtado, *Destroyer of the Gods: Early Christian Distinctiveness in the Roman World* (Baylor University Press, 2017); Tom Holland, *Dominion: How the Christian Revolution Remade the World* (Basic Books, 2019).

84. See Cory C. Brock and N. Gray Sutanto, *Neo-Calvinism: A Theological Introduction* (Lexham, 2023), esp. chaps. 2–3.

85. Andrew Ong, "World Christianity," in *T&T Clark Handbook of Neo-Calvinism*, ed. Nathaniel Gray Sutanto and Cory Brock (Bloomsbury T&T Clark, 2024), 426–38.

Sixth, what do these affirmations concerning the corporate character of humanity and the catholicity of the church entail with respect to our local congregations? We cannot do everything, and we are finite creatures—the task of the church as an institution is to preach the word and administer the sacraments. It is the confession of our God's name and acts that make us distinct (Ps. 145). At the very least, however, I am suggesting that our local congregations should represent the demographics of the place in which we find ourselves. If we focus on the values and message of the gospel, then we would attract anyone whom God has called, regardless of their background, because the gospel addresses humans as sinners. If the local context in which we find ourselves is ethnic-specific, then our churches may well comprise members mainly of that ethnicity.[86] However, in many cases (if not most), there will be visitors and members from a minority culture in our context, and in those moments we should be asking hard questions about whether our community is a welcoming and hospitable environment for those who are coming from different backgrounds. Having members and qualified leaders from a diversity of backgrounds is beneficial to the church because they will expose us to the cultural blind spots that we have and values that we take for granted (e.g., values concerning time, hospitality, family, food, or dress), many of which have become invisible to us because they form the air we breathe. In my view, while contemporary analyses of race could be helpful at spotting some real problems that have caused subjugation or discrimination in the past or present, they are less successful at offering solutions that may foster mutual embrace, understanding, reconciliation, and unity.[87] At worst, we might be tempted to reify our cultural backgrounds into *identities* that demarcate in-groups and out-groups, and fail to recognize that our identity and mutual solidarity is grounded in Christ, who "has broken down in his flesh the dividing wall of hostility" (Eph. 2:14). Mutual cultural understanding,

86. For a theological exploration of ethnic-specific churches, see Andrew Ong, "Neo-Calvinism and Ethnic Churches in Multiethnic Contexts," *Journal of Reformed Theology* 12, no. 3 (October 2018): 296–320.

87. "The attraction of critical theories for Christians is that they grasp an aspect of the truth." Carl Trueman, foreword to *Critical Dilemma: The Rise of Critical Theories and Social Justice Ideology—Implications for the Church and Society*, by Neil Shenvi and Pat Sawyer (Harvest House, 2023). As Neil Shenvi and Pat Sawyer maintain: "The Bible offers better answers to questions about race, class, gender, sexuality, justice, oppression, and a host of other hot-button issues." *Critical Dilemma*, 30.

even the recognition of the wrongs of the past, must be coupled with a desire for greater unity rather than further ghettoization or separation.

It is impossible to sketch all the practical implications, and this section has only scratched at the surface. Its goal was to provide a positive theological framework for corporate diversity without reifying race. Christianity's catholicity pushes us toward a unity that far transcends the cultural boundaries that have been raised due to sin—and the work toward that unity is hard but worth it and made possible by the Spirit.

CONCLUSION

This book has introduced the biblical contours and dogmatic articulations of a Reformed theological anthropology, and it has then applied that anthropology to the two contemporary issues of sex and race. As an introduction, however, I hope that the volume whets the appetite of readers to take the sketches canvassed here as a starting point for further reading and research. It is my prayer that this book also serves as an invitation to consider the ways in which the Bible and the Reformed tradition present a vision of humanity that is rich and full of generative implications. Indeed, Christianity is good news because it makes us into the kind of humans that God has always intended us to be.

FURTHER READING

Brock, Cory, and N. Gray Sutanto. *Neo-Calvinism: A Theological Introduction*. Lexham, 2023. This work introduces in greater depth the emphasis on the catholicity of the Christian church and its implications for cultural understanding from the neo-Calvinist tradition of Herman Bavinck.

Ong, Andrew. "World Christianity." In *T&T Clark Handbook of Neo-Calvinism*, edited by Nathaniel Gray Sutanto and Cory Brock. Bloomsbury T&T Clark, 2024. Ong's chapter is a persuasive argument that shows the ways in which the Reformed tradition and the discipline of world Christianity are complementary and fruitful when taken together.

Bacote, Vincent. *Reckoning with Race and Performing the Good News: In Search of a Better Evangelical Theology*. Brill, 2020. Bacote shows, from a broadly evangelical perspective, how to think well about race without reifying it.

CONCLUSION

TWELVE THESES ON HUMANITY AS CREATED AND FALLEN

THIS BOOK IS MERELY an entryway into the depth and width of the biblical teachings on theological anthropology. I hope that it provides not merely an introduction but also an invitation to think more deeply about what it means to be human and to image God. I have also covered much ground—from biblical-theological material on human beings as created, fallen, and redeemed to a panoramic overview of human nature in dogmatic development, then to some reflections on the difficult topics of sexuality and cultural diversity. I thus end this work with twelve theses that summarize, in capsule form, the main points covered in the work. After presenting the theses, I then provide a brief and summative exposition of each.

1. All human beings are made in the image of the Triune God and are thus called to represent, enjoy, and glorify God forever.
2. The doctrine of the image of God entails both ontological and ethical affirmations. God creates humans as embodied souls with intellectual and volitional capacities, and he calls humans to represent him by a proper exercise of those faculties in righteousness, holiness, and true knowledge.
3. Just as the visible creation witnesses to the invisible God, the image of God includes the body, as shown in its created goodness, dependence,

and fittingness for the soul, for the incarnation, and for communion with God.

4. The image of God entails the stewarding and cultivating of creation: the cultural mandate.
5. The image of God refers to humanity as a single corporate whole, united under a federal head, and thus it has a teleological orientation for a consummate existence of perfect and everlasting fellowship with God in a sanctified and perfected cosmos.
6. Adam was the federal head of humanity, and his originating sin resulted in the imputation of guilt and the transmission of corruption to humanity as a whole.
7. Original corruption refers to the loss of original righteousness and the illicit concupiscence that now marks fallen human nature, the source of all actual sins.
8. Death is the just wage of sin and is the unnatural separation of the soul from the body.
9. Christ's human obedience is the exemplar for the restored and sanctified image of God.
10. Regeneration of the "inner self" is a definite starting point for the renewal of human nature and is a guarantee for a resurrected, glorified, and consummated human nature.
11. Humanity is created male and female, and this sexed complementary difference is good, witnessing to Christ and the church, whether in marriage or in faithful singleness.
12. Human cultural diversity, though often leading to division due to sin, is a creational good, and the kingdom of God will comprise a diversity of cultures with a common confession of the Triune God.

TWELVE THESES

1. All human beings are made in the image of the Triune God and are thus called to represent, enjoy, and glorify God forever.

   God creates each individual according to his own image. The first person plural in Genesis 1:26, and other passages like Colossians 1:15–17, indicate that the whole Triune God is the archetype for the human being, for each person of the Trinity shares a singular divine substance. Humans are thus religious creatures who are created to have communion with the Triune God, and each human being, therefore, *as such* is created good, with dignity and agency.

2. The doctrine of the image of God entails both ontological and ethical affirmations. God creates humans as embodied souls with intellectual and volitional capacities, and he calls humans to represent him by a proper exercise of those faculties in righteousness, holiness, and true knowledge.

   The *image* of God has two connotations: metaphysics and ethics. We are ontologically image-bearers and thus have distinct personalities, with an immortal and indivisible soul with the faculties of knowing and willing. We are meant to exercise those faculties (potencies) to represent God in true virtue: in righteousness (obedience to God), in wisdom (thinking God's thoughts after him), and as representations of God on a creaturely level. Humans are prophets, priests, and kings meant to communicate and represent God in their cultivation of the world.

3. Just as the visible creation witnesses to the invisible God, the image of God includes the body, as shown in its created goodness, dependence, and fittingness for the soul, for the incarnation, and for communion with God.

   The body is a fitting home for the soul, and the soul is, in turn, the form of the body. As embodied souls, humans image God through their sexed bodies, and their personalities are communicated by way of embodiment. Unlike angelic or artificial intelligences, human bodies signify our ethical and physical bonds and our moral solidarity. God, after all, has created our bodies *good*, has assumed it in the incarnation, and is committed to resurrect it in the consummation of the new creation. The body is thus a reminder of humanity's humility and exaltation (Ps. 8)—humans represent God and yet are absolutely dependent on God.

4. The image of God entails the stewarding and cultivating of creation: the cultural mandate.

   The cultural mandate is the vocational aspect of the image of God. God calls human beings to be fruitful and multiply, and this involves not merely procreation but the cultivation of creation through the formation of culture. As human beings spread across the globe, so is the glory of God spreading through human representation—this natural development leads to the affirmation that cultural diversity itself is good. Given the fall, however, cultural diversity leads to much conflict and division, and the cultural mandate is carried out not merely by the natural course of the family but by the preaching of the gospel and the work of ecclesial discipleship. The gospel is the means through which humans are reformed to represent God properly, and it orients regenerate cultures to the glory of God.

5. The image of God refers to humanity as a single corporate whole, united under a federal head, and thus it has a teleological orientation for a consummate existence of perfect and everlasting fellowship with God in a sanctified and perfected cosmos.

   Though God creates each individual in his image, God's absolute perfection can never be reflected by mere individuals. It is humanity, taken together as a corporate whole, that is called to image God in his fullness. God thus desires the cultures, united under the confession of his lordship, to be consummated, and no single Christianized culture in any time or place is coterminous with the kingdom of God. God calls Christians to bear a chastened, transformational witness to the way of the kingdom now.

6. Adam was the federal head of humanity, and his originating sin resulted in the imputation of guilt and the transmission of corruption to humanity as a whole.

   God has designed human beings to be diverse individuals united by a singular federal head, either in Adam or in Christ. If Adam had offered perfect, personal, and perpetual obedience in the state of innocence, he would have transmitted original righteousness to his progeny. Adam, however, fell, and thus God imputes his guilt and ensuing corruption to his progeny.

7. Original corruption refers to the loss of original righteousness and the illicit concupiscence that now marks human nature, the source of all actual sins.

The corruption humanity inherits results in concupiscence, such that humanity is now predisposed toward acts of sin. The loss of original righteousness refers not to a mere absence but to the privation of natural qualities that humanity was called to actualize. The privation of wisdom leads to folly, privation of righteousness to wickedness, and privation of holiness to animality. This predisposition and tendency toward sin is itself culpable, for it is that from which all actual sins arise. The unregenerate person is thus totally depraved: Sin has marred the whole of human nature, and it is only by God's common grace that humans are not utterly sinful. Fallen humanity thus has no internal resources to prepare itself to receive salvation, and the grace of effectual regeneration is necessary for humans to have faith in Christ.

8. Death is the just wage of sin and is the unnatural separation of the soul from the body.

   Having sinned against God, humans are now destined to die. Death is the separation of the soul from the body—and this is not God's creational intention. Thus, God is committed to resurrect the body, and humans are incomplete without the body.

9. Christ's human obedience is the exemplar for the restored and sanctified image of God.

   The divine Son of God is the unique divine image of God. As the incarnate one, however, he is patterned after our human nature, being made like us in every way so that he might be the second Adam, the federal head that represents humanity. Through his obedience, humans are made right with God, and it is his example that humans ought to follow in their sanctification.

10. Regeneration of the "inner self" is a definite starting point for the renewal of human nature and is a guarantee for a resurrected, glorified, and consummated human nature.

    Regeneration is the result of God's effectual calling, through which he restores our nature, such that we are enabled once again to obey God in holiness. God regenerates the "inner self," that is, the center of human personality that directs the whole person. Regeneration is a down payment for the glorified human nature that Christians will receive in the resurrection—what God has begun in us he will complete (Phil. 1:6). Though Christians still struggle with indwelling sin now, they can, by the power of the Spirit, obey God, and in the last day, Christian righteousness is confirmed such that the presence of sin shall be no more.

11. Humanity is created male and female, and this sexed complementary difference is good, witnessing to Christ and the church, whether in marriage or in faithful singleness.

    Human beings are sexed, embodied creatures, created male and female. This sexed distinction is *good*—males and females complement each other, as seen in the fruitfulness of procreation and companionship. Our bodies are thus authorities that one must heed, and our basic identity is *given* rather than constructed by our own sincerity, psychological inner sense, or desires. Marriage points to Christ and his church and will thus be no more in the consummated order, where his church will see God in Christ face to face. Therefore, singleness, as such, has eschatological significance.

12. Human cultural diversity, though often leading to division due to sin, is a creational good, and the kingdom of God will comprise a diversity of cultures with a common confession of the Triune God.

    "Race" is a social construct raised by sinful imagination, and the differences one sees among the peoples are cultural, not ontological. These cultural differences arise naturally due to the geographical and historical distribution of humanity and result in conflict and division only after the entrance of sin. In the last day, the kingdom of God will comprise a diversity of tribes, tongues, and nations, with a common confession of the Triune God. We should witness to this eschatological vision now by not mistaking cultural preferences for theological essentials and by practicing hospitality and a love of neighbor that crosses cultural boundaries.

Learning about a Christian theological anthropology is no mere academic exercise. It gets to the heart of who we are, explains daily experience, and pushes us toward the love of neighbor and the common good. May this work be yet another instrument by which God makes his love known to us. May it thus cause us to be secure in our identity as his image-bearers, chosen in Christ, such that all fleshly boundaries we raise are torn down: "For in Christ Jesus you are all sons of God, through faith. For as many of you as were baptized into Christ have put on Christ. There is neither Jew nor Greek, there is neither slave nor free, there is no male and female, for you are all one in Christ Jesus" (Gal. 3:26–28). Amen!

GLOSSARY

Active and passive potency: The scholastic categories used to designate the ontological grounds from which a particular capacity arises (whether or not that capacity is actualized) in order to distinguish the ontology of one kind of thing from another. For instance, unborn infants, as humans, possess the potency for reasoning and willing, and female humans possess the potency for bearing children, even if these capacities are never physically realized or actualized.

Antithesis: Refers to the absolute ethical (not ontological) opposition that exists in principle (not always in practice) between those in Adam and those in Christ, the seed of the woman and the seed of the serpent. The antithesis will one day be eschatologically realized as common grace is suspended in the last day, where believing and unbelieving individuals and cultures cannot coexist (Matt. 13:24–30).

Archetypal theology: The unique wisdom of the divine-on-divine matters—God perfectly knows himself in the divine mode; we confess and adore this theology and do not search it out.

Biological determinism: The view that one's sexed body not only determines one's gender but also a specific set of (easily identifiable) norms to which one should adhere.

Chastened transformational witness: The view on the relationship between the church and culture that says Christians do not bring about an eschatological transformation of culture by their vocational labors. Instead, having been transformed by regeneration (2 Cor. 5:17), they now in principle engage with all of life in a rightly ordered way, meaning their works give a (often unwelcome) glimpse to the unbelieving world of what the transformed cosmos will look like under Christ's consummate rule.

Common grace: The grace of God at work in the realm of unbelief, which, while not salvific, restrains humankind's capacities for sin and grants the gifts of life and breath as well as moral and epistemic goods, delaying the eschatological culmination of the antithesis. Common grace accounts for the civic virtues and achievements made by unregenerate human beings in spite of unbelief and ultimately serves for the preservation of humanity and the elect (cf. Gen. 4:20–22; 8:15–9:17; 11:8; Matt. 5:45; Acts 14:6–7; James 1:17; 2 Pet. 3:9).

Concupiscence: A desire for some sinful object that arises from the human heart prior to the conscious consent of the will. Reformed theologians, often drawing from texts such as James 1:15, have traditionally viewed this desire itself as sinful.

Corruptionism: A theory of the disembodied soul in the intermediate state that says though the soul survives bodily death, it exists in an incomplete state and lacks the full status of personhood apart from the body.

Creationism (*contra* traducianism): The view on the origin of the soul that says God creates the soul *de novo* at the moment a new human person is conceived.

Cultural mandate: The call given to human beings by God to be fruitful and multiply, to fill the earth and subdue it (Gen. 1:28; cf. Ps. 104:14–15) in association with their image-bearing status. This entails humanity stewarding, cultivating, and forming what God has made into that which brings about human flourishing in obedience to God's word and in a manner that reflects his holy character.

Ectypal theology: The knowledge of God according to finite human capacities, this is further divided into three: (1) the knowledge of union (which is the knowledge that the incarnate Christ has uniquely), (2) the knowledge of revelation (disclosed to the pilgrim church on earth), and (3) the knowledge of vision (which the church triumphant enjoys in the beatific vision).

Faculties (of the soul): Historically posited as the capacities inherent in the soul by which it performs activities of cognition and volition. Theologians and philosophers have most commonly posited two faculties: the intellect and the will.

Federalism (with respect to original sin): A forensic account of sin and justification that asserts redemptive history is structured around two federal heads—Adam and Christ—with original sin imputed to all of humanity through the former and righteousness imputed to the elect through the latter. In terms of the transmission of original sin, federalism holds that both Adam's guilt and corrupt nature are imputed to his progeny. (Cf. Rom. 5:12–21; 1 Cor. 15:22.)

Functional model (of the image of God): Also known as the vocational model, this account defines the image of God in terms of humanity's representational and/or ruling function.

Gender constructivism: The view that gender is something other than biological sex, and not determined by it, thus making gender into something constructed via social norms.

Gender essentialism: The view that gender is a consequence of or identical with biological sex.

Holistic dualism: A view of human nature which asserts that though humans are composed of both body and soul, they come together to form a harmonious whole and functional unity.

Hylomorphism: An Aristotelian account of forms existing in matter, as that which shapes and imbues identity to a particular material thing. Applied to anthropology, it identifies the soul as the form of the body. In Aristotle and Thomas Aquinas, souls are tiered with vegetative, sensitive, and rational powers of the soul.

Image of God: The doctrine that each individual person and humanity corporately relate to and analogically represent the Triune God, created in dignity, and are called to reflect God in his righteousness and holiness in their entire being (in personality, body, soul, and faculties), worship, vocations, and creaturely endeavors (cf. Gen. 1:28; 5:1; 9:6; Eph. 4:24; Col. 3:19; James 3:9).

Image of God in the broad sense: Refers to the ontology of the human being as a whole in the image of God, both before and after the fall (Gen. 1:26–28; 9:6; James 3:9).

Image of God in the narrow sense: Refers to the ethical component of the image of God, the righteousness and holiness that is a natural quality bestowed on human beings at creation but lost in the fall and renewed in Christ (Eph. 4:24; Col. 3:10).

Manichaeism: An ancient sect that believed the struggle between good and evil was an eternal opposition and saw evil as residing in matter.

Monism: The view that all of reality is composed of a single substance.

Neoplatonism: A system Augustine engaged with that asserts the primacy of the One, where pure, absolute being resides and from which all other beings emanate. There is a hierarchy between being and nonbeing, where the One is pure being, and mind, soul, nature, matter, and nonbeing are ranked successively. Humanity is a composite of soul and body, and the soul, which looks upward to the mind and longs to achieve union with higher forms of being, is dragged downward by the body, which is the material, lower form of being.

***Nephesh*:** A Hebrew word with a wide semantic range, including "life," "soul," "throat," and others. In terms of the anthropology of the Old Testament, this term likely should not be construed as referring to the independent substance of the soul in the Greek or Cartesian sense but as representing the whole person.

Ontology: The study concerned with the nature of *being*, inquiring into the essential and accidental properties of things and what distinguishes one thing from another.

Original righteousness: The perfect righteousness, holiness, and proper orientation toward God and neighbor that characterized humanity at creation and was lost in the fall. According to the Reformed tradition, this original righteousness is an inherent and concreated attribute of human nature as created.

Pelagianism: An ancient heresy that denied original sin and posited the primacy of free will in human beings by which they could choose to obey God's commands so as to earn salvation.

Personality (in Herman Bavinck): That which accounts for the unity of the person in body and soul, that incommunicable property that distinguishes one individual person from another and also provides the direction of human individuality.

Privation: The absence of a natural quality. A tree with the absence of sight is not called blind, because sight is not a natural quality of trees. A squirrel that fails to pray is not unrighteous, because it was never in its nature to have the potency to pray. A human without sight, however, is blind, and a human who fails to commune with God is unrighteous.

Race essentialism: The view that race is essential and demarcates one human's ontology from another's, rather than it being a social or geographical reality.

Realism (with respect to original sin): Maintains that original sin is transmitted to all of Adam's progeny because all people are really *in* Adam; the transmission of original sin is thus held to take place either immediately (because all of humanity was present in Adam metaphysically and thus in some sense commits his sin with him) or mediately (such that all necessarily sin by virtue of the corrupt nature they inherit).

Relational model (of the image of God): An account of the image of God that defines the image in terms of the human being's relation to God and/or others.

Sex/gender distinction: Holds that "sex" is a biological reality (referring to the kinds of gametes one produces), while "gender" refers to the norms associated with sex.

In contemporary approaches to the topic, it is often held that gender is simply the set of norms chosen for oneself and not necessarily contingent upon biological sex.

Structural model (of the image of God): An account of the image of God that locates the image in the substance of humanity itself or a particular component of human nature, often the rational soul.

Substance dualism: The view that the human being is a compound of two distinct substances: an immaterial soul and a material body. It is usually accompanied by the further claim that the soul is the source of our identity.

Superadded gift (*donum superadditum*) in Roman Catholicism: A Roman Catholic view of original righteousness that construes it as not inherent to humanity's created nature but as a supernatural gift that elevates human nature by bridling the natural conflict between flesh and spirit in created humanity. Under this conception, humanity's fall from the state of innocence is not one from nature to corrupted nature, but of elevated nature to a normal, mortal condition.

Survivalism: An account of the disembodied soul in the intermediate state that, identifying the person with the soul, asserts a person has a complete existence apart from the body (in contrast to corruptionists).

Total depravity: The doctrine explaining the scope of sin as (1) infecting the entirety of the human race; (2) corrupting the entirety of human nature in body, soul, and all its faculties, including both the conscious and unconscious directions of thinking and willing, stemming from a fallen heart as the wellspring of life (Prov. 4:23); and (3) characterizing every human action. Total depravity does not mean that all sins are equally heinous or that humans are always as bad as they can possibly be. (Cf. Gen. 8:21; Jer. 17:9; Mark 7:21; Rom. 3:9–18; Eph. 2:1–3.)

Traducianism: The view on the origin of the soul that says the soul is not created anew each time a new person comes into being but is propagated from parent to child.

The "trans-inclusion" problem: Refers to revisionist definitions of what it means to be a woman that are intended to be trans-inclusionary but result in circular definitions: These define "woman" in terms of adopting for oneself a certain number of norms associated with women, thereby placing the term in the definition.

Trichotomy: The view that there are three parts to human nature: body, soul, and spirit (often with reference to 1 Thess. 5:23 and Heb. 4:12).

BIBLIOGRAPHY

Allen, Michael. *Ephesians*. BTCB. Brazos, 2022.

Allen, Prudence. *The Concept of Woman*, vol. 3, *The Search for Communion of Persons, 1500–2015*. Eerdmans, 2016.

Anderson, James, and Paul Manata. "Determined to Come Most Freely: Some Challenges for Libertarian Calvinism." *Journal of Reformed Theology* 11 (2017): 272–97.

Ansberry, Christopher B. "Writings." In *T&T Clark Companion to the Doctrine of Sin*, edited by Keith L. Johnson and David Tauber. Bloomsbury T&T Clark, 2016.

Aubert, Annette G. *The German Roots of Nineteenth-Century American Theology*. Oxford University Press, 2013.

Augustine. *The City of God*. Translated by Marcus Dods. Random House, 1993.

———. *Confessions*. Translated by Henry Chadwick. Oxford University Press, 2008.

———. "Letter 37, to Simplician." In *Responses to Miscellaneous Questions*, translated by Boniface Ramsey, edited by Raymond Canning. New City Press, 2008.

———. *The Literal Meaning of Genesis*. Volume 1. Translated by John Hammond Taylor. Paulist Press, 1982.

———. *The Trinity*. Translated by Edmund Hill. New City Press, 1991.

Babcock, William. "Augustine's Interpretation of Romans (A.D. 394–396)." *Augustinian Studies* 10 (1979): 55–74.

Bacote, Vincent. "Erasing Race: Racial Identity and Theological Anthropology." In *Black Scholars in White Space: New Vistas in African American Studies from the Christian Academy*, edited by Anthony Bradley. Pickwick, 2015.

———. "Kuyper and Race." In *Calvinism for a Secular Age: A Twenty-First Century Reading of Kuyper's Stone Lectures*, edited by Jessica and Robert Joustra. IVP Academic, 2022.

———. *Reckoning with Race and Performing the Good News: In Search of a Better Evangelical Theology*. Brill, 2020.

Bahnsen, Greg L. "The Crucial Concept of Self-Deception in Presuppositional Apologetics." *Westminster Theological Journal* 57 (1995): 1–31.

Barth, Karl. *Church Dogmatics* III/1. Edited by Geoffrey W. Bromiley and T. F. Torrance. T&T Clark, 2004.

Bauckham, Richard. *The Theology of the Book of Revelation*. Cambridge University Press, 1993.

Bavinck, Herman. *Biblical and Religious Psychology*. Translated by Herman Hanko. Edited by Gregory Parker Jr. Reformed Free, 2023.

———. "Calvin and Common Grace." In *Calvin and the Reformation: Four Studies*, edited by William Park Armstrong. Revell, 1909.

———. "The Catholicity of Christianity and the Church." Translated by John Bolt. *Calvin Theological Journal* 27 (1992): 220–51.

———. *The Christian Family*. Christian's Library Press, 2012.

———. *Christianity and Science*. Translated and edited by N. Gray Sutanto, James Eglinton, and Cory C. Brock. Crossway, 2023.

———. *Christian Worldview*. Edited and translated by N. Gray Sutanto, James Eglinton, and Cory Brock. Crossway, 2019.

———. "Common Grace." Translated by Raymond van Leeuwen. *Calvin Theological Journal* (1989): 35–65.

———. *De Vrouw in de Hedendaagsche Maatschappij*. Kok, 1918.

———. "Foundations of Psychology." Edited by John Bolt. Translated by Jack Vanden Born, Nelson Kloosterman, and John Bolt. *The Bavinck Review* 9 (2018).

———. *Gereformeerde Dogmatiek*. 3rd ed. 4 vols. Kok, 1918.

———. *Guidebook for Instruction in the Christian Religion*. Edited and translated by Gregory Parker Jr. and Cameron Clausing. Hendrickson, 2022.

———. "Hoofd en Hart." In *Christophilus: Jaarboekje Nederlandsch Jongelings-Verbond* (1892): 71–75. English translation: "Head and Heart." Translated by Gregory Parker Jr. *Modern Reformation*, November 21, 2021. https://modernreformation.org/resource-library/articles/head-and-heart.

———. "The Kingdom of God, the Highest Good." Translated by Nelson D. Kloosterman. *The Bavinck Review* 2 (2011): 133–70.

———. *Over het onbewuste: Wetenschappelijke samenkomst op 7 juli 1915*. Kirchner, 1915.

———. *Philosophy of Revelation: A New Annotated Edition*. Edited by Cory Brock and N. Gray Sutanto. Hendrickson, 2018.

———. "The Primacy of the Intellect or the Will." In *Essays on Religion, Science, and Society*, edited by John Bolt, translated by Harry Boonstra and Gerrit Sheeres. Baker Academic, 2008.

———. *Reformed Dogmatics*, vol. 2, *God and Creation*. Edited by John Bolt. Translated by John Vriend. Baker Academic, 2004.

———. *Reformed Dogmatics*, vol. 3, *Sin and Salvation in Christ*. Edited by John Bolt. Translated by John Vriend. Baker Academic, 2006.

———. *Reformed Dogmatics*, vol. 4, *Holy Spirit, Church, and New Creation*. Baker Academic, 2008.

———. *Reformed Ethics*, vol. 1, *Created, Fallen, and Converted Humanity*. Edited and translated by John Bolt. Baker Academic, 2019.

———. *Reformed Ethics*, vol. 2, *The Duties of the Christian Life*. Edited and translated by John Bolt, Jessica Joustra, Nelson D. Kloosterman, Antoine Theron, and Dirk van Keulen. Baker Academic, 2022.

———. "The Unconscious." In *Essays on Religion, Science, and Society*, edited by John Bolt, translated by Harry Boonstra and Gerrit Sheeres. Baker Academic, 2008.

———. *Wonderful Works of God*. Translated by Henry Zylstra. Westminster Seminary Press, 2020.

Bavinck, Johan Herman. *Between the Beginning and the End: A Radical Kingdom Vision*. Translated by Bert Hielema. Eerdmans, 2014.

———. "Religious Consciousness and Christian Faith." In *The J. H. Bavinck Reader*, edited by John Bolt, James D. Bratt, and Paul J. Visser. Eerdmans, 2013.

Beale, G. K. *The Temple and the Church's Mission: A Biblical Theology of the Dwelling Place of God*. IVP Academic, 2004.

———. *We Become What We Worship: A Biblical-Theology of Idolatry*. IVP Academic, 2008.

Beale, G. K., and Mitchell Kim. *God Dwells Among Us: A Biblical Theology of Temple*. IVP Academic, 2021.

Behr, John. "Humanity." In *New Cambridge Companion to Christian Doctrine*, edited by Michael Allen. Cambridge University Press, 2022.

Berkouwer, G. C. *Man: The Image of God*. Translated by Dirk Jellema. Eerdmans, 1962.

———. *Sin*. Translated by Philip C. Holtrop. Eerdmans, 1971.

Bettcher, Talia Mae. "Through the Looking Glass: Trans Theory Meets Feminist Philosophy." In *Routledge Companion to Feminist Philosophy*, edited by Ann Garry, Serene Khader, and Alison Stone. Routledge, 2017.

Black, C. Clifton. "Synoptic Gospels." In *T&T Clark Companion to the Doctrine of Sin*, edited by Keith L. Johnson and David Tauber. Bloomsbury T&T Clark, 2016.

Blocher, Henri. *Original Sin: Illumining a Riddle*. IVP Academic, 1997.

Boda, Mark. "Prophets." In *T&T Clark Companion to the Doctrine of Sin*, edited by Keith L. Johnson and David Tauber. Bloomsbury T&T Clark, 2016.

———. *A Severe Mercy: Sin and Its Remedy in the Old Testament*. Eisenbrauns, 2009.

Boersma, Gerald. *Augustine's Early Theology of Image*. Oxford University Press, 2016.

Boersma, Hans. *Seeing God: The Beatific Vision in Christian Tradition*. Eerdmans, 2018.

Bogardus, Tomás. "Evaluating Arguments for the Sex/Gender Distinction." *Philosophia* (2020): 1–20.

———. "Some Internal Problems with Revisionary Gender Concepts." *Philosophia* (2019): 1–21.

———. "Why the Trans Inclusion Problem Cannot Be Solved." *Philosophia* (2022): 1–26.

Bolt, John. *Bavinck on the Christian Life*. Crossway, 2015.
Bonaventure. *Breviloquium*. Translated by Dominic V. Monti. Franciscan Institute, 2005.
———. *Collations on the Ten Commandments*. Translated by Paul J. Spaeth. The Franciscan Institute, 1995.
———. *Disputed Questions on the Mystery of the Trinity*. Edited by George Marcil. Translated by Zachary Hayes. The Franciscan Institute, 1979.
———. *Itinerarium Mentis in Deum*. Edited by Philotheus Boehner and Zachary Hayes. Translated by Zachary Hayes. The Franciscan Institute, 2002.
Bonner, Gerald. "Pelagianism and Augustine." *Augustinian Studies* 23 (1992): 33–51.
Brink, G. A. van den. *The Transfer of Sin: The Debate on Imputation in the English Antinomian Controversy (1690–1700) in Its International and Interconfessional Context.* Brill, 2025.
Brock, Cory C. *Orthodox yet Modern: Herman Bavinck's Use of Schleiermacher*. Lexham, 2020.
Brock, Cory C., and N. Gray Sutanto. *Neo-Calvinism: A Theological Introduction*. Lexham, 2023.
Budziszewski, J. *On the Meaning of Sex*. Intercollegiate Studies Institute, 2014.
Bullinger, Heinrich. "The Second Helvetic Confession." In *The Second Helvetic Confession*. Jazzybee Verlag, 2012.
Burge, Gary M. "The Gospel and Epistles of John." In *T&T Clark Companion to the Doctrine of Sin*, edited by Keith L. Johnson and David Tauber. Bloomsbury T&T Clark, 2016.
Burgess, Anthony. *A Treatise on Original Sin: Proving That It Is, by Pregnant Texts of Scripture, and Vindicated from False Glosses*. Anchora Spei, 1658.
Burkett, Elinor. "What Makes a Woman?" *New York Times*, June 6, 2015. https://www.nytimes.com/2015/06/07/opinion/sunday/what-makes-a-woman.html.
Butler, Judith. *Gender Trouble*. 2nd ed. Routledge: 1999.
———. "Performative Acts and Gender Constitution: An Essay in Phenomenology and Feminist Theory." *Theater Journal* 40 (1988): 519–31.
Byrne, Alex. "The Origin of 'Gender Identity.'" *Archives of Sexual Behavior* (2023): 1–2.
Calvin, John. *Commentaries on the First Book of Moses, Called Genesis*. Translated by John King. Printed for the Calvin Translation Society, 1850.
———. *Institutes of the Christian Religion*. Translated by Ford Lewis Battles. Edited by John T. McNeill. Westminster, 1960.
Carter, J. Kameron. *Race: A Theological Account*. Oxford University Press, 2008.
"Catechism of the Catholic Church." The Holy See. https://www.vatican.va/archive/ENG0015/__P1C.HTM. Accessed February 14, 2023.
Cavadini, John. *Visioning Augustine*. Wiley-Blackwell, 2019.
Chaplin, Jonathan. *Faith in Democracy: Framing Politics of Deep Diversity*. SCM, 2021.

Clausing, Cameron. *Theology and History in the Methodology of Herman Bavinck: Revelation, Confession, and Christian Consciousness*. Oxford University Press, 2023.

Cohick, Lynn. *The Letter to the Ephesians*. NICNT. Eerdmans, 2020.

Coleman, Stephen M. "The Folly, Mystery, and Absurdity of Sin in the Wisdom Literature." In *Ruined Sinners to Reclaim: Human Corruption in Historical, Biblical, Theological, and Pastoral Perspective*, edited by David Gibson and Jonathan Gibson. Crossway, 2024.

Cooper, John. *Body, Soul, and Life Everlasting: Biblical Anthropology and the Monism-Dualism Debate*. Eerdmans, 2000.

Cortez, Marc. *Christological Anthropology in Historical Perspective: Ancient and Contemporary Approaches to Theological Anthropology*. Zondervan, 2016.

———. *Resourcing Theological Anthropology: A Constructive Account of Humanity in Light of Christ*. Zondervan Academic, 2017.

———. *Theological Anthropology: A Guide for the Perplexed*. Bloomsbury T&T Clark, 2010.

Cortez, Marc, and Michael P. Jensen. "Human Ontology." In *T&T Clark Reader in Theological Anthropology*, edited by Marc Cortez and Michael P. Jensen. Bloomsbury T&T Clark, 2018.

Couenhoven, Jesse. *Stricken by Sin, Cured by Christ: Agency, Necessity, and Culpability in Augustinian Theology*. Oxford University Press, 2013.

Crisp, Oliver D. "Federalism vs Realism: Charles Hodge, Augustus Strong, and William Shedd on the Imputation of Sin." *International Journal of Systematic Theology* 8 (2006): 55–71.

———. "On Original Sin." *International Journal of Systematic Theology* 17 (2015): 252–66.

———. "Original Sin and Atonement." In *The Oxford Handbook of Philosophical Theology*, edited by Thomas P. Flint and Michael C. Rea. Oxford University Press, 2009.

———. "Sin." In *Christian Dogmatics: Reformed Theology for the Church Catholic*, edited by Michael Allen and Scott R. Swain. Baker Academic, 2016.

———. *The Word Enfleshed: Exploring the Person and Work of Christ*. Baker Academic, 2016.

Crowe, Brandon. *The Last Adam: A Theology of the Obedient Life of Jesus in the Gospels*. Baker Academic, 2017.

———. *The Lord Jesus Christ: The Biblical Doctrine of the Person and Work of Christ*. Lexham, 2023.

———. *The Obedient Son: Deuteronomy and Christology in the Gospel of Matthew*. De Gruyter, 2012.

Davis, Stephen T. "Redemption, the Resurrected Body, and Human Nature." In *The Ashgate Companion to Theological Anthropology*, edited by Joshua R. Farris and Charles Taliaferro. Routledge, 2016.

De Haan, Daniel D., and Brandon Dahm. "After Survivalism and Corruptionism: Separated Souls as Incomplete Persons." *Quaestiones Disputatae* 10 (2020): 161–76.

De Jong, Marinus. "The Church Is the Means, the World Is the End: The Development of Klaas Schilder's Thought on the Relationship Between the Church and the World." PhD thesis, Kampen Theological University, 2019.

Dembroff, Robin. "Why Be Non-Binary?" *Aeon* (2018): https://philarchive.org/archive/DEMWBNv1.

Dempster, Stephen G. *Dominion and Dynasty: A Theology of the Hebrew Bible*. IVP Academic, 2003.

Dodaro, Robert, and George Lawless, eds. *Augustine and His Critics*. Routledge, 2000.

Douma, Jochem. *Common Grace in Kuyper, Schilder, and Calvin: Exposition, Composition, and Evaluation*. Translated by Albert H. Oosterhoff. Edited by William Helder. Lucerna, 2017.

Doyle, Dominic. "From Image to Indwelling: Aquinas' Theological Anthropology." In *T&T Clark Handbook to Theological Anthropology*, edited by Ann Hinsdale and Stephen Okey. Bloomsbury T&T Clark, 2021.

Do Vale, Fellipe. "Cappadoccian or Augustinian? Adjudicating Debates on Gender in the Resurrection." *International Journal of Systematic Theology* 21 (2019): 182–98.

———. *Gender as Love: A Theological Account of Human Identity, Embodied Desire, and Our Social Worlds*. Baker Academic, 2023.

Drever, Matthew. *Image, Identity, and the Forming of the Augustinian Soul*. Oxford University Press, 2013.

Duby, Steven J. *Jesus and the God of Classical Theism*. Baker Academic, 2023.

Edgar, William. *Created and Creating: A Biblical Theology of Culture*. IVP Academic, 2016.

Eglinton, James. *Bavinck: A Critical Biography*. Baker Academic, 2020.

———. "'Indignation Would Arise Within You': Herman Bavinck on Racial Injustice in Europe and North America." In *Social Christianity in Scotland and Beyond, 1800–2000: Essays in Honour of Stewart J. Brown*, edited by Andrew Kloes and Laura M. Mair. Edinburgh University Press, 2024.

———. "Planting Tulips in Rainforests: Herman and Johan Bavinck on Christianity in East and West." *Journal of Biblical and Theological Studies* 6 (2021): 277–92.

———. *Trinity and Organism: Toward a New Reading of Herman Bavinck's Organic Motif*. Bloomsbury T&T Clark, 2010.

Engelke, Matthew. *How to Think Like an Anthropologist*. Princeton University Press, 2018.

Everhart, D. T. "Communal Reconciliation: Corporate Responsibility and Opposition to Systemic Sin." *International Journal of Systematic Theology* 25, no. 1 (2023): 134–56.

Farris, Joshua Ryan. *An Introduction to Theological Anthropology: Humans, Both Creaturely and Divine*. Baker Academic, 2020.

Favale, Abigale. *Genesis of Gender: A Christian Theory*. Ignatius, 2022.

Feingold, Laurence. *The Natural Desire to See God according to St. Thomas Aquinas and His Interpreters*. 2nd ed. Sapientia, 2010.

Feser, Edward. *Scholastic Metaphysics: A Contemporary Introduction*. Editiones Scholasticae, 2014.

Fesko, J. V. *Death in Adam, Life in Christ: The Doctrine of Imputation*. Christian Focus, 2016.

Finn, Douglas. "Soul, Body, and the Miraculous Excess of the Human Being: Augustine's Theological Anthropology." In *T&T Clark Handbook to Theological Anthropology*, edited by Mary Ann Hinsdale and Stephen Okey. Bloomsbury T&T Clark, 2021.

Gaffin, Richard B., Jr. *In the Fullness of Time: An Introduction to the Biblical Theology of Acts and Paul*. Crossway, 2022.

Goldingay, John. *Psalms*, vol. 1, *Psalms 1–41*. Baker Academic, 2006.

Gombis, Timothy G. "Paul." In *T&T Clark Companion to the Doctrine of Sin*, edited by Keith L. Johnson and David Tauber. Bloomsbury T&T Clark, 2016.

Gregory of Nyssa. "On the Making of Man." In *A Select Library of Nicene and Post-Nicene Fathers of the Christian Church*, 2nd series, edited by Philip Schaff and Henry Wace. Vol. 5 of 14. Christian Literature, 1890–1900. Reprint, Hendrickson, 1994.

Grumett, David. "De Lubac, Grace, and the Pure Nature Debate." *Modern Theology* 31 (2015): 123–46.

Hamilton, Victor P. *The Book of Genesis, Chapters 1–17*. NICOT. Eerdmans, 1990.

Harinck, George. "Calvinism Isn't the Only Truth: Herman Bavinck's Impressions of the USA." In *The Sesquicentennial of Dutch Immigration: 150 Years of Ethnic Heritage; Proceedings of the 11th Biennial Conference of the Association for the Advancement of Dutch American Studies*, edited by Larry J. Wagenaar and Robert P. Swierenga. The Joint Archives of Holland, Hope College, 1998.

———. "'Wipe Out Lines of Division (Not Distinctions)': Bennie Keet, Neo-Calvinism and the Struggle Against Apartheid." *Journal of Reformed Theology* 11 (2017): 81–88.

Harris, Harriett A. "Should We Say That Personhood Is Relational?" *Scottish Journal of Theology* 51 (1998): 214–38.

Harrison, Carol. *Rethinking Augustine's Early Theology: An Argument for Continuity*. Oxford University Press, 2008.

Hartley, John. *The Book of Job*. NICOT. Eerdmans, 1988.

Haslanger, Sally. "Gender and Race: (What) Are They? (What) Do We Want Them to Be?" *Noûs* 34 (2000): 31–55.

Helm, Paul. *Human Nature from Calvin to Edwards*. Reformation Heritage Books, 2018.

Hereth, Blake. "The Shape of Trans Afterlife Justice." In *Voices from the Edge: Centering Marginalized Perspectives in Analytic Theology*, edited by Michelle Panchuk and Michael Rea. Oxford University Press, 2020.

Hiestand, Gerald. "Put Pain Like That Beyond My Power: A Christocentric Theodicy with Respect to the Inequality of Male and Female Power." In *Beauty, Order, and*

Mystery: A Christian Vision of Human Sexuality, edited by Gerald Hiestand and Todd Wilson. IVP Academic, 2017.

Hildebrand, Pierrick. *The Zurich Origins of Reformed Covenant Theology*. Oxford University Press, 2024.

Hill, Daniel J. "Union, Distinction and Creaturely Perfections: Petrus van Mastricht's Rejection of Deification." *Scottish Journal of Theology* 78 (2025): 189–201.

Hodge, Archibald A. *A Commentary of the Confession of Faith: With Questions for Theological Students and Bible Classes*. Presbyterian Board of Education, 1869.

Hodge, Caspar W. "Imputation." In *The International Standard Bible Encyclopedia*, edited by James Orr. Eerdmans, 1974.

Hodge, Charles. "Inquiries Respecting the Doctrine of Imputation." *The Biblical Repertory and Theological Review* 2 (1830): 425–71.

———. *Systematic Theology*, vol. 2, *Anthropology*. London: Thomas Nelson and Sons, 1872.

Holland, Tom. *Dominion: How the Christian Revolution Remade the World*. Basic Books, 2019.

Horton, Michael. *The Christian Faith: A Systematic Theology for Pilgrims on the Way*. Zondervan, 2011.

———. "Image and Office: Human Personhood and the Covenant." In *Personal Identity in Theological Perspective*, edited by Michael S. Horton and Mark R. Talbot. Eerdmans, 2006.

———. "Image and Office: Human Personhood and the Covenant." In *T&T Clark Reader in Theological Anthropology*, edited by Marc Cortez and Michael P. Jensen. Bloomsbury T&T Clark, 2018.

Hunter, Justus H. *If Adam Had Not Sinned: The Reasons for the Incarnation from Anselm to Scotus*. Catholic University of America Press, 2020.

Hurtado, Larry. *Destroyer of the Gods: Early Christian Distinctiveness in the Roman World*. Baylor University Press, 2017.

Imes, Carmen. *Being God's Image: Why Creation Still Matters*. InterVarsity, 2023.

Ince, Irwyn. *The Beautiful Community: Unity, Diversity, and the Church at Its Best*. InterVarsity, 2020.

Jenkins, Katherine. "Amelioration and Inclusion: Gender Identity and the Concept of Woman." *Ethics* 126 (2016): 394–421.

———. "Black Theology." In *The New Cambridge Companion to Christian Doctrine*, edited by Michael Allen. Cambridge University Press, 2022.

Jennings, Willie James. *The Christian Imagination: Theology and the Origins of Race*. Yale University Press, 2010.

Johnson, Dennis E. "The Function of Romans 7:13–25 in Paul's Argument for the Law's Impotence and the Spirit's Power, and Its Bearing on the Identity of the Schizophrenic 'I.'" In *Resurrection and Eschatology: Theology in Service of the Church; Essays in Honor of Richard B. Gaffin Jr.*, edited by Lane G. Tipton and Jeffrey C. Waddington. P&R, 2004.

Johnson, Keith L., and David Lauber, eds. *T&T Clark Companion to the Doctrine of Sin*. Bloomsbury T&T Clark, 2016.

Jones, Serene. *Feminist Theory and Christian Theology: Cartographies of Grace*. Fortress, 2000.

Joustra, Jessica. "An Embodied Imago Dei: How Herman Bavinck's Understanding of the Image of God Can Help Inform Conversations on Race." *Journal of Reformed Theology* 11 (2017): 9–23.

Junius, Franciscus. *A Treatise on True Theology*. Translated by David C. Noe. Reformation Heritage Books, 2014.

Kantzer Komline, Han-Luen. *Augustine on the Will: A Theological Account*. Oxford University Press, 2020.

Kapic, Kelly. "Anthropology." In *Christian Dogmatics: Reformed Theology for the Church Catholic*, edited by Michael Allen and Scott R. Swain. Baker Academic, 2016.

Kelsey, David. *Eccentric Existence: A Theological Anthropology*. Volume 1. Westminster John Knox, 2009.

Kilner, John F. *Dignity and Destiny: Humanity in the Image of God*. Eerdmans, 2015.

Kleinig, John. *Wonderfully Made: A Protestant Theology of the Body*. Lexham, 2021.

Klink, Edward W., III. "Genesis Revealed: Second Adam Christology in the Fourth Gospel." *Bulletin of Ecclesial Theology* 5 (2018): 27–42.

———. *John*. Zondervan Exegetical Commentary on the New Testament. Zondervan Academic, 2017.

Koyzis, David. *Political Visions and Illusions: A Survey and Christian Critique of Contemporary Ideologies*. 2nd ed. IVP Academic, 2019.

Kuyper, Abraham. *Common Grace*, vol. 1, *God's Gifts for a Fallen World*. Translated by Nelson D. Kloosterman and Ed M. van der Maas. Edited by Jordan Ballor. Lexham, 2015.

———. *Lectures on Calvinism*. Eerdmans, 1999.

Lapine, Matthew A. *The Logic of the Body: Retrieving Theological Psychology*. Lexham, 2020.

Lawford-Smith, Holly. *Gender-Critical Feminism*. Oxford University Press, 2022.

Lefebvre, Michael. "Adam Reigns in Eden: Genesis and the Origins of Kingship." *Bulletin of Ecclesial Theology* 5 (2018): 23–57.

Leidenhag, Joanna. "The Challenge of Autism for Relational Approaches to Theological Anthropology." *International Journal of Systematic Theology* 23 (2021): 109–34.

Leslie, Andrew M. "Retrieving a Mature Reformed Doctrine of Original Sin: A Conversation with Some Recent Proposals." *International Journal of Systematic Theology* 22 (2020): 336–60.

Levering, Matthew. "Israel." In *The New Cambridge Companion to Christian Doctrine*, edited by Michael Allen. Cambridge University Press, 2023.

———. "Thomas Aquinas on Sexual Ethics." In *Beauty, Order, and Mystery: A Christian Vision of Human Sexuality*, edited by Gerald Hiestand and Todd Wilson. IVP Academic, 2017.

Lints, Richard. *Identity and Idolatry: The Image of God and Its Inversion*. IVP Academic, 2015.

———. *Uncommon Unity: Wisdom for the Church in an Age of Division*. Lexham, 2022.

Liou, Jeff. "Taking Up #blacklivesmatter: A Neo-Kuyperian Engagement with Critical Race Theory." *Journal of Reformed Theology* 11 (2017): 99–120.

Long, Steven A. "Creation ad Imaginem Dei: The Obediential Potency of the Human Person to Grace and Glory." *Nova et Vetera* 14 (2016): 1175–92.

Madueme, Hans. "Mea Culpa: An Apology for Original Guilt." *Mid-America Journal of Theology* 32 (2021): 7–34.

Marcus, Joel. "Son of Man as Son of Adam." *Revue biblique* 110 (2003): 36–61.

———. "Son of Man as Son of Adam, Part 2: Exegesis." *Revue biblique* 110 (2003): 370–86.

Marías, Julián. *Metaphysical Anthropology: The Empirical Structure of Human Life*. Translated by Francis M. López Morllias. Pennsylvania State University Press, 1971.

Mason, Matthew. "The Authority of the Body: Discovering Natural Manhood and Womanhood." *Bulletin of Ecclesial Theology* 4 (2017): 39–57.

———. "The Wounded It Heals: Gender Dysphoria and the Resurrection of the Body." In *Beauty, Order, and Mystery: A Christian Vision of Human Sexuality*, edited by Gerald Hiestand and Todd Wilson. IVP Academic, 2017.

Mathewes, Charles. *Evil and the Augustinian Tradition*. Cambridge University Press, 2001.

Matter, E. Ann. "Christ, God and Woman in the Thought of St. Augustine." In *Augustine and His Critics*, edited by Robert Dodaro and George Lawless. Routledge, 2000.

Mattson, Brian. *Restored to Our Destiny: Eschatology and the Image of God in Herman Bavinck's Reformed Dogmatics*. Brill, 2011.

McCall, Thomas H. *Against God and Nature: The Doctrine of Sin*. Crossway, 2019.

McCormack, Bruce. *The Humility of the Eternal Son: Reformed Kenoticism and the Repair of Chalcedon*. Cambridge University Press, 2021.

McFadyen, Alistair. *Bound to Sin: Abuse, Holocaust, and the Christian Doctrine of Sin*. Cambridge University Press, 2009.

McFarland, Ian. *In Adam's Fall: A Meditation on the Christian Doctrine of Original Sin*. Blackwell, 2010.

McKirland, Christa. *God's Provision, Humanity's Need: The Gift of Our Dependence*. Baker Academic, 2022.

McLaughlin, Rebecca. *Secular Creed: Engaging Five Contemporary Claims*. The Gospel Coalition, 2021.

Meador, Jake. *What Are Christians Good For? Life Together at the End of the World*. InterVarsity, 2022.

Middleton, J. Richard. *The Liberating Image: The Imago Dei in Genesis 1*. Brazos, 2005.

Mikkola, Mari. "Gender Essentialism and Anti-Essentialism." In *Routledge Companion to Feminist Philosophy*, edited by Ann Garry, Serene Khader, and Alison Stone. Routledge, 2017.

Moo, Douglas. *The Letter to the Romans*. 2nd ed. NICNT. Eerdmans, 2018.

Morales, Michael. *Who Shall Ascend the Mountain of the Lord? A Biblical Theology of the Book of Leviticus*. IVP Academic, 2015.

Mouw, Richard. *Abraham Kuyper: A Short and Personal Introduction*. Eerdmans, 2011.

Muller, Richard. *Calvin and the Reformed Tradition: The Work of Christ and the Order of Salvation*. Baker Academic, 2003.

———. *Divine Will and Human Choice: Freedom, Contingency, and Necessity in Early Modern Reformed Thought*. Baker Academic, 2017.

———. *God, Creation, and Providence in the Thought of Jacob Arminius: Sources and Directions of Scholastic Protestantism in the Era of Early Orthodoxy*. Baker, 1991.

Murray, John. *Collected Writings of John Murray*, vol. 2, *Systematic Theology*. Banner of Truth, 1977.

———. *The Epistle to the Romans*. Eerdmans, 1997.

———. *The Imputation of Adam's Sin*. Presbyterian and Reformed, 1959.

———. *Redemption Accomplished and Applied*. Eerdmans, 2015.

Nelson, Derek R. *Sin: A Guide for the Perplexed*. Bloomsbury T&T Clark, 2011.

———. *What's Wrong with Sin: Sin in Individual and Social Perspective from Schleiermacher to Theologies of Liberation*. T&T Clark, 2009.

Noe, David C. "Suppress or Retain? Theodore Beza, Natural Theology, and the Translation of Romans 1:18." In *Theodore Beza at 500: New Perspectives on an Old Reformer*, edited by Kirk Summers and Scott M. Manetsch. Vandenhoeck & Ruprecht, 2021.

Ong, Andrew. "Neo-Calvinism and Ethnic Churches in Multiethnic Contexts." *Journal of Reformed Theology* 12, no. 3 (October 2018): 296–320.

———. "World Christianity." In *T&T Clark Handbook of Neo-Calvinism*, edited by Nathaniel Gray Sutanto and Cory Brock. Bloomsbury T&T Clark, 2024.

Panchuk, Michelle. "Gender and Justice: Human and Divine Gender in Analytic Theology." In *T&T Clark Handbook of Analytic Theology*, edited by James Arcadi and James T. Turner Jr. Bloomsbury T&T Clark, 2021.

Paul, John II. *Man and Woman He Created Them: A Theology of the Body*. Translated by Michael Waldstein. Pauline Books & Media, 2006.

Pedersen, Daniel. *Schleiermacher's Theology of Sin and Nature: Agency, Value, and Modern Theology*. Routledge, 2020.

Peeler, Amy. "Imaging Glory: 1 Corinthians 11, Gender, and Bodies at Worship." In *Beauty, Order, and Mystery: A Christian Vision of Human Sexuality*, edited by Gerald Hiestand and Todd Wilson. IVP Academic, 2017.

Peppiatt, Lucy. *Imago Dei: Humanity Made in the Image of God*. Cascade Books, 2022.

Perkins, Harrison. *Righteous by Design: Covenantal Merit and Adam's Original Integrity*. Christian Focus, 2024.

Peterson, David. *The Acts of the Apostles*. Pillar New Testament Commentary. Eerdmans, 2009.

Peterson, Ryan S. *The Imago Dei as Human Identity: A Theological Interpretation*. Eisenbrauns, 2016.

Plantinga, Alvin. *Where the Conflict Really Lies: Science, Religion, and Naturalism*. Oxford University Press, 2012.

Plantinga, Cornelius, Jr. *Not the Way It's Supposed to Be: A Breviary of Sin*. Eerdmans, 1995.

Powery, Luke A. *Becoming Human: The Holy Spirit and the Rhetoric of Race*. Westminster John Knox, 2022.

Poythress, Vern. *Making Sense of Man: Using Biblical Perspectives to Develop a Theology of Humanity*. P&R, 2024.

Pruss, Alexander. *One Body: An Essay in Christian Sexual Ethics*. University of Notre Dame Press, 2013.

Reno, R. R. *Genesis*. BTCB. Brazos, 2017.

Ridderbos, Herman. *Paul: An Outline of His Theology*. Eerdmans, 1975.

Roberts, Matthew. *Pride: Identity and the Worship of Self*. Christian Focus, 2023.

Romero, Robert Chao, and Jeff Liou. *Christianity and Critical Race Theory: A Faithful and Constructive Conversation*. Baker Academic, 2023.

Schilder, Klaas. *Christ and Culture*. Translated by Williem Helder and Albert H. Oosterhoff. Lucerna, 2016.

———. "Culture and Common Grace." In *The Klaas Schilder Reader: The Essential Theological Writings*, edited by George Harinck, Marinus de Jong, and Richard Mouw, translated by Albert Gootjes and Albert Oosterhoff. Lexham, 2022.

———. "'No' to Natural Theology (1939)." In *The Klaas Schilder Reader: The Essential Theological Writings*, edited by George Harinck, Marinus de Jong, and Richard Mouw, translated by Albert Gootjes and Albert Oosterhoff. Lexham, 2022.

Schleiermacher, Friedrich. *Christian Faith: A New Translation and Critical Edition*. Edited by Catherine L. Kelsey and Terrence N. Tice. Translated by Terrence N. Tice, Catherine L. Kelsey, and Edwina Lawler. Westminster John Knox, 2016.

———. *On Religion: Speeches to Its Cultured Despisers*. 3rd ed. Translated by John Oman. Paul, Trench, Trubner, 1893.

Schreiner, Thomas. *Romans*. 2nd ed. Baker Exegetical Commentary on the New Testament. Baker Academic, 2018.

Shenvi, Neil, and Pat Sawyer. *Critical Dilemma: The Rise of Critical Theories and Social Justice Ideology—Implications for the Church and Society*. Harvest House, 2023.

Shrier, Abigail. *Irreversible Damage: The Transgender Craze Seducing Our Daughters*. Regnery, 2020.

Siddiqui, Mona. *Christians, Muslims, and Jesus*. Yale University Press, 2013.

Sklar, Jay. "Pentateuch." In *T&T Clark Companion to the Doctrine of Sin*, edited by Keith L. Johnson and David Tauber. Bloomsbury T&T Clark, 2016.

Smith, Murray J. "'Everyone Who Practices Sin is a Slave to Sin': Sin in the Johannine Literature." In *Ruined Sinners to Reclaim: Human Corruption in Historical, Biblical, Theological, and Pastoral Perspective*, edited by David Gibson and Jonathan Gibson. Crossway, 2024.

Spaemann, Robert. *Persons: The Difference Between "Someone" and "Something."* Translated by Oliver O' Donovan. Oxford University Press, 2017.

Spencer, Mark. "Survivalist, Platonist, Thomistic Hylomorphism: A Reply to Daniel De Haan and Brandon Dahm." *Quaestiones Disputatae* 10 (2020): 177–84.

Steenberg, M. C. *Of God and Man: Theology as Anthropology from Irenaeus to Athanasius*. Bloomsbury T&T Clark, 2009.

Steffaniak, Jordan. "Retrieving Reformed Philosophy of Mind: Herman Bavinck's Eclectic Harmonism as Gateway to Neo-Aristotelianism." *Evangelical Quarterly* 94 (2023): 26–50.

Sung, Elizabeth. "'Racial Realism' in Biblical Interpretation and Theological Anthropology: A Systematic-Theological Evaluation of Recent Accounts." *Ex Auditu* 31 (2015): 3–21.

Sutanto, N. Gray. "Consummation Anyway: A Reformed Proposal." *Journal of Analytic Theology* 9 (2021): 223–37.

———. "*Gevoel* and Illumination: Bavinck, Augustine, and Bonaventure on Awareness of God." *Pro Ecclesia* 30 (2021): 265–78.

———. *God and Humanity: Herman Bavinck and Theological Anthropology*. Bloomsbury T&T Clark, 2024.

———. *God and Knowledge: Herman Bavinck's Theological Epistemology*. Bloomsbury T&T Clark, 2020.

———. "Herman Bavinck on the Beatific Vision." *International Journal of Systematic Theology* 26, no. 1 (2022): 1–17.

———. "Herman Bavinck on the Image of God and Original Sin." *International Journal of Systematic Theology* 18 (2016): 174–90.

———. "Original Sin in Modern Theology: Charles Hodge and Herman Bavinck on Friedrich Schleiermacher." In *Ruined Sinners to Reclaim: Sin in Historical, Biblical, Theological, and Pastoral Perspective*, edited by David Gibson and Jonathan Gibson. Crossway, 2024.

———. "Questioning Bonaventure's Augustinianism?: On the Noetic Effects of Sin." *New Blackfriars* 102 (2021): 401–17.

———. *A Sense of the Divine: An Affective Model of General Revelation from the Reformed Tradition*. Cambridge University Press, 2025.

Swain, Scott. *The Trinity: An Introduction*. Crossway, 2020.

Synod of Dort. *The Articles of the Canons of Dort*. Faith Alive Christian Resources, Christian Reformed Church in North America, 2011.

Synopsis of a Purer Theology: Latin Text and English Translation. 3 vols. Edited by Dolf te Velde. Translated by Riemer A. Faber. Brill, 2013–20.

Thiselton, Anthony. *1 Corinthians*. NIGTC. Eerdmans, 2006.

Thomas, Gabrielle. *The Image of God in the Theology Gregory of Nazianzus*. Cambridge University Press, 2019.

Thomas Aquinas. *Summa Theologiae*. Translated by the Fathers of the Dominican Province. 1920. Available at https://www.newadvent.org/summa.

Timmins, William N. *Romans 7 and Christian Identity: A Study of the "I" in Its Literary Context*. Cambridge University Press, 2017.

Treweek, Danielle. *The Meaning of Singleness: Retrieving an Eschatological Vision for the Contemporary Church*. IVP Academic, 2023.

Trueman, Carl. Foreword to *Critical Dilemma: The Rise of Critical Theories and Social Justice Ideology—Implications for the Church and Society*, by Neil Shenvi and Pat Sawyer. Harvest House, 2023.

———. *Rise and Triumph of the Modern Self: Cultural Amnesia, Expressive Individualism, and the Road to Sexual Revolution*. Crossway, 2019.

Turretin, Francis. *Institutes of Elenctic Theology*, vol. 1, *First Through Tenth Topics*. Edited by James T. Dennison. Translated by George Musgrave Giger. P&R, 1992.

Tylor, Edward. *Primitive Culture: Researches into the Early History of Mankind and the Development of Civilization*. John Murray, 1865.

Tyra, Steven. *"Neither the Spirit Without the Flesh": John Calvin's Doctrine of the Beatific Vision*. Bloomsbury T&T Clark, 2024.

Vanhoozer, Kevin J. *Mere Christian Hermeneutics: Transfiguring What It Means to Read the Bible Theologically*. Zondervan, 2024.

Van Asselt, Willem J., T. Theo J. Pleizier, and Pieter L. Rouwendal. *Introduction to Reformed Scholasticism*. Translated by Albert Gootjes. Reformed Historical-Theological Studies. Reformation Heritage Books, 2011.

Van den Brink, Gijsbert. *Reformed Theology and Evolutionary Theory*. Eerdmans, 2020.

Van Mastricht, Petrus. *Novitatum Cartesianum Gangrena*. Jansson-Waesburg, 1677.

———. *Theoretical-Practical Theology*, vol. 2, *Faith in the Triune God*. Translated by Todd M. Rester. Edited by Joel R. Beeke. Reformation Heritage Books, 2019.

———. *Theoretical-Practical Theology*, vol. 3, *The Works of God and the Fall of Man*. Edited by Joel Beeke. Translated by Todd M. Rester. Reformation Heritage Books, 2018.

Van Til, Cornelius. "Nature and Scripture." In *The Infallible Word: A Symposium by Members of Westminster Theological Seminary*, edited by N. B. Stonehouse and Paul Woolley. P&R, 2003.

———. "Why I Believe in God." Reformed.org. 1996. https://reformed.org/apologetics/why-i-believe-in-god-by-cornelius-van-til.

Van Til, Henry R. *The Calvinistic Concept of Culture*. Presbyterian and Reformed, 1959.

Vater, Carl A. *God's Knowledge of the World: Medieval Theories of Divine Ideas from Bonaventure to Ockham*. Catholic University of America Press, 2022.

Vermigli, Peter Martyr. *On Original Sin*. Translated by Kirk Summers. Davenant, 2019.

———. *Philosophical Works: On the Relation of Philosophy to Theology*. Edited and translated by Joseph C. McLelland. Davenant, 2018.

Viret, Andre. "Testimonies on the Doctrine of Imputation." *The Princeton Review* 4 (1839): 553–79.

von Rad, Gerhard. *Old Testament Theology*. Volumes 1 and 2. Translated by D. M. G. Stalker. Prince, 2005.

Vos, Geerhardus. "The Eschatological Aspect of the Pauline Conception of the Spirit." *In Redemptive History and Biblical Interpretation: The Shorter Writings of Geerhardus Vos*, edited by Richard B. Gaffin. Presbyterian and Reformed, 1980.

———. *Reformed Dogmatics*, vol. 2, *Anthropology*. Translated by Richard B. Gaffin. Lexham, 2014.

Waters, Guy Prentiss. "Ephesians." In *A Biblical-Theological Introduction to the New Testament: The Gospel Realized*, edited by Michael J. Kruger. Crossway, 2016.

———. "Romans." In *A Biblical-Theological Introduction to the New Testament: The Gospel Realized*, edited by Michael J. Kruger. Crossway: 2016.

Watkin, Christopher. *Biblical Critical Theory: How the Bible's Unfolding Story Makes Sense of Modern Life and Culture*. Zondervan, 2022.

Webster, John. "The Dignity of Creatures." In *God Without Measure: Working Papers in Christian Theology*, vol. 2, *Virtue and Intellect*. Bloomsbury T&T Clark, 2016.

———. "The Human Person." In *The Cambridge Companion to Postmodern Theology*, edited by Kevin J. Vanhoozer. Cambridge University Press, 2006.

———. "The Place of Christology in Systematic Theology." In *The Oxford Handbook of Christology*, edited by Francesca Murphy. Oxford University Press, 2015.

Wenham, Gordon. *Genesis 1–15*. WBC. Zondervan, 1987.

Westminster Assembly. *Annotations Upon All the Books of the Old and New Testaments: This Third, Above the First and Second, Edition So Enlarged, as They Make Commentary on the Sacred Scripture, Never Before Published in English*. Evan Tyler, 1657.

———. *The Westminster Confession of Faith*. 3rd ed. Committee for Christian Education and Publications, 1990.

Whitney, Isaac. "The Body and the Image of God in Bavinck and the Reformed Orthodox." *Scottish Journal of Theology* (2024): 1–12.

Wiley, Tatha. *Original Sin: Origins, Developments, Contemporary Meanings*. Paulist Press, 2002.

Williams, Rowan. *On Augustine*. Bloomsbury, 2016.

Wolff, Hans Walter. *Anthropology of the Old Testament*. Translated by Margaret Kohl. SCM, 1947.

Wolters, Al. *Creation Regained: Biblical Basics for a Reformational Worldview*. Eerdmans, 2005.

Wolterstorff, Nicholas. *Justice: Rights and Wrongs*. Princeton University Press, 2008.

Wood, Adam. *Thomas Aquinas on the Immateriality of the Intellect*. Catholic University of America Press, 2020.

Wood, William M. "Breaching the Covenant: Sin in the Prophets." In *Ruined Sinners to Reclaim: Human Corruption in Historical, Biblical, Theological, and Pastoral Perspective*, edited by David Gibson and Jonathan Gibson. Crossway, 2024.

———. "Sin as Self-Deception." In *T&T Clark Handbook of Analytic Theology*, edited by James M. Arcadi and James T. Turner Jr. Bloomsbury T&T Clark, 2021.

Yarhouse, Mark. *Understanding Gender Dysphoria: Navigating Transgender Issues in a Changing Culture*. IVP Academic, 2015.

Zahl, Simeon. *The Holy Spirit and Christian Experience*. Oxford University Press, 2021.

Ziegler, Philip. "'Those He Also Glorified': Some Reformed Perspectives on Human Nature and Destiny." *Studies in Christian Ethics* 32 (2019): 165–76.

SCRIPTURE INDEX

Old Testament

Genesis

Exodus

1 Peter

2 Peter

1 John

Jude

Revelation

AUTHOR INDEX

SUBJECT INDEX